BEHAVIORAL DIAGNOSTIC GUIDE

for *Developmental Disabilities*

A. GEDYE, Ph.D.

Board of Clinical Advisors
JIM W. BODFISH, PhD
ELSPETH A. BRADLEY, MBB'
BRUCE D. McCREARY, N
JIM E. RUSSELL, MD

DIAGNOSTIC BOOKS ☞ Vancouver

DISCLAIMER

This book describes features and symptoms that may be associated with certain medical conditions or adverse effects of medication. I have written this book to serve as an information guide and reference source for both professionals and nonprofessionals. Neither the author nor the publisher can accept medical or legal responsibility for having the contents of this book used as a substitute for the judgment of medical or other health professionals. The information in this book is intended to be useful to physicians, but is not intended to be a substitute for the medical judgment of physicians.

Gedye, Angela 1948 -
    Behavioral Diagnostic Guide for Developmental Disabilities / Angela Gedye

    Includes bibliographical references.
    ISBN 0-9683155-0-X

    1. Mental retardation. 2. Behavioral assessment. I. Title.

RC570.G42 1998   616.85'88047   C 97-911077-7

ACKNOWLEDGMENTS

The author is very grateful for the assistance of four clinicians who specialize in research and clinical work in persons with mental retardation. Psychiatrist Bruce McCreary, MD, Professor, Queen's University, Kingston, Ontario, Canada, has specialized in clinical services and research in this field for 30 years. Psychiatrist Elspeth Bradley, BSc, MBBS, PhD, Department of Psychiatry, University of Toronto, Ontario, has done research and provided psychiatric services in this field for over ten years. Physician Jim Russell, MD of Victoria, British Columbia, Canada is the provincial director for medical services to this population, and has provided direct clinical services for over 30 years. These dedicated physicians served as medical advisors on this book and gave generously of their time. Psychologist and researcher Jim Bodfish, PhD, Department of Psychology, Western Carolina Center, Morganton, North Carolina, also carefully reviewed parts of the book.

A very special thanks goes to psychologist Claude de Martino, PhD, who served as editor and spent myriad hours toward improving this book.

I also wish to thank psychologist Tonnar Brace, MA, administrator Jacinta Eni, BA, and psychiatric nurse Joyce Procure, RPN, for sharing their insightful comments and helpful suggestions.

The idea for this book came from a desire to help individuals with difficult behaviors who were being misdiagnosed, wrongly treated for conditions they did not have, and who continued to suffer from unrecognized conditions. To these individuals, I dedicate this book.

PREFACE

Undetected medical conditions. Undiagnosed seizures and psychiatric disorders. Unrecognized adverse effects of medication. Researchers are reporting these errors in more and more studies of people with developmental disabilities (Benage et al., 1995; Bosch et al., 1997; Ryan & Sunada, 1997; Ziring, 1987). These errors reflect the reason this book was written.

Such unrecognized conditions often present as "behavioral problems" in this population. Clinicians and caregivers need better, more systematic ways to identify difficult-to-recognize conditions which may underlie behavioral problems. Where does one start with someone who is nonverbal, unpredictably aggressive, and already taking 3 or 4 medications? What does aggression during acute pain look like in a person who cannot talk? What does aggression during a traumatic flashback look like? How is it different from other causes of aggression? What does medication-induced delirium look like, and are people aggressive in such a state? What are the clues that can lead to the correct diagnosis of a puzzling clinical presentation?

Sometimes "clues" to the underlying cause can be found in the neurological literature, pharmacology literature, psychiatric and medical literature, food allergy literature, or even the parasitology literature. Sometimes the clues are in journal articles describing people with a particular syndrome e.g., Fragile X, Prader-Willi, or Down syndrome. Clues can also come from your own experience with certain disorders or from hearing of a similar case that had a particular condition.

What if someone put together clues both from published research covering a broad range of disciplines and from considerable clinical experience? What if someone compiled a "catalog of clues" that would direct caregivers and clinicians to the types of features to look for? Hmmm. We would want such a "catalog" to be organized so one could turn to the relevant pages quickly.

The busy clinician needs clues to know *what* to screen for. Alternatively, a physician can run a battery of 30-40 tests and hope some answers surface. (Though that approach may encounter resistance from health insurers who balk at casting such a wide net.) If there were a way to narrow the search for *which conditions to test for*, *which factors to rule out*, this would shorten the time taken to make the correct diagnosis, and thereby shorten the time without proper treatment.

In creating the ***Behavioral Diagnostic Guide***, I have amassed a broad range of literature and clinical experience and organized it into over 70 diagnostic categories. I was fortunate to have excellent feedback from several experts in the field. Two prominent psychiatrists who specialize in this field and a physician with over 30 years in this area have enriched and clarified parts of this book. A prolific researcher and psychologist has also provided input. Other dedicated professionals have contributed to this undertaking. It is the first book of its kind for those working with developmentally disabled people. If this book leads you, the reader, to finally uncover the conditions underlying severe behaviors in even one individual, then acquiring this book will have been worthwhile.

A. Gedye, Ph.D.,
Vancouver, B.C., Canada
December 1997

TABLE OF CONTENTS

INTRODUCTION

A mind that is stretched by a new idea can never go back to its original dimensions.
Oliver Wendall Holmes.

Not all disruptive behaviors in people with developmental disabilities are learned and done deliberately. In fact, many disruptive behaviors in this population are caused by undiagnosed conditions and unrecognized disorders. Making accurate diagnoses can be very difficult, however, because clinicians cannot rely on patient interviews or self-report in this population, especially in persons with little or no speech. Instead, professionals and caregivers often need "detective skills" to figure out what underlies certain behaviors. Knowing what clues to look for can be crucial to finding the answer.

This book is a **catalogue of clues** to help clinicians determine what conditions underlie certain problem behaviors. It addresses seven major behavioral concerns in the developmentally disabled population. These are: Aggression; Self-Injury; Screaming; Sleep and Eating Disturbances; Dementia; and Falls. These behavioral concerns can be caused by *unrecognized* and *undiagnosed* medical conditions, illness, physical pain, nonconvulsive seizures, side effects of medication, withdrawal from medication, psychiatric conditions, nutritional deficiencies, and environmental factors. Although dementia and falls are not behavioral problems per se, they can result in changes in behavior that may be difficult to understand until the correct diagnosis is made. Therefore, dementia and unusual falls have been included in this book.

Although this book often refers to published reports of *medication-induced* adverse effects on behavior in some people, readers should be reminded that many other people do very well on the same medications.

The main purpose of this book is to assist clinicians in diagnosing conditions that underlie certain "behaviors" in people with developmental disabilities. This book is a guide for making diagnoses, but is not a book of strict diagnostic criteria. As a diagnostic guide, it is structured to assist clinicians in ruling out certain conditions and ruling in others for further investigation. It draws attention to a *wider range of differential diagnoses for behavioral concerns* in people with developmental disabilities than has previously been done. This approach contrasts sharply with theories that presume that disruptive behaviors in this population are done intentionally to inflict pain, communicate messages, solicit attention, or provide self-stimulation. While this book does not cover every explanation for disruptive behavior, it does provide a rational and systematic way to investigate such concerns.

Readers will find it easier to use this book once they understand how it is organized. For the following discussion, please refer to the next two pages. There are 7 chapters, each addressing a **Presenting Concern**. For each Presenting Concern, e.g., Aggression, there may be 10 or more differential diagnoses. The differential diagnoses have been divided into categories called **Diagnostic Categories**. In some cases, there are several etiologies for a particular Diagnostic Category, and in others cases only one etiology. Each Diagnostic (Dx) Category has been further divided into 8 **Sections** which provide a structure for systematically investigating the cause or causes of that particular problem. This structure is repeated throughout the book and is illustrated on the next two pages. The book also includes symptom checklists and practical suggestions for gathering information used in this ruling in/ruling out process.

Improving diagnostic accuracy reduces the risk of people being misdiagnosed and treated for a disorder they do not have while an unrecognized condition that negatively affects behavior goes untreated.

Presenting Concern: *example* **PHYSICAL AGGRESSION**
Dx Category   AG: *1, 2, 3, etc.* _____

---

1. ❏ *COMMON FORMS*

- This section provides descriptions of how the Presenting Concern (e.g., aggression) can appear for a particular Diagnostic (Dx) Category. Descriptions of *COMMON FORMS* may be similar across different Dx Categories, but readers can look at the *DISTINGUISHING FEATURES* section for clues that help differentiate one Dx Category from another.
- If several possible forms are listed, that does not mean that they all apply to any one person.

---

2. ❏ *VARIATIONS*

- Other versions for that particular Dx Category are given.
- If several possible variations are listed, that does not mean that they all apply to any one person.

---

3. ❏ *DISTINGUISHING FEATURES FOR AG.1*

- This section lists features that *may* help distinguish one particular Dx Category or condition from other Dx Categories. A distinguishing feature refers in some cases to a laboratory test that can confirm the diagnosis (e.g., thyroxin deficiency). In other cases it refers to features that point to a particular condition for which definitive tests are not yet available.
- Any one person would not likely have all the features listed in this section. The features listed are "clues" to help readers rule out or rule in certain conditions for further investigation.
- The "distinguishing features" listed are not intended to be diagnostic criteria, but merely clues to help the ruling in/ruling out process.

---

4. ❏ *FACTORS THAT MAY WORSEN THE CONDITION*

- This section lists factors that could exacerbate that particular condition (i.e., Dx Category).
- Identifying exacerbating factors might help in making a diagnosis.
- Identifying stressors and agents that worsen a condition can alert those involved to reduce or eliminate those stressors.

5. ❑ *PERSONS WHO MAY BE AT RISK*

- People who have certain syndromes, characteristics, medical histories, or who take certain medications *may* be at greater risk than others for a particular Dx Category.
- The risk factors listed come from published sources and clues from clinical experience.

6. ❑ *SUGGESTIONS FOR COLLECTING INFORMATION*

- This section lists practical suggestions for types of information to gather. It also refers to symptom checklists* that are provided in the Appendix.
- The information collected may provide clues to the cause of the "behavior" in question.
- The information collected is to be given to the clinicians involved to aid them in ruling out some conditions and ruling in others for further investigation.

    * *A chart or checklist listed in italics in this section can be found in the Appendix.*

7. ❑ *MEDICAL TESTING / SCREENING AG.1*

- This section lists medical tests that may assist physicians or other clinicians in making diagnoses.
- This section also cites possible adverse effects of certain medications on behavior or on particular conditions.
- The suggestions were reviewed by two or more medical experts who specialize in developmental disabilities. However, these are suggestions only and *not intended as a substitute for the medical judgment of physicians*.

8. ❑ *POSSIBLE BIOCHEMICAL / ANATOMICAL INVOLVEMENT*

- This section serves to emphasize that certain "behaviors" reflect biochemical dysfunction and are not merely learned or deliberate misbehaviors. However, the comments in this section are not intended to be comprehensive or a substitute for neuroscience textbooks.
- Readers who want more detail are referred to medical journals and medical textbooks.
- Readers not interested in such details can easily omit this section when using the book.

THIS GUIDE FOCUSES ON DIAGNOSIS

Some readers will wonder why there is no section specifically on treatment. The purpose of this book is to *improve treatment* by first *improving diagnosis* of what underlies certain behaviors. If a person's behavioral problem is caused by an unrecognized illness, then almost any behavioral treatment tried will not help while the medical illness continues unrecognized and untreated. First things first.

Are unrecognized illnesses and incorrect diagnoses likely to occur in this population? Yes. Studies of people with developmental disabilities have found many medical conditions and adverse effects of medication that were not previously detected. For example, 11% of adults with development disabilities seen for medical screening had adverse effects of drug treatment and 50% had medication levels outside the therapeutic drug range (Benage et al., 1995). Among the 202 adults, there was "an average of 5.4 medical disorders per person, half of which had not been detected previously" (Benage et al., 1995, p. 595). Among 729 people with developmental disabilities, Ziring (1987) found "many previously undiagnosed conditions" (p.207). Among 25 people with self-injurious behaviors, 28% had at least one untreated medical problem likely to cause pain (Bosch et al., 1997). Almost 75% of 1135 adults with mental retardation had undiagnosed or undertreated medical conditions (Ryan & Sunada, 1997). Even in the general population, both physicians and community nurses showed surprisingly high rates of misdiagnosing dementia in elderly patients (who were actually depressed or had a psychiatric disorder), and underdiagnosing dementia in elderly people who did have the condition (McCartney & Palmateer, 1985; O'Connor et al., 1988).

The process of correctly identifying a disease state, nutritional deficiency, or medication side effect in developmentally disabled people can require dogged determination, many medical tests, and considerable time. Compare this to patients who can clearly describe the nature, location, and duration of their symptoms. Correct diagnosis of a *primary problem* that causes a *secondary problem*--the behavioral concern--is crucial in treating people unable to self-report.

- **Correct identification of a painful, previously unrecognized illness points to medical treatment of that particular illness.** If self-hitting movements result from an underlying disease, once that medical condition is identified, treating the disease--the primary problem--is "the treatment" for the self-hitting.

- **Correct identification of a nutritional deficiency underlying a behavioral concern points to treatment of the deficiency.** If an eating disturbance or pica is due to a mineral deficiency, once it is identified, treating that condition--the primary problem--should ameliorate the secondary problem.

- **Correct identification of medication-induced behavior deterioration points to removal of the offending medication.** If agitation, aggression, or psychiatric symptoms are due to medication known to cause those effects (Medical Letter,1993), eliminating the offending medication becomes "the treatment."

- **Correct identification of an underlying neurochemical/psychiatric disorder points to treatment of that neurochemical imbalance.** If aggression to caregivers occurs when they interrupt a person unable to inhibit compulsions, once the neurochemical imbalance/psychiatric condition is recognized, treating it becomes the primary issue. The aggression results from difficulty inhibiting compulsions.

- **Correct identification of a health condition underlying a behavioral change--even if no successful treatment is available--points to better understanding of the issue, avoids misdiagnosis and improper treatments based on misdiagnosis.** If cognitive deterioration turns out to be caused by sleep deprivation from severe sleep apnea, even if the condition cannot be corrected medically, this avoids misdiagnosing the person with Alzheimer disease or other type of dementia. If rage attacks turn out to be nonconvulsive seizures, even if standard anticonvulsants are ineffective, this avoids misdiagnosing the person as deliberately aggressive and using negative reinforcement. If mania turns out to be due to a medication (e.g., vigabatrin/Sabril) or hyperthyroidism, this avoids inappropriate treatment with anti-manic drugs such as lithium, carbamazepine, or valproic acid.

An important part of treatment is the elimination of factors that worsen the condition. All 75 diagnostic categories have a section on *FACTORS THAT MAY WORSEN THE CONDITION* to assist clinicians and caregivers in identifying exacerbating factors.

A NOTE ON PERSONS DIAGNOSED WITH AUTISM

While persons with autism or Asperger syndrome show some of the behavioral concerns listed in this book, they might represent a special subgroup. Research indicates that 80-90% of persons with autism from 7 countries have intestinal peptides (opioids) that are toxic to the brain (Reichelt et al., 1997). Before using this guide for someone with autism, first consider the following. Determine if the person has (a) an overgrowth of intestinal yeast, (b) high levels of casein/gluten antibodies in the blood or peptides in the urine, or (c) multiple food allergies (immunoglobulin testing or elimination diet, not skin testing). I refer readers to work by Baker and Pangborn (1997) and Shaw et al. (1998). In brief, the steps to consider are:

1. Control an overgrowth of intestinal yeast--if present--which can follow antibiotic use (Crook, 1992; Danna et al., 1991; Shaw et al., 1998).
2. Correct a leaky gut. Allergenic foods cause alterations in intestinal permeability which allow unwanted substances to enter the bloodstream (Baker, 1997, p. 119). The colonization of yeast on the intestinal wall and repeated use of antibiotics can also cause a leaky gut (Shaw et al., 1998).
3. Restore normal gut flora (the "good bacteria"), especially after antibiotic use.
4. Remove sources of opioids or other food allergens from the diet, e.g., casein (milk), gluten (wheat).
5. Correct any vitamin or mineral deficiency resulting from a leaky gut.
6. Promote detoxification and avoid exposure to biologic, synthetic, or elemental toxins (Baker, 1997).
7. If encephalopathy is suspected, consider testing for a stealth virus causing autism (Martin, 1995;1996).

Because the above health concerns may be undiagnosed and untreated in some people with autism (see Shaw et al., 1998), these need to be addressed *first* before trying to use this diagnostic guide.

COMMENTS ON THE FORMAT AND TERMINOLOGY

To the extent that this book is a "catalogue of clues," the information is presented in an easy-to-access format. For example, the text is in point-form. And the eight subsections for each diagnostic category have been positioned in a uniform manner throughout the book.

The words used to refer to people who have mental retardation require extra sensitivity because social acceptability of terms varies over time and varies between countries. Rather than using "client," "person with a developmental disability," "person with mental retardation," or "person with DD or MR," the word "person" is used in the text to refer to someone with a developmental disability. At times, use of this referent also includes people from the general population as in "a person at risk for ulcers." Most users of this book will have in mind *an individual who has both a developmental disability and a behavioral concern.* A short way to say that countless times in this book has been to use the word "person."

COMMENTS ON USING THE CHECKLISTS

Sometimes knowing what questions to ask leads directly to the correct diagnosis. Sets of questions have been organized into "symptom checklists" to aid clinicians in gathering information. I suggest that clinicians or consultants complete the checklists by interviewing people very familiar with the individual. If interviewing is not feasible, caregivers and families could fill out checklists and return them to the clinician. If families or caregivers decide on their own to fill out a checklist, they should not try to make clinical diagnoses themselves. The information gathered needs to be evaluated by a clinician who determines if certain diagnostic criteria have been met. Symptom checklists help in gathering information that might otherwise have been overlooked, and in eliciting specific information from caregivers and family. They can assist clinicians in evaluating if diagnostic criteria have been met (e.g., obsessive-compulsive disorder) and in deciding to request further investigation (e.g., sleep studies, neurologic assessment). These checklists are *guides* for collecting information; they are not standardized tests with norms and scoring criteria.

USERS OF THIS GUIDE

The **Behavioral Diagnostic Guide** is intended for psychologists, behavioral consultants, physicians, psychiatric nurses, and allied professionals who work with people who have developmental disabilities. Different parts will be of more interest to some than others. It was also written with direct-care staff and families in mind, as it can help in formulating questions to ask the professionals. Instructors of university or college courses on special education could use this book as a textbook or workbook.

This book addresses behavioral concerns mostly in *adults* with developmental disabilities, but clinicians may find it useful for children with developmental disabilities or some adults without mental retardation.

WAYS TO USE THIS GUIDE

Unlike a book that one reads from the first to the last page, this book was designed to be read selectively depending on the clinical concern. I recommend a "step-by-step" approach for *ruling out* unlikely explanations and *narrowing* the categories to consider. Here are steps that a psychologist or behavioral consultant could take when using this guide.

PREPARATION: Choose one person at a time when working through a case.
> Obtain a detailed description of each "Presenting Concern" for the person, i.e., aggression, self-injury, screaming, sleep or eating disturbance, cognitive decline, and/or falls. Examples for Aggression, Self-Injurious Movements, and Sleep are found in the appendix.
> Have familiar caregivers and/or family provide details of the Presenting Concern.
> Add your own observations.
> List each medication the person takes and the "class" it is in, e.g., anticholinergic, anticonvulsant, benzodiazepine, beta blocker, histamine type 2 blocker, neuroleptic (antipsychotic).

STEP 1. Choose one Presenting Concern at a time (e.g., Aggression) to work through.
> Read **COMMON FORMS   VARIATIONS &   DISTINGUISHING FEATURES**
> for all Diagnostic Categories in that Chapter (e.g., AG.1 - AG.11).
> Rule out Categories that do not apply, or set them aside temporarily.
> Select about 2 - 4 Categories for further consideration (e.g., AG.1, AG.3, AG.6).

STEP 2. Read **FACTORS THAT MAY WORSEN THE CONDITION &**
> **PERSONS WHO MAY BE AT RISK**   for all the Categories selected in STEP 1.
> Narrow the selection to 1-2 Categories for that Presenting Concern (e.g., AG.1, AG.6).
> If other Presenting Concerns apply (e.g., Screaming, Sleep Disturbance), repeat STEPS 1 and 2
> by working through one concern at a time (e.g., SC.1 - SC.7 first, then SD.1 - SD. 13).
> Narrow the selection of Categories as much as possible at this stage.
> Keep in mind that people can have more than one "unrecognized condition" affecting behavior.

STEP 3. Read **SUGGESTIONS FOR COLLECTING INFORMATION** on the 1-2 Categories chosen.
> Collect information as suggested. Check additional sources for relevant information.
> Read **FACTORS THAT MAY WORSEN THE CONDITION** and list factors that apply.
> Read **MEDICAL TESTING / SCREENING**   and list any medical tests, etc. already done.
> Optional: obtain relevant literature from the library.

STEP 4. Provide the information collected (or a summary) to clinicians involved, especially physicians.
> Discuss ways to reduce or eliminate factors that could be worsening the condition.
> Physicians may decide to request further medical investigation.
> Monitor the outcome of any treatments tried, medication changes, and so on.

Physicians might first ask others to get the detailed descriptions and collect information for STEP 3, then focus on *MEDICAL TESTING / SCREENING* and *FACTORS THAT MAY WORSEN THE CONDITION*.
    A depiction of these steps is given on the next page.

PREPARATION: Get a thorough description of the Presenting Concern.
List each medication the person takes and the "class" it is in.

STEP 1.

Read these.
Narrow
the field.

AG.1	AG.2	AG.3	AG.4	AG.5	AG.6	AG.7	AG.8	AG.9	AG.10	AG.11
COMMON FORMS **VARIATIONS** **DISTINGUISHING** **FEATURES**										

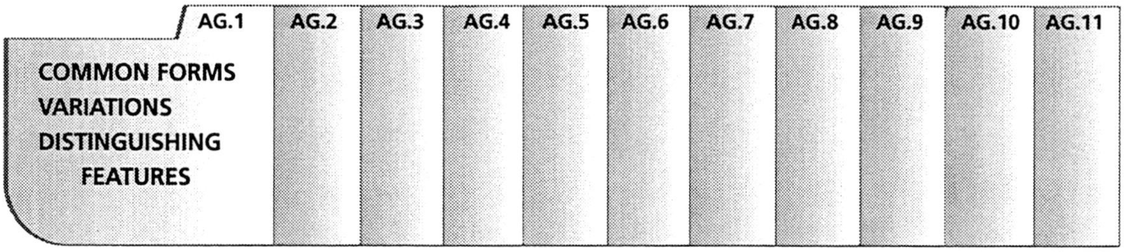

STEP 2.

Read these.
Narrow
the field.

AG.1	AG.6	AG.8
FACTORS...WORSEN **PERSONS WHO MAY** **BE AT RISK**		

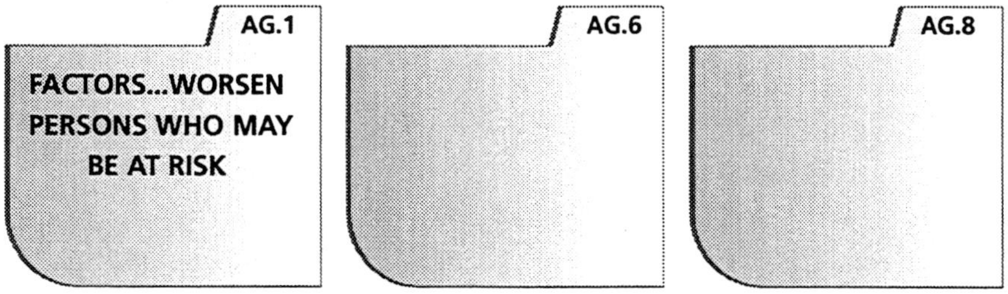

If the person also
screams often,
do STEPS 1 & 2
for SC.1 to SC.7,
or other Presenting
Concerns.

STEP 3.

Narrow to
1-2 Dx Cat.
for each
Presenting
Concern.

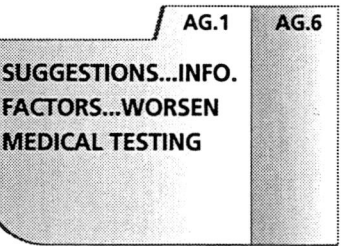

AG.1	AG.6
SUGGESTIONS...INFO. **FACTORS...WORSEN** **MEDICAL TESTING**	

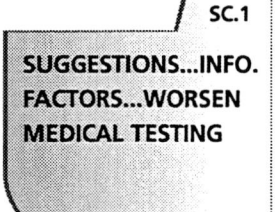

SC.1
SUGGESTIONS...INFO. **FACTORS...WORSEN** **MEDICAL TESTING**

→ Collect info. suggested.
→ List factors that apply.
→ List medical tests completed.

STEP 4.

Provide the physician or professional team with the information collected.
Discuss ways to reduce exacerbating factors.
Consider further medical investigation, if warranted.
Monitor the effect of changes in treatment.

While the ***Behavioral Diagnostic Guide*** does not cover every explanation for disruptive behavior and cognitive decline, it does provide a rational and systematic way to investigate such concerns in people unable to report symptoms.

Chapter I

PHYSICAL AGGRESSION

AG.1. Aggressive Response To Pain From An Illness or Medical Condition

AG.2. Aggressive Response To A Painful Transient Condition

AG.3. Aggression When Others Interfere With Compulsions

AG.4. Ictal Aggression During Nonconvulsive Frontal Lobe Seizures

AG.5. Ictal Or Interictal Aggression In Persons With Temporal Lobe Seizures

AG.6. Drug-Induced Aggression

AG.7. Aggression Associated With Hallucinations And/Or Delirium

AG.8. Flashback-Related Aggression In Persons With Post-Traumatic Stress Disorder

AG.9. Reactive Aggression

AG.10. Pre-Meditated Aggression

AG.11. Learned Behavior From Observing Others Or Being Rewarded For Aggressive Responses

Presenting Concern: **PHYSICAL AGGRESSION**
Dx Category   AG.1: *AGGRESSIVE RESPONSE TO PAIN FROM AN ILLNESS*
                     OR MEDICAL CONDITION

❑ COMMON FORMS
- the person uses one hand to hit someone once or a few times.
- grabbing another forcefully and digging one's fingers into the other's skin.
- biting others who approach to provide care or examine the person.
- hitting others who attempt to provide care or examine painful areas.
- if the person is verbal, telling others to go away or threatening verbally before hitting out and throwing things.
- guarding an area of the body, then hitting out when someone comes near or tries to examine the area being guarded.

❑ VARIATIONS
- running up to a caregiver, while appearing to be in pain, and squeezing the caregiver's arm forcefully.
- grabbing someone while crying, vocalizing, or whincing.
- grabbing someone with one hand while pressing the other hand somewhere on their own body.
- if the person is nonverbal, hitting or grabbing only caregivers (not peers) in an attempt to get the caregiver to help relieve the pain.
- if an ear infection is present, the person hits or grabs others and may also hit his/her own head or ears.
- violent and threatening actions in persons who are hyperactive, impulsive, and unresponsive to neuroleptic medication can be due to iron deficiency anemia (Tu et al., 1994).

❑ DISTINGUISHING FEATURES FOR AG.1
- the aggressive episodes stop after treatment (e.g., antibiotics, iron supplements) corrects the illness or medical condition.
- the aggressive episodes stop during periods when pain-relieving measures are in effect (e.g., for inflammation).
- the timing of the aggression is associated with eating or digesting food, in a person with esophageal reflux, stomach ulcers, or other gastrointestinal problems.

❑ FACTORS THAT MAY WORSEN THE CONDITION
- an infection that continues undetected or is quite extensive by the time it is discovered.
- increased pressure to perform activities that the person enjoys when well, but not when ill.
- increased pressure to perform tasks that previously were done easily, but have become difficult due to pain, declining hearing, or declining vision.
- noisy environments.
- caffeinated drugs, food, or beverages.
- if the person has reflux esophagitis: wearing tight clothing; eating before going to bed; sleeping on a level bed (instead of one with the head raised six inches); eating large meals; consuming citrus juices, tomatoes, hot spicy foods, caffeine, hot liquids, alcohol, chocolate, sweets, or high fat foods.
- discomfort from increased photosensitivity that can occur in persons taking a phenothiazine type of neuroleptic (e.g., chlorpromazine/Thorazine, thioridazine/Mellaril).
- using anticholinergics (e.g., benztropine/Cogentin, procyclidine/Procyclid), antispasmotics, or muscle relaxants in a person with reflux as these medications decrease tone of the esophageal sphincter.

❏ *PERSONS WHO MAY BE AT RISK*

- a person who is unable to report pain or physical symptoms, e.g., has no speech or is in the severe or profound range of intelligence.
- a nonverbal person with a history of ear infections, urinary infections, yeast infections, etc.
- persons with Down syndrome have increased susceptibility to infections (Lang, 1992).
- a person with reduced mobility (e.g., severe cerebral palsy) as this can lead to upper gastrointestinal problems such as esophageal reflux, feedings by nasogastric tube, and other feeding difficulties.
- a person with a leaky gut or a history of stomach or intestinal ulcers.
- a person at risk for developing an ulcer, e.g., a person with mental retardation due to phenylketonuria (PKU) who is on a regular diet with no protein restrictions.
- someone with undiagnosed ulcers taking ASA/Aspirin, anti-inflammatory medication, or valproic acid/ Depakene.
- someone with a metabolic disorder involving food, e.g., milk or wheat (casein-gluten peptiduria).
- persons with Down syndrome are at risk for celiac disease (a disorder involving gluten) that can cause bowel pain, diarrhea, constipation, and anemia (George et al., 1996; Simila & Kokkonen, 1990).
- a person in the late teens or early twenties who may have impacted wisdom teeth.
- a person with a history of poor dental hygiene or possible dental decay.
- a person with a condition associated with sensory impairments, e.g., Down syndrome, Meniere's disease. Meniere's disease is a recurrent and often progressive set of symptoms such as progressive deafness, ringing in the ears, dizziness, and a sensation of pressure in the ears (Thomas, 1993, p. 1191).

❏ *SUGGESTIONS FOR COLLECTING INFORMATION*

- obtain details about the nature of the aggression using the *Checklist for Describing Physical Aggression.**
- use the *Discomfort Scale** (Hurley et al., 1992) to assess a noncommunicative person for pain.
- rule out physical pain from transient conditions such as constipation or menstrual pain (see AG.2).
- tally the type and frequency of infections in the past 2-5 years to assess risk of recurrence.
- provide the person's temperature, pulse, and respirations per minute to the nurse and/or physician.
- if there are *unexplained* persistent gastrointestinal problems, collect information using the *Risk Factors for Casein-Gluten Peptiduria.**
- check family history for irritable bowel syndrome, celiac disease, and wheat or milk intolerance.

* *A chart or checklist listed in italics in this section can be found in the Appendix.*

❏ *MEDICAL TESTING / SCREENING AG.1*

- check for infection, especially in the ears, urinary tract, chest, and check the mouth for possible pain.
- check for symptoms suggestive of ulcers, bowel impaction, gall stones, kidney stones, etc.
- if there is a history of *unexplained* persistent gastrointestinal problems, test for intestinal parasites, yeast overgrowth, serum antibodies to common foods, especially casein-gluten antibodies in serum or casein-gluten peptides in urine. Test for celiac disease in Down syndrome (George et al., 1996).
- check if the person has dental examinations regularly and if daily oral hygiene is considered adequate.
- rule out recurring transient conditions as discussed in AG.2 (e.g., headaches, seasonal allergies, constipation, etc.)
- test for iron deficiency anemia (ferritin, serum iron, mean cell volume, etc.) if hemoglobin is borderline or low (Tu et al., 1994).

❏ *POSSIBLE BIOCHEMICAL / ANATOMICAL INVOLVEMENT*

- there may be an increase in cortisol, due to infection and/or physical pain, that activates the enzyme tryptophan pyrrolase (dioxygenase) leading to increased production of neuroexcitatory agents such as kynurenine and quinolinic acid and decreased production of serotonin (Stone, 1989).
- conditions such as esophagitis, esophageal reflux or stricture, stomach or duodenal ulcer can cause pain.

Examples include painful constipation, menstrual discomfort, histamine reaction to pollens, other allergens, or an exaggerated response to insect bites.

❏ *COMMON FORMS*
- the person uses one hand to hit someone once or a few times.
- grabbing another forcefully, digging one's fingers into the other's skin.
- guarding an area of the body, then hitting out when someone comes near or tries to examine the area being guarded.

❏ *VARIATIONS*
- if the person is nonverbal, hitting or grabbing only caregivers (not peers) in an attempt to get the caregiver to help relieve the pain.
- the hitting, kicking, or grabbing at others is accompanied by crying, screaming, or irritability that is unusual for that person.

❏ *DISTINGUISHING FEATURES FOR AG.2*
- the aggression or agitation ceases after the painful transient condition passes.
- the timing of the episodes coincides with the premenstrual or menstrual phase of the woman's cycle.
- the aggressive or agitated moments occur mostly within the hour before having--or trying to have--a bowel movement; the person strains to pass stool and/or has hard stool.
- the aggression/agitation stops and mood improves after passing stool or after menstrual pain is alleviated.

❏ *FACTORS THAT MAY WORSEN THE CONDITION*
- using medication that suppresses bowel functioning (e.g., phenothiazines such as thioridazine/Mellaril, chlorpromazine/Largactil, mesoridazine/Serentil, methotrimeprazine/Nozinan) (De Silva et al., 1992) in a person with frequent constipation.
- using a tricyclic antidepressant (e.g., clomipramine/Anafranil, imipramine/Tofranil) in an elderly person who has constipation as this can suppress bowel functioning (paralytic ileus).
- a high fiber diet with a low intake of water in a person with constipation.
- a wasp/spider bite or multiple mosquito bites in a person who has histamine overreactions to insect bites.
- eating foods that cause an allergic reaction.

❑ *PERSONS WHO MAY BE AT RISK*

- a person who is unable to report pain or physical symptoms, e.g., has no speech or is in the severe or profound range of intelligence.
- a person with reduced mobility (e.g., severe cerebral palsy) as this can lead to pressure sores, joint pain, stiffness, and muscle contractures.
- a person taking a phenothiazine medication as this increases the risk of paralytic ileus, megacolon, constipation, and other bowel problems (De Silva et al., 1992).
- a person taking two or more medications that have constipation as a possible adverse effect.
- a person with a history of bowel problems or constipation. Constipation is a frequent finding in Williams syndrome (Bradley & Udwin, 1989).
- a person who has taken laxatives continuously for many years.
- a woman in the menopausal years when hormonal changes can be marked.
- a person with allergies or a family history of allergies.
- a person with a family history of migraines who also has clusters of features such as: seeking a darkened area, covering the eyes, being extra sensitive to noise, wanting to lie still, refusing to eat or do activities, with occasional vomiting.
- persons with Down syndrome have increased susceptibility to infections (Lang, 1992).

❑ *SUGGESTIONS FOR COLLECTING INFORMATION*

- obtain details about the nature of the aggression using the *Checklist for Describing Physical Aggression*.
- use the *Discomfort Scale* (Hurley et al., 1992) to assess a noncommunicative person for pain.
- chart the day and hour of aggressive episodes. Chart the day and hour of bowel movements and attempts to pass stool; rate unusual size, firmness, and color of stool passed, or signs suggesting constipation.
- record juice and water intake for one or more weeks if the person has a history of constipation.
- chart the timing of aggression and the onset and duration of menses; collect information using the *Menstrual Distress Chart*. With women able to be interviewed, consider using the "Menstrual Distress Questionnaire" (Moos, 1968).
- chart the timing of aggression to see if it is associated with food intake.
- review the history for past response to insect bites, possible allergic responses to food, family history of allergies, or seasonal recurrence of nasal congestion and red eyes.
- check family history for migraines and allergies.
- provide the person's temperature, pulse, and respirations per minute to the nurse and/or physician.

❑ *MEDICAL TESTING / SCREENING AG.2*

- check for bowel parasites if the person has constipation and is unable to indicate pain reliably.
- check stools for occult blood (a chemical test or microscopic examination for blood in feces which is not seen on visual inspection).
- request a dietitian to evaluate the person's current intake of fiber and water.
- check if the aggression is seasonal or associated with stuffy nose, red eyes, or other known allergic responses suggestive of chronic or seasonal allergies.
- test for allergies if risk factors are present and the assessment supports this.
- consider a trial of analgesics or anti-migraine medication to help diagnose suspected headaches.

❑ *POSSIBLE BIOCHEMICAL / ANATOMICAL INVOLVEMENT*

- there may be low intake of water with high intake of fiber causing hard-to-pass stools and/or suppression of bowel function from phenothiazine type neuroleptics (De Silva et al., 1992).
- there may be an increase in cortisol, due to infection or physical pain, that activates the enzyme tryptophan pyrrolase (dioxygenase) leading to increased production of neuroexcitatory agents such as kynurenine and quinolinic acid and decreased production of serotonin (Stone, 1989).
- there may be an increased release of prostaglandins during menstruation or migraine associated with pain.

Presenting Concern: **PHYSICAL AGGRESSION**
Dx Category AG.3: *AGGRESSION WHEN OTHERS INTERFERE WITH COMPULSIONS*

❏ *COMMON FORMS*

- the anger or aggression is directed at anyone who tries to prevent the person from doing compulsive activities (Barak et al., 1995; Gedye, 1992a; 1996a).
- the aggressive motions of pushing, kicking, and hitting another are directed at trying "to remove the obstacle" impeding the person from completing a ritual or compulsive activity.

❏ *VARIATIONS*

- the hitting and kicking stop when the intervener stops preventing the person from doing compulsive activities or obsessive talking.
- the person has been insisting on doing a certain activity or doing something in a fixed way, and the insistence escalates into an argument with the caregiver. Frustration increases, voices rise, then the person runs after the caregiver to hit, kick, push, or cause injury.
- the person has been demanding that someone else do such-and-such (which is dangerous or not feasible). The obsessive talking escalates into loud yelling of these demands. If caregivers approach at that time, they get hit or pushed.
- compulsive stalking and hitting.

❏ *DISTINGUISHING FEATURES FOR AG.3*

- the aggression occurs when the person is engaged in obsessive talking or compulsive activity.
- the person fits the criteria for obsessive-compulsive disorder (OCD) as applicable to people with young mental ages (DSM-IV, 1994; Gedye, 1992a; 1996a; McDougle et al., 1995).
- the person's anger and aggression are directed at the individual who tries to prevent the person from performing compulsions.
- the aggression may be a single hit or kick in an attempt to remove the block, so the compulsive activity can resume.
- the duration of aggression is usually brief, lasting seconds or no more than two minutes, *unless* the intervener continues to argue with or interrupt the person.

❏ *FACTORS THAT MAY WORSEN THE CONDITION*

- expecting the person to be able to stop the obsessions or compulsions immediately, and reprimanding the person when he/she does not comply.
- exposing the person to triggering stimuli such as objects that elicit the person's compulsions or raising topics that elicit obsessive talk. (This does not refer to exposure where one tries to desensitize the person).
- dietary factors that reduce serotonin production, e.g., high protein diet, caffeinated drinks (Gedye, 1990; 1991d; 1991e).
- medications that reduce the production and release of serotonin such as benzodiazepines (e.g., diazepam/ Valium, lorazepam/Ativan) (Essman & Essman, 1986; Green, 1986; Pei et al., 1989; Saner & Pletscher, 1979; Wise et al., 1972).
- most neuroleptics/antipsychotics as they are ineffective with OCD or can worsen OCD (Baker et al., 1992; Baldwin et al., 1992; Vitiello et al., 1989).
- medication that can induce or worsen obsessive-compulsive symptoms such as clozapine/Clozaril (Baker et al., 1992; Patel & Tandon, 1993; Patil, 1992) or clothiapine (Toren et al., 1995).

❏ *PERSONS WHO MAY BE AT RISK*

- a person with a family history of OCD (Rasmussen & Eisen, 1990).
- adults with Down syndrome are at risk for OCD (Prasher & Day, 1995) or subclinical OCD.
- a person who hoards, cleans excessively, insists on arranging objects, and takes a traditional neuroleptic and/or a benzodiazepine. These medications risk worsening obsessive-compulsive disorder (Baker et al., 1992; Baldwin et al., 1992; Vitiello et al., 1989).
- persons with Fragile X syndrome are at risk for obsessive-compulsive behavior (Dorn et al., 1994).
- a person on clozapine, as it can induce obsessive-compulsive symptoms in those with no prior symptoms.
- a person with a history of frontal head injury, as OCD may develop thereafter (Donovan & Barry, 1994).
- a person with Asperger syndrome (Scragg & Shah, 1994).

❏ *SUGGESTIONS FOR COLLECTING INFORMATION*

- obtain details about the nature of the aggression using the *Checklist for Describing Physical Aggression*.
- use the *Compulsive Behavior Checklist* as a guide for collecting information in persons with mental retardation to see if the diagnostic criteria (DSM-IV, 1994) for OCD are met. The "lack of recognition of the diversity of presenting symptoms in OCD by professionals, misdiagnosis, failure to ask OCD screening questions in the routine mental status examination" have contributed to OCD cases going unrecognized (Rasmussen & Eisen, 1990, p. 10). (See also Gedye, 1992a; 1996a).
- with persons able to converse, use the *Obsessive Speech Checklist* for collecting information in this population.
- use the *OCD Severity Scale* (Vitiello et al., 1989) to rate severity of obsessive-compulsive features in persons with developmental disabilities.
- check family history for obsessive-compulsive disorder and depression.
- assess for depression as a contributing factor using instruments or criteria appropriate for this population (e.g., Cooper & Collacott, 1994; Sovner, 1986). Use the *Checklist of Observable Signs of Depression*.
- for those able to read and label different emotional states, the "Children's Depression Inventory" (Kovacs, 1985) has been used for screening depression in developmentally disabled people (Meins, 1993).

❏ *MEDICAL TESTING / SCREENING AG.3*

- if the person is already on anti-obsessional medication, be aware that "OCD patients tend to respond to medication with only 30% to 60% symptom reduction and patients tend to remain chronically symptomatic to some degree despite the best of pharmacological interventions." (Jenike, 1992, p. 895).
- review medications for ones that risk causing obsessive-compulsive symptoms (e.g., clozapine), that are ineffective, or that can worsen symptoms (e.g., neuroleptics, benzodiazepines) (Baker et al., 1992; Baldwin et al., 1992).
- PET scans of OCD patients during exposure to triggering stimuli can show abnormalities in the frontal and basal ganglia area, but these are expensive and require very cooperative patients.

❏ *POSSIBLE BIOCHEMICAL / ANATOMICAL INVOLVEMENT*

- frontal-subcortical circuits, i.e., orbital frontal (often left), bilateral caudate, and thalamus, are involved in OCD (Ames et al., 1994; Baxter, 1992; 1994; Galderisi et al., 1995; Mega & Cummings, 1994; Rapoport, 1989a).
- central serotonin deficiency is strongly implicated in OCD (Baldwin et al., 1992; De Groot et al., 1995; Jenike et al., 1990; Zohar et al.,1987) and possibly dopamine involvement in some cases (Goodman et al., 1990).

❑ *COMMON FORMS*

- there are repetitive, bilateral arm motions that result in striking hard surfaces (walls, doors) or someone nearby, accompanied by intense facial expressions, rapid breathing, and intense vocalizations.
- the hitting continues for 2-5 minutes or up to 30 minutes; in unusual cases the person continues the hitting/kicking/vocalizing on and off for hours.
- during outbursts with hitting or kicking, often there is staring, a vacant or wild look, head and eyes look to the side, grimacing, teeth clenched, jaw jutting, intense vocalizations, occasional biting or spitting.
- during outbursts with hitting or kicking, the person often has rapid or noisy breathing, facial flushing or pallor, pupil dilation; sometimes there is excessive saliva or drooling, incontinence, or sweating.

❑ *VARIATIONS*

- the person throws nearby objects or destroys nearby objects during sudden outbursts.
- the person may have little or no awareness of what happened during the "attack" (Munari et al., 1981; Waterman et al., 1987).
- if the person has awareness of events during an intense outburst, he or she often shows remorse or apologizes for hurting another, saying that he or she did not mean to hurt anyone.

❑ *DISTINGUISHING FEATURES FOR AG.4*

- the episode can follow anger and frustration or occur "out-of-the-blue," i.e., without provocation. Ictal aggression is often unprovoked (Creaby et al., 1993).
- the person seems to be physically stronger than usual during these involuntary outbursts.
- there is an abrupt onset of intense motor movements, vocalizations, with autonomic changes such as facial flushing or pallor, pupil dilation, and/or sweating (references in Gedye, 1989a; 1991a; 1996b). See list of 60 possible ictal signs by Gedye (1996b) in the Appendix.
- often there is intense staring, a vacant or wild look in the eyes, head and eyes look left at times, grimacing, teeth clenched or jaw jutting, intense vocalizations, and occasional biting or spitting.
- often there is noisy breathing or accelerated breathing, facial flushing or pallor, pupil dilation; sometimes there is excessive saliva or drooling, incontinence, or sweating.
- the person may also display minor versions of the intense outbursts such as head-turning, fixed staring with drooling, or grimacing with a vacant look.
- often there are body movements inconsistent with deliberate aggressive intent such as: repeated head-turning; arms flailing in mid-air; eyes looking up at the ceiling repeatedly; hitting one's own face, chest or leg during an episode; backward head-thrusting in mid-air; or twirling (Gedye, 1996b).
- standard antiepileptic drugs may be ineffective or worsen nonconvulsive frontal lobe seizures (Delgado et al., 1991; Fusco et al., 1990; Horn et al., 1986; Stores et al., 1991).
- the person resumes pre-outburst activity without bearing grudges or making angry comments.

❑ *FACTORS THAT MAY WORSEN THE CONDITION*

- criticizing or trying to argue with the person during an involuntary outburst.
- trying forcefully to stop the arm movements.
- dietary factors that reduce serotonin production, e.g., high protein diet, caffeinated food or drink (Gedye, 1990; 1991d; 1991e).
- medications that reduce the production and release of serotonin such as benzodiazepines (e.g., diazepam/ Valium, lorazepam/Ativan) (Essman & Essman, 1986; Green, 1986; Pei et al., 1989; Saner & Pletscher, 1979; Wise et al., 1972).
- medication that can worsen frontal lobe seizures, e.g., carbamazepine/Tegretol (Horn et al., 1986).
- standard anticonvulsants can worsen frontal lobe seizures in some people (Delgado et al., 1991; Fusco et al., 1990; Horn et al., 1986; Stores et al., 1991).
- phenobarbital can exacerbate certain types of aggression in this population (Hanzel et al., 1992).

- medication that lowers the seizure threshold, e.g., neuroleptics (haloperidol/Haldol, thioridazine/ Mellaril).
- the following are possible stressors and times of risk, especially for intense episodes of involuntary movements: high noise level or a startling event; bright sunlight or flickering light; lacking sleep or being overtired; low blood sugar, missing a meal or a history of hypoglycemia; allergic reactions to pollens, etc. or an exaggerated response to insect bites; highly emotional events, positive or negative; anger or emotional frustration; stress or pressure to perform; a change in plans or in routine sequence; premenstrual or menstrual phase; in the waking hours of the morning or when falling asleep (times when consciousness is shifting); late afternoon; mealtime (breakfast, lunch, or supper). (See references in Gedye, 1991b; 1996b). The 1996b article is reprinted in the Appendix.

❏ *PERSONS WHO MAY BE AT RISK*
- a person with temporal lobe seizures (because temporal discharges can spread to the frontal area) (Lieb et al., 1991; Luciano, 1993; Quesney et al., 1995; Veilleux et al., 1992; Williamson, 1995).
- a person with Tuberous Sclerosis who has tubers in the frontal area.
- a person with known frontal lobe abnormality or frontal lobe seizures (Gedye 1989a; Shah, 1992).
- a person with a history of head injury or physical abuse that might have caused head trauma.
- a person with a leaky gut, food allergies, and/or intestinal yeast overgrowth.
- a person who wakes from sleep with hand-biting (Mizuno et al.,1979), head-thrusting, or the person's hand is hitting their head.
- a person with frequent involuntary movements that are sometimes called "stereotypic movements."
- a person with an etiology known to have low levels of serotonin, e.g., Cornelia De Lange syndrome, Down syndrome, histidinemia, phenylketonuria (PKU) (Coleman, 1973; Greenberg & Coleman, 1973; Lou et al., 1985; Tu & Partington, 1972).
- a person with a history of birth trauma, anoxia, encephalitis, rubella, tuberous sclerosis, or head injury, who was diagnosed with Tourette syndrome and has no family history of this syndrome (Gedye, 1991c).

❏ *SUGGESTIONS FOR COLLECTING INFORMATION*
- obtain details about the nature of the aggression using the *Checklist for Describing Physical Aggression*.
- videotape the person during outbursts to help detect observable involuntary phenomena.
- check for a high number of ictal signs during outbursts using the *Nonconvulsive Ictal Signs Checklist* (Gedye, 1996b); carefully review the high risk times and stressors identified on that Checklist. If there are high-risk times and stressors, inform caregivers of these.

❏ *MEDICAL TESTING / SCREENING AG.4*
- consider an EEG and neurological investigation for frontal lobe seizures. However, scalp or sphenoidal EEGs are often normal during seizures and between seizures (Luciano, 1993; Stores et al., 1991); see literature review (Gedye, 1991b; 1996b).
- obtain a thorough listing of unusual features (possible ictal features) that occur during the person's aggressive episodes. The observable pattern of features during these seizures was the basis for diagnosis by neurologists experienced with nonconvulsive frontal lobe seizures (Fusco et al., 1990; Takeda, 1988; Williamson, 1995).
- review medications for ones that can lower the seizure threshold.
- rule out food allergies by testing for serum antibodies to common foods.

❏ *POSSIBLE BIOCHEMICAL / ANATOMICAL INVOLVEMENT*
- the mesial-basal area of the frontal lobes is often involved in frontal lobe seizures (Quesney et al., 1984; Waterman et al., 1987).
- central serotonin deficiency and possibly GABA may be involved in involuntary muscle contractions (Paul & Krishnamoorthy, 1990).
- adverse effects on the central nervous system from multiple food allergies can cause nonconvulsive seizures (Gobbi et al., 1992).

Presenting Concern: **PHYSICAL AGGRESSION**
Dx Category   AG.5: *ICTAL OR INTERICTAL AGGRESSION IN PERSONS WITH TEMPORAL*
LOBE SEIZURES

❏ *COMMON FORMS*
- the person has "unpredictable outbursts or rage and aggression" (Gillberg et al., 1996).
- the episodes may begin with blank expression or look of disgust and unnatural posturing of leg or arm, followed by head and body turning to one side (Hiyoshi et al., 1989).
- aggression can occur during a seizure, after a seizure (postictal), or between seizures (interictal).
- during a postictal disoriented state, the person may hit anyone nearby or anyone who tries to restrain the person.
- during aggressive acts between seizures (the interictal period), the person is alert, attentive, and may become angry over trivial events.

❏ *VARIATIONS*
- the person suddenly becomes glassy-eyed, flails one arm, grabs people's hair, shows no anger or fear, seems confused, is unresponsive when told to stop, and is slow to resume his or her usual level of alertness (Ryan, 1996b).
- there may be sudden attacks of flushing, heart racing, sweating, and feelings of fear or rage.
- the ictal events may begin with unilateral movements such as unnatural posturing of one arm or leg, head and body turning to one side, one eye blinking, and/or facial asymmetry (Kotagal et al., 1989).
- the person may be awakened at night by intense episodes of involuntary movements.
- seizure-related phenomena can last over two hours. Postictal psychosis can last many days (Kanemoto et al., 1996).
- aggression during postictal psychosis can warrant police making arrests (Kanemoto et al., 1996).
- between seizures, the person may feel an urge to hit someone.
- between seizures, the person may develop a delusional state, be suspicious of others, may plan actions to harm another person, or may target certain staff or new arrivals.

❏ *DISTINGUISHING FEATURES FOR AG.5*
- there is consistency in the way involuntary features present for each person over time (Tucker et al., 1986).
- during seizures, the person suddenly shows several features listed above in the *VARIATIONS* section.
- recall of actions/speech during the episode can be patchy, minimal, or reflect complete amnesia. If there is recall, the person may apologize or show remorse.
- temporal lobe epilepsy is diagnosed (Tucker et al., 1986; Varney et al., 1992).
- when aggressive behaviors occur in the period between temporal lobe seizures (not during seizures), the person has frequent feelings of anger (Tucker et al., 1986).
- aggressive behavior during postictal psychosis can occur without confusion or impaired consciousness (Kanemoto et al., 1996).

❏ *FACTORS THAT MAY WORSEN THE CONDITION*
- interpersonal stress (Tucker et al., 1986).
- premenstrual changes (Tucker et al., 1986).
- bright sunlight (Ryan, 1996b, p. 33).
- restraining the person during the postictal period of a temporal lobe seizure (Devinsky & Bear, 1984).
- misdiagnosing the person as psychotic as such people are "often placed on antipsychotic medication which may even exacerbate the symptoms" of temporal lobe epilepsy (Farber et al., 1986, p. 78).
- medication that lowers the seizure threshold such as neuroleptics or tricyclics (e.g., imipramine/Tofranil) (Tucker et al., 1986), or using tricyclic antidepressants in slow metabolizers (Dailey & Naritoku, 1996).

❏ *PERSONS WHO MAY BE AT RISK*
- a person with temporal lobe epilepsy (Tucker et al.,1986; Varney et al.,1992) or complex partial seizures.
- a person with a history of head injury (Varney et al., 1992) or head injury before age 5 years (Marks et al., 1995).
- a person with a history of encephalitis, e.g., herpes simplex encephalitis (Sanders et al., 1997).
- someone who reports distortions of time speeding up or slowing down, distortions of uncanny familiarity or not recognizing the familiar, distortions of personal reality, illusions of size of a body part (micropsia, macropsia), seeing or hearing things that others do not (Farber et al., 1986; Tucker et al., 1986).
- someone who shows panic-like anxiety or sudden depressive moods unrelated to any precipitant (McNamara & Fogel, 1990; Tucker et al., 1986).
- someone with a history of smelling things that others do not, suggestive of olfactory hallucinations (Luciano, 1993).
- someone who draws, prints, or writes excessively especially if very large (hypergraphia) or very small (micrographia).
- persons who present with postictal psychosis may also show disinhibited sexual behavior and elevated mood (Kanemoto et al., 1996).

❏ *SUGGESTIONS FOR COLLECTING INFORMATION*
- obtain details about the nature of the aggression using the *Checklist for Describing Physical Aggression*.
- videotape the person during outbursts to help detect observable involuntary phenomena.
- if the person is verbal, check for signs of temporal lobe dysfunction using the "Structured Clinical Interview for Complex Partial Seizure Symptoms" (Roberts et al., 1992; Varney et al., 1992).
- check if the person reports phenomena suggestive of time illusions; distortions of personal awareness; somatic distortions of size or shape (arm seems huge or tiny); visual, auditory or olfactory illusions. These can be indicative of temporal lobe dysfunction.
- temporal lobe seizures can spread to the frontal lobe (Luciano, 1993; Munari et al., 1981) and vice versa, so also use the *Nonconvulsive Ictal Signs Checklist* as some episodes reflect frontal and temporal signs.
- assess for sudden-onset depression in relation to signs of temporal lobe disturbance (Tucker et al., 1986).
- rule out psychosis; collect information using the *Checklist of Observable Signs of Psychosis in Persons with Mental Retardation*. (See also Ryan, 1996b).
- if relentless writing and/or drawing is present, rule out obsessive-compulsive disorder as the explanation; collect information using the *Compulsive Behavior Checklist*.

❏ *MEDICAL TESTING / SCREENING AG.5*
- request an EEG (sleep EEG if possible) and neurologic investigation for temporal lobe epilepsy or temporal lobe dysfunction. The "medial temporal lobe focus might well escape detection by the surface EEG, while dysrythmias conducted to the cortex would be observed." (Devinsky & Bear, 1984, p. 653). EEG theta bursts may correlate with an abundance of seizure-like symptoms (Varney et al., 1992). Neurologic exams and CT scans can be normal in temporal lobe epileptics (Tucker et al., 1986). Not all temporal lobe epileptics improve on anticonvulsant trials (Sperling et al., 1996). The majority of temporal lobe epileptics are not overtly violent people.
- review medications for possible lowering of the seizure threshold, if seizures are involved.
- rule out repeated bouts of hypoglycemia (Guberman et al., 1986).

❏ *POSSIBLE BIOCHEMICAL / ANATOMICAL INVOLVEMENT*
- aggression can occur during temporal lobe seizures and possibly between seizures (Tucker et al., 1986).
- the amygdala-hippocampus may be involved in non-ictal episodes of rage and aggression (Sachdev et al., 1992) and in ictal aggression (Saint-Hilaire et al., 1980); the lateral hypothalamus and amygdala seem to facilitate defensive and predatory aggression (Pinel, 1990, p. 362).
- in some cases, the epileptic discharge spreads from the temporal lobe to orbital pre-frontal cortex, thus impairing socially acquired inhibitory control over aggressive impulses (Devinsky & Bear, 1984, p. 654.)

❑ *COMMON FORMS*
- the person starts to show aggression, agitation, or hyperactivity after a medication is introduced or increased.
- pre-existing aggression and agitation worsen after a medication is introduced or increased.
- the person has marked motor restlessness and may strike others indiscriminately when walking by them.
- a previously friendly, well-behaved person starts breaking objects, throwing self to the floor, pinching, biting others, pulling people's hair, and spitting on others (Commander et al., 1991).

❑ *VARIATIONS*
- hyperactivity or motor restlessness may appear with the onset or worsening of aggression.
- if on triazolam/Halcion, the person may show fearfulness and strange behaviors that are unusual for the person.
- the aggressive actions occur after using alcohol, street drugs, or benzodiazepines.

❑ *DISTINGUISHING FEATURES FOR AG.6*
- the frequency of hitting (or other physical aggression) returns to its previously lower level after the offending medication is reduced or withdrawn.
- if any features (e.g., motor restlessness) began about the same time period when the hitting began, both the aggression and concurrent features cease when the offending medication is withdrawn.

❑ *FACTORS THAT MAY WORSEN THE CONDITION*
- increasing the dose of the offending medication (e.g., carbamazepine/Tegretol).
- adding another medication that slows the clearance of the offending medication e.g., adding a neuroleptic to carbamazepine increases the risk of neurotoxicity of both medications.
- using valproic acid/Depakene with carbamazepine (Friedman et al., 1992).
- providing caffeinated foods or beverages (Podboy & Mallory, 1977).

❏ *PERSONS WHO MAY BE AT RISK*
- a person taking "ordinary doses" of propranolol/Inderal (Gershon et al., 1979).
- a person taking a benzodiazepine, especially clonazepam/Rivotril/Klonopin (Rivinus, 1982).
- a person taking phenytoin/Dilantin or sodium valproate/Epival (Bhatara & Carrera, 1994; Rivinus,1982).
- a person taking vigabatrin/Sabril (Aldenkamp et al., 1994; Matilainen et al., 1989).
- a person with reduced intake of food related to difficulty staying seated at meals due to continuous motor restlessness (not a loss of appetite) who is taking psychotropic or anticonvulsant medication.
- a person taking medication that increases the risk of neurotoxicity of carbamazepine (e.g., neuroleptics).
- a person taking valproic acid with carbamazepine (Friedman et al., 1992).
- severely or profoundly developmentally disabled adults with long-standing self-injury, irritability, stripping, and noisiness who are taking carbamazepine (Reid et al., 1981).
- a person with mental retardation taking carbamazepine (Friedman et al., 1992; Silverstein et al., 1982).
- a person with therapeutic blood levels of carbamazepine (Friedman et al., 1992; Pleak et al., 1988; Silverstein et al., 1982; Snead & Hosey, 1985).
- persons with prior adverse reactions to tricyclic antidepressants (e.g., clomipramine/Anafranil, imipramine/Tofranil) may be at increased risk on carbamazepine because of structural similarities of these medications (Friedman et al., 1992).
- a child with mental retardation who previously showed aggression and behavior deterioration on valproic acid may be at risk for a similar drug-induced reaction to carbamazepine (Bhatara & Carrera, 1994).

❏ *SUGGESTIONS FOR COLLECTING INFORMATION*
- obtain details about the nature of the aggression using the *Checklist for Describing Physical Aggression*.
- review records for start or increase in medication related to the onset or worsening of aggression and/or agitation.
- check if there are risk factors for carbamazepine-induced behavior deterioration such as the presence of mental retardation (Mathew, 1988; Reid et al., 1981; Silverstein et al., 1982); severe and profound mental retardation with long-standing self-injury, irritability, stripping or screaming (Reid et al., 1981); having mental retardation and receiving carbamazepine solely for behavior, not for epilepsy (Friedman et al., 1992); or concurrent use of valproic acid or thioridazine/Mellaril (Friedman et al., 1992).

❏ *MEDICAL TESTING / SCREENING AG.6*
- review medications for ones with aggression or rage as a possible side effect, e.g., anticonvulsants, benzodiazepines, bromocriptine/Parlodel, naloxone/Narcan, phenelzine/Nardil (Medical Letter, 1993; Rivinus, 1982). Note that behavior deterioration due to carbamazepine frequently occurred at therapeutic blood levels (Mathew, 1988; Pleak et al., 1988; Silverstein et al., 1982).
- consider a trial off suspected medication(s) and request systematic charting of the target features in order to evaluate medication changes.

❏ *POSSIBLE BIOCHEMICAL / ANATOMICAL INVOLVEMENT*
- medication such as benzodiazepines can cause disinhibition (Estroff & Gold, 1986).
- withdrawal psychosis can occur after discontinuing alcohol or sedatives; reactions to withdrawal may be delayed with some long-acting drugs such as diazepam/Valium (Medical Letter, 1993).
- adverse neurochemical effects from one drug or from drug interactions (Buchannan, 1992) can cause behavior deterioration, even at therapeutic drug levels (Bezchlibnyk-Butler et al., 1994; Friedman et al., 1992).
- in some people, carbamazepine activates epileptiform discharges evident on EEGs (Pleak et al., 1988; Snead & Hosey, 1985).
- another possibility is that some medications are associated with increased bodily discomfort (e.g., constipation, akathisia, epigastric activity) that in turn increases irritability and the risk for striking out.

Presenting Concern: **PHYSICAL AGGRESSION**
Dx Category   AG.7:   *AGGRESSION ASSOCIATED WITH DELIRIUM AND/OR*
                            HALLUCINATIONS

❑ *COMMON FORMS*

- the person, within a short period of time (usually hours or days), shows signs of delirium, i.e., a reduced level of awareness, reduced ability to focus, disorientation, language or memory or perceptual disturbance. In this state, the person is easily angered and might kick, push, or hit out.
- persons who have recently become disoriented push or strike a caregiver who enters their personal space.
- the person, unlike his/her usual self, is physically resistive during routine care and hits or pushes others.
- the person grabs the arm of a caregiver or supervisor while giving the appearance of needing something.

❑ *VARIATIONS*

- a person showing signs of delirium might misperceive others as threatening and attack them.
- the person wakes at night, is disoriented to time and place, does not recognize caregivers, and may hit out.
- the person who is delirious has motor restlessness, paces often, and may hit, kick or push staff when they intervene.
- aggression, delusions, and confusion start after a tonic clonic (grand mal) seizure in a person who is in nonconvulsive status epilepticus--which can last 1-7 days (Kaplan, 1996).

❑ *DISTINGUISHING FEATURES FOR AG.7*

- hallucinations can be caused by delirium, schizophrenia, or adverse effects of medication.
- a person with auditory hallucinations may have a running conversation that includes speaking what the voices are saying.
- the hallucinations are genuine as opposed to imaginary friends, an active fantasized social life, post-traumatic flashbacks, or echolalic speech misinterpreted as conversing with non-existent people.
- the person may fit the diagnostic criteria for delirium (e.g., DSM-IV, 1994).
- the delirium clears after the acute or chronic medical illness causing it is successfully treated (Raskind & Risse, 1986).
- if the delirium is drug-induced, the cognitive decline reverses after the toxic state is eliminated (e.g., the offending medication is discontinued).
- a person with epilepsy can be confused, delusional, and aggressive while in nonconvulsive status epilepticus lasting 1-7 days; it resolves with appropriate antiseizure treatment (Kaplan, 1996).
- the person may show unambiguous features of schizophrenia (Ryan, 1996b), especially if there is a family history of schizophrenia.

❑ *FACTORS THAT MAY WORSEN THE CONDITION*

- threatening the person or otherwise increasing the person's fear.
- arguing with the person about whether what they perceive is real or not.
- unstructured, unpredictable environments, especially in persons with dementia (Raskind & Risse, 1986).
- "delirious patients often worsen during the night" (Hales & Hershey, 1984, p. 822).
- lack of normal sleep and having abnormal REM (rapid eye movement) periods may exacerbate symptoms of delirium (Hales & Hershey, 1984).
- cognitively-impairing drugs (e.g., neuroleptics) can worsen a delirium (Raskind & Risse, 1986).
- benzodiazepine medications can worsen a delirium.
- "withdrawal from an anti-anxiety agent or hypnotic agent can precipitate or exacerbate delirium in the elderly patient" (Raskind & Risse, 1986, p. 21).

❑ *PERSONS WHO MAY BE AT RISK*

- a person with advanced age, brain damage, polypharmacy, surgery and immobilization, and sensory under- or over-stimulation (Jain, 1996, p. 59).
- a person in a postoperative state (Raskind & Risse, 1986).
- a person with a history of delirium.

- a person with a family history of hallucinations.
- a person taking tricyclic medication as it increases the risk for delirium (Lowenthal & Nadeau, 1991).
- someone taking barbiturates.
- a person undergoing medication changes that may produce toxicity or withdrawal effects.
- a person with mild chronic organic brain syndrome or mild mental retardation as this appears to increase sensitivity to the toxic effects of anticonvulsants and to drug-induced psychosis (Franks & Richter,1979).
- persons taking anticonvulsants can show psychotic features such as "paranoid delusions and auditory, visual, and tactile hallucinations that are indistinguishable from schizophrenia or mania." (Estroff & Gold, 1986, p. 172).

❑ *SUGGESTIONS FOR COLLECTING INFORMATION*
- obtain details about the nature of the aggression using the *Checklist for Describing Physical Aggression*.
- check for reduced ability to maintain attention or shift attention, as well as memory impairment compared to previous functioning, and disorientation to time, place, or person, i.e., look for signs of delirium.
- chart the timing of aggression to see if it is related to a disoriented state, a disturbed sleep pattern, medication increases, untreated infection, fever, or other health conditions.
- check for recent onset of command hallucinations, delusions, and other psychotic features; collect information using the *Checklist of Observable Signs of Psychosis in Persons with Mental Retardation*.
- check for features (such as an active fantasy life) that can be misinterpreted as hallucinations in this population (DesNoyers Hurley, 1996).
- check if the diagnostic criteria for delirium (DSM-IV, 1994) have been met.
- provide the person's temperature, pulse, and respirations per minute to the nurse and/or physician.

❑ *MEDICAL TESTING / SCREENING AG.7*
- check for a medical condition causing delirium such as dehydration, heart failure, systemic bacterial, fungal or viral infections, especially bladder, chest, vaginal or ear infections (complete blood count).
- review medications for drug-induced delirium. Drugs with established and frequent associations with delirium are benzodiazepines, non-steroidal anti-inflammatory drugs, opioid analgesics, and sedative withdrawal. Other medications associated with delirium are anticholinergics, anticonvulsants, anti-depressants, antipsychotics, lithium, beta blockers, and histamine type 2 receptor blockers (Jain, 1996; Medical Letter, 1993). "A toxic delirium associated with confusion, inattention, and visual hallucinations may be seen with higher doses of both neuroleptics and tricyclic agents, particularly when anticholinergic drugs have also been used to treat extrapyramidal side effects. This delirium may produce a paradoxical worsening of psychoses." (Lowenthal & Nadeau, 1991, p.1S-29).
- review medications for drug-induced hallucinations. Drugs frequently reported are antidepressants, benzodiazepines, digitalis, ephedrine, levodopa, methylphenidate/Ritalin, propranolol/Inderal, pentazocine/Talwin (Jain, 1996).
- check for drug-induced psychosis. Drugs frequently reported to induce psychoses are anabolic steroids, anticholinergics, benzodiazepines, corticosteroids, and withdrawal from neuroleptics (Jain, 1996). Medication-induced psychosis has been reported due to propranolol (Gershon, 1979), carbamazepine/ Tegretol (Mathew 1988), clobazam/Frisium, vigabatrin/Sabril (Sander et al., 1991), and other anticonvulsants (Franks & Richter, 1979).

❑ *POSSIBLE BIOCHEMICAL / ANATOMICAL INVOLVEMENT*
- delirium has been associated with high fever, infection, and medication toxicity.
- "The combination of antipsychotics with other drugs possessing anticholinergic properties can be syner-gistic, causing anticholinergic delirium that may be misinterpreted as the worsening of the psychosis." (Estroff & Gold, 1986, p. 169). "Anticonvulsants can also cause acute delirium." (Ibid., p. 172).
- central cholinergic functioning is disturbed in delirious patients (Lowenthal & Nadeau, 1991; Raskind & Risse, 1986).
- on brain scans using positron emission tomography (PET), visual and auditory hallucinations were associated with increased cerebral blood flow in the vision association cortex (specialized for higher-order visual perception) and auditory-linguistic association cortex (specialized for speech perception); Boca's speech area was not involved (Silbersweig et al., 1995).

Presenting Concern: **PHYSICAL AGGRESSION**
Dx Category   AG.8:   *FLASHBACK-RELATED AGGRESSION IN PERSONS WITH*
                                    POST-TRAUMATIC STRESS DISORDER

❑ *COMMON FORMS*

- the person kicks, punches, scratches, or bites staff who touch or approach the person during a flashback.
- the person starts to hit, kick, scratch, or push someone who asks questions that remind the person of past traumas ("Has anyone ever hurt you?").
- the person startles when touched or approached from behind, then strikes out.
- the person may show inexplicable explosive violence that risks serious harm to others.
- the aggressive actions require coordinated hand movements such as holding a victim's hair/head in one hand and injuring the face with the other hand. The movements are not simply repetitive synchronized motions of both arms.

❑ *VARIATIONS*

- attacking a favorite caregiver, calling the caregiver by a different name, one associated with past traumas.
- the person erupts with anger and attacks someone weaker/smaller after somebody makes a minor criticism.
- the aggression is not just repetitive pounding on someone but suggests an intent to injure, e.g., by pulling on the skin near the eyes, scratching the other's face deeply, or putting a hand down another's throat.
- the person may be very personable and social when "lucid," compared to when he/she is re-living traumatic memories of another time and place.
- the person returns to the "here-and-now" and can be reasoned with after an episode when he/she could not be reasoned with, was oriented to a different time, different place, and was addressing people not present.
- the person might alternate between aggressive motions (kicking, hitting) and defensive postures (hands over face), even though no one is standing near.
- during an aggressive episode, the person speaks both sides of a victim-perpetrator scene, e.g., pleading "No! don't, don't." then "You're going to be tied up." "I didn't mean to." then "You'll be put in that room."
- the person may suddenly run up to any man and aggressively fondle him (Ryan, 1994).
- the person abruptly begins crying, screaming, using foul language, looking angry or appearing "numb" with a mask-like face. Then the person bolts across the room, runs up to someone and scratches, pinches, or pulls their hair, and speaks of people and places from the past.

❑ *DISTINGUISHING FEATURES FOR AG.8*

- aggression is provoked by unusual triggers, e.g., certain smells or sounds, certain rooms, certain people.
- during the episodes the person might not be fully oriented, i.e., may know who he is but not where he is.
- the person might be hitting or scratching someone familiar, yet call them by a different name.
- the person might become less interactive with others in the 1-2 days before a flashback. Or the person might have been talking about the perpetrators in the days leading up to a flashback.
- after visits with abusers the person may become hyperactive, incontinent of urine and feces, and hit or kick caregivers (Ryan, 1996a).

❑ *FACTORS THAT MAY WORSEN THE CONDITION*

- forcing the person to have contact with someone he/she does not want to see at that time (Ryan, 1996a).
- noisy environments, lack of privacy, or lack of safety and comfort (Ryan, 1996a).
- caregivers who physically remind the person of abusers (Ryan, 1996a).
- engaging in power struggles with a person who has been traumatized.
- caregivers ignoring the person during flashbacks, blaming the person for the traumatic events, or "pretending like nothing happened" (Ryan, 1996a, p. 50).
- psychotherapy that inadvertently causes "emotional flooding" of traumatic memories leading to increased dissociation and/or decompensation (McCann & Pearlman, 1990, p. 92-93).
- being questioned about painful past events by other people, especially a clinician unfamiliar to the person.
- the frequency of flashbacks may increase on special holidays that remind the person of past traumas, or after exposure to people or places that trigger traumatic memories, e.g., visiting a former home or city.

- cognitively-impairing medication e.g., neuroleptics can increase the frequency of flashbacks (Ryan,1996a).
- in a person with post-traumatic stress disorder, medications such as beta blockers, histamine type 2 receptor blockers, barbiturate anticonvulsants, diuretics, and neuroleptics can interfere with the healing process and/or worsen some post-traumatic stress symptoms (Ryan, 1996a).

❑ *PERSONS WHO MAY BE AT RISK*
- a person with a history of sexual abuse, physical trauma, and/or ritualistic abuse.
- a person with a history of witnessing traumatic events or natural disasters (Koopman et al., 1994).
- a person who has symbols cut into the skin, disfiguring marks, or unusual scarring on areas out-of-reach for that person (e.g., on the back or buttocks).
- someone with a history of being cruel to animals or insects.
- someone who assumes a defensive or cowering posture when startled, frightened, or feeling threatened.
- someone who is usually hypervigilant and becomes rigid when anyone new enters the room, and who only has cheery, relaxed moments when with very close individuals.
- someone who often stands with his/her back to the wall, wants a fixed distance between self and anyone unfamiliar, and makes sure no one stands in a doorway blocking an exit.
- someone who shows numbness, a frozen mask-like face, and no eye contact when examined by a physician.
- someone who slips into dissociative states such as moments with no eye contact, a frozen mask-like face, and numbness, and shows signs of re-experiencing past traumas (flashbacks).
- someone who is hypervigilant, feels very unsafe at night, and fears the dark.
- persons who show dissociative symptoms following a severe trauma are much more likely to develop post-traumatic stress symptoms than those who show anxiety or loss of personal autonomy after a severe trauma (Koopman et al., 1994).
- a person with mental retardation caused by head injury at a young age, possibly from physical abuse.
- a person with prior hospitalizations and/or a history of invasive procedures.
- a person, able to dress properly, sometimes wears trousers backwards with the zipper at the back, wears extra underpants, or does similar things with clothing that suggest extra protection of the genital area.

❑ *SUGGESTIONS FOR COLLECTING INFORMATION*
- obtain details about the nature of the aggression using the *Checklist for Describing Physical Aggression*.
- review aggressive episodes in detail; determine if the onset was related to a reminder of possible traumas.
- assess for signs of dissociative states, numbing, and flashbacks.
- review records for nightmares, anxious fearful states at bedtime, or sleeping in day for fear of the dark.
- assess for post-traumatic stress disorder (PTSD) using diagnostic criteria (DSM-IV, 1994; Ryan, 1994).
- try to identify distinct sounds that trigger fearful or protective responses. Then have staff minimize the occurrence of these triggering cues. Also plan ways to desensitize the person to these triggers.
- assess for depression using criteria appropriate for this population (Cooper & Collacott, 1994; Sovner, 1986). Use the *Checklist of Observable Signs of Depression*.

❑ *MEDICAL TESTING / SCREENING AG.8*
- list scarred areas and indicate which are anatomically incompatible with self-inflicted wounds.
- list areas of possible burns, possible cutting, past fractures, especially if multiple (there may be no previous written record to confirm suspected physical abuse).
- with PTSD, review medications as some interfere with the healing process or worsen symptoms, e.g., beta blockers, histamine type 2 blockers, barbiturate anticonvulsants, diuretics, neuroleptics (Ryan,1996a).

❑ *POSSIBLE BIOCHEMICAL / ANATOMICAL INVOLVEMENT*
- chronic stress and traumatization can result in low cortisol levels, even decades after the chronic stress has ended (Resnick et al., 1995; Yehuda et al., 1993a; Yehuda et al., 1993b; Yehuda et al., 1995).
- persons with PTSD had high concentrations of lymphocyte glucocorticoid receptors and low urinary cortisol excretion, compared to those with major depression who had high levels of urinary cortisol (Yehuda et al., 1993b).
- serotonergic dysregulation is present in some people with post-traumatic stress disorder (Nagy et al., 1993).

❏ *COMMON FORMS*

- the person started throwing objects, hitting, grabbing, or kicking others when his/her wishes were thwarted.
- the person makes angry comments and threatening gestures to "warn" staff. If these warnings are not heeded, then the person becomes physically aggressive.
- after being physically aggressive to others, the person continues to express anger by frowning and glaring at others, making threatening gestures, or complaining.
- the aggression does not appear to require advance planning or forethought.
- insomnia and/or loss of appetite may have started about the time when the aggression started.

❏ *VARIATIONS*

- the person continues to talk about what upset him/her for hours or days after the hitting or kicking episode.
- the person hits or kicks others who are less able to fight back, e.g., a smaller, weaker developmentally disabled individual, a vulnerable caregiver (e.g., pregnant or recently injured), a cat or dog.
- persons with dementia might start to express anger physically rather than verbally, as their language and comprehension skills decline.
- the person becomes aggressive after taking an agent that lowers inhibitions, e.g., alcohol, street drugs, benzodiazepines.

❏ *DISTINGUISHING FEATURES FOR AG.9*

- the person shows increasing levels of frustration progressing from verbal complaints or threats, threatening gestures, to anger toward objects, then physical aggression toward people.
- if the circumstances causing distress to the person are not dealt with, then the aggressive displays escalate in severity, i.e., more force is used, additional people are attacked, or the attacks follow increasingly minor concerns.
- the aggressive act could be interpreted as a way of asserting dominance or intimidating others so they let the person have his/her way or leave the person alone.
- anger, aggression, and poor control over one's behavior can occur with depression. This has been called "affective aggression" which occurs with "high autonomic arousal, poor modulation of behavior and is apparently unplanned." (Vitiello et al., 1990, p. 189; Vitiello & Stoff, 1997).

❏ *FACTORS THAT MAY WORSEN THE CONDITION*

- letting everyday interactions with the person become power struggles with that person.
- forcing ultimatums on the person.
- insisting on conformity and inflexible adherence to rules.
- using medication that can cause depression in someone who is already depressed.

❏ *PERSONS WHO MAY BE AT RISK*
- a person with poor impulse control and a low tolerance for frustration.
- a person with a history of being subjected to cruelty, neglect or frequent physical abuse.
- a person who demonstrates a strong need to be the one in charge.
- someone with a long history of using manipulative behaviors for getting one's wishes or needs met.
- someone who holds grudges for a long time.
- a person with poor articulation of speech who gets very frustrated when unable to make his/her words understood by others.
- a person with access to disinhibiting substances such as alcohol or street drugs.
- persons with Fragile X are at risk for having difficulty inhibiting behavior (Cohen, 1995); persons with both Fragile X and autism are more likely to be aggressive than those with only Fragile X (Cohen, 1995).
- persons with fetal alcohol syndrome are at risk for depression and emotional disorders (Steinhausen et al., 1994).
- a person with mental retardation who is depressed (Lowry, 1995; Reiss & Rojahn, 1993).

❏ *SUGGESTIONS FOR COLLECTING INFORMATION*
- obtain details about the nature of the aggression using the *Checklist for Describing Physical Aggression.*
- assess for depression using instruments or criteria appropriate for this population (e.g., Cooper & Collacott, 1994; Sovner, 1986). Use the *Checklist of Observable Signs of Depression.*
- for those able to read and label different emotional states, the "Children's Depression Inventory" (Kovacs, 1985) has been used for screening depression in developmentally disabled people (Benavidez & Matson, 1993; Meins, 1993).
- review the person's history for past physical or sexual abuse, and assess for post-traumatic stress disorder.
- check for observable signs of disinhibition and poor impulse control; also check if the person has access to disinhibiting substances, e.g., alcohol or street drugs.

❏ *MEDICAL TESTING / SCREENING AG.9*
- with depression, rule out medical conditions that can cause depressive symptoms such as: endocrine disorders (hypothyroidism, hyperthyroidism, diabetes mellitus); infections (hepatitis, influenza, mononucleosis); nutrition (B_{12}, B_6, folate, thiamine deficiencies); metabolic (acute porphyria); and electrolyte disturbance (Hales & Hershey, 1984; Wise & Taylor, 1990).
- review medications for one's that can cause depressive symptoms, e.g., propranolol/Inderal, indomethacin/Indotec, oral contraceptives, clonidine/Catapres, corticosteroids, benzodiazepines, cimetidine/Tagamet, ranitidine/Zantac, and barbiturates (Hales & Hershey, 1984; Wise & Taylor, 1990).
- assess for post-traumatic stress disorder; see screening considerations AG.8.
- rule out Fragile X by chromosomal testing if the cause of the person's mental retardation is not known.

❏ *POSSIBLE BIOCHEMICAL / ANATOMICAL INVOLVEMENT*
- "Dopamine has been found to facilitate affective aggression, GABA to inhibit it, and serotonin--probably through different receptors--to inhibit both affective and predatory types." (Vitiello et al., 1990, p. 189).
- if aggression occurs as a sign of depression, then serotonin, noradrenalin, and/or free thyroxin may be low (e.g., Dorn et al., 1996; Rao et al., 1994).
- the frontal lobe areas that control social inhibition may be involved (Stuss & Benson, 1986) if the aggression is related to difficulty inhibiting socially acceptable responses to anger.
- impulsive violent offenders had significantly lower cerebrospinal levels of a serotonin metabolite than nonimpulsive violent offenders (Linnoila et al., 1983). See also Chafetz (1990) and Coccaro (1989).

❑ *COMMON FORMS*
- the aggressive acts may cause or risk major property losses such as fire-setting.
- the aggressive acts may be directed toward the property (clothing, keys, vehicle) of a supervisor disliked by the person.
- the destruction of property or harm to others may be delayed, i.e., not when the person's wishes are denied, but minutes, hours, or a few days later. The hostile and destructive acts require some forethought or planning.

❑ *VARIATIONS*
- the aggressive acts may be directed toward another resident in the same living unit, perhaps someone less able to defend self or someone who gets a lot of staff attention.
- setting a fire in one's bedroom to force being relocated to another area or facility with different staff.
- taking valuable items from others then disposing of them, e.g., flushing keys down a toilet, putting someone's wallet in the garbage.
- slashing the tires or scratching the paint on the vehicle owned by someone that the person dislikes.
- a person with a long history of lying, stealing, and brutality who does not have awareness that such behaviors are socially unacceptable (Reiss, 1994, p. 72).

❑ *DISTINGUISHING FEATURES FOR AG.10*
- the aggressive act requires planning, e.g., waiting for caregivers to go on their breaks, waiting for supervisors to leave an area, or waiting until no male staff are around.
- the aggressive acts tend to follow incidents in which the person's wishes are thwarted, sometimes by minutes, hours or days later.
- the person shows little or no remorse if others were injured by the person's actions.
- the actions may have caused major property losses, e.g., fire-setting, destruction of documents or possessions that the person knows are valued by others.
- this is also called "predatory aggression," characterized by goal-oriented behavior, planning, secrecy, and low autonomic arousal (Vitiello et al., 1990).

❑ *FACTORS THAT MAY WORSEN THE CONDITION*
- staff continuing to talk about the dramatic (antisocial) event in front of the person, who gets satisfaction from all the attention and discussion it generated and from hearing how much this upset others.
- the reinforcing excitement of firemen coming to the scene (if applicable), of witnesses responding dramatically to a fire, and of staff continuing to talk about the event. The person observes how upset this makes others, and might enjoy all of this in a vengeful way.

❑ *PERSONS WHO MAY BE AT RISK*
- someone with a history of antisocial acts (Simeon et al., 1992; Virkkunen, 1976) and showing no remorse if others have been injured.
- a person in the moderate range of intelligence with a personality disorder (Linaker, 1994).
- a person in the moderate range of intelligence with a psychosexual disorder (Linaker, 1994).
- a person in the severe range of intelligence or higher with a conduct disorder and/or social inadequacy (Davidson et al., 1994).
- a person with a history of destructive behavior who functions in the low moderate range intellectually or higher, as forethought and planning are required (Linaker, 1994).
- someone with a history of being sexually or physically abused.
- someone with a history of being cruel to animals.
- someone with an impaired ability to empathize or see the world from other people's perspective.
- someone with a psychopathic personality or many psychopathic traits such as lack of remorse or guilt, lack of empathy, shallow emotions, deceitful and manipulative, impulsive, poor behavior control, early behavior problems, adult antisocial behavior (Hare, 1993a, p. 34).

❑ *SUGGESTIONS FOR COLLECTING INFORMATION*
- obtain details about the nature of the aggression using the *Checklist for Describing Physical Aggression*.
- review the history for antisocial acts and other evidence characteristic of antisocial personality.
- check for a history of repeated physical abuse or a rigid authoritarian up-bringing.
- if psychopathy is suspected, locate a professional who is qualified to use the "Hare Psychopathy Checklist-Revised" (Hare, 1993b).

❑ *MEDICAL TESTING / SCREENING AG.10*
- consider a psychiatric evaluation for a personality disorder, if not previously diagnosed.
- if psychopathy is suspected, refer to a qualified professional to assess the person using rigorous criteria, namely, the "Hare Psychopathy Checklist - Revised" (Hare, 1993b).
- check for evidence that suggests self-cutting or past physical abuse.
- rule out post-traumatic stress disorder; see screening considerations in AG.8.

❑ *POSSIBLE BIOCHEMICAL / ANATOMICAL INVOLVEMENT*
- the lateral hypothalamus and amygdala can facilitate predatory aggression, and the septum, medial accumbens, medial hypothalamus, and raphe nuclei appear to inhibit defensive predatory aggression (Pinel, 1990, p. 362).
- psychopaths differ from non psychopaths in the pattern of relative cerebral blood flow in frontal-temporal areas bilaterally during processing of emotional words (Intrator et al., 1997).

Presenting Concern: **PHYSICAL AGGRESSION**
Dx Category AG.11: *LEARNED BEHAVIOR FROM OBSERVING OTHERS OR BEING REWARDED FOR AGGRESSIVE RESPONSES*

❑ *COMMON FORMS*

Learned behaviors are repeated and not random. Behavior is said to be learned when the consequence is rewarding to the individual. Learning can also occur by observing this process in others, and this is called "modeling."

- the aggression (e.g., hitting, kicking, pulling people's hair, throwing things) occurs when the person is forced to do something unpleasant (e.g., difficult work, cleaning, etc.).
- the aggression occurs when the person is stopped from doing something pleasurable (e.g., watching TV/videos, socializing).
- the aggression occurs when the person wants to escape from a particular individual or setting (e.g., a seat near a noisy peer, a work table).

❑ *VARIATIONS*

- hitting a staff member who is trying to enforce work or house rules that the person does not like.
- the person tends to attack weaker individuals and avoids confronting anyone who has physically overpowered them in the past.
- a person, who dislikes noise and commotion, has learned that hitting someone results in going to a quiet room.
- the person pushes over a work table or destroys work materials when not allowed to stop work.

❑ *DISTINGUISHING FEATURES FOR AG.11*

- the aggressive episode stops when the person is allowed to escape work, be left alone, go to a different area, or do preferred activities.
- the aggression may have been learned by imitating aggressive models (Bandura, 1973).

❑ *FACTORS THAT MAY WORSEN THE CONDITION*

- inconsistently reinforcing the aggressive acts can increase their frequency because random reinforcement strengthens the learned association.
- staff failing to find tasks more suitable to the person's mental or physical limitations.
- caregivers failing to teach nonaggressive ways to ask for a break, ask for quiet, or other basic needs.
- failing to teach the hand-sign for "No" to a nonverbal person who is capable of learning a small number of hand signs.

❏ *PERSONS WHO MAY BE AT RISK*

- a person who has learned aggressive responses in other settings and situations.
- someone who has witnessed others using brute strength to get their own way, e.g., in a prison or forensic correctional facility.
- a person who has learned to intimidate others through verbal or gestural threats.
- persons with an imposing size or strength that enables them to overpower others physically.

❏ *SUGGESTIONS FOR COLLECTING INFORMATION*

- obtain details about the nature of the aggression using the *Checklist for Describing Physical Aggression.*
- chart antecedent and consequent variables to analyze what might be reinforcing the learned behavior.
- review the person's history to see if there is a strong pattern of using aggression to manipulate others in order to get what the person wants.
- rule out pain as a contributing factor; use the *Discomfort Scale* (Hurley et al., 1992) to assess a noncommunicative person.
- rule out other possibilities such as depression-related aggression (see AG.9) and ictal phenomena (see AG.4 and AG.5).

❏ *MEDICAL TESTING / SCREENING AG.11*

- consider an assessment for depression if aggression is atypical for the person until recently.
- rule out illness and physical causes of pain; see considerations in AG.1 and AG.2.

❏ *POSSIBLE BIOCHEMICAL / ANATOMICAL INVOLVEMENT*

- the association cortex refers to the areas of the cortex that receive input from more than one sensory system. The association cortex mediates "complex cognitive activities such as thinking and remembering." (Pinel, 1990, p. 203).

Chapter II

SELF-INJURY

SI.1.   Self-Hitting Related To Localized Pain Or Discomfort

SI.2.   Injurious Eye-Poking Or Attempts To Remove The Eye

SI.3.   Injurious Self-Rubbing

SI.4.   Frontal Lobe Ictal Movements That Are Self-Injurious

SI.5.   Self-Injury Related To Temporal Lobe Seizures Or Temporal Lobe Dysfunction

SI.6.   Intrusive Urges To Harm Oneself (Horrific Temptations)

SI.7.   Compulsive Self-Injurious Actions In Persons With Obsessive-Compulsive Disorder

SI.8.   Self-Injurious Acts During Depressed And/Or Dissociative States

SI.9.   Self-Injurious Acts Associated With Intense Anger

SI.10. Self-Mutilation In A Delusional Or Psychotic State

❏ *COMMON FORMS*
- the person often presses on and/or pokes at a particular area of the body; this may be accompanied by moaning, screaming, or whincing.
- the person's hand hits an area of the body where localized pain occurs or is suspected, e.g., hitting the ear when an ear infection is present (but not diagnosed), or hitting the jaw when tooth pain is present.

❏ *VARIATIONS*
- often hitting or pressing on one's abdominal area, and gastrointestinal problems are later discovered.
- hitting one's hip area repeatedly, and bone degeneration is later found to be causing severe pain there.
- relentlessly scratching the rectal area causing bleeding and eventual thickening of the skin, caused by a pinworm infestation or, in rare cases, rectal cancer.
- screaming or whincing as if in pain might accompany the self-hitting movements at times.
- stuffing objects into one's ears to reduce ringing in the ears (tinnitus), possibly in a nonverbal person taking medication that can cause tinnitus (e.g., carbamazepine/Tegretol); the ear stuffing stops after the offending medication is stopped.
- scratching the stomach area, and peptic ulcer disease is later discovered (Ryan, 1996b, p. 48).
- hand-mouthing, rumination, bad breath, and increased self-injurious actions at mealtimes could mean reflux is causing esophagitis and pain (Bosch et al., 1997).
- pushing one or more fingers on or behind an eyeball, and a painful eye condition is later found (see SI.2).
- the person inflicts pain in one area of the body to shift the focus of pain away from an area with unbearable pain, e.g., banging one's head on a hard surface in a person with advanced intestinal cancer.

❏ *DISTINGUISHING FEATURES FOR SI.1*
- a medical condition is identified (e.g., cancer, degenerative bone condition, cystitis, bowel loop, or esophagitis) that can cause intense pain in the area being repeatedly hit.
- hitting a particular body area ceases after that area is no longer painful, e.g., an ear infection is treated, a hip is x-rayed and treatment provided, a painful intestinal condition is diagnosed and treated.
- a dental condition is identified (e.g., abscessed tooth, impacted wisdom tooth, temporal mandibular joint problems) that can cause pain to the area being hit.
- the onset of this self-injury can be associated in time with an accident, injury, mealtimes (if gastro-intestinal problems), or onset of a painful condition.
- the frequency of pain-related self-injury varies, but can be daily until relief from the pain occurs.

❏ *FACTORS THAT MAY WORSEN THE CONDITION*
- regarding these self-hitting actions as a self-induced "endorphin high" and failing to investigate possible sources of pain.
- interpreting these actions as "communication," e.g., "I want to stop working" or "I want to leave" and focusing on training alternate ways to "communicate messages," while neglecting to investigate possible sources of pain.
- allowing a serious physical condition to go undiagnosed a long time, increasing the risk that the condition worsens and/or becomes more difficult to treat.
- caregivers touching an area (later discovered to be painful) when moving the person or providing care.
- stopping treatment for gastrointestinal problems in persons who self-hit and headbang (Bosch et al.,1997).
- "As a general rule, any medication that can cause sedation, dysphoria, depression, irritability, or restless-ness can cause or aggravate self-injurious behavior [in mentally retarded people] (Gualtieri, 1989, p.358).

❏ *PERSONS WHO MAY BE AT RISK*
- a person unable to report pain or physical symptoms (e.g., is nonverbal or in the severe or profound range of intelligence).

- a person with a leaky gut or history of painful conditions.
- a person with a history of eye infections or marked changes in appearance of the eyes.
- a person with a family history of "difficult-to-palpate" types of cancer (e.g., bone cancer, bowel cancer) or other painful diseases.

❏ *SUGGESTIONS FOR COLLECTING INFORMATION*
- use the *Discomfort Scale** (Hurley et al., 1992) to assess a noncommunicative person for pain.
- check if the person has a history of difficulty in reporting pain or unreliability in answering questions about pain. In the former case, the person may have been discouraged years earlier from reporting pain and "trained" not to complain. In the latter, the person complains about "every little thing," making it difficult to distinguish when serious pain is being reported.
- chart over days/weeks for possible *antecedents* to intense self-hitting, e.g. certain physical activities, certain types of physical care, repositioning, contacting certain body areas, how long since previous bowel movement or meal, during or after meals. Chart changes in the usual level of nighttime and daytime activity.
- if there is a history of *unexplained* persistent gastrointestinal problems, collect information using the *Risk Factors for Casein-Gluten Peptiduria.**
- provide the person's temperature, pulse, and respirations per minute to the nurse and/or physician.
- rule out involuntary self-injurious movements; collect information using the *Checklist of Intentional Self-Restraint and Involuntary Self-Injurious Movements.** See also SI.4 and SI.5.
- check family history for irritable bowel syndrome, cancer, and other painful conditions.
- in women, check for menstrual worsening; collect information using the *Menstrual Distress Chart.** With women able to be interviewed, consider using the "Menstrual Distress Questionnaire" (Moos,1968).

* A chart or checklist listed in italics in this section can be found in the Appendix.*

❏ *MEDICAL TESTING / SCREENING SI.1*
- investigate thoroughly for physical sites of pain, then do follow-up screening for possible medical conditions that could account for the painful areas. Gualtieri (1989) reports that self-injurious behavior "was the consequence of undetected physical disorders: migraine, otitis, peptic ulcer disease, esophagitis, hypoglycemia, endometriosis, premenstrual distress, menopause, cystitis." (p. 358).
- check ears, teeth, and mouth. Check for systemic infection, urinary tract or other infection.
- investigate for possible gastrointestinal problems, e.g., ulcers, bowel impaction/obstruction, foreign objects.
- with severe inconsolable screaming and oozing stool, consider ruling out obstructed or twisted bowel.
- with severe inconsolable screaming for hours daily, consider ruling out gall stones and kidney stones.
- if there is a history of *unexplained* persistent gastrointestinal problems, test for intestinal yeast overgrowth, serum antibodies to common foods, especially casein-gluten antibodies or casein-gluten peptides in urine. Test for celiac disease in Down syndrome (George et al., 1996).
- check for intestinal parasites, e.g., Giardia lamblia, Blastocystis hominis, pinworms, etc. (Pinworms emerge from the rectum to lay eggs in the perianal region usually at night; diagnosis can be done by microsopic examination of a strip of cellophane tape that captures the eggs from the skin.)
- review medications because self-injurious behavior "may be the result of behavioral toxicity. The most common culprits are the sedative anticonvulsants, phenobarbital, primidone, phenytoin, and ethosuccimide. [also] the xanthines, theophylline, and caffeine; and the neuroleptics like haloperidol, which can cause akathisia and dysphoria." (Gualtieri, 1989, p. 358).
- if a trial on pain medication reduced the self-hitting, investigate further for possible sources of pain.
- check for cancer if the family history or other signs warrant it.

❏ *POSSIBLE BIOCHEMICAL / ANATOMICAL INVOLVEMENT*
- an underlying condition is causing localized pain or sensations in the area targeted by the person.
- the adverse effects of certain medications on neurotransmitters, e.g., dopamine, opiates, serotonin, GABA, and adenosine, can result in self-injurious behavior (Gualtieri, 1991).

___

❑ *COMMON FORMS*

- repeatedly pushing on one's eyeball with one or more fingers.
- repeatedly pushing one's finger near the back of the eyeball.
- frequently hitting one or both eyes forcefully, which can result in detaching the retina and blindness (Coleman, 1994).
- "eye-poking" has been defined as chronically and episodically exerting "intense pressure with the tips of their fingers on the side of one or both globes, thereby causing self-directed and eventual tissue damage." (Jan et al., 1994b, p. 321).
- eye-poking with eventual tissue damage can occur in sighted persons who have transient or chronic eye pathology or intolerable eye sensations related to hypocalcinuria (Coleman, 1994). The ocular self-abuse can result in blindness or impaired vision.
- attempts by a child with autism to remove his or her own eyeball may be related to intolerable eye sensations and a desire to end such discomfort by removing the eye (Coleman, 1994).
- injurious rubbing of the eye(s), causing blindness, can occur in a person in the severe or profound range of intelligence after cataract-removal surgery if measures are not taken to prevent post-operative eye-rubbing.

___

❑ *VARIATIONS*

- "eye-pressing" has been defined as "a steady prolonged, non-painful pressure on one or both globes in an individual style, with fingers, knuckles or fists" (Jan et al., 1994b, p. 321). This occurs in congenitally blind or visually-impaired children, usually not resulting in injury (Jan et al., 1994b).
- eye-pressing without tissue damage can occur in blind or visually impaired people who function in the profound range of intelligence.
- deliberately crossing one's eyes, patting and hitting the eyes, sometimes saying that the eye hurts, or making comments like "take the eye out" (Coleman, 1994).
- trying to remove one's eyeball with a sharp implement.
- the person actually removed the eyeball by cutting it out or pulling it out (Coleman, 1994).
- traumatizing the corneas of the eyes with one's fingers, toys, and food causing corneal scarring (Mader & Stulting, 1992).
- infrequently a person with obsessive-compulsive disorder will compulsively rub his/her eyes; see SI.7.
- ocular self-abuse can occur during a psychotic, delusional state; see SI.10.

___

❑ *DISTINGUISHING FEATURES FOR SI.2*

- if disease, injury, or some mineral deficiency causes ocular self-abuse, a distinguishing feature is that this behavior stops when the cause is diagnosed and treated.
- if hitting and/or poking the eyes is caused by eye disease, it stops after the disease is diagnosed, treated, and fully healed.
- ocular self-abuse stops after hypocalcinuria is diagnosed, treated (with calcium supplements), and urine levels of calcium reach the normal range (Coleman, 1994). Self-inflicted eye damage related to calcium deficiency usually starts in childhood (Coleman, 1994).
- the person who pushes on his/her eyes may also be relatively insensitive to pain, noise, and light (Coleman, 1994; Mader & Stulting, 1992).
- eye-poking or eye-hitting can start after eye disease develops or after having eye surgery.
- the person may halt eye-pressing or eye-poking temporarily when asked to stop, but resumes it later.

___

❑ *FACTORS THAT MAY WORSEN THE CONDITION*

- transient eye infections.
- very low intake of calcium-containing foods if hypocalcinuria is present.

❏ *PERSONS WHO MAY BE AT RISK*

- a person with a history of eye infections or marked changes in the appearance of the eyes.
- a person diagnosed with autism who has hypocalcinuria and a profound language delay (Coleman, 1994).
- a person with both mental retardation and a pre-existing visual impairment has a higher risk for eye-gouging than mental peers without visual impairment (Hyman et al., 1990).
- a person in the profound range of intelligence with a visual impairment is at risk for eye-poking (Jan et al., 1994b).
- a person in the profound range of intelligence with multiple disabilities with or without blindness (Jan et al., 1994b).
- a person with other self-injurious movements (Jan et al., 1994b).
- a person with congenital sensory neuropathy and indifference to painful stimuli (Mader & Stulting, 1992).
- a person who rubs several different areas of the body might also rub his/her eyes repeatedly; see SI.3.

❏ *SUGGESTIONS FOR COLLECTING INFORMATION*

- review records for the onset of eye-poking or eye-hitting in relation to possible eye disease, in sighted or visually-impaired individuals.
- screen for an inability to report pain or unreliability in answering questions about pain.
- chart the self-injury for time of day, location, indoors or out, etc. to identify factors that may worsen it.
- use the *Discomfort Scale* (Hurley et al., 1992) to assess a noncommunicative person for pain.
- rule out obsessive-compulsive disorder as underlying the eye-pushing or eye-rubbing; collect information using the *Compulsive Behavior Checklist* and, if applicable, the *Obsessive Speech Checklist.* See SI.7.
- rule out a psychotic explanation for the ocular self-abuse; see considerations in SI.10.
- provide the person's temperature, pulse, and respirations per minute to the nurse and/or physician.

❏ *MEDICAL TESTING / SCREENING SI.2*

- screen for pathologic changes in or behind the eye, as these might be causing intolerable sensations or pain that can lead to eye-poking, especially in persons in the profound range of intelligence (Jan et al., 1994b).
- request a 24-hour urine test for calcium deficiency; serum calcium usually shows normal results in affected individuals with ocular self-abuse (Coleman, 1994). "Most patients with autism and hypocalcinuria do not have ocular self-abuse" (Coleman, 1994, p. 66). In Coleman's study (1994), the children with autism, hypocalcinuria, and severe eye-poking showed normal urine levels of phosphorus, magnesium, creatinine, uric acid, sodium, and potassium, and also their CT scans showed no calcifications in the basal ganglia.
- rule out a psychotic explanation for the ocular self-abuse. Franks & Richter (1979) reported that forceful rubbing of the eyes along with a psychosis was induced by carbamazepine/Tegretol in a person in the borderline range of intelligence; both resolved when the drug was discontinued.
- if the person rubs several body areas other than the eyes, consider ruling out congenital sensory neuropathy. See SI.3.

❏ *POSSIBLE BIOCHEMICAL / ANATOMICAL INVOLVEMENT*

- in some cases, a calcium deficiency results in intolerable sensations in or behind the eye. Not all people with autism and hypocalcinuria show ocular abuse (Coleman, 1994).
- these actions may be attempts to end "intolerable sensations" from eye disease or post-operative discomfort by people who are unable to understand the long-term consequences of rubbing, pressing, or hitting one's eyes.
- also read the last point in the *POSSIBLE BIOCHEMICAL / ANATOMICAL INVOLVEMENT* section for SI.3.

___

❑ *COMMON FORMS*
- the person rubs any two body surfaces together for hours at a time if not prevented.
- using one's hand to rub any exposed part of the body.
- rubbing the skin off areas that are rubbed relentlessly.
- rubbing one's back on a stationery object like a bed or back of a chair.
- rubbing or pressing on one's eyes. Also see SI.2.

___

❑ *VARIATIONS*
- repeatedly rubbing one hand on the forearm of the other arm, the heel of one hand against the back of the other hand, or one finger against another finger.
- repeatedly rubbing the elbow against one's stomach or other body area.
- repeatedly rubbing the back of the head on a hard surface such as the floor.
- repeatedly rubbing one foot on top of the other foot, or rubbing the knees together.
- rubbing one body part on another then shifting to other areas of body; this is not simply the midline hand-rubbing typical of people with Rett syndrome.
- a person wraps his arms tightly around himself; this looks like a "self-hug" or trying to warm oneself.
- the person severely scratches his or her skin in addition to severely rubbing it.
- in addition to severe self-rubbing, the person may also bite his/her fingers, lips, shoulders, arms, knees, any area the person can reach with his/her mouth, especially in a person with Lesch-Nyhan syndrome or De Lange syndrome (Anderson & Ernst, 1994; Bryson et al., 1971; Shear et al., 1971).
- in addition to self-rubbing, the person may also pull off his/her finger nails or toe nails.
- repetitive rubbing mainly on the ends of the fingers (or toes) in persons with Familial Dysautonomia.

___

❑ *DISTINGUISHING FEATURES FOR SI.3*
- the person vigorously rubs one body part on another, or rubs an area of the body against a hard surface.
- the person may have histamine hypersensitivity and/or a dermatological condition that causes severe itchiness and chronic rubbing (Hanifan, 1991).
- the person may have a condition that causes peripheral neuropathy, numbness, tingling, or loss of sensation in hands, feet, or areas being rubbed (Roach et al., 1985).
- the person may have severe itchiness (pruritus) caused by certain parasites (e.g., blastocystis hominis) (O'Gorman et al.,1993; Ponce de Leon et al.,1991) or tardive cutaneous porphyria (Bonnetblanc et al., 1986).
- the person may have a history of elevated porphyrins or diagnosis of a porphyria disorder.
- the person may be able to inhibit the self-rubbing contingent on a predictable and forceful consequence.
- the person may have blotchy skin, signs suggesting defective thermoregulation, and/or diminished thermal sensitivity (Daniel et al., 1980; Domingues et al., 1994; Hageman et al., 1992; Mass & Gadoth, 1994).

___

❑ *FACTORS THAT MAY WORSEN THE CONDITION*
- any condition that increases itchiness such as allergic reactions to food, seasonal pollens, grasses.
- drops in blood sugar can trigger porphyria attacks.
- certain medications can worsen porphyria, e.g., alcohol, barbiturates, benzodiazepines, carbamazepine, estrogens, imipramine/Tofranil, phenytoin/Dilantin, progesterones, tolbutamide/Mobenol, valproic acid/ Depakene, verapamil/Calan/Isoptin, and other medications.

___

❑ *PERSONS WHO MAY BE AT RISK*
- persons who eat feces are at risk for an initial infestation or recurrence of intestinal parasites that can cause pruritus (severe itchiness).
- a person with Lesch-Nyhan syndrome (Anderson & Ernst, 1994) or Cornelia de Lange syndrome (Bryson et al., 1971).
- a person in the severe or profound range who cannot report pain, coldness, or "intolerable sensations."

- people with certain types of metabolic disorders may be at increased risk for self-rubbing, e.g., Noonan syndrome or a porphyria disorder.
- a person with congenital sensory neuropathy (Daniel et al., 1980; Domingues et al, 1994; Ishli et al., 1988; Mader & Stulting, 1992; Rosemberg et al., 1994) or acquired sensory neuropathy (Roach et al., 1985) may do severe self-rubbing and/or severe biting of the lips, tongue and finger tips. A person who is indifferent to painful stimuli, who self-mutilates fingers or lips, has recurrent unexplained fever, and is unable to sweat may have congenital sensory and autonomic neuropathy with anhidrosis (an inability to sweat) (Daniel et al., 1980; Rosemberg et al., 1994).

❏ *SUGGESTIONS FOR COLLECTING INFORMATION*
- review history for rashes, skin reactions, and histamine hypersensitivity.
- assess the person for a history of inability to report pain, or an absence of sensitivity to pain.
- use the *Discomfort Scale* (Hurley et al., 1992) to assess a noncommunicative person for pain.
- check records for prior parasite infestations as they could have recurred.
- check family history for congenital sensory neuropathies, porphyria disorders, skin disorders, and check for consanguinity of the parents (a risk factor for congenital sensory neuropathy, Domingues et al.,1994).

❏ *MEDICAL TESTING / SCREENING SI.3*
- check for rashes or skin disorders, and refer to a dermatologist if warranted. Generalized pruritus (severe itchiness) can occur with tardive cutaneous porphyria and the pruritus does not correlate with levels of urinary porphyrins (Bonnetblanc et al., 1986).
- check for histamine over-reactivity or relief of symptoms when taking a histamine type 1 blocker.
- check for intestinal parasites if severe rubbing occurs in a person with unexplained persistent abdominal pain, excessive abdominal gas, and diarrhea. If stool results are negative in a person with severe rubbing and persistent abdominal symptoms, consider sending stool to a different laboratory. (A severely developmentally delayed child with very severe self-rubbing, abdominal pain, excessive gas, diarrhea, and constipation over 5 years finally had *three* different parasites detected by a particular laboratory (Great Smokies Lab, North Carolina) after years of no parasites being detected in the numerous stool samples sent to laboratories in *two other states*.)
- check for pinworms and blastocystis hominis as both parasites can cause severe itchiness. B. hominis is more likely to cause symptoms in immunocompromised individuals (Stenzel & Boreham, 1996). It can also infect synovial fluid in joints and cause severe joint pain and arthritis (Lee et al., 1990).
- check for sensory neuropathy in persons who mutilate their lips, tongue, and/or finger tips by severe biting, who are indifferent to painful stimuli, and who may be unable to sweat.
- if thermal dysregulation symptoms are present, check for signs of hypothalamic dysfunction, porphyria disorders, sensory neuropathies, and other disorders that can cause thermal dysregulation.
- rule out Lesch-Nyhan syndrome in males by chromosomal testing or other tests.
- most persons with Familial Dysautonomia are in the normal range of intelligence. The features include severe rubbing of the fingers, self-mutilation of the fingers and tongue, inappropriate or decreased pain sensation, impaired temperature and blood pressure regulation, lack of tearing of the eyes, and Ashkenazi Jewish extraction (Mass et al., 1992; Mass & Gadoth, 1994).

❏ *POSSIBLE BIOCHEMICAL / ANATOMICAL INVOLVEMENT*
- there may be pain, itchiness, or intolerable sensations in the areas forcefully rubbed/scratched; this can result from sensory neuropathy, altered pain perception, skin disorders, or pruritus from certain parasites.
- in gluten-related disorders, IgA deposits under the skin can cause itching or burning (Garioch et al., 1994).
- in persons with thermal regulation abnormalities and severe self-rubbing, there may be abnormal functioning of the preoptic and anterior hypothalamus which contain thermoreceptors that are involved in regulating body temperature (Guyton, 1986, p. 853; Pinel, 1990, p. 362). That area is behind the eyes. Interestingly, Domingues et al. (1994) reported a hyperactive, mentally retarded girl with congenital sensory neuropathy who self-mutilated her fingers and who had a "decrease in heart rate from 92 to 76 beats per minute after pressure to the eyeball" (p. 233).

❑ *COMMON FORMS*

- slapping one's ears or head, i.e., the arm adducts with an open or closed hand to contact the head and/or ear area, usually done repeatedly.
- both arms hit one's ears or the side of one's head, i.e., the arms adduct symmetrically to contact the ears, side of the head, or neck; this usually occurs repeatedly.
- hand-biting or hitting self on the chin, i.e., the arm adducts with the wrist in the "palm down" position, contacting the mouth/chin; the muscles and nerves involved are discussed elsewhere (Gedye, 1992b).
- head-thrusting, headbanging (if objects are contacted), or lunging: the neck muscles and upper shoulder muscles contract alternately causing forward and backward head-thrusting.

❑ *VARIATIONS*

- slapping one's neck, i.e., the arm adducts with an open hand and forcefully contacts the neck area.
- slapping one's chest, i.e., the arm adducts with an open or closed hand to contact the chest area.
- forceful knee-to-face contact as this can result in bruises or a black eye.
- scratching one's face or arms.

❑ *DISTINGUISHING FEATURES FOR SI.4*

- the involuntary contractions can occur without provocation.
- the anatomical topography shows consistency over years or even decades, i.e. the limbs/hands contact the same body area repeatedly; there may be permanent tissue damage such as scarring, callus formation, cauliflower ears, loosening of teeth, or detached retinas (Hyman et al., 1990).
- self-restraining actions are common in people with involuntary muscle contractions that cause pain (Gedye, 1992b). People restrain their limbs by: tucking arms under one's shirt; pulling sleeves over one's hands; wrapping a shirt around one's hand/arm; entangling hands/arms in the rungs of a chair or other furniture; stiffly holding an object with both hands for hours; covering one's head or whole body with a blanket in the daytime; sitting on one's hands; lying facedown on one's arms; crossing one's arms then leaning on them while sitting; or walking with stiffened arms.
- the movements involve forceful involuntary muscle contractions, in contrast to self-injury that involves forethought or planning (e.g., obtaining objects for cutting, burning, or poisoning self).
- the frequency of these self-injurious movements can be weekly, daily, or up to 100's of times an hour.
- the onset of these involuntary self-injurious movements is usually before age 10 (often age 3-4 years) or in the year following head trauma that affected the frontal lobe area.

❑ *FACTORS THAT MAY WORSEN THE CONDITION*

- criticizing or trying to argue with the person during these movements.
- not providing loose-fitting clothing that can be used for self-restraint in persons who restrain their limbs.
- physical illness or pain from otitis media (Hyman et al., 1990), other infections, migraine, esophagitis, cystitis, menstrual cramps (Gualtieri, 1991), impacted wisdom teeth, gastrointestinal disorders, etc.
- some anticonvulsants worsen self-injurious movements, e.g., carbamazepine/Tegretol alone or with valproic acid/Depakene, phenobarbital (Gualtieri, 1991, p.168; Hanzel et al., 1992; Kalachnik et al., 1995; Mayhew et al., 1992).
- drugs that can worsen frontal lobe seizures, e.g., carbamazepine (Horn et al., 1986; Stores et al., 1991).
- long-term use of medication that lowers the seizure threshold, e.g., neuroleptics.
- opiate blockers (naltrexone/Trexan) have worsened self-injurious movements (Benjamin et al., 1995).
- medications that reduce the production and release of serotonin, e.g., benzodiazepines (Gardos, 1980).
- dietary factors that reduce serotonin production, e.g., high protein diet, caffeinated food (Gedye, 1990; 1991e).
- the following are possible stressors and times of risk, especially for intense episodes of involuntary movements: high noise level or a startling event, bright sunlight or flickering light; lacking sleep or being overtired; low blood sugar, missing a meal or a history of hypoglycemia; allergic reactions to pollens, etc. or an exaggerated response to insect bites; a highly emotional event, positive or negative; emotional

frustration or anger; stress or pressure to perform; stress associated with removal of protective device such as a helmet or clothing that is used to self-restrain; a change in plans or in routine sequence; premenstrual or menstrual phase; during the waking hours of the morning or when falling asleep (times when consciousness is shifting); late afternoon; mealtime (breakfast, lunch, supper).

❑ *PERSONS WHO MAY BE AT RISK*
- a person with a history of head injury or physical abuse that might have caused head trauma.
- a person with Tuberous Sclerosis who has tubers in the frontal lobe area.
- a person who has frontal lobe seizures or frontal lobe abnormality (Gedye, 1989b; 1991b; 1996b).
- a person who has frequent involuntary movements, sometimes called "stereotypic movements."
- a person who wakes from sleep with head-thrusting movements or one of his hands is hitting his head.
- a person with an etiology known to have low levels of serotonin, e.g., untreated phenylketonuria (PKU) (Neilsen et al., 1988; Tu & Partington, 1972), de Lange syndrome (Greenberg & Coleman, 1973).
- a person with mental retardation due to birth trauma or anoxia, encephalitis, rubella, Tuberous Sclerosis, or head injury (references given in Gedye, 1991c).
- a person diagnosed with "Tourette syndrome" and has no family history of Tourette syndrome.
- persons with mental retardation due to PKU who are not on a low-protein diet (Harper & Reid, 1987).
- people with autism have been reported to self-hit, self-bite, headbang (Gillberg & Coleman, 1992, p. 31).
- those forms of self-injurious movements have been reported in Lesch-Nyhan syndrome (Anderson & Ernst, 1994), de Lange syndrome (Bryson et al., 1971; Dossetor et al., 1991; Shear et al., 1971; Singh & Pulman, 1979), Rett syndrome, Down syndrome, a history of infantile spasms (Hyman et al., 1990).
- a person on carbamazepine/Tegretol alone or with valproic acid/Depakene (Friedman et al., 1992).

❑ *SUGGESTIONS FOR COLLECTING INFORMATION*
- videotape the person during outbursts to help detect observable involuntary phenomena.
- check for a high number of ictal signs during intense episodes (and relatively calm moments) using the *Nonconvulsive Ictal Signs Checklist.*
- carefully review the high risk times and stressors identified on the *Nonconvulsive Ictal Signs Checklist.*
- check if a high percentage of waking hours is spent doing self-restraining actions with clothing, furniture, people, or body postures that restrict limb movements. Collect information using the *Checklist of Intentional Self-Restraint and Involuntary Self-Injurious Movements.*
- review the history as to onset as these forms of self-injury often start in childhood or follow head injury.

❑ *MEDICAL TESTING / SCREENING SI.4*
- review medications: "phenobarb, primidone, phenytoin, ethosuximide, xanthine, caffeine, neuroleptics, ...can cause or aggravate self-injurious behavior" [in mentally retarded people] (Gualtieri, 1991, p. 168).
- consider an EEG and neurological investigation for frontal lobe seizures, although scalp or sphenoidal EEGs are often normal during seizures and between seizures (Luciano, 1993; Stores et al., 1991); see literature review (Gedye, 1991b; 1996b).
- MRI and PET scans sometimes show frontal lobe abnormalities but are very costly for routine screening.
- rule out food allergies by testing for serum antibodies; food allergies can cause nonconvulsive seizures.
- rule out pain-related self-hitting as given in SI.1.

❑ *POSSIBLE BIOCHEMICAL / ANATOMICAL INVOLVEMENT*
- certain metabolic abnormalities adversely affect central serotonin levels, e.g., PKU, persons with casein/ gluten peptiduria (Knivsberg et al.,1990; 1995; Rimland & Baker,1996; Tu & Partington,1972).
- there could be a deficiency in central serotonin or GABA (Gedye,1992c; Paul & Krishnamoorthy, 1990).
- opioids/endorphins may adversely affect dopaminergic activity in persons with self-injurious movements (e.g., Sandyk & Bamford, 1987) and also affect serotonergic neurotransmission (Reichelt et al., 1994). Opioid levels may be abnormal in some who have repetitive self-hitting (e.g., Sandman et al., 1990).
- adverse effects on the central nervous system from food allergy can cause nonconvulsive seizures (Gobbi et al., 1992).
- the mesiobasal frontal area is often involved in frontal lobe seizures (Quesney et al., 1984; Waterman et al., 1987).

❑ *COMMON FORMS*

- using a sharp object to cut one's arms or other area of the body.
- burning oneself by holding a lit cigarette to the skin.
- an attempt to kill oneself.
- becoming suddenly very depressed without any precipitant in one's life and, just as quickly, the depression (which is an interictal seizure-like phenomenon) disappears (Tucker et al., 1986).
- the person may be his or her usual self between episodes, i.e., sociable and not depressed (Tucker et al., 1986).
- showing some of the following features: lip smacking, chewing, swallowing, pouting lips, pursed lips, licking lips, yawning, and expressionless stare; these may be accompanied by urinary or fecal incontinence, sweating, and heart racing (Farber et al., 1986; Kotagal et al., 1989; Luciano, 1993).

❑ *VARIATIONS*

- the person also has "staring spells" with a blank look (Tucker et al., 1986) or sometimes has an unnatural posturing of a leg or arm, followed by the head and body turning to one side (Hiyoshi et al, 1989).
- a look of disgust may accompany oral-alimentary movements (i.e., chewing, lip smacking, or swallowing when the person is not eating) (Hiyoshi et al., 1989).
- the person may have "thought crowding" or intrusive thoughts, and anxiety symptoms as part of the temporal lobe aura (Kroll, 1993).
- the person may report simple visual hallucinations such as flashes of light, spots, and lines, or complex ones such as cars, trees, or faces (Tucker et al., 1986).
- the person may have episodes of being extra sensitive to sound (hyperacusis), hearing sounds that others do not hear (bells, phones, musical refrains, voices), or experiencing "odd" smells (Tucker et al., 1986).
- with ictal events, recall of actions or speech during an episode can be patchy, minimal, or reflect total amnesia.
- ictal events may begin with unilateral movements such as unnatural posturing of one arm or leg, head and body turning to one side, one eye blinking, and/or facial asymmetry (Kotagal et al., 1989).
- the person might hear voices commanding injurious or suicidal behavior such as to burn, cut, or kill oneself (Tucker et al., 1986). See also SI.6.

❑ *DISTINGUISHING FEATURES FOR SI.5*

- there is an overall consistency in the presentation of the involuntary movements for each individual over time (Tucker et al., 1986).
- "During the post-ictal period, recovery is often progressive, as opposed to the generally rapid recovery seen after frontal seizures." (Luciano, 1993, p. 812).
- complex partial seizures or temporal lobe epilepsy is diagnosed.
- many, but not all, temporal lobe epileptics respond to anticonvulsant treatment (Farber et al., 1986; Sperling et al., 1996).
- the person can have symptom-free intervals of being one's usual self (e.g., sociable and not depressed) between episodes which include some of the unusual symptoms described in *COMMON FORMS* and *VARIATIONS* (Tucker et al., 1986).
- the onset of self-injury during temporal lobe seizures has been reported in people from ages 16 years to 62 years (Tucker et al., 1986).
- regarding frequency, temporal lobe ictal self-injurious actions tend to occur as distinct episodes, not as a daily phenomenon.
- the majority of temporal lobe epileptics do not cut, burn, or attempt to kill themselves during seizures.

❏ *FACTORS THAT MAY WORSEN THE CONDITION*
- interpersonal stress (Tucker et al., 1986).
- premenstrual changes (Tucker et al., 1986).
- medication that lowers the seizure threshold such as neuroleptics or tricyclic antidepressants (imipramine/Tofranil) (Tucker et al., 1986), or tricyclic antidepressants in people who are slow metabolizers (Dailey & Naritoku, 1996).
- if a misdiagnosis is made, the patient is "often placed on anti-psychotic medication which may even exacerbate the symptoms" of temporal lobe epilepsy (Farber et al., 1986, p. 78).

❏ *PERSONS WHO MAY BE AT RISK*
- a person with temporal lobe epilepsy (Tucker et al., 1986) or complex partial seizures.
- a person with a history of head injury before age 5 years (Marks et al., 1995).
- a person with a history of encephalitis, e.g., herpes simplex encephalitis (Sanders et al., 1997).
- a person who reports distortions of time speeding up or slowing down, distortions of uncanny familiarity or not recognizing what is familiar, distortions of personal reality, illusions of size of a body part, seeing or hearing things that others do not (Farber et al., 1986; Tucker et al., 1986).
- a person who reports smelling things that others do not, suggestive of olfactory hallucinations (Luciano, 1993).
- a person showing panic-like anxiety or sudden depressive moods unrelated to any precipitant (Tucker et al., 1986).

❏ *SUGGESTIONS FOR COLLECTING INFORMATION*
- if the person is verbal, check for signs of temporal lobe dysfunction using the "Structured Clinical Interview for Complex Partial Seizure Symptoms" (Roberts et al., 1992; Varney et al., 1992).
- check if the person has reported phenomena suggestive of time illusions; distortions of personal awareness; somatic distortions of size or shape (macrospia, microspia); visual, auditory, or olfactory hallucinations.
- videotape the person during outbursts to help detect observable involuntary phenomena. These can be indicative of temporal lobe dysfunction.
- if relentless writing and/or drawing is present, rule out obsessive-compulsive disorder as the explanation; collect information using the *Compulsive Behavior Checklist*.
- consider using the *Checklist of Intentional Self-Restraint and Involuntary Self-Injurious Movements*.
- in women, check for premenstrual worsening; collect information using the *Menstrual Distress Chart*. With women able to be interviewed, consider using the "Menstrual Distress Questionnaire" (Moos, 1968).

❏ *MEDICAL TESTING / SCREENING SI.5*
- request an EEG (sleep EEG if possible) and neurologic investigation for temporal lobe epilepsy or temporal lobe dysfunction. The "medial temporal lobe focus might well escape detection by the surface EEG, while dysrythmias conducted to the cortex would be observed." (Devinsky & Bear, 1984, p. 653). Neurologic exams and CT scans can be normal in temporal lobe epileptics (Tucker et al., 1986). Not all temporal lobe epileptics improve on anticonvulsant trials (Sperling et al., 1996).
- review medications for possible lowering of the seizure threshold, if seizures are involved.
- rule out repeated bouts of hypoglycemia (Guberman et al., 1986).

❏ *POSSIBLE BIOCHEMICAL / ANATOMICAL INVOLVEMENT*
- the self-injury could result from temporal lobe seizure activity or possibly interictal (between seizures) activity (Tucker et al., 1986).

❑ *COMMON FORMS*

- the person, who is not psychotic, has intrusive urges, ideas, or impulses to harm self or kill self but resists doing these.
- the person reports feeling compelled to do a life-threatening act, but also indicates this is an unwanted and *intrusive urge*, not a desire or death-wish.

❑ *VARIATIONS*

- the person--who is not psychotic--might have urges to harm self or others, or have images of harming a loved one, but is horrified by these thoughts and feelings (Primeau & Fontaine, 1987).
- the person, who is not psychotic, feels an urge to jump into traffic but is horrified by this urge or feeling and may ask others to help prevent such an act.
- the person reports feeling compelled to jump out of a moving vehicle, but also reports this is an urge, not a real desire, and asks for help to reduce the opportunity to enact such an urge.

❑ *DISTINGUISHING FEATURES FOR SI.6*

- horrific temptations can occur in persons with obsessive-compulsive disorder, atypical temporal lobe seizures, or psychosis.
- the person has a strong feeling of not wanting to do these acts and may actively resist these intrusive thoughts of harming self or others.
- the person may seek help from others to reduce the opportunities for him/her to carry out such self-harming urges.
- the onset of these self-harming urges can be in childhood (e.g., Anderson & Ernst, 1994).
- the person has other intrusive thoughts that are unrelated to harming self.
- if this is viewed as part of an obsessive-compulsive spectrum, the focus is on *intrusive urges/thoughts with self-injurious content*. As these people cannot control intrusive thoughts, they may ask for help to prevent themselves from enacting such self-injurious urges. They may also engage in compulsions or rituals designed to prevent themselves from obtaining the means to harm self or others, e.g., hide all knives, sharp objects, or other objects that they associate with doing harm.

❑ *FACTORS THAT MAY WORSEN THE CONDITION*

- repeated exposure to stimuli that are associated with the person's self-harming intrusive thoughts (e.g., sharp objects).
- medication that lowers the seizure threshold in a person whose "forced thinking" occurs in relation to temporal lobe seizures.
- medication that can induce or worsen obsessive-compulsive symptoms such as clozapine/Clozaril (Baker et al., 1992; Patel & Tandon, 1993; Patil, 1992) or clothiapine (Toren et al., 1995).

❑ *PERSONS WHO MAY BE AT RISK*

- a person with obsessive-compulsive disorder.
- a person who talks obsessively but has few or no compulsions.
- a person with temporal lobe epilepsy (Tucker et al., 1986).
- a person who reports smelling things that others do not detect (suggestive of olfactory hallucinations) might have temporal lobe epilepsy (Luciano, 1993).
- a person who shows panic-like anxiety or sudden onset of depressive moods unrelated to any precipitant might have temporal lobe epilepsy (Tucker et al., 1986).
- a person with Lesch-Nyhan syndrome (Anderson & Ernst, 1994).

❑ *SUGGESTIONS FOR COLLECTING INFORMATION*

- screen for obsessive-compulsive disorder or other evidence of "forced thoughts." Collect information using the *Obsessive Speech Checklist* and *Compulsive Behavior Checklist* for persons with mental retardation.
- check if the person has reported phenomena suggestive of: time illusions; personal awareness distortions; somatic distortions of size or shape; visual, auditory, or olfactory hallucinations.
- if the person is verbal, check for signs of temporal lobe dysfunction using the "Structured Clinical Interview for Complex Partial Seizure Symptoms" (Roberts et al., 1992; Varney et al., 1992).
- if cognitive testing is done, there may be no classic neuropsychological testing difficulties in temporal lobe epileptics (Tucker et al., 1986).
- temporal lobe seizures can spread to the frontal lobe (Luciano, 1993; Munari et al., 1981) and vice versa, so use the *Nonconvulsive Ictal Signs Checklist* as some episodes may also reflect frontal ictal signs.
- check for signs of schizophrenia or psychotic disorders. Collect information using the *Checklist of Observable Signs of Psychosis in Persons with Mental Retardation* to help rule this out or rule it in for further investigation.

❑ *MEDICAL TESTING / SCREENING SI.6*

- request an EEG (sleep EEG if possible) and neurologic investigation for temporal lobe epilepsy or temporal lobe dysfunction. Neurologic exam and CT scans can be normal in temporal lobe epileptics (Tucker et al., 1986). The "medial temporal lobe focus might well escape detection by the surface EEG, while dysrythmias conducted to the cortex would be observed." (Devinsky & Bear, 1984, p. 653). The majority of people with temporal lobe epilepsy do not cut, burn, or attempt to kill themselves during seizures. Not all temporal lobe epileptics improve on anticonvulsant trials (Farber et al., 1986; Sperling et al., 1996).
- review medications for possible lowering of the seizure threshold, if seizures are involved.
- review medications for possible medication-induced obsessive-compulsive symptoms such as clozapine.
- consider a psychiatric evaluation if psychosis is suspected.

❑ *POSSIBLE BIOCHEMICAL / ANATOMICAL INVOLVEMENT*

- the left orbital-frontal area has been implicated in intrusive thoughts and "forced thinking," and is part of the orbital-caudate-thalamus circuit which is involved in obsessive-compulsive disorder (Ames et al., 1994; Mega & Cummings, 1994).
- command hallucinations to injure or kill oneself and the sudden onset of depression--unrelated to any precipitant--can occur during temporal lobe seizures (Tucker et al., 1986).

❑ *COMMON FORMS*

- the person uses an implement to perform the self-injurious action, e.g., a lit cigarette, sharp-edged material, a knife or fork for cutting or stabbing self (Lipinski, 1991; Primeau & Fontaine, 1987).
- repeatedly picking at one's skin or wounds, severely scratching the skin, or severely biting fingernail beds.
- calmly pulling out head hair or eyebrows (not hair-pulling during screaming outbursts) causing baldness or bald patches (Primeau & Fontaine, 1987). "Trichotillomania" is hair-pulling in the absence of other compulsions (Rapoport, 1989b).
- repeatedly picking or pulling at one's lips, picking one's nose and/or skin.

❑ *VARIATIONS*

- a history of jumping off stairs, jumping into an elevator shaft, jumping into pits or holes.
- frequent repetitive door slamming (e.g., bedroom door, refrigerator door) that eventually causes shoulder pain or injury.
- the person feels an urge to hit an arm or leg against the doorframe when going through doorways, feels compelled to jump out of one's wheelchair, feels compelled to touch hot objects and does so, e.g., in persons with Lesch-Nyhan syndrome (Anderson & Ernst, 1994).
- a person, who has a strong tendency to imitate actions seen, repeatedly mimics an injurious act that he or she witnessed, e.g., repeatedly falling in a dramatic fashion after seeing a close friend fall and be injured.
- having obsessive thoughts of wanting to gouge out one's eyes or teeth, and later calmly doing this (Goodhart & Savitsky, 1933).
- the person inserts objects into his or her body orifices.

❑ *DISTINGUISHING FEATURES FOR SI.7*

- objects are often involved in the self-injury, e.g., sharp objects, hot objects, door frames.
- the injurious acts are usually intended to harm oneself, not to kill oneself.
- the person fits the criteria for obsessive-compulsive disorder (OCD) (Bodfish et al., 1995; Gedye, 1992a; 1996a; Lipinski, 1991).
- relief of mounting anxiety is stated as the reason why some obsessive-complusive people injure themselves (Gardener & Gardener, 1975).
- the frequency of the self-injurious acts varies with the severity of OCD or depression, if present.
- obsessive-compulsive behaviors usually have a chronic course.
- the onset of OCD is often in the late teens or twenties (Rasmussen & Eisen, 1990) but can be in childhood (Rapoport, 1989a).
- if this is viewed as part of an obsessive-compulsive spectrum, the focus is on *compulsive acts with self-injurious effect*, and these can occur periodically or daily.

❑ *FACTORS THAT MAY WORSEN THE CONDITION*

- access to stimuli such as sharp objects, i.e., objects that elicit the person's self-injurious obsessive thoughts or compulsions.
- expecting the person to be able to inhibit his/her obsessions or compulsions immediately, and reprimanding the person when he or she does not comply.
- dietary factors that reduce serotonin production, e.g., high protein diet, caffeinated food/beverages.
- medication that can induce or worsen obsessive-compulsiveness such as clozapine/Clozaril (Baker et al., 1992; Patel & Tandon, 1993; Patil, 1992) or clothiapine (Toren et al., 1995).
- medication that reduces the production and release of serotonin, e.g., benzodiazepines (diazepam/ Valium, lorazepam/Ativan) (Essman & Essman, 1986; Green, 1986; Pei et al., 1989; Saner & Pletscher, 1979; Wise et al., 1972).

❑ *PERSONS WHO MAY BE AT RISK*
- a person with obsessive-compulsive disorder (OCD), possibly not yet diagnosed.
- a person with OCD and major depression.
- a person with a family history of OCD.
- persons with Fragile X syndrome are at risk for obsessive-compulsive behavior (Dorn et al., 1994).
- adults with Prader-Willi syndrome are at risk for compulsive scratching and picking at their skin (Clarke, 1993; Dykens et al., 1992) and for OCD (Benjamin & Buot-Smith, 1993).
- adults with Down syndrome are at risk for OCD (Prasher & Day, 1995) or "subclinical" OCD.
- some persons with Smith-Magenis syndrome insert objects into their body orifices (Dykens et al., 1997).
- a person with OCD taking one or more traditional neuroleptics plus a benzodiazepine.
- a person taking clozapine as it can induce obsessive-compulsive symptoms in someone with no prior OCD symptoms (Baker et al., 1992; Patel & Tandon, 1993; Patil, 1992).

❑ *SUGGESTIONS FOR COLLECTING INFORMATION*
- assess for obsessive-compulsive disorder using the DSM-IV diagnostic criteria. Collect information using the *Compulsive Behavior Checklist* and, if applicable, the *Obsessive Speech Checklist*.
- use the *OCD Severity Scale* (Vitiello et al., 1989) to rate the severity of obsessive-compulsive features in persons with developmental disabilities.
- check family history for obsessive-compulsive disorder and depression.
- assess the person's access to sharp objects, cigarettes, matches, etc., and if there is a risk for cutting or burning self, restrict access to such items in all settings.
- assess for depression as a contributing factor in persons who cut or burn themselves, or do similar acts; use instruments or criteria appropriate for this population (e.g., Cooper & Collacott, 1994; Sovner, 1986). Collect information using the *Checklist of Observable Signs of Depression*.
- for those able to read and label different emotional states, the "Children's Depression Inventory" (Kovacs, 1985) has been used to screen depression in developmentally disabled people (Meins, 1993).
- assess dietary factors that reduce serotonin production, e.g., high protein diet, caffeinated food or drinks.
- rule out involuntary forms of self-injurious movements. Collect information using the *Checklist of Intentional Self-Restraint and Involuntary Self-Injurious Movements*.

❑ *MEDICAL TESTING / SCREENING SI.7*
- "OCD patients tend to respond to medication with only 30% to 60% symptom reduction and patients tend to remain chronically symptomatic to some degree despite the best of pharmacological interventions." (Jenike, 1992, p. 895).
- PET scans during exposure to triggering stimuli can show abnormalities in the frontal and/or basal ganglia area (Baxter, 1994), but these are expensive and require very cooperative patients.
- review medications for ones that risk causing obsessive-compulsive symptoms (e.g., clozapine), that risk being ineffective or worsening symptoms (e.g., neuroleptics, benzodiazepines) (Baker et al., 1992; Baldwin et al., 1992).

❑ *POSSIBLE BIOCHEMICAL / ANATOMICAL INVOLVEMENT*
- analgesias (absence of normal sense of pain) can occur in these people during states of intense emotion (Gardener & Gardener, 1975; Goodhart & Savitsky, 1933, p. 682; Winchel & Stanley, 1991).
- central serotonin deficiency is strongly implicated in OCD (Baldwin et al., 1992; De Groot et al., 1995; Jenike et al., 1990; Zohar et al., 1987) and possibly dopamine in some cases (Goodman et al., 1990).
- frontal-subcortical circuits, i.e., orbital frontal, bilateral caudate, and thalamus, are involved in OCD (Ames et al., 1994; Baxter, 1992; 1994; Galderisi et al., 1995; Mega & Cummings, 1994; Rapoport, 1989a).

Presenting Concern: **SELF-INJURY**
Dx Category   Sl. 8:   *SELF-INJURIOUS ACTS DURING DEPRESSED AND/OR*
                        DISSOCIATIVE STATES

❑ *COMMON FORMS*
- using a piercing object to stab or cut oneself in the arm or leg (Berman, 1992; Sternlicht et al., 1969).
- hanging or strangling oneself (Sternlicht et al., 1969).
- jumping from a high place (Sternlicht et al., 1969) such as a roof, a bridge, or out a window.
- the person risks being assaulted or killed, e.g., someone with post-traumatic stress disorder talks of suicide and repeatedly goes to a dangerous area at night where he/she was previously severely assaulted.
- a person, who talks of feeling rejected or hopeless, steals matches/lighter and sets self on fire by lighting one's clothes (see Shah, 1992).

❑ *VARIATIONS*
- the person makes comments about wanting to end one's life or threatening to kill oneself.
- a person, who has been talking of killing him or herself, runs in front of moving vehicles and is hit.
- a person, who has been talking of suicide, lies on the road and risks being killed (Sternlicht et al., 1969).
- a person, who had been talking about jumping off a particular bridge, finally jumps off and dies.
- overdosing on medication or shooting oneself are common forms in people from the general population, but less likely in people with no access to guns or large amounts of medication.

❑ *DISTINGUISHING FEATURES FOR SI.8*
- The person may be numb or indifferent to self-inflicted pain due to dissociation (Orbach, 1994; Russ et al., 1993; van der Kolk, 1988). "Dissociation can be defined as a state of mind characterized by a break in the continuity of the conscious experience. There are two essential processes in the dissociative experience: ...detachment [numbing] and... loss of ability to monitor behavior" (Orbach, 1994, p. 69).
- the person, who is known to dissociate, may be undergoing acute interpersonal stress or emotional flooding of traumatic memories (e.g., talking often about those memories and about dying).
- if viewed as a continuum of severity, the person moves from verbal threats to harm self (with no intention to kill self), to acts of harming self, verbal comments about suicidal actions, then suicidal attempts.
- the action might follow intense feelings of rejection in a "rejection-sensitive" person, acute interpersonal stress, worsening of a depression, or flooding of traumatic memories in a person with a traumatic history.
- the frequency of suicidal attempts can be rare, once or perhaps a couple of attempts in a lifetime. The frequency of self-harming acts (e.g., cutting or burning self) might be occasional.
- assess the risk of death. "When a patient has an accurate conception of the lethality of his suicidal act, the resulting degree of danger to his life is proportional to his suicidal intent." (Beck et al., 1975, p. 287).

❑ *FACTORS THAT MAY WORSEN THE CONDITION*
- accumulated sleep deprivation.
- hypoglycemia (Braly, 1992, p. 343).
- an intestinal yeast overgrowth (Candida albicans infection) can worsen depression (Crook, 1996).
- high intake of caffeine (especially in a person with insomnia), alcohol, or disinhibiting street drugs.
- failing to recognize dissociative states and/or criticizing the person when dissociated for "ignoring" staff.
- prompting the person to think or talk about past traumas when he or she is too emotionally fragile, already talking of suicide, and at risk for decompensating (McCann & Pearlman, 1990, p. 92-93).
- an untrained counselor who elicits traumatic memories in a fragile client, precipitating emotional flooding and an inability to halt re-experiencing past traumas.
- the additional emotional intensity and environmental stressors of having a close relative who is dying.

❑ *PERSONS WHO MAY BE AT RISK*
- those who had intrusive and repeated sexual abuse as a child (Romans et al., 1995; Shaunesey et al., 1993), a history of trauma, or a diagnosis of post-traumatic stress disorder (McCann & Pearlman, 1990).
- a person who is numb or indifferent to pain, impulsive, or dissociates (Russ et al., 1993); early traumatic

experiences can lead to decreased pain sensitivity and dissociative symptoms (Russ et al., 1993).
- a person in the mild range of intelligence, with feelings of inadequacy and worthlessness, who shows severe anxiety from a recent death of a loved one or other provoking stressor (Sternlicht et al., 1969).
- someone who talks of death, feels hopeless, has become severely depressed, or is often rejected socially.
- someone who has had "substantial suicidal ideation at some stage of their lives" (Romans et al., 1995).
- persons who can plan a suicidal act, obtain the means (matches, razor, pills), and endanger themselves (run out in traffic): those in the mild range of intelligence (Barrett & Walters,1992;Sternlicht et al.,1969).
- a person who used to be healthy but has developed a severe, painful chronic illness (Kellner et al., 1985).
- a person with Prader-Willi syndrome who is under extreme stress (Bartolucci & Young, 1994).

❏ SUGGESTIONS FOR COLLECTING INFORMATION
- assess for signs of dissociation, numbing, and flashbacks; check for access to a large quantity of pills.
- assess for post-traumatic stress disorder (PTSD) (e.g., DSM-IV) or evidence of a traumatic history.
- assess for depression using criteria appropriate for this population (e.g., Cooper & Collacott, 1994; Sovner, 1986). Collect information using the *Checklist of Observable Signs of Depression.*
- check family history for depression and suicide; check if a close friend attempted or committed suicide.
- assess level of suicidal risk: past attempts; vague vs. specific comments on methods; access to means; level of impulsiveness; risk times for being unsupervised or evading supervision; current level of stress and negative interactions; level of support. (See also "Suicide Intent Scale" by Beck et al., 1974.)
- check for signs of temporal lobe dysfunction in a suicidal person with staring spells and illusory distortions, visual, auditory, olfactory or other hallucinations; see considerations in SI.5.
- rule out a psychotic explanation for self-mutilation of the body; see considerations in SI.10.

❏ MEDICAL TESTING / SCREENING SI.8
- rule out medical causes of depression, e.g., hypothyroidism, hepatitis, electrolyte imbalances (Wise & Taylor, 1990).
- review medication for risk of causing/worsening depression, e.g., propranolol/Inderal, benzodiazepines, barbiturates, anticonvulsants, oral contraceptives, ranitidine/Zantac, cimetidine (Wise &Taylor, 1990).
- consider a trial on a different antidepressant if the current one has been tried long enough and is not yielding satisfactory improvement in the target symptoms (e.g., sleep, appetite, energy level, mood).
- list scarred areas; indicate which are anatomically compatible with self-inflicted wounds, which are not.
- list areas of possible burns, possible cutting, past fractures, especially if multiple.
- with PTSD, review medications as some can interfere with the healing process or worsen symptoms, e.g., beta blockers, histamine type 2 blockers, barbiturate anticonvulsants, diuretics, neuroleptics (Ryan, 1996).
- check for signs of temporal lobe epilepsy as sudden-onset depression and related suicidal acts can occur with temporal lobe ictal activity (Tucker et al., 1986). Request a neurological investigation if warranted.
- if both psychotic and depressed symptoms present, rule out vitamin B_{12} deficiency (Zucker et al., 1981).

❏ POSSIBLE BIOCHEMICAL / ANATOMICAL INVOLVEMENT
- low central serotonin (Asberg et al. 1986; Mann et al., 1992; Rao et al., 1994), low central serotonin due to abnormalities of platelet serotonin type 2 receptors (Pandey et al., 1995), and low blood levels of serotonin have all been found in acutely suicidal patients (Rao et al., 1994).
- adults who do not experience pain during self-injury are more likely to have depression, anxiety, dissociation, and a history of sexual abuse and suicide attempts (Russ et al., 1993; Winchel & Stanley, 1991). A history of dissociating may mean the person has no recall (amnesia) for the self-injurious act.
- self-mutilation may induce an analgesia associated with the release of endogenous opioids as well as an altered state of consciousness. A traumatized patient's urge to harm oneself is often associated with the emergence of traumatic memories (McCann & Pearlman, 1990, p. 258).
- "early and continuous stress lead to the simultaneous development of dissociative tendencies (including indifference to the body and pain) and heightened vulnerability to stress."(Orbach, 1994, p. 68).
- diminished central dopamine activity may occur in suicidal behavior in depressives; there may be dys-regulation of the hypothalamic-pituitary-adrenal axis in those who attempt violent suicide (Roy, 1994).

Presenting Concern: **SELF-INJURY**
Dx Category   SI. 9:   *SELF-INJURIOUS ACTS ASSOCIATED WITH INTENSE ANGER*

❑ *COMMON FORMS*

- this category of self-injury might be more common in people from the general population than people with mental retardation.
- someone who makes multiple cuts on his or her skin using a razor blade, knife, or scissor edge.
- the person burns self with a lit cigarette.

❑ *VARIATIONS*

- stabbing oneself in the arm with a fork or similar sharp object.
- smashing one's hand on a hard surface and causing a bone fracture, in the hours or day following an event that angered the person.
- pouring corrosive substances onto one's skin.
- mutilating one's body.
- the person cuts symbols, numbers, or words into his or her skin.
- someone who is not ready to ask for help may continue to self-cut/self-injure in secret any time (any shift if living in a group home or facility). Someone who may be seeking help to stop this behavior might self-cut only when a favorite or trusted caregiver is on shift (as a gesture to ask for help when asking for help in words is emotionally too difficult).

❑ *DISTINGUISHING FEATURES FOR SI.9*

- "psychological motivations include venting anger, establishing control, ...responding to self-hatred or guilt, discharging sexual feelings, and seeking euphoria" (Simeon et al., 1992, p. 221).
- relief of mounting anxiety has been stated as the reason for self-mutilation in individuals with chronic anger, impulsivity, anxiety, and a history of antisocial acts (Simeon et al., 1992).
- the acts have a low risk of fatality and are not intended to end the person's life.
- the person who has a history of abuse feels intense emotional pain leading up to the acts of self-cutting, self-burning, or other self-injuring.
- among affected individuals from the general population, some report feeling physical pain during the self-cutting/burning, but that it is much less than the emotional pain felt at that time *or* it actually induces a pleasant feeling. Others report not feeling physical pain during the self-cutting/injuring as they dissociate from the intense emotional pain.
- adults, even from the general population, may have no idea why they do this and may not have told anyone close to them about being abused as a child (before they receive appropriate treatment).

❑ *FACTORS THAT MAY WORSEN THE CONDITION*

- exposure to others who self-injure, e.g., living with prison inmates (Winchel & Stanley, 1991).
- isolation and/or confinement (Winchel & Stanley, 1991).
- escalating stress and rejection in a person sensitive to rejection (Simeon et al, 1992).
- regarding this as mere "attention-seeking behavior" and ignoring the person who is experiencing intense emotional pain (with anger or self-hatred) prior to engaging in these acts.
- exposure to triggers that evoke the emotional pain such as special holidays, certain smells, certain types of movies, or hearing about ways that others use to injure themselves.
- professionals (e.g., police, ambulance attendants, nurses) telling the person to just stop the self-cutting or threatening the individual with negative consequences (e.g., full restraint, isolation or confinement).
- entering into a therapeutic relationship with the individual then (a) trying to control the person's behavior, (b) breaking their trust (e.g., telling a lie to the individual, not following through on what you promised, breaking your appointment time because someone else's crisis is "more important"), or (c) prematurely ending the relationship soon after the individual stops self-injuring.
- in a person with post-traumatic stress disorder, medications such as beta blockers, histamine type 2 receptor blockers, barbiturate anticonvulsants, diuretics, and neuroleptics can interfere with the healing process and/or worsen some post-traumatic stress disorder symptoms (Ryan, 1996a).

❑ *PERSONS WHO MAY BE AT RISK*

- someone who was physically and/or sexually abused as a child and has extensive scarring on the body.
- someone who was physically and/or sexually abused as a child and has become clinically depressed.
- a person with post-traumatic stress disorder or a history of repeated abuse.
- someone who provides less and less believable explanations for having many new cuts on their body.
- someone with chronic anger, impulsiveness, anxiety, and a history of antisocial acts (Simeon et al., 1992).
- someone with antisocial personality who has a history of frequent fighting, aggression, intense anger, and anxiety (Virkkunen, 1976).
- someone who has been diagnosed with a severe form of "character disorder" (e.g., borderline personality disorder, sociopathy) and has chronic anger, anxiety, and impulsiveness (Simeon et al., 1992).
- a person with a history of exhibiting "superhuman strength" during bouts of intense anger such as twisting metal bars, lifting and smashing extremely heavy objects.

❑ *SUGGESTIONS FOR COLLECTING INFORMATION*

- review the history for physical and/or sexual abuse as a child.
- assess for post-traumatic stress disorder; see SI.8.
- assess for a history of chronic anger (e.g., directed acts of hostility and verbal aggression) and general level of anxiety.
- assess for antisocial tendencies or a diagnosis of borderline personality (or other "character" disorder).
- assess for depression using instruments or criteria appropriate for this population (e.g., Cooper & Collacott, 1994; Sovner, 1986). Use the *Checklist of Observable Signs of Depression.*
- for those able to read and label different emotional states, the "Children's Depression Inventory" (Kovacs, 1985) has been used to screen depression in developmentally disabled people (Meins, 1993).
- rule out a psychotic explanation for self-mutilation of the body; see considerations in SI.10.

❑ *MEDICAL TESTING / SCREENING SI.9*

- do a careful listing of scarred areas that are compatible with self-inflicted wounds.
- evaluate for depression and post-traumatic stress disorder; if warranted also evaluate for antisocial tendencies and antisocial personality disorder.
- assess the level of suicidal intent as it may be much higher in self-abusers when they are depressed.
- review medications for ones that might adversely affect depression or post-traumatic stress if present. See considerations in SI.8.

❑ *POSSIBLE BIOCHEMICAL / ANATOMICAL INVOLVEMENT*

- a severe form of behavioral dyscontrol involving the serotonin system occurs among habitually violent people with mental retardation or with neuropsychological dysfunction (Hillbrand, 1992).
- Simeon and associates found that self-mutilators had reduced numbers of serotonin type 2 receptor binding sites on blood platelets, which may reflect central serotonergic dysfunction, reduced presynaptic serotonin release, and possibly lower cerebrospinal fluid levels of a serotonin metabolite (5-HIAA) (Simeon et al., 1992, p. 226).
- Orbach suggested that "early and continuous stress lead to the simultaneous development of dissociative tendencies (including indifference to the body and pain) and heightened vulnerability to stress." (Orbach, 1994, p. 68).

❏ *COMMON FORMS*

Most of the examples in this category are from reports of people without mental retardation, but the examples are worth noting since they could also occur in high functioning individuals with mental retardation.
- the person, who is in a psychotic state, reacts to a command hallucination to kill oneself, e.g., by overdosing on medication.
- these command hallucinations to kill oneself are often religious in nature (Winchel & Stanley, 1991)
- stuffing one's ears with objects in an attempt to block hearing voices in person with psychosis (Lauerma, 1994).

❏ *VARIATIONS*

- some acts risk a permanent loss of tissue or an organ during a deluded act of atonement or self-punishment, but do not include the intent to kill oneself. Examples from people who are not mentally retarded include schizophrenics removing one's teeth or eyeballs, or cutting off one's genitals (Ashkenazi et al., 1992; Goodhart & Savitsky, 1933; Jones, 1990; Winchel & Stanley, 1991), and removing the fillings from one's teeth--believed to be radio transmitters--to "end the annoyance caused by auditory hallucinations" (Paterson et al., 1992).
- other acts pose a high risk of death and may include the intent to kill oneself, e.g., pounding a three-inch nail into one's skull when in a delusional state (Puri et al., 1994).

❏ *DISTINGUISHING FEATURES FOR SI.10*

- the person meets strict diagnostic criteria for a chronic psychotic disorder and was delusional at the time of the self-injurious act (Ashkenazi et al., 1992; Pies, 1992; Winchel & Stanley, 1991).
- the onset of this type of self-injury coincides with an acute psychotic state with delusions.
- the frequency of these acts is usually very rare and may occur only once in the person's lifetime.

❏ *FACTORS THAT MAY WORSEN THE CONDITION*

- drug-induced psychosis has lead to enucleation (removing one's eyeball) during a paranoid delusional state (Jones, 1990).

❑ *PERSONS WHO MAY BE AT RISK*

- a person who is acutely psychotic and has a history of self-inflicted injuries or pain insensitivity.
- a person with schizoaffective psychosis and a severe disturbance of body image (MacLean & Robertson, 1976).
- a person who is acutely psychotic and having religious delusions with reference to quotations such as "an eye for an eye" or "If thy right eye offend thee, pluck it out" (Goodhart & Savitsky, 1993; Winchel & Stanley, 1991).
- a person who has a family history of schizophrenia and has food sensitivities to gluten is at risk for schizophrenia (Reichelt et al., 1996), but not necessarily severe self-mutilation.

❑ *SUGGESTIONS FOR COLLECTING INFORMATION*

- check family history for psychosis or schizophrenia.
- screen for features of a psychotic disorder, especially if there is a family history of schizophrenia. Collect information using the *Checklist of Observable Signs of Psychosis in Persons with Mental Retardation*.
- if the person who stuffs his/her ears with objects can speak, ask the reason why he/she does that. (If the person is trying to block out "voices," safe alternatives such as ear plugs can be tried.)
- review the history for past instances of self-harm; if possible, identify body areas at risk.

❑ *MEDICAL TESTING / SCREENING SI.10*

- if a psychotic patient stuffs his/her ears, rule out tinnitus (ringing in the ears) caused by medication or a medical condition, or try to obtain better pharmacological control over the auditory hallucinations.
- if a psychotic patient is acutely delusional and has a history of self-harm or severe disturbance of body image, consider continuous protective supervision during the acute phase.
- in persons with temporal lobe seizures presenting as atypical psychosis and unexplained depression, antipsychotics or tricyclic antidepressants can worsen the person's symptoms (Farber et al., 1986; Tucker et al., 1986). See considerations for SI.5.
- review medications for drug-induced hallucinations, e.g., antidepressants, benzodiazepines, digitalis, ephedrine, levodopa, methlyphenidate/Ritalin, propranolol/Inderal, and pentazocine/Talwin (Jain, 1996). Drugs frequently reported to induce psychoses are anabolic steroids, anticholinergics, benzodiazepines, corticosteroids, and withdrawal from neuroleptics (Jain, 1996). Medication-induced psychosis has been reported due to propranolol (Gershon, 1979), carbamazepine/Tegretol (Mathew 1988), clobazam/ Frisium, vigabatrin/Sabril (Sander et al., 1991), and other anticonvulsants (Franks & Richter, 1979).
- test for elevated casein or gluten antibodies in the blood or elevated casein-gluten peptides in the urine (Reichelt et al., 1996).

❑ *POSSIBLE BIOCHEMICAL / ANATOMICAL INVOLVEMENT*

- there may be intestinal permeability and insufficient breakdown of dietary peptides such as gluten, which then result in excessive peptides absorbed into the blood and interference with central nervous system functioning in some persons with schizophrenia (Reichelt et al., 1996).
- "Ocular self-mutilation in psychotic patients tends to be particularly cold-blooded suggesting distorted pain perception and body image. A nonpsychotic [person] with self-injury would be overwhelmed by pain before completing an action such as a corneal or scleral perforation." (Ashkenazi et al., 1992, p. 650). Other types of self-mutilation in psychotic patients also reflect distorted pain perception when carrying out the self-mutilation.

Chapter III

SCREAMING

Presenting Concern: **SCREAMING**
Dx Category   SC.1:   *SCREAMING IN RESPONSE TO PHYSICAL PAIN OR DISCOMFORT*

❑ *COMMON FORMS*
- the person does prolonged loud screaming that is accompanied by tears or perspiration.
- the screaming can last for hours every day, and can persist into the night.
- the prolonged screaming started one day and has continued almost daily since then.

❑ *VARIATIONS*
- the person makes an abrupt, sharp, high-pitched shrill or rapid shrieks only when touched or repositioned by others.
- the person who screams shows minor shock symptoms consistent with severe pain such as shallow guarded breathing, pallor or greyness, body coolness or clamminess.
- the person used to be friendly and happy, then became moody and would moan or scream when repositioned.
- the person often has tears in the eyes and a painful, pleading expression when silent or when screaming.
- a person with a pattern of daily screaming lasting 15-30 minutes starts to scream for many hours (8-14) every day; later, a very painful condition such as gall or kidney stones is discovered.
- if the person does not have the lung capacity for loud screaming due to a physical condition, there may be a steady droning sound like a cry at a low volume, a low "ahhhh," or sobbing with tears.

❑ *DISTINGUISHING FEATURES FOR SC.1*
- the person is not consoled when given extra attention or offered special activities and treats.
- the screaming ends once the source of pain has been eliminated, i.e., the disease/condition has been treated.
- if the screaming lessens when pain medication is given, the screaming returns as the pain killer wears off.
- the person is unable to report physical pain, or has a history of not reporting pain even though he or she is verbally capable of doing so.
- a person with a rib or pelvic fracture, or stomach/abdominal pain, might show only shallow breathing.
- screaming associated with pain can occur day and night, hence may cause insomnia.

❑ *FACTORS THAT MAY WORSEN THE CONDITION*
- physically moving the person or touching an area that is painful to the person.
- repositioning the person when this inadvertently increases pressure on the affected body part.
- acute illness, seasonal allergies, or sores in addition to whatever painful condition causes the screaming.

❑ *PERSONS WHO MAY BE AT RISK*
- a person who is unable to report pain or symptoms (e.g., in the severe or profound range of intelligence).
- a person with a family history of arthritis or other conditions that appear to be associated with early onset of arthritis, e.g., Down syndrome, scoliosis, kyphosis or other musculo-skeletal disorder.
- a person with a family history of "difficult-to-palpate" types of cancer (e.g., bone cancer, bowel cancer).
- a person who is at risk for serious bowel dysfunction, e.g., a person with a history of megacolon or paralytic ileus who also takes a phenothiazine-type neuroleptic (De Silva et al., 1992).
- someone with chronic constipation, especially if he or she takes a phenothiazine-type neuroleptic, e.g., thioridiazine/Mellaril, methotrimeprazine/Nozinan, chlorpromazine/Largactil.
- someone at risk for gastrointestinal problems such as a person with PKU (phenylketonuria) who is not on a low-protein diet, or a person with impaired breakdown of certain proteins (e.g., casein/gluten peptides) who is not on a modified diet.

- persons with Down syndrome are at risk for celiac disease (a disorder involving gluten) that can cause, bowel pain, diarrhea, constipation, and anemia (George et al., 1996; Simila & Kokkonen, 1990).
- a person with a leaky gut or history of food allergies, sinus headaches, migraines, or sensitivities to food additives.
- a person with pain or discomfort from gastro-tubes, muscle contractures, bed sores, etc.
- a person who has the mental age of a young child and eats inedibles is at risk for gastrointestinal obstruction.
- someone with a dramatic weight loss who has become very lethargic and seeks to lie down more often.
- an elderly person who is at risk for bone fractures and is unable to report pain.
- a person who is nonambulatory or medically fragile, as these increase the risk for osteoporosis and other painful medical conditions.

❑ SUGGESTIONS FOR COLLECTING INFORMATION
- use the *Discomfort Scale** (Hurley et al., 1992) to assess a noncommunicative person for pain.
- check if the person has a history of difficulty in reporting pain or unreliability in answering questions about pain. In the former case, the person may have been discouraged years earlier from reporting pain and "trained" not to complain. In the latter, the person complains about "every little thing" making it difficult to distinguish when serious pain is being reported.
- interview caregivers for possible *antecedents* to the screaming, e.g., certain physical activities, certain types of physical care, repositioning, touching certain body areas, during or after meals, the timing in relation to bowel movements or refusals to eat. Chart changes in the usual level of nighttime and daytime activity.
- observe the person's response to noise and light during screaming episodes (e.g., covering ears, covering eyes, seeking a darkened room) for possible signs of migraine. Also check family history for migraine.
- review records for dramatic weight loss, signs of pain or discomfort, and marked lethargy.
- review the history to see if there are patterns suggesting that the screaming is related to illness or pain.
- in women, check for menstrual worsening; collect information using the *Menstrual Distress Chart.** With those who can be interviewed, consider using the "Menstrual Distress Questionnaire" (Moos,1968).
- check family history for arthritic conditions, allergies, cancer, and migraines.
- provide the person's temperature, pulse, and respirations per minute to the nurse and/or physician.
- if there is a history of *unexplained* persistent gastrointestinal problems, collect information using the *Risk Factors for Casein-Gluten Peptiduria.**

* A chart or checklist listed in *italics* in this section can be found in the Appendix.

❑ MEDICAL TESTING / SCREENING SC.1
- investigate thoroughly for sites of pain, then do follow-up screening for conditions that could account for the acutely sensitive organs or areas.
- check ears, teeth, and mouth. Check for urinary tract infections, vulval or vaginal infections.
- investigate for possible gastrointestinal problems (e.g., ulcers, bowel impaction or obstruction, foreign objects).
- if there is a history of *unexplained* persistent gastrointestinal problems, test for intestinal parasites, yeast overgrowth, serum antibodies to common foods, especially casein-gluten antibodies in serum or casein-gluten peptides in urine. Test for celiac disease in Down syndrome (George et al., 1996).
- with severe inconsolable screaming and oozing stool, consider ruling out obstructed or twisted bowel.
- with severe inconsolable screaming for hours daily, consider ruling out gall stones and kidney stones.
- check for cancer if the family history or other signs warrant it.
- check for inflammatory conditions such as arthritis and painful joints.

❑ POSSIBLE BIOCHEMICAL / ANATOMICAL INVOLVEMENT
- screaming and crying are understandable responses to severe physical pain.

Presenting Concern: **SCREAMING**
Dx Category   SC.2: *SCREAMING TO COMMUNICATE ANGER OR DISTRESS*

❏ *COMMON FORMS*
- the screaming starts when a particular individual enters the area and stops when that individual leaves.
- the above pattern of screaming can occur for weeks if no effort is made to uncover and resolve the "dispute" between the two parties.
- the person points at a particular individual while screaming.
- the screaming coincides with the start of a particular activity, and may end when that activity ends.
- the person screams while showing an angry look or making an angry gesture.

❏ *VARIATIONS*
- the screaming stops after caregivers reassure the person that no harm will occur to them or theft of their belongings.
- the person screaming makes gestures toward a particular individual to "go away."

❏ *DISTINGUISHING FEATURES FOR SC.2*
- the screaming starts when a particular individual enters the area and stops when that individual leaves.
- the screaming diminishes or stops after the concern between the screamer and "other" is resolved, or when that individual is away (e.g., on vacation, sick leave, or relocates).

❏ *FACTORS THAT MAY WORSEN THE CONDITION*
- if the individual whose presence evokes screaming makes eye contact with or approaches the person screaming.
- if the individual whose presence evokes screaming touches food or valued possessions of the person screaming.
- caregivers failing to identify the underlying concern or interpersonal dynamic that created this person's stressful reaction.
- caregivers failing to resolve or eliminate the underlying stressor that upsets the person.

❑ *PERSONS WHO MAY BE AT RISK*

- a person who cannot communicate in words the nature of a concern that is associated with a particular individual or activity.
- a small person with little or no speech who is in dispute with a much larger individual.
- nonambulatory persons who are unable to prevent others from taking their food or possessions.
- a nonambulatory person who is unable to protect self from individuals with a history of aggression or taking others' possessions.

❑ *SUGGESTIONS FOR COLLECTING INFORMATION*

- chart the screaming for onset and offset related to individuals nearby, people arriving and departing, activities started and ended, and peers' behavior that could be upsetting to the person (e.g., stealing other's food or possessions, unprovoked hitting).
- chart the screaming for time of day and possible worsening with illness, menstrual phase, hunger, thirst, or recent medication change.
- review history to see if the screaming occurred only after a change in housemate, staffing, living arrangements, work demands, medication, major life event, and so on.
- identify what tends to upset the person and identify what nonverbal gestures and facial expressions the person uses to convey disapproval or anger; inform all caregivers of these nonverbal clues.
- identify what tends to upset the person and plan ways to reduce or eliminate triggers where possible.
- rule out physical pain as a contributing factor; use the *Discomfort Scale* (Hurley et al., 1992) to assess a noncommunicative person for pain.
- assess for depression using instruments or criteria appropriate for this population (e.g., Cooper & Collacott, 1994; Sovner, 1986). Use the *Checklist of Observable Signs of Depression.*
- rule out screaming in response to hallucinations in a person with schizophrenia; collect information using the *Checklist of Observable Signs of Psychosis in Persons with Mental Retardation.*
- if there is a history of past trauma, check if the screaming is related to the *presence* of a past abuser or if the screaming has features consistent with a flashback. See SC.7.
- check if there are signs suggesting that the screaming is related to pain (see SC.1), a need to escape (see SC.3), or asking for basic care (see SC.4).

❑ *MEDICAL TESTING / SCREENING SC.2*

- rule out physical sources of pain; see considerations in SC.1.
- rule out increases or decreases in screaming that parallel changes in medication; see SC.5.
- if there is a history of trauma, see SC.7 for comments about medications that can worsen flashbacks.

❑ *POSSIBLE BIOCHEMICAL / ANATOMICAL INVOLVEMENT*

- this category of screaming is regarded as intentional behavior, i.e., a nonverbal way to communicate anger, emotional distress, or fear.

Presenting Concern: **SCREAMING**
Dx Category   SC.3: *SCREAMING TO ESCAPE OR AVOID SOMETHING*

❑ *COMMON FORMS*
- the screaming starts during demand-related activities such as self-care tasks.
- the screaming stops when a demand ends.
- the screaming occurs during tasks that are difficult or frustrating for the person.
- the screaming starts after a task or activity has gone on "too long," beyond the person's tolerance.
- the person screams then throws or pushes away objects that are associated with a task or activity.
- the screaming starts when the person tries to leave an area and is prevented from leaving.
- the screaming may be associated with heights, enclosed spaces, medical labs, people in lab coats, doctors, dentists, etc.

❑ *VARIATIONS*
- the screaming stops after caregivers reassure the person that no more task demands will be made at that time.
- the screaming stops after caregivers reassure the person that no harm will come to him or her.
- the screaming might be an attempt to escape from auditory distortions associated with ear disease (McCreary, 1997).

❑ *DISTINGUISHING FEATURES FOR SC.3*
- the timing of the person's screaming is connected with a particular task, activity, or individual previously associated with failure.
- the screaming stops when the person is allowed to escape or avoid something, or is made to feel protected and safe.
- the screaming might be a phobic response to stimuli (heights, enclosed spaces, dogs, etc.) that provoke an immediate anxiety response.

❑ *FACTORS THAT MAY WORSEN THE CONDITION*
- introducing new tasks or more difficult tasks.
- having staff who do not accommodate well to those with multiple disabilities work closely with the person.
- having time constraints on getting certain tasks or activities done.
- if the individual whose presence evokes screaming makes eye contact with or approaches the person screaming.
- failure of caregivers to identify the underlying concern that created the person's desire to escape.
- expecting the person to learn tasks beyond his or her level of comprehension.

❏ *PERSONS WHO MAY BE AT RISK*

- a person with a low level of skill in the particular task or activity.
- a nonverbal person with a new home, school, workplace, or type of work.
- a person who cannot communicate in words the nature of a concern that is associated with a particular individual or activity.
- a person who has dementia and is losing the ability to communicate with words.
- a small person who is in dispute with a much larger individual.
- a nonambulatory person who is unable to protect self from others who have a history of hitting peers.
- persons who have physical limitations that reduce their ability to leave a room on their own.
- a person who has been handled roughly by or hurt by someone who still has occasional contact with the person.
- blind people, with little or no speech who rely on sounds and voices to orient themselves, when they are placed in noisy environments.
- a person with a fear of heights, confined spaces, medical procedures, or anxiety-provoking stimuli.

❏ *SUGGESTIONS FOR COLLECTING INFORMATION*

- chart the screaming for onset and offset related to individuals nearby, people arriving and departing, activities started and ended, peers' behaviors that the person might want to escape from (e.g., hitting).
- review the history to see if screaming occurred prior to the current housemate, staff, and living arrangements.
- chart the screaming in relation to the person not being able to escape from a task, activity, noisy setting, medical procedures, or certain kinds of people.
- analyze the screaming for communicative function (Donnellan et al., 1984).
- check if there are signs suggesting that the screaming is related to pain (see SC.1), anger (see SC.2), or asking for basic care (see SC.4).
- rule out screaming associated with illness, menstrual phase, hunger, thirst, or recent medication change. In women, check for menstrual worsening; collect information using the *Menstrual Distress Chart*. With women able to be interviewed, consider using the "Menstrual Distress Questionnaire" (Moos, 1968).
- rule out physical pain as a contributing factor using the *Discomfort Scale* (Hurley et al., 1992) to assess a noncommunicative person.
- assess for depression as a contributing factor using instruments or criteria appropriate for this population (e.g., Cooper & Collacott, 1994; Sovner, 1986). Use the *Checklist of Observable Signs of Depression*.
- check for features of a specific phobia (DSM-IV, 1994) if there is a marked and persistent morbid anxiety to a defined object or situation. A diagnosis of phobia requires that the avoidance, fear, or anxious anticipation of encountering the phobic stimulus interferes significantly with the person's daily routine, work, or social life.

❏ *MEDICAL TESTING / SCREENING SC.3*

- if the screaming is associated with a particular activity, evaluate if the movements involved in the activity could be causing pain.
- check for anxiety disorders, phobias, and/or a need to be desensitized to certain stimuli.
- rule out flashback-related screaming if post-traumatic stress disorder is present or suspected.
- rule out physical sources of pain generally; see considerations in SC.1.
- rule out increases or decreases in screaming that parallel changes in medication; see SC.5.

❏ *POSSIBLE BIOCHEMICAL / ANATOMICAL INVOLVEMENT*

- this category of screaming is regarded as intentional behavior, i.e., as a nonverbal way to communicate the desire to leave an area or to avoid something or someone.

Presenting Concern: **SCREAMING**
Dx Category   SC.4: *SCREAMING FOR CARE AND ATTENTION*

___

❏ *COMMON FORMS*

- the screaming starts when the individual giving care says "Goodbye" or leaves the person.
- the screaming starts when caregivers try to release the person's grip on their hand, or indicate that they are about to leave.
- in a person who can speak, the screaming includes spoken pleas such as "Don't leave me."
- the screaming stops when the person's favorite caregiver comes near or provides physical contact.
- the screaming stops when sympathetic attention is provided.

___

❏ *VARIATIONS*

- the person might scream for 5-10 minutes before pausing to "catch their breath," but the screaming does not continue longer than half an hour without pause.

___

❏ *DISTINGUISHING FEATURES FOR SC.4*

- the screaming usually starts when caregivers stop a particular activity, break off physical contact, or indicate they are about to leave.
- the screaming bouts diminish or stop when the person learns that personal attention and/or affection will be provided frequently.
- the screaming bouts diminish when the person learns that his or her personal needs (e.g., hunger, thirst, warmth, diaper change needed, repositioning needed, etc.) will be identified and met more often than before.

___

❏ *FACTORS THAT MAY WORSEN THE CONDITION*

- leaving the person for 2-3 hours without physical contact on a frequent basis, especially if nonambulatory.
- having a favorite caregiver away for several days or longer, e.g., on vacation or medical leave.

❑ *PERSONS WHO MAY BE AT RISK*

- a nonverbal, blind person who is not receiving very much physical touch or social contact.
- a nonverbal, nonambulatory person who is unable to initiate social and physical contact by walking up to people.
- a person who has little or no speech and cannot ask someone in words for care or comfort.
- a nonverbal person with a new school, home, workplace, or new type of work.
- a nonverbal person who has new staff providing personal care.
- a person who has little or no speech and shows signs of depression.
- a person with dementia who is losing the ability to communicate with words.

❑ *SUGGESTIONS FOR COLLECTING INFORMATION*

- chart the screaming for timing, duration, people nearby, people arriving and departing, activities started and ended, and other factors that increase or decrease the screaming.
- collect data on the effects of providing attention/activities continent upon so many minutes without screaming and "time-out from attention" contingent on screaming.
- rule out physical pain as a contributing factor; use the *Discomfort Scale* (Hurley et al., 1992) to assess a noncommunicative person for pain.
- in women, check for menstrual worsening; collect information using the *Menstrual Distress Chart*. With women able to be interviewed, consider using the "Menstrual Distress Questionnaire" (Moos, 1968).
- check if there are signs suggesting that the screaming is due to pain (see SC.1), anger (see SC.2), a need to escape (see SC.3), or other communicative function (Donnellan et al., 1984).
- assess for depression using instruments or criteria appropriate for this population (e.g., Cooper & Collacott, 1994; Sovner, 1986). Use *Checklist of Observable Signs of Depression*.

❑ *MEDICAL TESTING / SCREENING SC.4*

- rule out physical sources of pain; see considerations in SC.1.
- rule out medication-related screaming; check for a pattern of increases and decreases in screaming that parallel changes in medication. See considerations in SC.5.

❑ *POSSIBLE BIOCHEMICAL / ANATOMICAL INVOLVEMENT*

- this category of screaming is regarded as intentional behavior, i.e., as a nonverbal way to ask others to continue an ongoing activity or to provide basic care, comfort, or physical contact.

Presenting Concern: **SCREAMING**
Dx Category   SC.5: *INTENSE INVOLUNTARY SCREAMING*

❏ *COMMON FORMS*
- the intense vocalizations tend to "run their course" before abating, regardless of the caregiver's efforts to distract, discourage, console, or provide personal care and attention.
- intense vocalizations and motor movements begin suddenly without provocation.
- repetitive striking motions of the arms, staring, and rapid breathing sometimes occur with the screaming.
- the screaming can be under 2 minutes, up to 5-30 minutes, or in unusual cases, go on and off for hours.

❏ *VARIATIONS*
- the person makes other vocalizations such as shrieking, humming, ah-ah-ah that can last many minutes.
- the person repeats a word, phrase, or syllable (ah-ah-ah) over and over during the screaming episode.
- the person makes a brief, loud sound at random intervals throughout the day, and the sound always has the same quality (e.g., a short sharp sound, a whoop, or brief vocalization); otherwise the person is silent and non-interactive the rest of the time.
- the person randomly makes a very loud, sharp sound that is "ear piercing" and startles others nearby .
- the person screaming sometimes does head turning, head weaving, fixed staring, or the eyes turn upward.
- there may be no obvious emotional distress such as fear or anger that accompanies the screaming.
- the person may have little or no awareness of what happened during a screaming attack, or the person may indicate afterward that he/she is sorry and did not mean to be disruptive.
- a person, who is unable to converse or use speech in a meaningful way, yells single words or phrases that have emotional content *only during screaming outbursts*.
- the screaming lasts 10-30 seconds with gasps for a breath between each scream, and can persist for 10-12 hours daily, often until the person is exhausted and wet with sweat (Pasion & Kirby, 1993).

❏ *DISTINGUISHING FEATURES FOR SC.5*
- the person rarely gets a hoarse voice from prolonged involuntary screaming.
- the episodes can occur without provocation, "out-of-the-blue."
- the episodes are inordinately intense or prolonged relative to the everyday frustrations that precede them.
- the person seems to be physically stronger than usual during these screaming outbursts.
- intense screaming starts suddenly and is accompanied by intense motor movements.
- there may be intense staring, a vacant look or wild look in the eyes, the head and eyes look left at times, grimacing, clenched teeth or jaw-jutting, and occasionally spitting or biting.
- there may be noisy breathing or accelerated breathing, facial flushing or pallor, pupil dilation; sometimes there is excessive saliva or drooling, incontinence, or sweating.
- often there are body movements that are inconsistent with deliberate anger or fearfulness.
- the person resumes his/her previous activity after the screaming stops, without bearing grudges or making angry comments, "as if the outburst did not happen."

❏ *FACTORS THAT MAY WORSEN THE CONDITION*
- criticizing or trying to argue with the person during screaming outbursts.
- trying to overpower the person during a screaming episode.
- dietary factors that reduce serotonin production, e.g., high protein diet, caffeinated food/beverages (Gedye, 1990; 1991d; 1991e).
- medication that reduces the production and release of serotonin, e.g., benzodiazepines (diazepam/ Valium, lorazepam/Ativan) (Essman & Essman, 1986; Green, 1986; Pei et al., 1989; Saner & Pletscher, 1979; Wise et al., 1972).
- medication that can worsen frontal lobe seizures, e.g., carbamazepine/Tegretol (Horn et al., 1986).
- long-term use of drugs that lower the seizure threshold such as neuroleptics (e.g., haloperidol/Haldol, thioridazine/Mellaril).

- the following are possible stressors or times of risk for involuntary episodes: high noise level or a startling event; bright sunlight or flickering light; lacking sleep or being overtired; low blood sugar, missing a meal or a history of hypoglycemia; allergic reactions to pollens, etc. or an exaggerated response to insect bites; highly emotional events, positive or negative; emotional frustration or anger; stress or pressure to perform; a change in plans or in routine sequence; premenstrual or menstrual phase; during the waking hours of the morning or when falling asleep (times when consciousness is shifting); late afternoon; mealtime (breakfast, lunch, supper). (See Gedye, 1991b; 1996b).

❏ *PERSONS WHO MAY BE AT RISK*
- a person with a history of head injury or physical abuse that might have caused head trauma.
- a person who has temporal lobe seizures (because temporal discharges can spread to the frontal area) (Lieb et al., 1991; Luciano, 1993; Quesney et al., 1995; Veilleux et al., 1992; Williamson, 1995).
- a person with Tuberous Sclerosis who has tubers in the frontal lobe area.
- a person with a known frontal lobe abnormality.
- a person with frequent involuntary movements, sometimes called "stereotypic movements".
- a person with an etiology known to have low levels of serotonin, e.g., Cornelia De Lange syndrome, Down syndrome, histidinemia, phenylketonuria (PKU) (Coleman, 1973; Greenberg & Coleman, 1973; Lou et al., 1985; Tu & Partington, 1972).
- a person with a family history of Tourette syndrome.

❏ *SUGGESTIONS FOR COLLECTING INFORMATION*
- videotape the person during screaming episodes to help detect involuntary phenomena.
- check for a high number of ictal signs during outbursts using the *Nonconvulsive Ictal Signs Checklist*.
- carefully review the high risk times and stressors identified on the *Nonconvulsive Ictal Signs Checklist*.
- assess for signs of Tourette syndrome, especially in persons with a strong family history of that disorder.
- check if there are signs suggesting that the screaming is related to pain (see SC.1), anger (see SC.2), a need to escape (see SC.3), or asking for basic care (see SC.4).
- assess for possible involuntary self-injurious movements accompanying the involuntary screaming or vocalizations. Collect information using the *Checklist of Intentional Self-Restraint and Involuntary Self-Injurious Movements*.
- if there is a history of *unexplained* persistent gastrointestinal problems, collect information using the *Risk Factors for Casein-Gluten Peptiduria*.

❏ *MEDICAL TESTING / SCREENING SC.5*
- rule out pain as the underlying reason; see considerations in SC.1.
- review medication for ones that adversely affect serotonin production and release, e.g., benzodiazepines.
- nonconvulsive status epilepticus can present with screaming, agitation, and confusion lasting 1-7 days (Kaplan, 1992). Consider an EEG and neurological investigation for frontal lobe seizures, although scalp or sphenoidal EEGs are often normal during and between seizures (Luciano, 1993; Stores et al., 1991). See literature review (Gedye, 1991b; 1996b).
- review medications for ones that risk lowering the seizure threshold.
- if there is a history of *unexplained* persistent gastrointestinal problems, test for intestinal parasites, yeast overgrowth, serum antibodies to common foods, especially casein-gluten antibodies in serum or casein-gluten peptides in urine. Test for celiac disease in Down syndrome (George et al., 1996).
- consider brain scans to rule out frontal tubers with Tuberous Sclerosis or identify frontal lobe pathology.

❏ *POSSIBLE BIOCHEMICAL / ANATOMICAL INVOLVEMENT*
- involuntary screaming can occur during frontal lobe seizures that affect the muscles involved in breathing and vocalizations (Maeda et al.,1992; Spencer et al.,1983; Stores et al.,1991; Waterman et al.,1987).
- the basal ganglia cannot be the sole site of dysfunction in persons diagnosed with Tourette syndrome *who have involuntary vocalizations*, because no speech functions are served there (Barabas, 1988).
- adverse effects on the central nervous system from a food allergy can cause nonconvulsive seizures (Gobbi et al., 1992).

❏ *COMMON FORMS*

- the person has bouts of screaming or intense vocalizations that last 5-30 minutes daily.
- the screaming bouts tend to occur at approximately the same hour each day, regardless of the activity involved.
- the screaming continues and "runs its course" despite caregivers offering attention and physical contact.

❏ *VARIATIONS*

- the person produces short screams throughout the day and occasionally strikes people when walking by them.
- the person who screams intermittently, walks about frequently and strikes people when walking by them.
- the person who screams intermittently, walks about frequently and has difficulty staying seated even for meals.
- the person makes loud hoots or short screams on and off throughout the day.
- the screaming increases when the person is pressured to do simple activities.

❏ *DISTINGUISHING FEATURES FOR SC.6*

- the screaming ceases after the offending medication is discontinued (e.g., carbamazepine/Tegretol).
- the short screams throughout the day and random hitting of others cease after stopping the offending medication.
- the person probably did not scream prior to taking a particular psychotropic medication.
- the screaming is not reduced by behavior modification programs.

❏ *FACTORS THAT MAY WORSEN THE CONDITION*

- increasing the dose of the offending medication.
- adding a drug that slows the clearance of the offending medication.
- adding neuroleptic medication to a person already taking carbamazepine.

❏ PERSONS WHO MAY BE AT RISK

- a person taking the anticonvulsant carbamazepine for "behavioral" control, not for seizure control.
- a person with pre-existing cerebral dysfunction who is taking carbamazepine (Reid et al., 1981).
- a person taking carbamazepine and a neuroleptic medication.
- a person with mental retardation who takes phenobarbital (Kalachnik et al., 1995).
- a person who had involuntary movements and involuntary vocalizations before any medication was introduced.

❏ SUGGESTIONS FOR COLLECTING INFORMATION

- chart the screaming for possible patterns related to the time of day, time when medication is given, and/or time when medication levels peak.
- review records to see if these screaming outbursts occurred before any medication was introduced, if the screaming started or worsened after certain medication changes, or if it stopped when the person was off certain medication.
- check if there are signs suggesting that the screaming is related to pain (see SC.1), anger (see SC.2), a need to escape (see SC.3), or asking for basic care (see SC.4).

❏ MEDICAL TESTING / SCREENING SC.6

- rule out physical sources of pain; see SC.1.
- check for a pattern of increases and decreases in screaming that parallel changes in medication.
- consider a trial off the suspected medication, and request detailed charting to see if there is a relationship between the time and duration of screaming and changes in medication.
- assess for ictal or involuntary screaming if this is suspected; see considerations in SC.5.

❏ POSSIBLE BIOCHEMICAL / ANATOMICAL INVOLVEMENT

- there may be involuntary activation of the nerves that control the vocal and breathing muscles.

Presenting Concern: **SCREAMING**
Dx Category   SC.7: *SCREAMING DURING FLASHBACKS*

❏ *COMMON FORMS*
- the screaming occurs with a fearful facial expression or when the person is cowering or assuming a protective posture.
- the screaming worsens if caregivers try to overpower the person.
- the person yells with intense anger or fear as if speaking to someone not present, e.g., No! Stop! Don't!
- there is an abrupt start to the screaming and yelling, and the yelling refers to people and places from the past.

❏ *VARIATIONS*
- the screaming occurs at night with or without the person reporting scary images or appearing to have nightmares.
- the person abruptly starts to cry, scream, yell foul language, and/or say angry comments that abusers might have said to the person, e.g., "Mary is a bad girl!"
- the person wakes up at night screaming, perhaps hides under the bed, and allows no one to come close (Ryan, 1996a).

❏ *DISTINGUISHING FEATURES FOR SC.7*
- screaming can occur during the re-living of traumatic memories in someone with post-traumatic stress.
- the screaming can be provoked by unusual triggers such as certain smells or sounds, certain rooms, certain people.
- during these episodes, the person might not be fully oriented, might know who he is but not where he is.
- the person calls others by names that are not their real names, but only during these episodes.
- the person might become less interactive with others in the 1-2 days before a flashback. The person may have been talking about the perpetrators in the days leading up to a flashback.
- after visits with abusers, the person may become hyperactive, incontinent of urine and feces, and hit or kick caregivers (Ryan, 1996a).

❏ *FACTORS THAT MAY WORSEN THE CONDITION*
- forcing the person to have contact with someone he or she does not want to see at that time (Ryan, 1996a).
- noisy environments, lack of privacy, or lack of safety and comfort (Ryan, 1996a).
- caregivers who physically remind the person of abusers (Ryan, 1996a).
- engaging in power struggles with a person who has been traumatized.
- caregivers ignoring the person during flashbacks or blaming the person for past traumatic events, or "pretend like nothing happened" (Ryan, 1996a, p. 50).
- psychotherapy that inadvertently causes "emotional flooding" of traumatic memories leading to increased dissociation and/or decompensation (McCann & Pearlman, 1990).
- the frequency of flashback-related screaming may increase after exposure to people or places that trigger traumatic memories, e.g., a visit to one's childhood house or hometown.
- special holidays that remind the person of past traumas.
- cognitively-impairing medication, e.g., neuroleptics can increase the intensity of flashbacks in a person with post-traumatic stress disorder (Ryan, 1996a).
- in a person with post-traumatic stress disorder, medications such as beta blockers, histamine type 2 receptor blockers, barbiturate anticonvulsants, diuretics, and neuroleptics can interfere with the healing process and/or worsen some PTSD symptoms (Ryan, 1996a).

❑ PERSONS WHO MAY BE AT RISK
- a person with a history of sexual abuse, physical trauma, and/or ritualistic abuse.
- a person with a history of witnessing traumatic events or natural disasters.
- a person who has symbols cut into the skin or disfiguring marks on body.
- a person with unusual scarring on areas out-of-reach for that person (e.g., on the back or buttocks).
- a person with a history of being cruel to animals or insects.
- a person who assumes a defensive or cowering posture when startled, frightened, or feeling threatened.
- a person who is hypervigilant at night, feels very unsafe at night, and fears the dark.
- a person who slips into dissociative states such as moments with no eye contact, a frozen mask-like face, numbness, and shows signs of re-experiencing past traumas (flashbacks).
- a person whose mental retardation was caused by head injury at a young age, possibly by physical abuse.
- a person whose history contains insufficient information on past events, but there are reasonable grounds to suspect past trauma.

❑ SUGGESTIONS FOR COLLECTING INFORMATION
- assess for signs of dissociative states, numbing, and flashbacks.
- chart sleep for nightmares, an anxious fearful state at bedtime, sleeping in the day because of fearing the dark, or other unusual features not typically associated with insomnia, i.e., check for signs of post-traumatic stress.
- assess for post-traumatic stress disorder using diagnostic criteria, e.g., DSM-IV (1994).
- assess for depression using instruments or criteria appropriate for this population (e.g., Cooper & Collacott, 1994; Sovner, 1986). Use the *Checklist of Observable Signs of Depression.*
- try to identify distinct sounds that trigger fearful or protective responses. Then have staff minimize the occurrence of these triggering cues. Also plan ways to desensitize the person to such triggers.
- review recent screaming episodes if possible; determine if the onset was related to a reminder of traumatizing events.
- rule out schizophrenia and screaming in response to hallucinations. Collect information using the *Checklist of Observable Signs of Psychosis in Persons with Mental Retardation.* (See also Ryan, 1996b).
- check if there are signs suggesting that the screaming is related to pain (see SC.1), anger at someone in the person's current life (see SC.2), or asking for basic care (see SC.4).

❑ MEDICAL TESTING / SCREENING SC.7
- do a careful listing of scarred areas that are anatomically compatible and which are incompatible with self-inflicted wounds; list areas of past fractures, especially if multiple.
- with post-traumatic stress disorder, review medications for those that can interfere with the healing process and/or worsen symptoms such as beta blockers, histamine type 2 blockers, barbiturate anticonvulsants, diuretics, and neuroleptics (Ryan, 1996a).

❑ POSSIBLE BIOCHEMICAL / ANATOMICAL INVOLVEMENT
- there may be involvement of the limbic system if the screaming was in response to fear associated with re-living past trauma.
- serotonergic dysregulation is present in some people with post-traumatic stress disorder (Nagy et al., 1993).

Chapter IV

SLEEP DISTURBANCES

SD.1. Pain-Related Sleep Disturbances

SD.2. Environmental And Sleep Hygiene Factors

SD.3. Insomnia Or Excessive Daytime Sleeping During Depression

SD.4. Mania And Sleep

SD.5. Hyperthyroidism And Sleep

SD.6. Medication-Induced Sleep Disturbances

SD.7. Insomnia During Neuroleptic Withdrawal

SD.8. Sleep Disturbances Related To Post-Traumatic Stress

SD.9. Nocturnal Anxiety And Nocturnal Panic Attacks

SD.10. Obstructive Sleep Apnea And/Or Central Sleep Apnea

SD.11. Hypothyroidism And Sleep

SD.12. Circadian Rhythm Sleep Disturbances

SD.13. Chronic Hyperventilation, Fibromyalgia Syndrome, And Sleep

Presenting Concern: **SLEEP DISTURBANCES**
Dx Category   SD.1: *PAIN-RELATED SLEEP DISTURBANCES*

❑ COMMON FORMS

- the person is having sleep disturbances that were not present before. Sometimes these disturbances are due to undetected pain.
- the person started screaming in the day or night, or had an increase in screaming spells around the time the sleeping difficulty began. He or she winces, moans, cries, or shows other signs suggestive of pain.
- the person has difficulty initiating sleep and/or has a pattern of waking from sleep that was not present before.
- a woman has a pattern of difficulty staying asleep which is related to her menstrual cycle.
- the person showed an increase in irritability and deterioration in overall mood around the time the sleeping difficulty started.

❑ VARIATIONS

- the person started refusing to do previously enjoyable activities that require physical exertion.
- the physical pain may be less in the day and magnified at night (Kryger & Shapiro, 1995) or when in a bed-rest position.

❑ DISTINGUISHING FEATURES FOR SD.1

- sleep improves after the source of pain is identified and successfully treated.
- sleep improves after the source of pain is identified and pain management measures taken.
- sleep does not improve as long as the painful condition persists.

❑ FACTORS THAT MAY WORSEN THE CONDITION

- eating spicy, acidic foods prior to sleep in a person with undetected stomach ulcers or reflux disease.
- daily stressors can worsen perimenstrual symptoms such as insomnia and pain (Woods et al., 1985).
- misinterpreting a painful medical condition (that eludes detection for a long time) as a behavior problem and neglecting to investigate for medical causes.
- misinterpreting a painful medical condition as a behavior problem and adding sedating medication.
- using a phenothiazine-type neuroleptic in a person whose sleep disturbance is due to bowel problems.

❑ PERSONS WHO MAY BE AT RISK

- persons who are unable to report (have little or no speech), typically deny pain, or cannot be relied on to report pain.
- a person who starts pressing on or repeatedly hitting a body area which is unusual for that person, e.g., pounding the hip (joint pain?), pressing on the jaw (tooth pain?), pressing on the eyes (eye disease?), hitting an ear (ear infection?), hitting the abdomen (parasites?). Hitting an area does not always mean that pain is the underlying reason, but a person who starts to hit or press a new area needs to be investigated for this possibility.
- a person with pica, especially nonfood pica, is at risk for throat lacerations, stomach or bowel obstruction which can be painful and interfere with sleep.
- a person with a hiatus hernia and/or esophageal reflux.
- a person at risk for ulcers, e.g., those with PKU (phenylketonuria) who are not on a low phenylalanine or low protein diet.
- a person with a long history of refusing fluids as this can increase the risk for urinary tract infections.
- a person taking a phenothiazine-type neuroleptic as it can adversely affect intestinal function and increase the risk for painful bowel problems (De Silva et al., 1992).
- a person with intestinal parasites or a history of bowel problems.

- a woman who has a history of pain related to her menstrual cycle or who is in the menopausal years.
- a woman whose menstrual cycle is not being charted by caregivers, thereby preventing clinicians from checking if symptoms are related to the menstrual cycle.
- a person who has skin irritations due to incontinence (Fleming, 1996).
- a person with difficulty moving and changing positions in bed (Fleming, 1996).
- a person with discomfort from muscle spasms, painful contractions, and/or deformities (Fleming, 1996).
- a person with fibromyaglia syndrome (see SD.13).
- a person with food allergies and nutritional imbalances (Braly, 1992, p. 393).

❑ SUGGESTIONS FOR COLLECTING INFORMATION
- use the *Discomfort Scale** (Hurley et al., 1992) to assess a noncommunicative person for pain.
- obtain a description of the sleep history, the type and onset of changes in daytime functioning, and chart the sleep pattern by using the *Monthly Sleep Chart** (Sovner & DesNoyers Hurley, 1990).
- check records for known sources of pain (e.g., menstrual pain, degenerative arthritic conditions) to aid the physician in screening.
- if the person has screaming spells, hits/presses on a body part, or has signs suggesting possible pain, identify when these began in relation to the worsening of their sleep.
- in women, check for menstrual worsening; collect information using the *Menstrual Distress Chart.** In women able to be interviewed, consider using the "Menstrual Distress Questionnaire" (Moos, 1968).
- identify and rule out external sources of noise, interruptions, or room discomfort that might cause awakenings.
- check for signs suggestive of sleep apnea as listed in the *Checklist of Overt Signs of Sleep Apnea.**
- chart bowel movements, oozing, unusual stool size, regularity. Chart fluid intake, vomiting episodes, and refusals of all food/fluid. Compare results with past patterns in these areas.
- check for signs suggesting food allergies, e.g., use the *Risk Factors for Casein-Gluten Peptiduria.**
- in persons with pica, record the variety of inedibles eaten, list changes in mood and functioning following previous swallowings of foreign objects, and check for a distinct onset of deterioration in mood and/or functioning.
- check for depressive features and when they became evident, then check if such features began after the onset of signs of pain. Use the *Checklist of Observable Signs of Depression.**
- provide the person's temperature, pulse, and respirations per minute to the nurse and/or physician.

A chart or checklist listed in italics in this section can be found in the Appendix.

❑ MEDICAL TESTING / SCREENING SD.1
- check for possible gastrointestinal problems such as hiatus hernia, hyperacidity, intestinal ulcers, bowel obstruction, parasites, appendicitis, gall stones (Kryger & Shapiro, 1995), and porphyria disorders.
- check for infections such as ear, sinus, throat, respiratory area, and urinary tract.
- rule out arthritic degenerative changes, neck pain, eye disease, nocturnal leg cramping (related to hypocalcemia, i.e., low calcium levels), and restless leg syndrome if suspected.
- check to see if the sleep disturbance is related to the menstrual cycle.
- in women over 40 years, determine if menopausal hormone changes are occurring because insomnia can be a symptom of premenopausal changes.
- in those with abdominal pain, light sensitivity, and thermal dysregulation symptoms, rule out porphyria.

❑ POSSIBLE BIOCHEMICAL / ANATOMICAL INVOLVEMENT
- an increase in cortisol during illness or pain may increase the stress response and arousal level, thereby interfering with sleep.
- discomfort from muscle spasms, painful contractions, and/or deformities can cause frequent wakenings (Fleming, 1996).
- in a person with food allergies, nighttime wakefulness may be in response to withdrawal symptoms (Braly, 1992, p. 393).

Presenting Concern: **SLEEP DISTURBANCES**
Dx Category   SD.2: *ENVIRONMENTAL AND SLEEP HYGIENE FACTORS*

❏ *COMMON FORMS*
- having a history of waking easily during sleep and being a "light sleeper" (Fleming & Shapiro, 1995a).
- having delays of 1-3 hours in falling asleep (sleep onset) (Fleming & Shapiro, 1995a).
- being able to fall asleep easily in a chair.
- showing excessive daytime sleepiness such as having 1-2 hour naps or multiple daytime naps.
- a person who has irritable mood and motivational disturbances, daytime fatigue and sleepiness, reduced attention, vigilance, and/or concentration.

❏ *VARIATIONS*
- getting up often to urinate at night and having difficulty falling asleep again.
- sleep difficulties in a person who drinks large quantities of caffeinated beverages when not restricted.
- the person frequently has extended periods in bed perhaps for passive activities such as watching TV, snacking or reading.
- having days of being unusually slowed down, less energetic, drowsy, and speech is slower or less clear than usual.

❏ *DISTINGUISHING FEATURES FOR SD.2*
- the person does activities that increase arousal prior to bedtime such as vigorous exercise in the 4 hours before bedtime; nonspecific stress and excitement; evening intake of caffeine, nicotine or alcohol; bedtime snacks (Fleming & Shapiro, 1995a).
- environmental factors that adversely affect sleep occur frequently such as noise (from peers, a nearby furnace, vehicles, neighborhood noise); interruptions by others (caregivers, peers, or pets); bedroom is not dark enough; bedroom temperature is too hot or too cold; uncomfortable mattress or inadequate blankets (Fleming & Shapiro, 1995a).
- removal of the environmental cause produces an immediate or gradual restoration of normal sleep (Fleming & Shapiro, 1995a).
- there are practices that interfere with the regular timing and duration of sleep and awake periods such as large variations in the timing of sleep and time for rising; frequent use of the bed for non-sleep activities like watching TV, reading, and snacking (Fleming & Shapiro, 1995a).
- there may be no evidence of a psychiatric or medical disorder that accounts for the sleep disturbance.

❏ *FACTORS THAT MAY WORSEN THE CONDITION*
- drinking fluids late in the evening thereby increasing nighttime urination.
- consuming a heavy evening meal that is rich in fats, complex carbohydrates, spicy food, or foods high in preservatives or monosodium glutamate.
- a urinary tract infection or enlarged prostate gland can increase nighttime urination.
- vigorous exercise in the four hours before bedtime (Fleming & Shapiro, 1995a; Hanly & Shapiro, 1995).
- an increase in noise, interruptions, or an uncomfortable room temperature during the sleep period.
- acute stress, conflict, relocation, or personal loss.
- physical pain.
- nocturnal seizures in a person with difficult-to-control epilepsy.
- caffeine (Leonard et al., 1987; Podboy & Mallory, 1977) or nicotine can delay sleep onset (Fleming & Shapiro, 1995a); alcohol can cause awakenings (Fleming & Shapiro, 1995a).
- hypnotic medication (sleeping pills) that adds to daytime drowsiness and further reduces REM sleep (Kales et al., 1983; Quine, 1991).
- undergoing drug withdrawal, e.g., recently taken off phenytoin/Dilantin or phenobarbital.

❏ *PERSONS WHO MAY BE AT RISK*

- a person who engages in exciting or emotionally upsetting activities (e.g., action movies) close to bedtime.
- a person who exercises too close to bedtime.
- someone who spends extended periods in bed.
- someone who consumes caffeinated beverages frequently and/or uses nicotine, especially in the evenings.
- someone whose bedtime and rising times vary considerably from the weekday schedule (e.g., group home) compared to weekends (e.g., regular visits with relatives).

❏ *SUGGESTIONS FOR COLLECTING INFORMATION*

- obtain a description of the sleep history, any seasonal patterns, the effect of inadequate sleep on daytime functioning; chart the sleep-wake cycle using the *Monthly Sleep Chart* (Sovner & DesNoyers Hurley, 1990).
- list the type and duration of typical evening activities over 2-3 weeks; rate for arousing or calming effect.
- list the frequency and amount of stimulants taken in the evening hours before bedtime.
- look for a relationship between the intake of spicy or fatty food at supper or bedtime snack, and wakefulness in the night; this could be due to pain or reflux in the night.
- identify the type and frequency of noise, interruptions, and other environmental factors that can cause awakenings from sleep.
- determine what the person does during nighttime wakenings, e.g., insists on arranging items or repetitive changing of clothes, if so screen for obsessive-compulsive disorder as this may be a complicating factor; use the *Compulsive Behavior Checklist* and, if applicable, the *Obsessive Speech Checklist*.
- check for daytime and nighttime signs suggestive of sleep apnea as listed on the *Checklist of Overt Signs of Sleep Apnea.*
- assess for depression using instruments or criteria appropriate for this population (e.g., Cooper & Collacott, 1994; Sovner, 1986). Use the *Checklist of Observable Signs of Depression.*
- for those able to read and label different emotional states, the "Children's Depression Inventory" (Kovacs, 1985) has been used for screening depression in developmentally disabled people (Meins, 1993).

❏ *MEDICAL TESTING / SCREENING SD.2*

- review medications for possible adverse effects; see SD.6.
- rule out infections, physical illness, and physical causes of pain; see SD.1.
- if the person urinates often at night, rule out urinary tract infections. With males, also rule out prostate infection or enlargement.
- rule out thyroid dysfunction such as hypothyroidism.
- rule out diabetes as postprandial sleepiness is frequent in persons with untreated diabetes mellitus (Hanly & Shapiro, 1995).

❏ *POSSIBLE BIOCHEMICAL / ANATOMICAL INVOLVEMENT*

- common substances like caffeine (cola drinks, coffee) and nicotine (smoking, cigarette pica) cause arousal and can affect "sleep architecture" (Fleming & Shapiro, 1995a).
- practices that interfere with the regular timing and duration of sleep may disturb the amount and quality of sleep (Fleming & Shapiro, 1995a).
- seizure activity can awaken people during sleep.

Presenting Concern: **SLEEP DISTURBANCES**
Dx Category   SD.3: *INSOMNIA OR EXCESSIVE DAYTIME SLEEPING DURING DEPRESSION*

❑ *COMMON FORMS*
- the person often wakes early in the morning and is unable to return to sleep (Fleming & Shapiro, 1995a).
- having difficulty falling asleep and/or waking frequently during the night.
- often feeling fatigued and sleepy in the day.
- the person who has insomnia is lethargic, irritable, and overactive in the day (Wiggs & Stores, 1996).

❑ *VARIATIONS*
- the person may not feel rested after excessive daytime sleeping (Fleming & Shapiro, 1995a).
- the person is excessively sleepy, apathetic, and has less interest in familiar activities.
- the person frequently sleeps until late morning or early afternoon.
- the person needs sleep but has difficulty getting more than a few hours at night, and daytime napping may not be restorative. This pattern has been occurring for several weeks or longer.

❑ *DISTINGUISHING FEATURES FOR SD.3*
- the person shows several of the following: depressed mood/sadness; spontaneous crying; reduced interest in activities; social withdrawal; reduced speech; slow speech; decreased energy; loss of self-care skills; impaired concentration; psychomotor retardation; increased anger or aggression (Burt et al., 1992; Cooper & Collacott, 1994; Pary et al., 1996; Prasher & Hall, 1996; Warren et al., 1989). Suicidal thought or action is rare.
- the time of onset of depressive features may be closely linked to a particular life event.
- the sleep disturbance began or worsened around the time that other signs of depression began.
- there is reduced time to the first episode of REM (rapid eye movement) (Avery et al., 1982).
- usually antidepressant treatment helps and sleep improves before mood does (Flanigan & Shapiro,1995).

❑ *FACTORS THAT MAY WORSEN THE CONDITION*
- intake of caffeine-containing drugs, food, or beverages, especially in the evening (Leonard et al., 1987).
- poor sleep hygiene practices as described in SD.1
- failing to meet the person's emotional/bereavement needs: not providing grief counseling or not adapting counseling to their mental level (photo and art therapy techniques can be used with nonverbal people).
- caregivers misinterpreting frequent crying as attention-seeking and "ignoring it" as a behavioral strategy.
- springtime for some persons with serotonin-related disorders (Brewerton, 1989).
- the shorter days of light during winter months, especially with seasonal affective type of depression.
- lack of regular exercise in a person with depression (Gabler-Halle et al., 1993; McNeil et al., 1991).
- misdiagnosing a depressed person with manic-depression, and using lithium (that can worsen depression, Estroff & Gold, 1986), carbamazepine or valproic acid/Depakene instead of an antidepressant.
- hypnotic medication/sleeping pills add to daytime drowsiness and reduce REM sleep (Kales et al., 1983).
- benzodiazepines, e.g., temazepam/Restoril can cause rebound insomnia (Bezchlibnyk-Butler et al.,1994).
- benzodiazepines in elderly depressed people can worsen depression (Thompson et al., 1983).
- antidepressants that reduce melatonin can cause insomnia, e.g., fluoxetine/Prozac (Childs et al., 1995).
- medication that lists insomnia as a possible side effect, e.g., carbamazepine/Tegretol, sertraline/Zoloft.
- medication that can cause depression e.g., benzodiazepines, beta blockers especially propranolol/Inderal, cimetidine/Tagamet, ranitidine/Zantac, oral contraceptives (Lowenthal & Nadeau,1991; Wise &Taylor,1990).

❑ *PERSONS WHO MAY BE AT RISK*
- adults with Down syndrome have an greater risk for depression than other adults with mental retardation (Collacott et al., 1992). The average age for onset of depression in Down syndrome is in the late 20's or early 30's (Collacott et al., 1992; Prasher & Hall, 1996).
- a person with apathy, lethargy, social withdrawal, less spontaneous activity, less interest in favorite activities, and/or a recent loss of appetite.
- a person with prior depressive episodes or a family history of depression or manic-depression.

- persons who recently moved or lost caregivers as this can also mean loss of familiar programming and lack of consistency in behavioral programming at both home and work settings. Such changes may be more stressful to people less able to understand the changes, i.e., those in the severe and profound range.
- those who had a personal loss, e.g., close caregiver, relative, home, major loss in vision/hearing/ health.
- someone with an intense reaction to minor stress might be reminded of a more serious ungrieved loss (Ryan, 1996b).
- persons with Prader-Willi syndrome who are overweight (Bartolucci & Younger, 1994).
- persons with Tuberous Sclerosis are at risk for insomnia and sleep problems in general (Hunt, 1993).
- persons with Fragile X are at risk for major depression and other mood disorders (Levitas, 1996).
- someone with Sanfilipo syndrome is at risk for severe insomnia (Stores, 1992).
- persons with fetal alcohol syndrome are at risk for sleep disorders and depression (Steinhausen et al.,1994).
- persons with Williams syndrome appear more capable than they are due to good spoken language and sociability. If others place unrealistic demands on them, depression can occur (Bradley & Udwin, 1989).
- persons with repeated contact (even if infrequent) with people or places associated with past traumas.
- a person under stress for a protracted period or showing signs of post-traumatic stress disorder.
- those at risk for hypothyroidism, elderly people (Goggans et al., 1986), or those with Down syndrome.
- a person in frequent contact with cats who shows excessive daytime fatigue, lethargy, anorexia, and fever of unknown origin, i.e., symptoms of cat scratch fever (Flexman et al., 1995; Margileth, 1992).
- a person taking the anticonvulsant vigabatrin/Sabril (Aldenkamp et al., 1994).

❑ *SUGGESTIONS FOR COLLECTING INFORMATION*
- obtain details of the sleep history and its effects on daytime functioning; chart the sleep-wake times using the *Monthly Sleep Chart* (Sovner & DesNoyers Hurley, 1990).
- check for family history of depression and manic-depression (bipolar disorder).
- assess for depression using DSM-IV criteria or criteria adapted for developmental disabilities (e.g., Cooper & Collacott, 1994; Sovner, 1986). Use the *Checklist of Observable Signs of Depression.*
- for those able to read and label emotions, the "Children's Depression Inventory" (Kovacs, 1985) has been used to screen depression in developmentally disabled people (Benavidez & Matson, 1993; Meins,1993).
- assess morning mood as insomnia may be associated with major depression (Fleming & Shapiro, 1995a)
- monitor weight, appetite increases or decreases, and eating patterns.
- assess for symptoms of seasonal effects on the sleeping pattern.
- assess for obsessive-compulsive disorder, anxiety, and post-traumatic stress as depression can co-occur.
- list the amount and frequency of stimulants and chocolate taken in the hours before bedtime.
- identify if there are interruptions, noise, or other environmental factors causing nighttime awakenings.
- list the type and duration of evening activities over 2-3 weeks; rate them for arousing or calming effect.
- screen for signs of sleep apnea using the *Checklist of Overt Signs of Sleep Apnea.*
- in women, check for menstrual worsening; collect information using the *Menstrual Distress Chart.* With women able to be interviewed, consider using the "Menstrual Distress Questionnaire" (Moos, 1968).

❑ *MEDICAL TESTING / SCREENING SD.3*
- review each medication for insomnia or hypersomnolence as possible adverse effects.
- rule out hypothyroidism, abnormally low serum iron/hemoglobin, vitamin B_{12} and folate deficiency.
- rule out diabetes as postprandial sleepiness is frequent in untreated diabetes mellitus (Hanly & Shapiro, 1995).
- rule out circadian rhythm disturbances in the sleep-wake cycle if seasonal affective disorder is suspected.
- rule out cat scratch fever if there is lethargy, fatigue, possibly unexplained fever, and contact with a cat.

❑ *POSSIBLE BIOCHEMICAL / ANATOMICAL INVOLVEMENT*
- low central serotonin and/or low noradrenalin in depressed patients can adversely affect sleep.
- plasma tryptophan (serotonin precursor) is markedly lower in some depressives than controls (Lucca et al., 1992).
- very low nighttime melatonin occurs in subgroups of depressed patients (Cavallo et al., 1987; Shafti et al., 1996).
- a thyroid abnormality may be involved in some cases (e.g., Dorn et al., 1996) given thyroxin's role in the onset of sleep and the beneficial response of some depressed patients to thyroxin treatment.

❑ *COMMON FORMS*

- being awake for 24-36 hour periods and being physically active during that time.
- the person is getting little sleep yet appears energized throughout the day (Fleming & Shapiro, 1995a).

❑ *VARIATIONS*

- going without sleep or naps for several consecutive days.
- the person talks more than usual during these sleepless periods.
- the person becomes hypersexual during the sleepless days and nights, e.g., long hours of masturbating.
- the person does not complain of sleep loss and appears energized during the day, despite having sleep disruptions and poor sleep efficiency (Fleming & Shapiro, 1995a).

❑ *DISTINGUISHING FEATURES FOR SD.4*

- in medication-induced mania, the sleep disturbance and manic symptoms resolve after the offending medication is stopped.
- diagnostic criteria for mania adapted for this population include (1) a mood disturbance characterized by elation, irritability, or excitability, and (2) four of the following symptoms: decreased need for sleep, overactivity, increase in the rate or frequency of verbalizations, onset or increase in distractibility, onset or increase in noncompliance, onset or increase in aggressiveness; if there is a first degree relative with manic-depression (bipolar disorder) then only three of the symptoms are required (Sovner, 1986).
- irritability and assaultiveness, rather than elation, can characterize the manic phase of persons with mania or manic-depression (bipolar disorder) caused by head injury (Shukla et al., 1987; Zwil et al., 1993).

❑ *FACTORS THAT MAY WORSEN THE CONDITION*

- medical conditions that can cause mania, e.g., hyperthyroidism, anemia, vitamin B_{12} deficiency, infections such as encephalitis or influenza, stroke (especially right hemisphere and thalamus), or cerebellar atrophy (Wise & Taylor, 1990).
- medication that can cause mania, e.g., benzodiazepines, corticosteroids, MAO inhibitors, thyroid hormones, tricyclic antidepressants such as clomipramine/Anafranil, serotonin reuptake inhibitor fluoxetine/Prozac, anticonvulsant vigabatrin/Sabril (Bezchlibnyck-Butler et al., 1994; Medical Letter, 1993; Naumann et al., 1994; Wise & Taylor, 1990).
- misinterpreting mania due to a medical condition as evidence for manic-depression (bipolar disorder), then adding a mood stabilizer (e.g., lithium, carbamazepine/Tegretol, or valproic acid/Depakane) rather than investigating to identify the medical cause.
- misinterpreting drug-induced mania as evidence for manic-depression (bipolar disorder), then adding a mood stabilizer rather than stopping the offending medication.
- caffeine can induce anxiety in some individuals (Orlikov & Ryzov, 1991).

❑ *PERSONS WHO MAY BE AT RISK*
- a person with a family history of manic-depression (bipolar disorder).
- a person with past episodes of medication-induced mania or hypomania due to a medical condition or adverse effects of medication.
- a person with a history of "paradoxical reactions" to behavioral medication.
- a person who has been taken off high doses of phenytoin/Dilantin or phenobarbital as such people can feel much more energized and have an elevated mood.
- some persons taking vigabatrin develop mania (Aldenkamp et al. 1994; Naumann et al., 1994).
- in rare cases, persons on carbamazepine develop manic symptoms and insomnia (Pleak et al., 1988).
- persons with Fragile X are at risk for mood disorders such as manic-depression (bipolar disorder) (Levitas, 1996).
- persons with postictal (post seizure) psychosis may also have disinhibited sexual behavior and elevated mood (Kanemoto et al., 1996).
- a person with manic-depression (bipolar disorder) who has been sleep deprived (Wehr, 1991).
- a previously healthy person who has been partially sleep deprived over four nights (Wright, 1993).
- a previously healthy person who started showing manic symptoms (and also manic-depression cycles) after a head injury (Pope et al., 1988; Shukla et al., 1987; Starkstein et al., 1987; Zwil et al., 1993).

❑ *SUGGESTIONS FOR COLLECTING INFORMATION*
- assess for a manic episode using criteria adapted for this population (see *DISTINGUISHING FEATURES* for SD.4) or the DSM-IV (1994).
- obtain details of the sleep history, effects of the sleep disturbance on daytime functioning, and chart the sleep-wake times using the *Monthly Sleep Chart* (Sovner & DesNoyers Hurley, 1990).
- review sleep records before and after certain medication was introduced or increased.
- review the history for other sleepless episodes when on certain medications.
- provide the person's temperature, pulse, and respirations per minute to the nurse and/or physician.
- check family history for depression or manic-depression (bipolar disorder).
- if the person has had head injury, check if the manic or manic-depressive symptoms began after the injury.

❑ *MEDICAL TESTING / SCREENING SD.4*
- rule out possible medical conditions that can cause mania, e.g., hyperthyroidism; anemia; vitamin B_{12} deficiency; systemic bacterial, fungal or viral infection (Wise & Taylor, 1990), and porphyria disorders.
- consider a trial off a suspected medication and request detailed recording of sleep in order to evaluate changes.
- rule out multiple food allergies with immunoglobulin testing.

❑ *POSSIBLE BIOCHEMICAL / ANATOMICAL INVOLVEMENT*
- dysregulation of central noradrenalin and/or serotonin can cause sleeplessness.
- plasma tryptophan (a precursor of serotonin) is significantly lower in people with manic-depression than non-depressed controls (Lucca et al., 1992).
- manic-depressives who switch from depression to mania when sleep-deprived are lacking non-REM sleep because "it is the non-REM component of sleep that is depressant and antimanic." (Wehr, 1991, p. 578).
- "head injury...may sometimes trigger ictal activity which manifests as bipolar symptoms" (Pope et al., 1988, p. 38).

❑ *COMMON FORMS*
- the person has difficulty sleeping more than a few hours at a time.
- occasionally the person is awake all night and the following day.
- the person is physically active when awake at night such as walking about, not just lying awake in bed.

❑ *VARIATIONS*
- the person is losing weight and appears to be physically ill, in addition to having sleeplessness.
- there is excessive sweating, perhaps soaking one's clothing or bed linens.

❑ *DISTINGUISHING FEATURES FOR SD.5*
- blood test results confirm hyperthyroidism or excessive dosing of thyroxin.
- the person may show sweating, a fast heart rate, weight loss, and indicate discomfort in the chest area.

❑ *FACTORS THAT MAY WORSEN THE CONDITION*
- mistaking "thyroid storm" for psychosis or mania.
- using medication that can elevate thyroxin levels.

❑ *PERSONS WHO MAY BE AT RISK*

- a person who has a diffuse non-tender goiter (from long-term use of lithium) as this can lead to hyperthyroidism.
- a person with a family history of thyroid dysfunction.
- a person on thyroxin supplement who has not had the blood level of thyroxin checked in over a year or since their sleep and health started to decline.
- a person who sweats excessively, is unusually active, and is resistant (fearful of needles) to giving a blood sample.

❑ *SUGGESTIONS FOR COLLECTING INFORMATION*

- chart the sleep-wake cycle using the *Monthly Sleep Chart* (Sovner & DesNoyers Hurley, 1990).
- review the recent history for sleeplessness, changes in overall level of activity, weight loss, and signs of ill health.
- review sleep records before and after certain medication was introduced (or dose changed) to rule out a medication-related effect.
- provide the person's temperature, pulse, and respirations per minute to the nurse and/or physician.
- check family history for thyroid disorders and sleep disorders.
- review the person's history for sleeplessness when on certain medications.
- find out what the person usually does during nighttime wakenings. If the person is hypervigilant and fearful, screen for post-traumatic stress as a complicating factor. If the person insists on arranging items or insists on changing clothes in the middle of the night, screen for obsessive-compulsive disorder as a complicating factor using the *Compulsive Behavior Checklist* and the *Obsessive Speech Checklist*.

❑ *MEDICAL TESTING / SCREENING SD.5*

- do thyroid function tests and repeat as necessary. Certain medications affect thyroid function test results (e.g., estrogen-containing oral contraceptives, carbamazepine/Tegretol) or affect thyroid function (e.g., lithium, many anticonvulsants).
- check for signs of heart dysfunction.
- rule out possible medical conditions that can cause mania such as anemia, vitamin B_{12} deficiency, and certain types of infection.
- rule out possible causes of physical pain contributing to the sleep disturbance (see SD.1).

❑ *POSSIBLE BIOCHEMICAL / ANATOMICAL INVOLVEMENT*

- the blood level of thyroxin is abnormally high due to a medical condition or excessive dosing of thyroxin.

❏ *COMMON FORMS*
- the person started having difficulty falling asleep in the days or weeks after a medication was introduced.
- the person has difficulty falling or staying asleep at night even though a hefty dose of a neuroleptic is given at bedtime. If this occurs, either the neuroleptic or another medication could be interfering with sleep.
- someone taking sleeping medication (e.g., zopiclone/Imovane or benzodiazepines such as flurazepam/ Durapam/Somnol, oxazepam/Serax) regularly for more than 2-4 months.
- the person tends to sleep in the day and has difficulty staying asleep at night, even though taking sleeping medication at bedtime.

❏ *VARIATIONS*
- a person on medication often lies down in the day and easily falls asleep anywhere (e.g., on a hard floor).
- the person takes medication at 8:00PM to aid sleep, yet regularly awakes about 4:30AM and is unable to return to sleep.
- the person sleeps well at night but is very sleepy in the hours after the morning (8:00AM) dose of benzodiazepine is given.
- the sleep-wake cycle is shifted forward several hours, e.g., the person tends to be awake until 1:00 or 2:00 AM and to rise about noon.
- the person is able to sleep when given chloral hydrate the first few times, but after about two weeks of continuous use, no further benefit is obtained and tolerance develops (Fleming & Shapiro, 1995b).
- the person, while on certain combinations of medication, starts to sleepwalk or become very confused and unaware of surroundings when up at night. Examples include: lithium with a traditional neuroleptic or with diazepam/Valium, oxazepam/Serax, or amitriptyline/Elavil; thioridazine/Mellaril with diphen-hydramine/Benadryl or with trichlorethanol; chlorpromazine/Largactil/Thorazine with amitriptyline or with fluphenazine/Prolixin, or haloperidol/Haldol; perphenazine/Trilafon with oxazepam or lithium; alcohol with methylphenidate/Ritalin or with diphenhydramine, or amitriptyline; amitriptyline with chlorpromazine (Flanigan & Shapiro, 1995).

❏ *DISTINGUISHING FEATURES FOR SD.6*
- the sleep disturbance resolves after the recently-introduced medication is reduced or withdrawn.
- the nighttime wakefulness and daytime sleeping resolve after the *timing* of certain medication is changed to reduce daytime sedation.
- the morning sleepiness resolves after the morning benzodiazepine is tapered and discontinued, or given late in the day.
- sleep improves after a gradual withdrawal from all benzodiazepines.
- if medication-induced mania is suspected, see SD.4.

❏ *FACTORS THAT MAY WORSEN THE CONDITION*
- increasing the dose of a medication that is causing or worsening insomnia.
- continuing to use chloral hydrate at bedtime when it no longer improves the person's sleep.
- adding another medication that lists insomnia as a possible adverse effect.
- drug interactions with nicotine or alcohol.
- frequent use of a benzodiazepine that was ordered for "occasional use" (p.r.n.) in a person already taking a benzodiazepine daily.

❏ *PERSONS WHO MAY BE AT RISK*

- a person taking medication that lists insomnia as an adverse effect in over 10% of patients, e.g., clomipramine/Anafranil, imipramine/Tofranil, sertraline/Zoloft, fluoxetine/Prozac (Bezchlibnyk-Butler et al., 1994).
- a person with a tendency for insomnia taking medication that lists insomnia as possible adverse effect.
- a person taking one or more benzodiazepines daily for many months or years.
- a person taking hypnotic medication (sleeping pills) that increases daytime drowsiness and further reduces REM sleep (Kales et al., 1983; Quine, 1991).
- a person taking both a major tranquilizer and a minor tranquilizer, e.g., a neuroleptic and benzodiazepine.
- a person taking two or more medications that can cause sedation.
- a person taking clobazam/Frisium, especially if nonambulatory.
- a person with a history of "paradoxical excitement," i.e., a reaction that is the opposite of what was expected to a particular medication. Some people have behavioral worsening on benzodiazepines or other hypnotic medications (Fleming & Shapiro, 1995b).
- a person taking fenfluramine, MAO-inhibitors, or beta blockers (Fleming & Shapiro, 1995a).
- a person undergoing drug withdrawal; see also SD.7.
- an elderly person on medication.

❏ *SUGGESTIONS FOR COLLECTING INFORMATION*

- chart the hours of sleep for 24-hour days for a month or longer using the *Monthly Sleep Chart* (Sovner & DesNoyers Hurley, 1990).
- record the time of day when the person seeks a place to sleep, actually falls asleep, and for how long.
- look for patterns in the time of early morning wakenings; the time of daytime sleeping and the time medications are given; the onset of a sleep disturbance and the start or increase in a medication; and the onset or worsening of a shift in the sleep-wake cycle and medication times or medication changes.
- screen for signs suggestive of sleep apnea as listed in the *Checklist of Overt Signs of Sleep Apnea*.

❏ *MEDICAL TESTING / SCREENING SD.6*

- rule out physical causes of pain as this could be underlying or worsening the insomnia (see SD.1).
- consider a trial off the suspected medication(s) and request a detailed recording of sleep in order to evaluate changes.
- consider changing the hour when medication is given if it appears to increase daytime sedation.
- if medication-induced mania is suspected, see SD.4.

❏ *POSSIBLE BIOCHEMICAL / ANATOMICAL INVOLVEMENT*

- daytime sedation may result in nighttime wakefulness.
- the additive effects or potentiating effects of two or more medications can result in excessive sedation.
- daily use of benzodiazepines can cause rebound insomnia (Bezchlibnyk-Butler et al., 1994) and reduce different stages of sleep.
- giving benzodiazepines in the morning or midday can result in daytime sleepiness and a reduced need for nighttime sleep.
- use of two or more benzodiazepines with different decay rates may cause daytime sleepiness.
- the short half-life of trazodone/Deseryl (about 4.5 hours) may be related to regular wakenings close to 4:30AM in a person who receives a modest dose of trazodone at 8:00PM. This might be corrected if trazodone were given later in the evening. If modest doses of trazodone are beneficial, higher doses could be counterproductive because it is an antagonist for serotonin type 2 receptors at low doses, but is an agonist at high doses (Maj et al., 1979).
- elderly people tend to have slower clearance rates for medication than younger adults.
- certain medications affect melatonin which is a hormone involved in sleep, e.g., fluoxetine decreases it, fluvoxamine/Luvox increases it (Childs et al., 1995; Demisch et al., 1986).

Presenting Concern: **SLEEP DISTURBANCES**
Dx Category   SD.7: *INSOMNIA DURING NEUROLEPTIC WITHDRAWAL*

❑ *COMMON FORMS*
- having difficulty falling asleep in the weeks after the person's neuroleptic medication was discontinued.
- sleeping only a few hours at night in the weeks following discontinuation of neuroleptic medication.
- the difficulty sleeping began along with a deterioration in behavior and increase in agitation soon after stopping neuroleptic medication (e.g., chlorpromazine/Largactil, haloperidol/Haldol, risperidone/ Risperdal, thioridazine/Mellaril, trifluoperazine/Stelazine).

❑ *VARIATIONS*
- the insomnia and motor restlessness began in the days and weeks after neuroleptic medication was tapered and stopped.
- anxiety and insomnia start five days after a decrease in thioridazine in someone being tapered off that medication (Sovner, 1995).
- "Nausea, vomiting, diarrhea, perspiration, restlessness, insomnia, shivering, headaches, increased appetite, and giddiness can occur ... as part of a neuroleptic withdrawal syndrome" (Estroff & Gold, 1986, p. 169).

❑ *DISTINGUISHING FEATURES FOR SD.7*
- the person may be awake all night the first or second day after the last dose of a neuroleptic following a period of tapering.
- the person did not have insomnia prior to the last dose of neuroleptic medication.
- the person's previous sleep disturbance worsened since the neuroleptic withdrawal period began.

❑ *FACTORS THAT MAY WORSEN THE CONDITION*
- using a neuroleptic intermittently (as a p.r.n.) in the 3-4 month period after the person was tapered off neuroleptic medication.
- drinking fluids late in the evening and thereby increasing nighttime urination.
- physical pain (see SD.1 *FACTORS*) or poor sleep hygiene practices (see SD.2 *FACTORS*).

❑ *PERSONS WHO MAY BE AT RISK*
- a person who recently received the last dose of neuroleptic medication after long-term use (Gualtieri et al., 1986).
- a person who was taken off a neuroleptic, put back on it after a month, then taken off, hence is undergoing a second neuroleptic withdrawal period in less than a year.
- a person who is being withdrawn from neuroleptics very rapidly.
- a person whose thioridazine is being tapered off (e.g., 5 mg. decreases at regular intervals) may present with anxiety and insomnia five days after a recent decrease (Sovner, 1995).

❑ *SUGGESTIONS FOR COLLECTING INFORMATION*
- chart monthly sleep times and duration; compare monthly patterns before neuroleptic withdrawal with the first month after withdrawal, second, third, and fourth month after withdrawal; use the *Monthly Sleep Chart* (Sovner & DesNoyers Hurley, 1990).
- assess for signs of Tardive Dyskinesia (e.g., use the "DISCUS" by Sprague & Kalachnik, 1991) because involuntary limb and neck movements--if temporarily severe--might increase nighttime awakenings.

❑ *MEDICAL TESTING / SCREENING SD.7*
- monitor drug levels of the neuroleptic and any other psychotropic medications during a neuroleptic taper because the neuroleptic can affect the blood level of other medications. Then if behavioral deterioration such as insomnia and anxiety occurs during the taper, one can evaluate whether the symptoms reflect neuroleptic withdrawal, or are caused by other psychotropic medications dropping below therapeutic drug levels (Sovner, 1995).
- rule out physical causes of pain as this could be underlying or worsening the insomnia.
- check if insomnia is listed as a possible adverse effect for any other medication the person takes.

❑ *POSSIBLE BIOCHEMICAL / ANATOMICAL INVOLVEMENT*
- the choline-dopamine balance is adversely affected by long-term dopamine receptor blockade by neuroleptic medication.

❑ *COMMON FORMS*

- the person is anxious, fearful, and not relaxed enough to fall asleep easily.
- the person is hypervigilant during the hours of darkness.
- the person wakes from sleep showing signs of fear, or if verbal, reports nightmares and fearful images.
- the person has frequent nightmares and often awakens early in the morning (Ryan, 1994).
- the person is a light sleeper and awakens easily during the night.
- the person wants the bedroom door left open and a nightlight left on.
- the person wanders about the house at night, possibly to avoid nightmares or flashbacks.

❑ *VARIATIONS*

- the person prefers to sleep in the daytime because of fearing the dark or being too hypervigilant to sleep in the evening hours.
- the person sleeps better when the favorite or most trusted caregivers are on shift in the evening.
- having a strong fear response to particular noises such as a door closing in the day or night.
- the person is often awake at night, sometimes wails or sobs loudly.

❑ *DISTINGUISHING FEATURES FOR SD.8*

- the person shows many features that suggest he or she is re-experiencing traumatic memories during the day or night.
- measures that increase the person's feeling of safety at night (nightlight on, quiet ensured) and feeling of control in one's life, help improve nighttime sleeping.

❑ *FACTORS THAT MAY WORSEN THE CONDITION*

- having a bedroom where nighttime traffic, voices, or street noise is easily heard, thereby increasing the person's level of vigilance and awakenings.
- evening staff who have the same gender and a similar size as the perpetrators of past traumas.
- engaging in power struggles with a person who has been traumatized.
- exposure to people or places that trigger traumatic memories (e.g., a visit to one's childhood house or hometown) as this may increase the frequency of flashbacks.
- special holidays that remind the person of past traumas.
- physical pain, see considerations in SD.1.
- cognitively-impairing medication, e.g., neuroleptics can increase the frequency of flashbacks (Ryan, 1996a).

❑ *PERSONS WHO MAY BE AT RISK*

- a person with a history of sexual abuse, physical trauma, and/or ritualistic abuse.
- a person with a history of witnessing traumatic events or natural disasters.
- someone who has symbols cut into the skin or disfiguring marks on the body.
- a person with unusual scarring on areas that are out-of-reach for the person (e.g., on back or buttocks).
- a person with a history of being cruel to animals or insects.
- a person who assumes a defensive or cowering posture when startled, frightened, or feeling threatened.
- a person who is usually hypervigilant and becomes rigid when anyone new enters the room, and who only has cheery, relaxed moments when with very close individuals.
- someone who often stands with his or her back to the wall, wants a fixed distance between self and any unfamiliar person, and will make sure no one stands in a doorway blocking an exit.
- a person who slips into dissociative states such as moments with no eye contact, a frozen mask-like face, numbness, and shows signs of re-experiencing past traumas (flashbacks).
- a person whose mental retardation was caused by head injury at a young age, possibly by physical abuse.
- a person whose history contains insufficient information on past events, but there are reasonable grounds to suspect past traumas.
- a person, capable of proper dressing, who sometimes wears trousers backwards with zipper at the back, wears extra underpants, or does similar things with clothing that suggest extra protection of the genital area.

❑ *SUGGESTIONS FOR COLLECTING INFORMATION*

- assess for signs of dissociative states, numbing, and flashbacks.
- assess for post-traumatic stress disorder (PTSD) and other anxiety disorders (Poindexter, 1996).
- chart sleep for nightmares, anxious fearful states at bedtime, sleeping in the day because of fearing the dark, or other unusual features not typically associated with insomnia. Also use the *Monthly Sleep Chart* (Sovner & DesNoyers Hurley, 1990).
- list the type and duration of nighttime noises inside and outside the house near where the person sleeps.
- try to identify distinct sounds that trigger fearful or protective responses. Then have staff minimize the occurrence of these triggering cues especially during bedtime hours.
- review the sleeping pattern over recent months, longer if possible; determine if there was a clear onset related to traumatizing events or strong reminders of past traumas.
- assess for depression as it is common among survivors of trauma (McCann & Pearlman, 1990); use instruments or criteria appropriate for this population (e.g., Cooper & Collacott, 1994; Sovner, 1986). Collect information using the *Checklist of Observable Signs of Depression*.

❑ *MEDICAL TESTING / SCREENING SD.8*

- list scarred areas and indicate which are anatomically incompatible with self-inflicted wounds.
- list areas of past fractures, especially if multiple.
- check for possible adverse effects of medication on sleep (see SD.6), cognitive functioning, or depression.
- rule out pain-related factors interfering with sleep (see SD.1).

❑ *POSSIBLE BIOCHEMICAL / ANATOMICAL INVOLVEMENT*

- physiological hyperarousal can interfere with the initiation of sleep.
- serotonergic dysregulation is present in some people with post-traumatic stress disorder (Nagy et al., 1993), and insomnia in such people has been treated successfully with sertonin-enhancing medication (Nagy et al., 1993).

Presenting Concern: **SLEEP DISTURBANCES**
Dx Category   SD.9: *NOCTURNAL ANXIETY AND NOCTURNAL PANIC ATTACKS*

❏ *COMMON FORMS*

- the person awakes from sleep in a panic attack or anxiety state and for several seconds or minutes shows sweating, trembling/shaking, facial flushing, pallor, heart racing, fearfulness, difficulty breathing, hyperventilation, and is easily startled. If verbal, the individuals may report features such as chest tightness or pain, stomach tightness or nausea, dizziness, a choking sensation, numbness or tingling, chills, hot flushes, or dry mouth (Wise & Taylor, 1990).

❏ *VARIATIONS*

- nocturnal panic attacks may be the only presenting symptom consistent with panic disorder (Kryger & Shapiro, 1995).
- the person sleeps only 2-3 hours at a time during the night.
- a person undergoing withdrawal from benzodiazepines may have a severe sleep disturbance, rebound anxiety, nausea, chills, headache, hallucinations, and may risk convulsive seizures (Kryger & Shapiro, 1995).
- the person may have middle-of-the-night insomnia and show daytime irritability, excessive talking, excessive worrying, heart pounding, poor concentration, poor appetite, and feeling overheated (Saliga et al., 1996).

❏ *DISTINGUISHING FEATURES FOR SD.9*

- the person may fit the DSM-IV (1994) criteria for panic attacks and/or "generalized anxiety disorder."
- in a person with post-traumatic stress disorder, the nocturnal disturbances may fit the criteria for panic attacks and occur in addition to nocturnal flashbacks (described in SD.8).
- if the nocturnal anxiety was caused by a physical illness, it ends after the illness is treated.
- if the nocturnal anxiety was medication-induced, it ends after the offending medication is stopped.
- "anxiety states are prominently represented among the interictal manifestations of TLE" (Post et al., 1986, p. 42) in a person with temporal lobe epilepsy (TLE).

❏ *FACTORS THAT MAY WORSEN THE CONDITION*

- substances that increase arousal, such as caffeine and nicotine, taken before bedtime (Fleming, 1996; Leonard et al., 1987).
- factors that increase level of arousal prior to bedtime such as a noisy environment, lack of privacy, and intense physical exercise in the hours before bedtime (see SD.2).
- lack of moderate and regular daytime exercise.
- a temporary worsening of anxiety during withdrawal from long-term use of benzodiazepines.
- nocturnal seizures in a person with difficult-to-control epilepsy.

❏ *PERSONS WHO MAY BE AT RISK*
- a person with a chronic infection.
- a person with poorly uncontrolled epilepsy (Kryger & Shapiro, 1995).
- a person who has panic attacks that are ictal manifestations of temporal lobe discharges (McNamara & Fogel, 1990; Post et al., 1986) or parietal lobe seizures (Alemayehu et al., 1995).
- a person who has been taking benzodiazepines for sleep for more than a few months.

❏ *SUGGESTIONS FOR COLLECTING INFORMATION*
- assess for panic attacks and anxiety disorders (e.g., generalized anxiety disorder, post-traumatic stress disorder, obsessive-compulsive disorder). Use the *Compulsive Behavior Checklist* and *Obsessive Speech Checklist* for collecting information on compulsions and obsessions in this population.
- assess for post-traumatic stress disorder using diagnostic criteria (DSM-IV, 1994); Ryan, 1994). If this disorder is present, check if the nocturnal phenomena are re-experiences of past traumas (flashbacks). Also check for signs of dissociative states and numbing in the night or day.
- review the records to see if the onset of anxiety or panic attack symptoms coincided with physical illness and/or a change in medication.
- obtain a description of the sleep history and chart the sleep-wake times using the *Monthly Sleep Chart* (Sovner & DesNoyers Hurley, 1990).
- in women, check for menstrual worsening; collect information using the *Menstrual Distress Chart*. With women able to be interviewed, consider using the "Menstrual Distress Questionnaire" (Moos, 1968).

❏ *MEDICAL TESTING / SCREENING SD.9*
- check for an underlying medical condition. The following have been identified as medical causes of anxiety: cerebral trauma, epilepsy, rheumatoid arthritis, alcohol and drug withdrawal, acetylsalicylic acid/Aspirin intolerance, caffeine or nicotine abuse, hyperthyroidism, parathyroid disorders, adrenal disorders, hypoglycemia, premenstrual syndrome, illnesses causing fever, chronic infections, irritable bowel syndrome, mitral valve prolapse, and reduced oxygen in the blood associated with lung disease, anemia or heart disease (Kryger & Shapiro, 1995).
- check for adverse effects of medication. The following medications have been identified as causing anxiety: anticholinergics, antihistamines, antihypertensives, caffeine, cocaine, dopamine, methlypheni-date/Ritalin, monosodium glutamate, neuroleptics (cause akathisia), nonsteroidal anti-inflammatory agents, steroids, thyroid preparations, and withdrawal from sedative-hypnotics (Medical Letter, 1993; Wise & Taylor, 1990).
- if temporal lobe seizures are suspected, request a 24-hour sleep-deprived EEG as it may be more revealing than a routine EEG (Post et al., 1986).

❏ *POSSIBLE BIOCHEMICAL / ANATOMICAL INVOLVEMENT*
- dysregulation of adrenergic functioning may be involved when people excessively scan their environment for possible threat and get overaroused if a threat is perceived (Abelson & Cameron, 1994).
- an aura of fear or ictal fear is produced by stimulation of the amygdala (Post et al., 1986).

❏ *COMMON FORMS*

- the person intermittently stops breathing during sleep (i.e., sleep apnea). The breathing stops for 10 seconds or longer on and off through the night (Flanigan & Shapiro, 1995; Hanly & Shapiro, 1995).
- the halted breathing (apnea) may be worse when people sleep on their back (Hanly & Shapiro, 1995).
- during sleep there is coughing, noisy breathing, loud snoring, and halted breathing lasting 10-40 seconds which is followed by a gasp or loud snort (Fleming, 1996).
- the person wakes frequently throughout the night.
- the person is slow to become fully alert after rising, may appear confused, or may report morning headache (Fleming & Shapiro, 1995a).
- the person does not feel refreshed after sleep, and has more difficulty than usual attending and comprehending.
- the person with poor sleep has daytime irritability, anxiety, and/or headache (Flanigan & Shapiro, 1995).
- daytime sleepiness persists despite adequate time spent in bed (Hanly & Shapiro, 1995).
- the person can easily fall asleep in the day while sitting in a vehicle or a chair.

❏ *VARIATIONS*

- the person can fall asleep in the day and remain motionless, unresponsive and catatonic-like for 30-60 minutes. If staff cross or uncross the person's legs during these motionless sleep spells, the person does not wake up. Unlike actual catatonia in which people can stand motionless and unsupported for hours, in these catatonic-like spells the person is motionless while being supported (sitting on a chair or the floor).
- nocturnal leg movements may occur after brief arousals from sleep due to the deep breaths or gasps in obstructive sleep apnea (Hanly & Shapiro, 1995).
- the person is very sleepy in the daytime and shows some of the following features at night: apnea, restless sleep, choking sounds, esophageal reflux, seizures, bedwetting (Hanly & Shapiro, 1995).
- a person with difficulty sleeping shows declines in daytime cognitive functioning, but it is not dementia.

❏ *DISTINGUISHING FEATURES FOR SD.10*

- the person shows observable *daytime* features such as being sleepy in the day, able to fall asleep easily in a chair, being slow to wake in the morning, reporting or appearing to have morning headaches, breathing through the mouth often in the day, and having a nasal voice at times.
- the person shows *nighttime* features such as snoring when asleep, noisy breathing when asleep, coughing frequently during the night in the absence of "cold symptoms," stopping breathing followed by a deep breath or gasping, periods of restlessness during the night, frequent wakenings through the night.
- with obstructive sleep apnea, the person has noisy breathing, shows an exaggerated effort to breathe, and snores in all sleep positions.
- sleep is not normalized by restricting daytime naps, by relaxation training, or using sleeping medication.
- weight reduction in obese people and avoiding sedating medication may relieve symptoms in persons with mild sleep apnea (Hanly & Shapiro, 1995).
- irregular breathing patterns are suggestive of impaired respiratory mechanics in central sleep apnea (Hanly & Shapiro, 1995).

❏ *FACTORS THAT MAY WORSEN THE CONDITION*

- marked obesity means added weight on the chest when people sleep on their back. Adults with Down syndrome are at a high risk for being overweight or obese (Prasher, 1995).
- a nasal obstruction, oversized tongue, or transient conditions affecting sinus passages, bronchi, or lungs.
- hypotonia (muscle weakness).
- hypothyroidism (Hanly & Shapiro, 1995).
- high daily intake of caffeine-containing foods, drugs, or beverages.
- sedating drugs or alcohol can increase the severity of obstructive sleep apnea (Hanly & Shapiro, 1995).

- taking medication that can suppress respiratory functioning in a person with central sleep apnea, e.g., benzodiazepines selectively reduce upper airway muscle tone (Hanly & Shapiro, 1995).
- medication that risks inducing or worsening insomnia, e.g., hypnotic medication (sleeping pills) can increase daytime drowsiness and further reduce REM sleep (Kales et al., 1983; Quine, 1991).

❏ *PERSONS WHO MAY BE AT RISK*
- persons with Down syndrome are at risk for both obstructive sleep apnea and central sleep apnea (Silverman, 1988; Strome & Strome, 1993).
- with obstructive sleep apnea, someone with a family member (parent or sibling) who snores or snored.
- an obese person, especially if male, as obesity increases the risk for obstructive sleep apnea (Hanly & Shapiro, 1995).
- a person with a fractured nose.
- a person with a congenital disorder that results in poor muscle tone or small airway (Stebbens et al., 1991).
- a person with enlarged tonsils and adenoids (Stebbens et al., 1991).
- a person with Prader-Willi syndrome who is extremely obese (Clarke et al., 1989).
- persons with Hunter syndrome, Hurler syndrome, or Morquio syndrome, Apert syndrome, or Pfeiffer syndrome (Mixter et al., 1990).
- a person with a combination of excessive sleepiness, snoring, and obesity.
- a person who has a long history of poor sleep and whose short-term memory and comprehension have become much worse, especially when overtired.

❏ *SUGGESTIONS FOR COLLECTING INFORMATION*
- check for daytime and nighttime signs of possible sleep apnea using the *Checklist of Overt Signs of Sleep Apnea.*
- do overnight charting (e.g., 5 consecutive nights) for signs of sleep apnea using a remote control room monitor or tape recorder. Use the *Overnight Chart for Signs of Sleep Apnea.*
- list the type and duration of evening activities in the past 2-3 weeks; rate for arousing or calming effects.
- list the type and duration of noise, interruptions, or other factors that cause wakenings (see SD.2).
- list the frequency and amount of stimulants taken in the evening hours before bedtime.
- assess for possible signs of cognitive deterioration (see DM.10).
- monitor the person's weight regularly because being markedly overweight can worsen sleep apnea.

❏ *MEDICAL TESTING / SCREENING SD.10*
- check if the person has had a tonsillectomy (e.g., from records or from the family).
- rule out a sinus condition or throat infection (Kryger & Shapiro, 1995).
- refer to an ear/nose/throat (ENT) specialist and to a sleep clinic for overnight polysomnographic recordings. "Central sleep apnea is not a single disease but a final pathway in a large group of heterogeneous disorders." (Hanly & Shapiro, 1995, p. 82).
- review the medications for possible sedation and effects on respiratory function.
- check the heart as obstructive sleep apnea can worsen pre-existing cardiac disease (myocardial ischemia and congestive heart failure) (Fleming, 1996) and, in persons with Down syndrome, worsen pulmonary hypertension.

❏ *POSSIBLE BIOCHEMICAL / ANATOMICAL INVOLVEMENT*
- with obstructive sleep apnea, the exaggerated respiratory muscular effort may be due to a structural abnormality such as decreased palatal width, micrognathia, or midfacial hypoplasia structurally impinging on the upper airway (Strome & Strome, 1992).
- malformations of the craniofacial bones, skull, cervical spine, and/or rib cage may contribute to obstructive sleep apnea (Fleming, 1996). A deviated nasal septum can also contribute to sleep apnea.
- lapses occur in the functioning of respiratory muscles in central sleep apnea, and an "abnormal hypoxic stimulus may serve as a pathway for centrally medicated sleep apnea" (Strome & Strome, 1992, p. 131).

❑ *COMMON FORMS*
- hypothyroidism can cause excessive sleepiness that affects daytime functioning.
- the person tires easily, seems sluggish, and needs more rest than used to be the case.
- the person often sleeps in the daytime in addition to a full night's sleep, as much as 14-16 hours a day (Guyton, 1986, p. 907).
- the person who shows excessive sleepiness may also show signs of hypothyroidism such as weight gain or weight fluctuations, extra sensitivity to the cold, dry skin and hair, marked lethargy, depression, and/or reversible cognitive decline.

❑ *VARIATIONS*
- the person who is excessively sleepy has been walking slower and for shorter distances before needing rest.
- the person who is excessively sleepy has become increasingly reluctant to do activities that require physical exertion, even favorite activities.

❑ *DISTINGUISHING FEATURES FOR SD.11*
- blood tests confirm hypothyroidism, insufficient dosing of thyroxin, or other thyroid dysfunction.
- in persons with Down syndrome who have hypothyroidism, there may be no overt signs of the condition such as weight gain, tiredness, lethargy, or sensitivity to cold temperatures (Korsager et al., 1978; Mani, 1988).
- the lethargy and excessive sleeping caused by hypothyroidism resolve after the condition is treated.

❑ *FACTORS THAT MAY WORSEN THE CONDITION*
- failing to check blood level of thyroxin at regular intervals in a person taking supplemental thyroxin because the person is very resistant to giving a blood sample (i.e., fearful of needles).
- the "bioavailability" of thyroxin medication is reduced when taken with food in the stomach.
- neuroleptics can lower serum thyroxin levels.
- hypnotic medication (sleeping pills) can add to daytime drowsiness and further reduce REM (rapid eye movement) sleep (Kales et al., 1983; Quine, 1991).
- taking lithium alone or taking it with a medication that potentates lithium (e.g., carbamazepine/Tegretol) as lithium can interfere with thyroid function.

❏ *PERSONS WHO MAY BE AT RISK*

- persons over age 60-65.
- a person with a family history of thyroid dysfunction.
- adults with Down syndrome are at increased risk for hypothyroidism (Dinani & Carpenter, 1990; Friedman et al., 1989) and the risk is even higher if they have Alzheimer disease (Lai & Williams, 1989).
- someone for whom testing thyroid function is not easy because the person is very resistant (fearful of needles) to giving a blood sample.
- someone who has become extra sensitive to cold temperatures and may be gaining weight easily.
- someone whose hair is dry and easily falls out.
- a person who started to show signs of depression (e.g., lethargy, social withdrawal, loss of daily living skills, change in appetite, etc.) about the same time as the increased need for sleep.
- a person taking lithium (Goggans et al., 1986) or taking lithium with carbamazepine.

❏ *SUGGESTIONS FOR COLLECTING INFORMATION*

- check family history for thyroid disorders.
- chart the sleep-wake cycle using the *Monthly Sleep Chart* (Sovner & DesNoyers Hurley, 1990).
- review the records for excessive sleeping over the past year or longer if records are available.
- review the history to see if the increased need for sleep occurred in the same overall period as changes in cognitive functioning, mood, appetite, weight, or medication.
- check to see if and how the sleep disturbance is affecting the person's daytime functioning.
- list the type and timing of medication given as it may produce drowsiness and/or sedation.
- rule out signs suggestive of sleep apnea as listed on the *Checklist of Overt Signs of Sleep Apnea.*
- consider tape recording the person's sleep sounds (e.g. snoring, gasping) to rule out sleep apnea.
- rule out depression using instruments or criteria appropriate for this population (e.g., Cooper & Collacott, 1994; Sovner, 1986). Use the *Checklist of Observable Signs of Depression.*

❏ *MEDICAL TESTING / SCREENING SD.11*

- do thyroid function tests and repeat as necessary if borderline results are obtained. Review possible effects of anticonvulsants on thyroid function (Gupta et al., 1992; Isojarvi et al., 1992; Tanaka et al., 1987).
- test the TSH level in persons with Down syndrome because they can have hypothyroidism yet show a normal T_4 level (Dinani & Carpenter, 1990).
- recheck blood level of thyroxin in a person on thyroxin supplementation to ensure adequate dosing.
- test serum iron, ferritin, and hemoglobin levels. Elevated cholesterol level is a supplementary blood test for investigating thyroid function.
- rule out an underlying medical condition such as systemic bacterial, fungal or viral infection (Hanly & Shapiro, 1995, p. 88).
- rule out diabetes as postprandial sleepiness is common in people with untreated diabetes mellitus (Hanly & Shapiro, 1995).
- rule out hypersomnolence due to head injury, brain tumors (e.g., in Tuberous Sclerosis) involving the pineal gland or upper brainstem (Hanly & Shapiro, 1995).

❏ *POSSIBLE BIOCHEMICAL / ANATOMICAL INVOLVEMENT*

- the blood levels of thyroxin may be too low because of auto-immune thyroiditis or other thyroid disorder (e.g., Percy et al., 1990).
- the dose of thyroxin supplement may be too low in persons already receiving treatment for hypothyroidism.
- lithium decreases iodine uptake by the thyroid which is important for thyroid functioning.

❑ *COMMON FORMS*

- the person often sleeps in the day and is awake at night, i.e., "reverses day and night," especially if blind.
- the person's sleep-wake cycle is not in synchrony with the 24-hour day (Czeisler & Shapiro, 1995).
- the person goes to sleep later and later (has successive delays in initiating sleep) and wakes later and later, and has periodic bouts of insomnia every 1-6 months (Czeisler & Shapiro, 1995).
- the person has marked difficulty in initiating sleep and in waking in the morning, but is not sleepy in the day once the person has become alert (Czeisler & Shapiro, 1995).
- the person has chronic difficulty falling asleep.

❑ *VARIATIONS*

- the person often falls asleep early in the evening and awakes too early in the morning, with peak alertness early in the day. This person may be disoriented and have reduced cognitive functioning in the evening hours.
- a sleep-wake diary reveals a 25-hour cycle in a blind person unable to detect light (Lapierre & Dumont, 1995). A 25-hour cycle is one in which a person sleeps at 12:00PM one night, 1:00AM the next night, 2:00AM the next, then 3:00AM, 4:00AM, and so on.

❑ *DISTINGUISHING FEATURES FOR SD.12*

- the sleep-wake cycle is disturbed suggestive of (a) delayed sleep-phase syndrome, (b) advanced sleep-phase syndrome, or (c) a non-24-hour day sleep-wake cycle.
- the overnight polysomnographic recording of sleep is typically normal in circadian rhythm sleep disorders, except for delayed sleep-phase syndrome (Czeisler & Shapiro, 1995).
- "For most patients with sleep-onset insomnia and difficulty awakening in the morning, *poor sleep hygiene* rather than an abnormality of the circadian pacemaker is responsible for the delayed circadian phase." (Czeisler & Shapiro, 1995, p. 201) (italics added).

❑ *FACTORS THAT MAY WORSEN THE CONDITION*

- having great variation in the time the person goes to sleep and time he/she is wakened in the morning, i.e., having no regularity in bedtime and wake times.
- stimulating and/or invigorating activities in the evening hours.
- travel involving time zone changes.
- afternoon napping may exacerbate the advanced sleep phase syndrome (Czeisler & Shapiro, 1995).
- motor restlessness or restless leg movements.
- nocturnal seizures in a person with difficult-to-control epilepsy.
- low serum vitamin B_{12} in persons with non-24 hour sleep-wake cycles (Okawa et al., 1991).
- scheduling the dose of an arousing medication late in the evening.
- hypnotic medication (sleeping pills) can add to daytime drowsiness and further reduce REM sleep (Kales et al., 1983; Quine, 1991).
- using medication that lowers melatonin such a fluoxetine/Prozac (Childs et al., 1995).

❑ *PERSONS WHO MAY BE AT RISK*

- a blind or visually impaired person with severe mental and neurological disabilities (Jan et al., 1994a; Lapierre & Dumont, 1995; Palm et al., 1991).
- multiply disabled individuals with or without blindness (Okawa et al., 1986).
- persons who are multiply disabled or have attention deficit disorder often have difficulty falling asleep (Jan et al., 1994a).
- a person with Rubella syndrome.
- a person with Tuberous Sclerosis, especially if a tuber affects the hypothalamic circadian pacemaker.
- persons over age 65 are at risk for showing early morning waking and early onset of sleep in the evening (Czeisler & Shapiro, 1995).

❑ *SUGGESTIONS FOR COLLECTING INFORMATION*

- chart the timing of sleep onset and offset (i.e., awakening) as accurately as possible for several weeks using the *Monthly Sleep Chart* (Sovner & DesNoyers Hurley, 1990).
- review sleep records for the past 12 months, longer if available.
- list the type and duration of typical evening activities over a month; rate them for arousing or calming effects.
- list the type and frequency of stimulants and the timing of sedatives taken in the evening hours.
- rule out nighttime noise, interruptions, and fear-provoking stimuli that might be affecting sleep.
- rule out depression with early morning wakening; assess for seasonal affective disorder. See SD.3 to assess for depression as a complicating factor. Alteration of circadian rhythms affects sleep in some depressed patients (Goodwin et al., 1982).

❑ *MEDICAL TESTING / SCREENING SD.12*

- verify if the person has a non-24-hour sleep-wake cycle by requesting sleep-wake recording, especially if the person is blind.
- rule out adverse effects of the *timing* of certain medication (e.g., that could be advancing the sleep phase).
- rule out physical pain associated with bed-rest positioning in persons with chronic difficulty falling asleep.

❑ *POSSIBLE BIOCHEMICAL / ANATOMICAL INVOLVEMENT*

- the brainstem ascending reticular formation is involved in wakefulness, the suprachiasmatic nucleus is involved in circadian sleep control, and the pontine and forebrain structures are involved in REM/ non-REM cycles (Cassone et al., 1986).
- "Loss of the synchronizing effect of light on the hypothalamic circadian pacemaker is presumably the basis for this condition in patients with severe eye damage." (Czeisler & Shapiro, 1995, p. 205); see also Lapierre & Dumont (1995) and Palm et al. (1991).
- there may be an age-related loss of neurons in the circadian pacemaker (suprachiasmatic nucleus) that causes shortening of the period of the pacemaker (Czeisler & Shapiro, 1995).
- receptors for the hormone melatonin have been found in the suprachiasmatic nucleus (Repperet et al., 1988) and this suggests that melatonin may have a direct effect on the circadian clock.
- the reduction in melatonin with age may shorten the sleep period in elderly people.
- circadian rhythms can be disturbed by disruptions of melatonin production in some severely neurologic- ally disabled children (Jan et al., 1994a) or when people travel across time zones (Claustrat et al., 1992).

Habitual hyperventilation is "breathing a volume of air which exceeds metabolic demands" (Lum, 1981, p. 2) and there is an absence of conspicuous overbreathing. The major symptoms of fibromyalgia are widespread musculo-skeletal pain, stiffness, fatigue, and several specific tender points. The chronic overbreathing, chronic fatigue, and pain symptoms might be different aspects of the same condition.

❑ *COMMON FORMS*
- the person often awakens within the first three hours of sleeping (Ley, 1988a). The wakenings are often between 1:30 - 3:30 AM, usually from a non-dreaming state (Ley, 1988a).
- the person is not rested on rising after sleep (nonrestorative sleep) and feels exhausted during the day.
- the person has pain and stiffness on awakening which may present as staggering or stumbling when first getting out of bed and that eases as the person walks around (Backstrom & Rubin, 1992).

❑ *VARIATIONS*
- the person awakens suddenly from sleep and appears startled.
- the person awakes suddenly from sleep with heart racing, irregular breathing, and appears afraid.
- the person has sudden "panic attacks" during sleep (Ley, 1988a).
- there is erratic breathing with irregular sighing during the night or during the day, and mostly shallow breathing with the upper chest area.

❑ *DISTINGUISHING FEATURES FOR SD.13*
- there is an *absence of conspicuous overbreathing* (Lum, 1981) but the respiratory rate is elevated at rest.
- minor physical or emotional stress evokes an exaggerated respiratory response with disproportionate increase in sighs and thoracic movement (Lum, 1981). "Once they start to [overbreathe] it is hard for them to stop" (Lum, 1981, p. 223). For example, they continue to overbreathe following moderate physical exertion long after the metabolic need for oxygen has been satisfied (Lum, 1976).
- the person shows some of these features: thoracic breathing, daily fatigue, dry mouth passages, unproductive cough, chest pain/heart racing, esophageal reflux, occasional intolerance of bright light, or extra-sensitive hearing, cold hands or feet, sweating at armpits and/or palms. If able to report, the person indicates some of the following: heaviness or numbness, muscle-joint pain, headaches (temporal, frontal or occipital), dizziness, faintness, unusual visual phenomena, depersonalization (Ley, 1988b; Lum,1981).
- the person has widespread pain in all four quadrants of the body, and the pain may be radiating, shooting, aching or burning, and not in an exact location (Backstrom & Rubin, 1992, p. 13).
- chronic fatigue patients with low red blood cell magnesium have shown improvement in the symptoms of fatigue, muscle pain, and emotional lability with magnesium treatment (Cox et al., 1991).
- a subgroup of people with fibromyalgia or chronic fatigue syndrome have a stealth virus causing the symptoms and encephalopathy (Martin, 1966).

❑ *FACTORS THAT MAY WORSEN THE CONDITION*
- physical exertion, physical illness, fear, or minor stress (Lum, 1976).
- wearing tight belts, tight trousers, girdles, or restrictive clothing which discourages diaphragm movement during breathing and which encourages the habit of excessive thoracic breathing (Lum, 1976).
- activities that result in tensing the upper chest, shoulder and neck muscles.
- developing an undiagnosed intestinal yeast overgrowth (Candida albicans infection) after one or more courses of antibiotic medication (Crook, 1996, p. 34-35).
- caffeine can increase the respiratory rate in non-caffeine users (Leonard et al., 1987).
- hypnotic medication (sleeping pills) can add to daytime drowsiness and further reduce REM (rapid eye movement) sleep (Kales et al., 1983; Quine, 1991).
- cold or humid weather in a person diagnosed with fibromyalgia syndrome (Backstrom & Rubin, 1992).

❑ *PERSONS WHO MAY BE AT RISK*

- a person who had an injury affecting the nerves that control the breathing muscles, e.g., a neck injury.
- a person who had a traumatic event earlier in life and has been under significant stress for a long period.
- a person with a history of panic attacks or a diagnosis of agoraphobia.
- persons who often look exhausted by their movements, facial expression, and poor recovery of breath after physical exertion.
- a person with chronic elevated respiration rates and magnesium deficiency (Galland, 1992).
- a person with a history of widespread pain in the upper and lower body for at least three months.
- a person with irritable bowel syndrome (Wolfe et al., 1995).
- a person who has had repeated antibiotic treatments (Crook, 1996).

❑ *SUGGESTIONS FOR COLLECTING INFORMATION*

- chart the sleep-wake cycle using the *Monthly Sleep Chart* (Sovner & DesNoyers Hurley, 1990) and check for a pattern of waking within 3 hours of falling asleep. Chart overnight sounds and wakenings using a remote control room monitor or tape recorder.
- assess a noncommunicative person for pain using the *Discomfort Scale* (Hurley et al., 1992).
- review the history for repeated antibiotic use and for pain (e.g., menstrual pain, degenerative arthritis).
- review the history for neck or shoulder injuries, past trauma, or severe protracted stress.
- in women, check for menstrual worsening; collect information using the *Menstrual Distress Chart*. With women able to be interviewed, consider using the "Menstrual Distress Questionnaire" (Moos, 1968).
- if there is widespread pain, identify when it began.
- list any arousing activities or stimulants taken in the hours before bedtime.
- check for overt signs of sleep apnea using the *Checklist of Overt Signs of Sleep Apnea* to help rule it out.
- record respirations per minute at rest at various times throughout the day and report this to the physician.

❑ *MEDICAL TESTING / SCREENING SD.13*

- do a physical examination, chest X-ray, and rule out a chronic airway obstruction causing disproportionate breathlessness; request an echocardiogram if warranted.
- rule out other causes of fatigue (e.g., anemia, a major illness) and pain (see SD.1).
- rule out magnesium deficiency; "the best test of Mg deficiency was a trial of oral Mg therapy." (Galland, 1992, p. 294). Serum Mg can be normal in magnesium deficient patients, so check erythrocyte Mg level.
- check for intestinal yeast overgrowth and excessive sugar intake (Crook, 1996, p. 33).
- if stealth virus encephalopathy is suspected, test for a stealth virus (Martin, 1995; 1996; Martin & Anderson, 1997).
- refer to a rheumatologist or medical practitioner with a specialty in fibromyaglia.
- capnography can identify the anaerobic threshold, by registering the respiratory response to the onset of metabolic acidosis, indicative of "effort syndrome" (Nixon, 1994). A low or abnormal blood level of carbon dioxide ($P\,CO_2$) is found in most hyperventilation patients at rest; all show abnormal $P\,CO_2$ after 2-3 minutes of heavy breathing after exercise or 2-3 minutes voluntary hyperventilating (Lum, 1981).

❑ *POSSIBLE BIOCHEMICAL / ANATOMICAL INVOLVEMENT*

- there are "profound sleep disturbances that follow depletion of the alkali reserves" (Rosen et al., 1990). "Hyperventilation is the commonest cause of depletion of the body's alkaline buffering system which presents to the physiologist as reduction of anaerobic threshold and to the clinician as effort syndrome." (Nixon, 1994, p. 161). Thoracic (shallow) breathing leads to abnormally low levels of arterial carbon dioxide which, if prolonged, leads to hypocapnia (Lum, 1976). "Respiratory alkalosis produces two major groups of symptoms, related (a) to cerebral vasoconstriction and hypoxia and (b) to its effect on peripheral nerves. That is, some symptoms are central, some peripheral." (Lum, 1976, p. 202). The cascade of physiological events following prolonged thoracic breathing can result in anxiety states (Lum, 1976) which can occur during sleep (Ley, 1988a).
- fibromyalgia patients have decreased pain thresholds (Wolfe et al., 1995) and may be low in serotonin which is involved in pain sensitivity and in regulating sleep.
- a subgroup of people with autism, fibromyalgia, or chronic fatigue syndrome have stealth virus encephalopathy (Martin, 1995; 1996; Martin & Anderson, 1997).

Chapter V

EATING DISTURBANCES

ED.1.   Eating Inedibles (Pica) Due To Nutritional Deficiencies Or Addictive Cravings

ED.2.   Pica In Persons Unable To Discriminate Inedibles From Edibles

ED.3.   Pica In Persons Able To Discriminate Inedibles From Edibles

ED.4.   Excessive Eating Or Hyperphagia

ED.5.   Excessive Water Drinking (Polydipsia) Due To A Medical Condition (e.g., Diabetes)

ED.6.   Medication-Related Polydipsia

ED.7.   Polydipsia As An Ictal Phenomenon

ED.8.   Polydipsia As An Obsessive-Compulsive Feature

ED.9.   Polydipsia In Persons With Psychosis

ED.10. Refusing To Eat In Persons With OCD Or Depression

ED.11. Long-Standing Refusals To Eat Or Drink

ED.12. Recent Onset Of Refusing To Eat

ED.13. Dysphagia Or Swallowing Difficulties

Presenting Concern: **EATING DISTURBANCES**

Dx Category   ED.1: *EATING INEDIBLES (PICA) DUE TO NUTRITIONAL DEFICIENCIES OR ADDICTIVE CRAVINGS*

Pica is the persistent ingestion of non-food or non-nutritive items. "Non-food" pica refers to ingesting inedibles such as paper, fabric, rubber, plastic, soap, metal, soil, twigs, and feces.

❑ *COMMON FORMS*
- eating feces (called coprophagia) (Bugle & Rubin, 1993; Danford & Huber, 1982; Lacey, 1990).
- eating cigarettes or butts (Danford & Huber, 1982; Lofts et al., 1990; Wakham et al., 1992)
- eating coffee grounds, packaged coffee, tea bags (Danford & Huber, 1982; Jawed et al., 1993).

❑ *VARIATIONS*
- searching constantly for pica items (Bugle and Rubin, 1993). Some search everyday for preferred pica items, while others search only when agitated.
- drinking urine or toilet water in addition to eating inedibles (Danford & Huber, 1982).
- eating clay, sand, mud or dirt (geophagia), i.e., substances containing phosphorus, iron, magnesium, and other minerals.
- eating grass, leaves, stones, and/or coins (Kinnel, 1985; Lacey, 1990).
- eating food dropped on the floor, vomit or urine (Danford & Huber, 1982).
- eating laundry starch (amylophagia) which contains amyloid, a source of protein (Lacey, 1990).
- eating paint chips where peeling paint containing lead is available (Sachdev & McDuff, 1989).
- eating large amounts of ice (pagophagia) is related to iron deficiency anemia (Coltman, 1969; Lacey, 1990).
- if iron deficient, the person may also be hyperactive, impulsive, violent, and unresponsive to neuroleptics (Tu et al., 1994).
- searching trash bins or dumpsters for caffeinated cola in discarded bottles.
- the person eats both cigarettes and soap bars (Danford & Huber, 1982).
- the person may become aggressive in the pursuit of pica items like cigarette butts (Bugle & Rubin, 1993; Danford & Huber, 1982; Sachdev & McDuff, 1989).

❑ *DISTINGUISHING FEATURES FOR ED.1*
- a person searches for and eats items that contain nutrients in which the person is deficient (e.g., zinc, iron, phosphorous, B vitamins) (Bugle & Rubin, 1993).
- there is a marked reduction in pica and/or pica complications after nutritional supplements are provided.
- persons who eat feces often have feces on their clothing or under their fingernails (Bugle & Rubin, 1993).
- a person who searches for items containing nicotine or caffeine might have pica only for those items.

❑ *FACTORS THAT MAY WORSEN THE CONDITION*
- having obsessive-compulsive features associated with food or eating.
- unrecognized, untreated depression in a person in the severe range of intelligence (Jawed et al., 1993).
- extended use of mineral oil for constipation may lower stored reserves of some fat-soluble vitamins.
- eating clay or laundry starch due to *one* deficiency can cause *another* deficiency as the clay and laundry starch can prevent iron being absorbed by the body (Lacey, 1990).
- neuroleptics can decrease serum iron and transferrin in people with motor restlessness (also called akathisia) (O'Loughlin et al., 1991).
- permitting free access to areas such as smoking lounges or waiting rooms with full ash trays.
- restricting access to cigarettes in developmentally disabled smokers may lead to eating cigarette butts.
- using cigarettes as a reward in a behavior modification program in a nicotine-addicted person.
- phenobarbital and/or phenytoin/Dilantin can lower red blood cell magnesium (see Galland, 1992).
- noise stress can lower red blood cell magnesium levels in magnesium deficient patients (Galland, 1992).

❑ *PERSONS WHO MAY BE AT RISK*
- nonfood pica is more common in those in the severe/profound level of intelligence (Danford & Huber, 1982).

- non-smokers with a tobacco odor on their breath or tobacco debris in their mouth (Wakham et al., 1992).
- a person who has a chronic infestation of intestinal parasites. Having both mental retardation and pica is a risk factor for intestinal parasites (Huminer et al., 1992).
- a person on a nutritionally complete diet who is unable to digest all the nutrients (Bugle & Rubin, 1993).
- a person with a leaky gut and/or food allergies.
- a person with a large portion of intestinal tract surgically removed, thereby reducing the absorption of minerals, vitamins, and water absorbed. This person might have both pica and excessive water drinking.
- a person with jittery, restless leg movements as this can be due to iron deficiency (Tu et al., 1994).
- a woman with long menstrual periods (hypermenorrhea) as this can cause iron deficiency anemia (Tu et al., 1994).
- persons on long-term traditional neuroleptics as this can lead to greater nicotine and caffeine intake. Atypical neuroleptics (clozapine/Clozaril, risperidol/Risperdal) are associated with reduced cigarette use.

❑ SUGGESTIONS FOR COLLECTING INFORMATION
- record the variety of inedibles eaten (or single-item pica) to assist the physician or dietitian in looking for possible nutritional deficiencies. Also record any excessive intake of fluids.
- chart when and where the "searching behavior" occurs. Chart the types of inedibles found in the person's mouth and look for patterns in the time of day, location, access to peers, etc. Also check if the searching or pica is related to deterioration in mood, appetite, or sleep.
- check for signs suggesting food allergies, e.g., use the *Risk Factors for Casein-Gluten Peptiduria.**
- rule out depression as a complicating factor. Use the *Checklist of Observable Signs of Depression.**
- rule out compulsions interfering with eating patterns. Collect information using the *Compulsive Behavior Checklist** and, if the person is verbal, the *Obsessive Speech Checklist.**
- * A chart or checklist listed in italics in this section can be found in the Appendix.*

❑ MEDICAL TESTING / SCREENING ED.1
- test for vitamin/mineral deficiencies (B vitamins, calcium, copper, iron, phosphorus, magnesium, zinc).
- monitor zinc levels in persons on zinc supplements as high daily doses (>100 mg. a day) can result in copper deficiency, macrocytic anemia, or neuropenia (Lofts et al., 1990).
- test serum lead level in a person who eats glossy magazine paper as this risks lead poisoning and also risks intestinal obstruction and intestinal perforation (McAlpine & Singh, 1986).
- test erythrocyte magnesium because serum magnesium can be normal in magnesium deficient patients (Galland, 1992).
- test hemoglobin because chronic mild blood loss resulting in low hemoglobin has occurred in persons with profound level of intelligence who have non-food pica (McLoughlin, 1988). "Hemoglobin...is not an adequate parameter" for iron deficiency anemia; if hemoglobin is borderline, test for ferritin, serum iron, mean cell volume, and other iron tests (Tu et al., 1994, p. 373).
- check for intestinal parasites if the person eats feces or soil where pets defecate, or has housemates with parasites (Huminer et al., 1992). Parasites can cause abdominal pain, diarrhea, excessive gas, anorexia, and in some cases severe itchiness (e.g., pruritus due to blastocystis hominis) (O'Gorman et al., 1993).
- check for gastrointestinal obstructions, perforations, and peptic ulcers if the person with pica has acute or chronic abdominal distress (Voitk, 1987). The presenting signs of an object obstructing the throat or esophagus include fever, excessive salivation with choking, vomiting, distension, prolonged constipation, and irritability (Decker, 1993).
- request follow-up charting of pica behavior if the nicotine patch is tried on those who eat cigarette butts.

❑ POSSIBLE BIOCHEMICAL / ANATOMICAL INVOLVEMENT
- pica can be due to a mineral deficiency, e.g., zinc, iron, or phosphorus deficiency (Lacey, 1990; Lofts et al.,1990) or a vitamin deficiency such as a B vitamin. Insufficient absorption of nutrients from food due to an undetected meta-bolic disorder (Bugle & Rubin, 1993). Zinc is a trace element responsible for taste sensitivity (Bhalla et al., 1983).
- the pica can be specific to addictive substances such as caffeine or nicotine.
- a severe deficit in dopamine release from the nucleus accumbens has been associated with drug withdrawal states related to addiction to nicotine, opiates, etc. (Lichtigfield & Gillman, 1996; Pontieri et al., 1996).

Presenting Concern: **EATING DISTURBANCES**
Dx Category   ED.2: *PICA IN PERSONS UNABLE TO DISCRIMINATE INEDIBLES*
                     FROM EDIBLES

❏ *COMMON FORMS*
- the person swallows solid items that he or she has been mouthing or chewing on, e.g., strings, rags, shoelaces, and/or clothing (Danford & Huber, 1982; Lacey, 1990; McAlpine & Singh, 1986).
- drinking urine or eating feces, vomit, paper, cigarettes, or soil (Danford & Huber, 1982; Lacey, 1990; McAlpine & Singh, 1986).
- consuming items that superficially look like food, e.g., soap, shampoo, hand cream, paint, other non-food liquids or semi-solids.
- eating paper, rags or cloth, or leaves (Lacey, 1990; Lofts et al., 1990).

❏ *VARIATIONS*
- eating small, inedible objects (screws, staples, paper clips, sewing needles, rubber gloves, rubber balls, toy building blocks) or chewing on things that the person can get reach with his or her mouth (leather shoes, foam padding, rubber sheets (Danford & Huber, 1982; Lacey, 1990).
- eating food off the floor (Danford & Huber, 1982).
- the person has had abdominal surgery for peptic ulcers, a perforation, or an obstruction due to foreign objects (Voitk, 1987).
- the person swallows hair frequently; a hairball (called a trichobezoar) may be unable to pass out of the stomach and can risk a bowel obstruction.

❏ *DISTINGUISHING FEATURES FOR ED.2*
- the person has mental development in the profound range and often mouths objects daily.
- the person has development arrested at a mental age under 2 years and lacks the capacity to discriminate inedibles from edibles, hence is unable to benefit from "training" not to eat inedibles.
- there is a marked reduction in pica and/or pica complications in settings that are rigorously monitored for potential pica items.
- the person has passed non-food items or foreign objects in stools, e.g., shoelaces, paper clips, fabric.

❏ *FACTORS THAT MAY WORSEN THE CONDITION*
- providing clothing with buttons or bows that can be pulled off and mouthed.
- providing toys or gifts with small pieces that can be chewed or broken off, and swallowed.
- permitting access to soaps, creams, or shampoo in the bathroom.
- free access to environments that are not rigorously monitored for small indigestible items.
- "...limited supervision of residents, and pica not being seen as a problem behavior which merits treatment" (McAlpine & Singh, 1986, p. 177).
- access to rubber gloves. Latex gloves usually pass without incident but "rubber gloves" not made of latex harden up when exposed to gastric acid and can cause internal bleeding or occasional bowel perforation (McCreary & Thompson, 1996).
- having addictive cravings, nutritional deficiencies, or insufficient absorption of nutrients in a person with intestinal parasites (see ED.2).

❏ *PERSONS WHO MAY BE AT RISK*
- persons in the severe or profound range of intelligence (Danford & Huber, 1982; McAlpine & Singh, 1986; Wakham et al., 1992) who often put things in their mouth.
- an adult with a young mental age who can finger feed, but not use utensils (Sachdev & McDuff, 1989).

- a person with cuts in the gums, under the tongue, or sharp objects lodged between the teeth (Wakham et al., 1992).
- a person in the severe or profound range with persistent vomiting (Danford & Huber, 1982) or persistent vomiting associated with eating paper, torn-up clothing, or sheets (McLoughlin, 1988).
- a person in the severe or profound range with persistent abdominal pain and dehydration (McAlpine & Singh, 1986).
- the person has a history of passing foreign objects in stools, e.g., shoelaces, paper clips, fabric.
- a person with a history of surgery to remove foreign objects from the stomach or gastrointestinal tract.
- a person with intestinal parasites who eats feces or soil contaminated by dog feces (Huminer et al.,1992).
- a person with Angelman syndrome who functions in the profound range (Summers et al., 1995).
- a person in the severe range of intelligence with the generic diagnosis of autism (Kinnel, 1985).

❑ *SUGGESTIONS FOR COLLECTING INFORMATION*
- review the records to ascertain whether or not the person's developmental age is equivalent to the 12-18 month level. Request a cognitive assessment if there has been no prior intelligence testing.
- chart to detect risk times of day, areas with high potential for pica, preferred objects, and so on.
- record the variety of inedibles mouthed or ingested. Evaluate them for risk of lacerations and perforations to the mouth, esophagus, stomach, etc. Provide this information to caregivers and clinicians.
- review the history for past X-rays and surgeries related to pica, objects passed in stool, age at onset of pica, and degree of success using special equipment or other measures to prevent pica.
- ask long-time caregivers to list the steps they take to restrict access to the types of objects likely to be eaten; provide the list to all caregivers.
- rule out obsessive-compulsive disorder as a contributing factor to eating inedibles.

❑ *MEDICAL TESTING / SCREENING ED.2*
- test the hemoglobin because chronic mild blood loss has occurred in persons with profound level of intelligence with non-food pica (McLoughlin, 1988). If the hemoglobin is borderline, test for iron deficiency anemia (Tu et al., 1994).
- test the serum lead level in a person who eats glossy magazine paper as this risks lead poisoning and also risks intestinal obstruction and intestinal perforation (McAlpine & Singh, 1986).
- check for gastrointestinal obstructions, perforations, and peptic ulcers if a person with pica has acute or chronic abdominal distress (Voitk, 1987). The presenting signs of a foreign body obstructing the throat or esophagus include excessive salivation with choking, vomiting, distension, prolonged constipation, irritability, and fever (Decker, 1993).
- check for intestinal parasites if the person eats feces or soil where pets defecate, or has housemates with parasites (Huminer et al., 1992). Parasites can cause abdominal pain, diarrhea, excessive gas, anorexia, and in some cases severe itchiness (e.g., pruritus due to blastocystis hominis) (O'Gorman et al., 1993).
- rule out mineral, vitamin, and other nutritional deficiencies (see ED.1).
- rule out Prader-Willi syndrome by chromosomal testing if clinical signs are present, i.e., neonatal hypotonia, obesity, short stature, small hands and feet, hypogonadism, mental retardation, and hyperphagia (Page et al., 1983). If Prader-Willi syndrome is present, the possible "complications include obesity hypoventilation syndrome, diabetes mellitus with a tendency to ketosis, atherosclerosis, glomerulosclerosis, and gastric perforation secondary to overeating" (Benjamin & Buot-Smith, 1993, p. 870).

❑ *POSSIBLE BIOCHEMICAL / ANATOMICAL INVOLVEMENT*
- children with mental ages of 12-18 months may display pica, but it is not considered pathological unless it persists past 18 months in a normally developing child (McAlpine & Singh, 1986; Wakham et al., 1992).

Presenting Concern: **EATING DISTURBANCES**
Dx Category   ED.3: *PICA IN PERSONS ABLE TO DISCRIMINATE INEDIBLES*
                      FROM EDIBLES

❏ *COMMON FORMS*
- the person searches for food in trash cans and eats it (Benjamin & Buot-Smith, 1993; Clarke, 1993; Danford & Huber, 1982; Page et al., 1983).
- eating food off the floor.
- eating uncooked or frozen foods.
- the person eats both inedible food (food pica: eating uncooked food, frozen food, pet food, rotting or discarded food) and inedible objects (non-food pica: eating plastic, metal, sand, leaves, etc.).

❏ *VARIATIONS*
- eating cat food (Clarke, 1993) or dogfood.
- eating rotting food (Clarke, 1993).
- the person relentlessly pursues one or two specific types of inedibles to eat.
- the person may become aggressive in searching for specific pica items (Benjamin & Buot-Smith, 1993).
- the person eats soap and paper during a reactive depression (Neville, 1959).

❏ *DISTINGUISHING FEATURES FOR ED.3*
- in depression-related pica, the pica remits after antidepressant treatment lifts the depressive symptoms (Jawed et al., 1993).
- in persons with obsessive-compulsive disorder, the compulsive urges involving inedible food (pica) remit after effective anti-obsessional treatment reduces the obsessive-compulsive symptoms (Deas-Nesmith & Brewerton, 1992).
- if the pica (with or without polydipsia) worsens during a depression, then the pica, mood, and sleep all improve after the depression is successfully treated (Jawed et al., 1993).

❏ *FACTORS THAT MAY WORSEN THE CONDITION*
- stress.
- trying to impose a calorie-reduced diet on an ambulatory person who is uncooperative to dieting.
- having untreated obsessive-compulsive disorder as the person may have strong compulsions about food.
- unrecognized and untreated depression as this can affect appetite, increasing it in some depressed people (Paykel, 1977).
- nutritional deficiencies or addictive cravings for caffeine or nicotine; see ED.2.
- using medication that increases the appetite, e.g., thioridazine/Mellaril, chlorpromazine/Largactil, tricyclic antidepressants such as clomipramine/Anafranil, imipramine/Tofranil; anticonvulsants such as valproic acid/Depakene.
- using medication that increases the appetite in a compulsive overeater, e.g., clomipramine (Benjamin & Buot-Smith, 1993).

❏ *PERSONS WHO MAY BE AT RISK*
- a person with obsessive-compulsive disorder who has compulsions regarding food.
- a person with obsessive-compulsive features and depression (Jawed et al., 1993; Neville, 1959).
- a person with Prader-Willi syndrome whose access to food is restricted (Benjamin & Buot-Smith, 1993; Clarke, 1993).

- a person with a history of neglect and deprivation, especially food deprivation.
- a person with a history of taking food belonging to others or food from stores.
- a person who overeats edible foods, or eats in secret or during the nighttime (see ED.4).

❑ *SUGGESTIONS FOR COLLECTING INFORMATION*
- chart to detect patterns in pica associated with time of day, changes in appetite, progressive weight gain or loss, agitated mood, co-occurring polydipsia, or lengthy periods of remission from pica.
- record the variety of inedibles eaten (or single-item pica) to assist the physician/dietitian.
- conduct room or person checks to discover stolen or hidden food items; record when the monitoring was done and the items discovered.
- assess for obsessive-compulsive disorder using the *Compulsive Behavior Checklist*; identify the variety of compulsions involving food.
- if the person is able to speak, use the *Obsessive Speech Checklist* for collecting information about obsessive thoughts, especially ones related to dieting, food, beverages, or inedibles.
- record if the person shows anxiety associated with urges to overeat or when asked to delay eating (many people with OCD have anxiety associated with their compulsions).
- use the *OCD Severity Scale* (Vitiello et al., 1989) to rate severity of obsessive-compulsive features in persons with developmental disabilities.
- assess for depression using instruments or criteria appropriate for this population (e.g., Cooper & Collacott, 1994; Sovner, 1986). Use the *Checklist of Observable Signs of Depression*.
- for those able to read and label different emotional states, the "Children's Depression Inventory" (Kovacs, 1985) has been used to screen depression in developmentally disabled people (Meins, 1993).

❑ *MEDICAL TESTING / SCREENING ED.3*
- review medications for possible adverse effects such as depression, weight gain, increasing appetite, or decreased absorption of vitamins or minerals.
- check for gastrointestinal obstructions, perforations, and peptic ulcers if a person with pica has acute or chronic abdominal distress (Voitk, 1987). The presenting signs of a foreign body obstructing the throat or esophagus include excessive salivation with choking, vomiting, distension, prolonged constipation, irritability, and fever (Decker, 1993).)
- check for intestinal parasites as a complicating factor, especially if there is abdominal pain, diarrhea, vomiting, and excessive gas (O'Gorman et al., 1993).
- rule out Prader-Willi syndrome by chromosomal testing if clinical signs are present, i.e., neonatal hypotonia, obesity, short stature, small hands and feet, hypogonadism, mental retardation, and hyper-phagia (Page et al., 1983). If Prader-Willi syndrome is present, the possible "complications include obesity hypoventilation syndrome, diabetes mellitus with a tendency to ketosis, atherosclerosis, glomeru-losclerosis, and gastric perforation secondary to overeating" (Benjamin & Buot-Smith, 1993, p. 870).
- rule out mineral, vitamin, and other nutritional deficiencies (see ED.1).

❑ *POSSIBLE BIOCHEMICAL / ANATOMICAL INVOLVEMENT*
- food pica and non-food pica have been associated with depression in severely mentally handicapped people (Jawed et al., 1993; Neville, 1959).
- there may be hypothalamic dysfunction affecting hormones that regulate food intake. The hormones insulin and cholecystokinin have receptors in the hypothalamus (Baskin et al., 1993; Pirke & Phillips, 1993).
- insufficient serotonin may be a contributing factor as serotonin modulates appetite (Blundell & Hill, 1987).
- insufficient serotonin is strongly implicated in obsessive-compulsive disorder (Baldwin et al., 1992; De Groot et al., 1995; Jenike et al., 1990; Zohar et al., 1987) and depression (e.g., Lucca et al., 1992).

❑ *COMMON FORMS*
- the person is continually searching for food (O'Brien & Whitehouse, 1990).
- the person consumes an excessive amount of sweet and/or high carbohydrate food (Glover et al., 1996), especially if depressed (O'Brien & Whitehouse, 1990).
- the person often steals food (Benjamin & Buot-Smith, 1993; Page et al., 1983) or hoards large quantities of food to ingest later.
- the person eats any time of day and in any location, not just in the kitchen or dining areas.
- the person eats edible food in secret.
- the person may have compulsive urges to eat excessively and/or drink fluids excessively when agitated.

❑ *VARIATIONS*
- the person eats discarded food or food left by others.
- the person might try to break locks on a refrigerator or remove a locked kitchen door from its hinges (Benjamin & Buot-Smith, 1993).
- taking--or trying to take--food from stores without paying.
- the person steals money, begs for money (Clarke, 1993), or prostitutes self to buy food (Bartolucci & Younger, 1994).

❑ *DISTINGUISHING FEATURES FOR ED.4*
- the person searches excessively for edible food.
- the person steals or hoards food to consume later.
- the person continues to gain weight even if the excessive eating is not observed (i.e., it is done secretly).
- with hyperphagia related to hypothalamic dysfunction, environmental control such as restricting access to food will likely be more successful than trying to teach the person self-control.

❑ *FACTORS THAT MAY WORSEN THE CONDITION*
- free access to the refrigerator, cupboards of food, kitchen, or cafeteria areas.
- depression in persons in the moderate or severe range of intelligence (O'Brien & Whitehouse, 1990).
- stress (Nathan, 1993).
- the desire for sweet foods during certain parts of a woman's menstrual cycle (Hennig et al., 1993).
- trying to impose a calorie-reduced diet on a person who is uncooperative to dieting.
- having untreated obsessive-compulsive disorder as the person may have strong compulsions about food.
- medication that increases appetite, e.g., thioridazine/Mellaril, tricyclic antidepressants, oral contraceptives.
- using medication for obsessive-compulsive disorder that increases appetite in an overeater, e.g., clomipramine/Anafranil (Benjamin & Buot-Smith, 1993).
- tricyclic antidepressants can also markedly lower the basal metabolic rate and contribute to weight gain.
- nutritional deficiencies or addictive cravings for caffeine or nicotine (see ED.1).

❑ *PERSONS WHO MAY BE AT RISK*

- a person with depression (O'Brien & Whitehouse, 1990), especially with depressive features such as lethargy, apathy, and an inability to enjoy activities (Paykel, 1977).
- a person with obsessive-compulsive features involving food, e.g., hoarding food, eating items in certain sequences.
- a person with Prader-Willi syndrome (Benjamin & Buot-Smith, 1993; Clarke, 1993).
- a person with a history of frequently trying to take food belonging to others or food from stores.
- a person who eats in secret or during the nighttime.
- a person who has a history of gaining weight easily and takes medication that increases appetite.
- a person with a history of eating uncooked food and/or frozen food; see ED.3.
- a person on a calorie-reduced diet.
- persons with temporal lobe epilepsy as periods of excessive eating have been associated with temporal lobe seizures (Tucker et al., 1986).

❑ *SUGGESTIONS FOR COLLECTING INFORMATION*

- check past weight charts to detect a possible pattern of weight gain during periods of free access to food compared to periods with restricted access to food; when taking certain medication; when depressed compared to non-depressed periods; or seasonal variations.
- record the types of "forbidden foods" eaten (junk foods, sweets), likely sources, and the results of room or personal checks for stolen or hidden food. Identify ways to control access to these across settings.
- assess for depression using instruments or criteria appropriate for this population (e.g., Cooper & Collacott, 1994; Sovner, 1986). Use the *Checklist of Observable Signs of Depression*.
- for those able to read and label different emotional states, the "Children's Depression Inventory" (Kovacs, 1985) has been used to screen depression in developmentally disabled people (Meins, 1993).
- assess for obsessive-compulsive disorder; collect information using the *Compulsive Behavior Checklist* and, if applicable, the *Obsessive Speech Checklist*. Identify the variety of compulsions involving food.

❑ *MEDICAL TESTING / SCREENING ED.4*

- rule out medical causes of marked weight gain such as hypothyroidism, diabetes mellitus, etc.
- rule out Prader-Willi syndrome by chromosomal testing if clinical signs are present, i.e., neonatal hypotonia, obesity, short stature, small hands and feet, hypogonadism, mental retardation, and hyperphagia (Page et al., 1983). If Prader-Willi syndrome is present, the possible "complications include obesity hypoventilation syndrome, diabetes mellitus with a tendency to ketosis, atherosclerosis, glomerulosclerosis, and gastric perforation secondary to overeating" (Benjamin & Buot-Smith, 1993, p. 870).
- review medications as a contributing factor in weight gain, increased appetite, or worsening depression.
- refer for EEG investigation of temporal lobe epilepsy if signs of ictal and interictal features are observed.
- evaluate the person for participation in regular physical exercise for weight loss and improving fitness.
- rule out pregnancy if this is suspected in a woman with a steady weight gain.

❑ *POSSIBLE BIOCHEMICAL / ANATOMICAL INVOLVEMENT*

- there may be hypothalamic dysfunction affecting the hormones that regulate food intake; the hormones insulin and cholecystokinin have receptors in the hypothalamus (Baskin et al., 1993; Pirke & Phillips, 1993).
- there may be dysregulation of cholecystokinin that controls short term satiety (Pirke & Phillips, 1993).
- there may be dysfunction of the mechanisms responsible for satiety (the feeling of fullness) in persons with Prader-Willi syndrome (Holland et al., 1995).
- serotonin deficiency may be involved as carbohydrate-loading is a way to increase central serotonin production (Nathan, 1993; Wurtman, 1982; 1993; Wurtman, 1987).
- the antihistamine effects of antidepressants can stimulate appetite.
- excessive eating can occur as ictal or interictal phenomena in temporal lobe epileptics (Tucker et al., 1986).

Presenting Concern: **EATING DISTURBANCES**
Dx Category   ED.5: *EXCESSIVE WATER DRINKING (POLYDIPSIA) DUE TO A*
                          MEDICAL CONDITION (e.g., Diabetes)

❑ *COMMON FORMS*
- the person urinates frequently (called polyuria).
- the person drinks water excessively (called polydipsia), i.e., liters or gallons of water daily if given free access.
- the person has excessive thirst, increased food intake, excessive urination, itching (frequently about the genitals), and sugar in the urine if diabetes mellitus is present (Thomas, 1993, p. 532).

Note: *COMMON FORMS* for polydipsia in one Diagnostic Category may appear similar to *COMMON FORMS* for polydipsia in other Diagnostic Categories.

❑ *VARIATIONS*
- putting one's head under the faucet to drink water.
- the person who drinks water excessively appears to be declining in vigor and general health.

❑ *DISTINGUISHING FEATURES FOR ED.5*
- the frequent urination and excessive water drinking stop once the underlying medical condition is identified and treated (Deb et al., 1994).
- a person with untreated diabetes mellitus in an advanced stage may have a sweet (acetone) odor, boils or carbuncles, eventual loss of weight, and debilitation.
- the appropriate blood sugar tests confirm diabetes mellitus (if present).
- the person has thirst, weakness, dry skin, and urine output of 5 to 10 liters per 24 hours with diabetes insipidus (Thomas, 1993, p. 532).
- "diabetes" refers to diseases characterized by excessive urination (Thomas, 1993, p. 532).

❑ *FACTORS THAT MAY WORSEN THE CONDITION*
- a poorly balanced diet, a high-sugar diet, going many hours without eating, obesity, and lack of exercise can worsen diabetes mellitus.
- restricting access to water in a person with diabetes insipidus can result in hypernatremia (a high blood level of sodium) and serious dehydration (Guyton, 1986, p. 458).
- using medication that can affect blood sugar or blood sodium levels.
- using medication that risks inducing diabetes mellitus or diabetes insipidus in a person with pre-existing diabetes mellitus or diabetes insipidus.

❑ *PERSONS WHO MAY BE AT RISK*
- a person under 30 years who has a family history of diabetes mellitus.
- a person over 40 years who has eaten high-sugar food in excess for many years as this can lead to diabetes mellitus.
- a person who started eating excessively around the same time as starting to urinate frequently.
- a person who has sudden changes in mood associated with intake of high-sugar food or drink (diabetes mellitus).
- a person with head trauma that affected the pituitary gland (diabetes insipidus) (Thomas, 1993, p. 532).
- a person with an essential fatty acid (EFA) deficiency may drink fluids excessively and have polyuria.

❑ *SUGGESTIONS FOR COLLECTING INFORMATION*
- check family history for diabetes.
- review records for age of onset of the excessive urination and water drinking (before age 30 or after age 40). Check the history for a poorly balanced diet, cravings for sweets, or signs of declining health starting with the onset of polyuria.
- weigh the person daily at the same time to monitor for water retention and hyponatremia (a low blood level of sodium) (Bremner & Regan, 1991).
- check for an increase in seizures in epileptics. Check for early signs of water intoxication which are listed below in *MEDICAL TESTING*.
- record the person's intake of fluids, and high-sugar foods and beverages for a week.
- assess for signs of psychosis to rule this in or out as a contributing factor. Collect information using the *Checklist of Observable Signs of Psychosis in Persons with Mental Retardation*.
- assess for obsessive-compulsive disorder to rule this in or out as a contributing factor. Collect information using the *Compulsive Behavior Checklist* and, if applicable, the *Obsessive Speech Checklist*.

❑ *MEDICAL TESTING / SCREENING ED.5*
- test serum sodium (often high in diabetes insipidus), electrolyte imbalances, plasma osmolality, anti-diuretic hormone, and specific urine gravity.
- test for medical causes such as adult-onset diabetes mellitus, inherited diabetes mellitus, neurogenic diabetes insipidus, nephrogenic diabetes insipidus, renal dysfunction, EFA deficiency, and other medical causes of excessive water drinking.
- rule out medication-related diabetes mellitus "brought on by administration of drugs such as cortico-steroids, certain diuretics, or birth control pills." (Thomas, 1993, p. 534). See ED.6.
- rule out medication-related diabetes insipidus such as lithium-induced nephrogenic-diabetes-insipidus-type syndrome.
- review medications for ones likely to affect salt and water regulation (i.e., hyponatremia, increased thirst, diuretic effects) such as lithium, carbamazepine, thiazide diuretics, and neuroleptics.
- water intoxication can be difficult to diagnose in persons with mental retardation *and* epilepsy because a generalized seizure is a frequent presentation of water intoxication (Bremner & Regan, 1991).
  water intoxication: early signs include headache, vomiting, diarrhea, excessive sweating, incoordination, slurred speech, unsteady gait, palpable urinary bladder, excitability; advanced signs include muscle twitching, delirium, lethargy, convulsive seizures, coma, and occasionally death (Bremner & Regan, 1991; Chinn, 1974).
- rule out Tardive Hypothalamic Syndrome in persons taking neuroleptics (Bezchlibnyk-Butler et al., 1994, p. 35).

❑ *POSSIBLE BIOCHEMICAL / ANATOMICAL INVOLVEMENT*
- polydipsia related to endocrine dysfunction can be due to adult-onset diabetes mellitus; inherited diabetes mellitus; neurogenic diabetes insipidus; nephrogenic diabetes insipidus; renal dysfunction; diseases of the pituitary, thyroid or adrenal glands; or other endocrine problems.
- in nephrogenic diabetes insipidus, the renal tubules in the kidneys do not respond well to antidiuretic hormone, resulting in large amounts of dilute urine being passed (Guyton, 1986).
- polydipsia can result from medical causes of inappropriate secretion of antidiuretic hormone (SIADH), low serum sodium (hyponatremia), or insufficient absorption of water after surgical removal of most of the large colon.
- diabetes insipidus following traumatic brain injury has been associated with symptoms of rage, hyper-phagia, and cognitive deterioration with damage to the posterior hypothalamus (Reeves & Plum, 1969).
- polydipsia was caused by a rare tumor that affected the hypothalamic-pituitary axis in a person with Cornelia de Lange syndrome (Sugita et al., 1986).

❏ *COMMON FORMS*
- the person drinks liters or gallons of water daily if given free access.
- putting one's head under the faucet to drink water.
- drinking excessive amounts of tea and/or other liquids available (Bremner & Regan, 1991).
- the weight gain over 12 hours can range from none to 7.5 kg (16.5 lb.) (Bremner & Regan, 1991).
- stealing or taking beverages from others if not restricted (Deb et al., 1994).
- the person urinates frequently.

❏ *VARIATIONS*
- the person goes to extraordinary lengths to drink fluid such as drinking from a toilet or bath tub, if access to water is restricted (Bremner & Regan, 1991).
- the person drinks aftershave liquids (Bremner & Regan, 1991).
- even if verbal, the person may be unable to give reasons for drinking excessively (Bremner & Regan, 1991).

❏ *DISTINGUISHING FEATURES FOR ED.6*
- the frequent searching for water and frequent drinking stop once the offending medication is withdrawn and water balance is restored.

❏ *FACTORS THAT MAY WORSEN THE CONDITION*
- having an unrecognized diabetic or pre-diabetic condition.
- increasing the dose of the offending medication.
- using one or more medications that cause increased thirst or diuretic effects.
- abrupt stopping of lithium (lithium opposes the antidiuretic effect of carbamazepine/Tegretol) in a schizophrenic person taking both carbamazepine and lithium as this may lead to severe low serum sodium (called hyponatremia) (Vieweg & Godleski, 1989).

❏ *PERSONS WHO MAY BE AT RISK*
- a person with a pre-existing medical cause for excessive water intake such as insufficient absorption of water in a person with most of the intestinal tract surgically removed.
- a person with pica (eating inedibles) who is taking lithium (Fukuda et al., 1986).
- a person taking lithium carbonate (Singh et al., 1985).
- a person with schizophrenia taking a thiazide diuretic (Smith & Clark, 1980).

❑ *SUGGESTIONS FOR COLLECTING INFORMATION*

- review records to see if the start of polydipsia and polyuria related to changes in medication or health.
- weigh the person every morning and evening, or once daily at the same time to monitor for water retention and hyponatremia (Bremner & Regan, 1991).
- if possible, record the amount and sources of fluids consumed, check for diurnal variations in drinking.
- check for an increase in seizures in epileptics. Check for early signs of water intoxication which are listed below in *MEDICAL TESTING*.
- assess for signs of psychosis as a possible contributing factor; collect information using the *Checklist of Observable Signs of Psychosis in Persons with Mental Retardation.*
- assess for obsessive-compulsive disorder underlying eating or drinking compulsions using the *Compulsive Behavior Checklist* and, if the person is verbal, the *Obsessive Speech Checklist*, as a possible contributing factor.

❑ *MEDICAL TESTING / SCREENING ED.6*

- test serum sodium, electrolytes, plasma osmolality, antidiuretic hormone, and specific urine gravity. "Blood samples taken in the afternoon, as opposed to the morning...allowed a greater chance of detecting significant hyponatremia." (Deb et al., 1994, p. 365).
- review medications for ones likely to affect salt and water regulation (causing hyponatremia, increased thirst, diuretic effects) such as lithium, carbamazepine, thiazide diuretics, and neuroleptics.
- rule out Tardive Hypothalamic syndrome in persons taking neuroleptics (Bezchlibnyk-Butler et al., 1994, p. 35).
- rule out medication-related diabetes mellitus "brought on by administration of drugs such as cortico-steroids, certain diuretics, or birth control pills" (Thomas, 1993, p. 534).
- rule out medical causes such as diabetes mellitus (hyperglycemia), diabetes insipidus, or renal dysfunction.
- water intoxication can be difficult to diagnose in persons with mental retardation *and* epilepsy because a generalized seizure is a frequent presentation of water intoxication (Bremner & Regan, 1991). *water intoxication*: early signs include headache, vomiting, diarrhea, excessive sweating, incoordination, slurred speech, unsteady gait, palpable urinary bladder, excitability; advanced signs include muscle twitching, delirium, lethargy, convulsive seizures, coma, and occasionally death (Bremner & Regan, 1991; Chinn, 1974).
- monitor for long term complications of chronic polydipsia such as "recurrent episodes of water intoxication, ...bowel and bladder dilatation, ...renal failure, malnutrition, projectile vomiting, cardiac failure, ...hernias, ...calcium loss" (Bremner & Regan, 1991, p. 244).

❑ *POSSIBLE BIOCHEMICAL / ANATOMICAL INVOLVEMENT*

- carbamazepine can cause low serum sodium (hyponatremia) and the risk for this may be elevated in a person with mental retardation and psychosis, leading to polydipsia (Kastener et al., 1992).
- lithium can have adverse effects on salt and water regulation (Fukuda et al., 1986).
- sudden stopping of lithium (lithium opposes the antidiuretic effect of carbamazepine) in a schizophrenic person on both carbamazepine and lithium can lead to severe hyponatremia (Vieweg & Godleski, 1989).
- "Lithium carbonate antagonizes the peripheral action of antidiuretic hormone thus resulting in polyuria and secondary polydipsia, but it never leads to water intoxication" (Singh et al., 1985, p. 130).
- there may be a direct effect on the hypothalamus from neuroleptics such as chlorpromazine/Largactil and thioridazine/Mellaril that affects the dopaminergic neurons which govern thirst, drinking, and anti-diuretic hormone secretion (Smith & Clark, 1980).
- medication-related diabetes mellitus may be "brought on by administration of drugs such as cortico-steroids, certain diuretics, or birth control pills." (Thomas, 1993, p. 534).

❏ COMMON FORMS
- the person runs to the sink, places his or her head under the faucet, or pours liquids into containers to consume 6-8 glasses of water during an episode (Cascino & Sutula, 1989).
- the consumption of large quantities of water is done with an urgency even if the person has recently finished eating and drinking (Cascino & Sutula, 1989).

❏ VARIATIONS
- the person wants a pitcher of water available at all times, but does not drink from it except during distinct episodes when he/she drinks with great urgency (Cascino & Sutula, 1989).
- the person who has episodes of excessive fluid and food intake (not a continuous daily search) also has episodes of abrupt cessation of motor activity, depersonalization, and mood lability (Tucker et al., 1986).
- the person runs about in terror if unable to locate water or fluids during a complex partial seizure.

❏ DISTINGUISHING FEATURES FOR ED.7
- the episodes of excessive drinking begin with a motionless stare followed by lip smacking and head-turning to one side.
- the person only drinks with urgency during distinct episodes, even if a pitcher of water is always available.
- the person shows several signs consistent with temporal lobe dysfunction or seizures.
- persons with polydipsia due to temporal lobe seizures can have normal electrolytes, serum and urine osmolality, and fasting blood glucose (Cascino & Sutula, 1989). The seizure is not terminated by ingesting fluids (Cascino & Sutula, 1989).

❏ FACTORS THAT MAY WORSEN THE CONDITION
- introducing medication that lowers the seizure threshold (e.g., neuroleptics, tricyclic antidepressants).
- stressors that increase the frequency of temporal lobe seizures such as interpersonal stress, premenstrual changes, or medications that lower the seizure threshold (Cascino & Sutula, 1989; Tucker et al., 1986).
- acute illness that results in excessive sweating and loss of body fluid.

❏ *PERSONS WHO MAY BE AT RISK*

- a person who has complex partial seizures or temporal lobe epilepsy (Tucker et al., 1986).
- a person who has not been diagnosed with temporal lobe epilepsy but has numerous features consistent with temporal lobe dysfunction (Roberts et al., 1992; Varney et al., 1992).

❏ *SUGGESTIONS FOR COLLECTING INFORMATION*

- videotape the person during outbursts of water drinking to help detect observable involuntary phenomena.
- if the person is verbal, check for signs of temporal lobe dysfunction using the "Structured Clinical Interview for Complex Partial Seizure Symptoms" (Roberts et al., 1992; Varney et al., 1992).
- temporal lobe seizures can spread to the frontal lobe (Luciano, 1993; Munari et al., 1981) and vice versa, so also use the *Nonconvulsive Ictal Signs Checklist* as some episodes reflect frontal and temporal signs.
- review records for onset or worsening of polydipsia associated with a change in the dose of a medication or the introduction of a medication that can lower the seizure threshold.
- review records for onset or worsening of polydipsia related to a change in anticonvulsant medication.
- check if the person has reported phenomena suggestive of temporal lobe dysfunction such as time illusions; personal awareness distortions; somatic distortions of size or shape; visual, auditory, or olfactory hallucinations.
- there may be an absence of classic signs on neuropsychological testing in temporal lobe epileptics (Tucker et al., 1986).
- rule out schizophrenia or psychotic disorders. Collect information using the *Checklist of Observable Signs of Psychosis in Persons with Mental Retardation*.
- assess for obsessive-compulsive disorder in case eating or drinking compulsions are a contributing factor. Collect information using the *Compulsive Behavior Checklist* and, if the person is verbal, the *Obsessive Speech Checklist*.

❏ *MEDICAL TESTING / SCREENING ED.7*

- test for low serum sodium, electrolytes, plasma osmolality, and related tests if polydipsia is suspected. Persons with polydipsia due to temporal lobe seizures can have normal electrolytes, serum and urine osmolality, and fasting blood glucose (Cascino & Sutula, 1989).
- request an EEG (sleep EEG if possible) and neurologic investigation for temporal lobe epilepsy or temporal lobe dysfunction. The neurologic exam and CT scans can be normal in temporal lobe epileptics (Tucker et al., 1986). The "medial temporal lobe focus might well escape detection by the surface EEG, while dysrythmias conducted to the cortex would be observed." (Devinsky & Bear, 1984, p. 653). The majority of people with temporal lobe epilepsy do not drink water/fluids excessively during seizures.
- not all temporal lobe epileptics improve on anticonvulsant trials (Farber et al., 1986; Sperling et al., 1996).
- review medications for ones that could lower the seizure threshold if the person has seizures.
- review medications for ones likely to affect salt and water regulation (causing hyponatremia, increased thirst, diuretic effects) such as lithium, carbamazepine, thiazide diuretics, neuroleptics.
- rule out medical causes such as diabetes mellitus (hyperglycemia), diabetes insipidus, or renal dysfunction.

❏ *POSSIBLE BIOCHEMICAL / ANATOMICAL INVOLVEMENT*

- the anterior and ventromedial hypothalamus are involved in thirst and water regulation. "Epileptiform activity generated in the temporal lobe may propagate into the hypothalamus and other structures implicated in thirst and water regulation, producing ictal manifestations of abnormal water seeking behavior." (Cascino & Sutula, 1989, p. 681).
- the mesiobasal area of the temporal lobe may be involved in the seizure activity (Cascino & Sutula, 1989).

❑ *COMMON FORMS*

- the person drinks water excessively during periods of agitation.
- drinking water from sink taps, the shower, or the toilet.
- the person has ritualistic behavior associated with drinking (e.g., rubs chest three times before drinking) (Deas-Nesmith & Brewerton, 1992).
- urinating frequently.

❑ *VARIATIONS*

- the person who drinks water excessively also has food pica (eats inedible unprepared food) (Deas-Nesmith & Brewerton, 1992) or non-food pica (eats buttons, metal objects, etc.) (Jawed et al., 1993).
- the person consumes food and fluids in a binge fashion such as two weeks of groceries at a time (Deas-Nesmith & Brewerton, 1992).
- the polydipsia and pica worsen during depressive illness (Jawed et al., 1993).
- the person becomes visibly anxious when others suggest that he or she not drink (Klonoff & Moore, 1984).
- if verbal, the person reports intrusive urges to drink (Deas-Nesmith & Brewerton, 1992).
- the person has probably had episodes of hyponatremia (low blood level of sodium) secondary to polydipsia (Deas-Nesmith & Brewerton, 1992; Jawed et al., 1993).

❑ *DISTINGUISHING FEATURES FOR ED.8*

- persons with obsessive-compulsive disorder (OCD) may have ritualistic behaviors that accompany the excessive intake of fluids (Deas-Nesmith & Brewerton, 1992).
- the person's feelings of thirst are relieved by fluid intake (Deas-Nesmith & Brewerton, 1992; Klonoff & Moore, 1984); the person reports intrusive urges to drink a lot of fluid (Deas-Nesmith & Brewerton, 1992).
- persons with OCD may have periods (several weeks) with polydipsia, then long periods without polydipsia.
- the person may have had obsessive-compulsive features (perhaps undiagnosed) for at least a few years before the excessive water drinking presented as a compulsive feature.
- if the polydipsia is related to anxiety based on a frightening experience (e.g., severe dehydration), it greatly diminishes with appropriate treatment for the anxiety-producing fear (e.g., response prevention, relaxation training, positive reinforcement) (Klonoff & Moore, 1984).
- medication for obsessive-compulsive disorder that reduces the person's overall obsessions and compulsions also reduces the compulsive water drinking (Deas-Nesmith & Brewerton, 1992).
- the polydipsia is not reduced by neuroleptics (Jawed et al., 1993; Klonoff & Moore, 1984).

❑ *FACTORS THAT MAY WORSEN THE CONDITION*

- free access to sink taps, showers, bathtubs, and toilet water.
- unsupervised meals.
- stress and anxiety-provoking situations.
- having acute illness that results in excessive sweating and loss of body fluid.
- using one or more medications that can cause dry mouth, increased thirst, or diuretic effects.
- using neuroleptic medication in a person who is not psychotic as it may cause electrolyte imbalances (Bezchlibnyk-Butler et al., 1994, p. 33, 37).

❏ *PERSONS WHO MAY BE AT RISK*

- a person with obsessive-compulsive disorder or anxiety disorder (Bremner & Regan, 1991).
- a person with obsessive-compulsive features (e.g., picks up threads, pieces of paper, bits of plastic on the carpet and puts them in the wastebasket) who eats discarded food or other inedibles (Jawed et al., 1993).
- persons with Fragile X syndrome are at risk for obsessive-compulsive behavior (Dorn et al., 1994).

❏ *SUGGESTIONS FOR COLLECTING INFORMATION*

- use the *Compulsive Behavior Checklist* as a guide for collecting information to see if the person meets the diagnostic criteria for obsessive-compulsive disorder. Try to determine the age when OCD began and if the polydipsia developed subsequently. List the person's compulsive features that involve food, drink, mealtime rituals, and obsessive talking about eating or drinking.
- if the person can converse, use the *Obsessive Speech Checklist* for collecting information about obsessive thoughts, especially ones related to water, thirst, beverages, food, and possible eating of inedibles.
- use the *OCD Severity Scale* (Vitiello et al., 1989) to rate severity of obsessive-compulsive features in persons with developmental disabilities.
- check if the person shows anxiety associated with urges to drink or when asked to delay drinking as many people with OCD show anxiety associated with their compulsions.
- weigh the person daily at the same time in order to monitor for water retention and possible hyponatremia (low blood level of sodium) (Bremner & Regan, 1991; Deas-Nesmith & Brewerton, 1992).
- record, if possible, the amount and sources of fluids consumed; evaluate which sources can be restricted.
- check for an increase in seizures in epileptics. Check for early signs of water intoxication (see below).
- assess for depression as a contributing factor using instruments or criteria appropriate for this population (e.g., Cooper & Collacott, 1994; Sovner, 1986). Use the *Checklist of Observable Signs of Depression*.
- for those able to read and label different emotional states, the "Children's Depression Inventory" (Kovacs, 1985) has been used to screen depression in developmentally disabled people (Meins, 1993).
- rule out psychosis as a possible contributing factor. Collect information using the *Checklist of Observable Signs of Psychosis in Persons with Mental Retardation*.

❏ *MEDICAL TESTING / SCREENING ED.8*

- test for low serum sodium, electrolytes, plasma osmolality, antidiuretic hormone, and specific urine gravity. "Blood samples taken in the afternoon, as opposed to the morning...allowed a greater chance of detecting significant hyponatremia." (Deb et al., 1994, p. 365).
- water intoxication can be difficult to diagnose in persons with mental retardation *and* epilepsy because a generalized seizure is a frequent presentation of water intoxication (Bremner & Regan, 1991). *water intoxication*: early signs include headache, vomiting, diarrhea, excessive sweating, incoordination, slurred speech, unsteady gait, palpable urinary bladder, excitability; advanced signs include muscle twitching, delirium, lethargy, convulsive seizures, coma, and occasionally death (Bremner & Regan, 1991; Chinn, 1974).
- review medications for ones likely to affect salt and water regulation (causing hyponatremia, increased thirst, diuretic effects) such as lithium, carbamazepine, thiazide diuretics, and neuroleptics.
- rule out medical causes, e.g., diabetes mellitus (hyperglycemia), diabetes insipidus, or renal dysfunction.
- check for long term complications of chronic polydipsia such as "recurrent episodes of water intoxication, ...bowel and bladder dilatation, ...renal failure, malnutrition, projectile vomiting, cardiac failure, ...hernias, ...calcium loss" (Bremner & Regan, 1991, p. 244).

❏ *POSSIBLE BIOCHEMICAL / ANATOMICAL INVOLVEMENT*

- serotonin is strongly implicated in obsessive-compulsive disorder (Baldwin et al., 1992; De Groot et al., 1995; Jenike et al., 1990; Zohar et al., 1987) and has a role in regulating thirst (Neill & Cooper, 1989).
- both polydipsia and obsessive-compulsive symptoms were reduced in a chronic schizophrenic treated with a selective serotonin agent, fluoxetine/Prozac when neuroleptics had not shown any benefit (Deas-Nesmith & Brewerton, 1992).

❏ *COMMON FORMS*

- the person drinks above average volumes of water, more than 3 liters of fluid per day (Deb et al., 1994) or more than 5 liters of water per day (Bremner & Regan, 1992).
- putting one's head under the faucet to drink water.
- drinking excessive amounts of tea and/or other liquids available (Bremner & Regan, 1991).
- the weight gain over 12 hours can range from none to 7.5 kg (16.5 lb.) (Bremner & Regan, 1991).
- taking or stealing beverages from others if not restricted (Deb et al., 1994).
- urinating frequently.
- searching for water sources frequently throughout the day.

❏ *VARIATIONS*

- a person with limited access to water will go to extraordinary lengths to drink fluid such as drinking from a toilet or bath tub (Bremner & Regan 1991).
- the person may become aggressive in demanding water (McNally et al., 1988) and drink clean toilet water or urine if access to water is restricted.
- a person who drinks urine or toilet water searches for many different sources of water.
- the person appears to drink in response to hallucinations as he/she talks to imaginary people and looks upward for no obvious reason during the periods when drinking excessively (Bremner & Regan, 1991).
- even if verbal, the person may be unable to give reasons for drinking a lot (Bremner & Regan, 1991).
- these people are vulnerable to episodes of water intoxication: early signs include headache, vomiting, diarrhea, excessive sweating, incoordination, slurred speech, unsteady gait, palpable urinary bladder, excitability; advanced signs include muscle twitching, delirium, lethargy, convulsive seizures, coma, and occasionally death (Bremner & Regan, 1991; Chinn, 1974).
- persons with delusional features may report drinking excessively to washout worms, other creatures, foul material or cancer, or to cleanse themselves from sin (Shah & Greenberg, 1992; Smith & Clark, 1980).

❏ *DISTINGUISHING FEATURES FOR ED.9*

- psychosis-related polydipsia can be due to inadequately treated psychosis (Bremner & Regan, 1991).
- if asked why they drink so much, they may report delusions that require "flushing out poisons," "baptizing," "dissolving food," or command hallucinations to drink plenty of fluids (Shah & Greenberg, 1992).
- in some persons with psychosis, the polydipsia diminishes with better treatment of the underlying psychosis, e.g., increasing or re-introducing neuroleptics (Bremner & Regan, 1991; Shah & Greenberg, 1992).
- in some persons with psychosis, the polydipsia diminishes with treatment for SIADH (syndrome of inappropriate secretion of antidiuretic hormone) (Singh et al., 1985).
- polydipsia with hyponatremia tends to be chronic when it occurs in schizophrenic patients with or without mental retardation (Shah & Greenberg, 1992).

❏ *FACTORS THAT MAY WORSEN THE CONDITION*

- adult-onset mild diabetes (Bremner & Regan, 1991).
- acute illness that results in excessive sweating and loss of body fluid.
- menstrual periods, as transient increases in agitation and fluid intake might occur (McNally et al., 1988).
- factors associated with SIADH include smoking, stress, neuroleptics, diuretics, and anticonvulsants such as carbamazepine (Shah & Greenberg, 1992; Singh et al., 1985).
- using carbamazepine in a person with both psychosis and polydipsia as this may increase the risk of hyponatremia (Kastener et al., 1992; Shah & Greenberg, 1992).
- low sodium diets and diuretics for hypertension exacerbated the polydipsia in schizophrenic patients who had polydipsia with hyponatremia (Shah & Greenberg, 1992).
- lowering the dose of a neuroleptic in a person with psychosis.
- using one or more medications that cause dry mouth, increased thirst, or diuretic effects.

- abrupt stopping of lithium (lithium opposes the antidiuretic effect of carbamazepine/Tegretol) in a schizophrenic person taking both carbamazepine and lithium, as this can lead to a severely low level of sodium in the blood (hyponatremia) (Vieweg & Godleski, 1989).

❑ *PERSONS WHO MAY BE AT RISK*
- persons with psychosis have an increased risk for water intoxication and polydipsia compared to those with non-psychotic behavior problems (Bremner & Regan, 1991).
- a person with mental retardation who also has pica (Deb et al., 1994).
- a person in the moderate, mild, or borderline range of intelligence is more likely to develop polydipsia than those in the severe or profound range (Bremner & Regan, 1991).
- a schizophrenic who vomits a lot of water after a generalized seizure (Vieweg & Karp, 1994).

❑ *SUGGESTIONS FOR COLLECTING INFORMATION*
- weigh the person every morning and evening, or once daily at the same time to monitor for water retention and hyponatremia (Bremner & Regan, 1991).
- record, if possible, the amount and sources of fluids consumed; evaluate which sources can be restricted.
- check for an increase in seizures in epileptics. Check for early signs of water intoxication (listed below).
- check family history for schizophrenia, obsessive-compulsive disorder, and diabetes.
- assess for signs of psychosis. Collect information using the *Checklist of Observable Signs of Psychosis in Persons with Mental Retardation* and determine if the diagnostic criteria (DSM-IV, 1994) are met.
- rule out obsessive-compulsive disorder underlying eating or drinking compulsions using the *Compulsive Behavior Checklist* and, if the person is verbal, the *Obsessive Speech Checklist*.

❑ *MEDICAL TESTING / SCREENING ED.9*
- test for low serum sodium, electrolytes, plasma osmolality, antidiuretic hormone, and specific urine gravity. "Blood samples taken in the afternoon, as opposed to the morning...allowed a greater chance of detecting significant hyponatremia." (Deb et al., 1994, p. 365).
- check if the person has "polydipsia with hyponatremia." The diagnostic criteria are excessive water intake and a serum sodium level of 125 mmol/L or less (Shah & Greenberg, 1992).
- review medications for ones likely to affect salt and water regulation (causing hyponatremia, increased thirst, diuretic effects) such as lithium, carbamazepine, thiazide diuretics, and neuroleptics.
- rule out Tardive Hypothalamic syndrome in those on neuroleptics (Bezchlibnyk-Butler et al.,1994, p.35).
- rule out medical causes, e.g., diabetes mellitus (hyperglycemia), diabetes insipidus, or renal dysfunction.
- water intoxication can be difficult to diagnose in persons with mental retardation *and* epilepsy because a generalized seizure is a frequent presentation of water intoxication (Bremner & Regan, 1991).
  water intoxication: early signs include headache, vomiting, diarrhea, excessive sweating, incoordination, slurred speech, unsteady gait, palpable urinary bladder, excitability; advanced signs include muscle twitching, delirium, lethargy, convulsive seizures, coma, and occasionally death (Bremner & Regan, 1991; Chinn, 1974).
- monitor for long term complications of chronic polydipsia such as "recurrent episodes of water intoxication, ...bowel and bladder dilatation, ...renal failure, malnutrition, projectile vomiting, cardiac failure, ...hernias, ...calcium loss" (Bremner & Regan, 1991, p. 244).

❑ *POSSIBLE BIOCHEMICAL / ANATOMICAL INVOLVEMENT*
- inappropriate secretion of antidiuretic hormone has been associated with acute psychosis and polydipsia (Kramer & Drake, 1983; Singh et al., 1985).
- normal water concentration, or osmolality, is controlled in the basal hypothalamic periventricular area (Shah & Greenberg, 1992). Hypothalamic dysregulation of thirst and water regulation might be related to hyperdopaminergic activity (Singh et al., 1985; Smith & Clark, 1980).
- "Water intoxication may occur either when polydipsia is so severe that renal water excretion is overwhelmed, or in conjunction with SIADH [inappropriate secretion of antidiuretic hormone], reset osmostat, or drug effects, all of which may be associated with psychosis." (Bremner & Regan, 1991).

❑ *COMMON FORMS*

- a person with compulsions, obsessions, or depression has a long-standing pattern of refusing to eat and/or drink.
- that person might also throw food, serving dishes, or utensils when refusing to eat.
- the person who refuses meals at times may have strong food preferences and may insist on a large quantity of only one item at a meal (e.g., three cans of peas for the meal, only chicken for the meal).

❑ *VARIATIONS*

- the person eats small portions, eats only certain foods, or eats items in a fixed sequence.
- if verbal, the person talks often about wanting not to eat too much, about staying thin, and/or the cost of groceries.
- the person who has food compulsions or dieting obsessions, exercises regularly and possibly excessively.
- refusing to eat in the presence of others and/or imposing a very strict diet on oneself (Clarke & Yapa, 1991).
- refusing to eat foods that the person thinks are high in calories.
- the person might become very agitated and angry if others try to make the person eat.

❑ *DISTINGUISHING FEATURES FOR ED.10*

- food refusal in persons with obsessive-compulsive disorder can reflect excessive concern about weight and/or compulsive behaviors involving food.
- if the person with food obsessions and compulsions is in the moderate or mild range of intelligence, he or she tends to remain thin.
- food refusal in persons who are depressed can be one of the symptoms of depression.
- the person may show several of the following features of depression: sadness; spontaneous crying; sleep disturbance; reduced interest in activities; social withdrawal; reduced speech; slow speech; decreased energy; loss of self-care skills; impaired concentration; psychomotor retardation; increased anger or aggression (Burt et al., 1992; Cooper & Collacott, 1994; Pary et al., 1996; Prasher & Hall, 1996; Warren et al., 1989).
- the reduced appetite began or worsened around the time that other signs of depression began, e.g., sleep disturbance, increased irritability, and aggression.
- if the weight loss and reduced appetite are due to depression, successful treatment for the depression restores the appetite to normal.
- for food refusals due to (1) organic impairment (e.g., anatomical defects, neurological dysfunction, metabolic imbalances), (2) pain, or (3) adverse effects of medication, see ED.11.

❑ *FACTORS THAT MAY WORSEN THE CONDITION*

- depression can adversely affect appetite in an obsessive-compulsive person who may already have compulsions involving types and amount of food eaten.
- medication that can suppress appetite.
- medication that can cause nausea and vomiting, e.g., anti-inflammatories, oral contraceptives alone or with other medications that also cause nausea such as carbamazepine/Tegretol and buspirone/Buspar.
- withdrawal from a neuroleptic, phenytoin/Dilantin, or phenobarb can cause a temporary loss of appetite, sometimes lasting weeks.

- a person who shows many compulsive features.
- if verbal, a person who often talks about dieting and not wanting to gain weight.
- someone showing signs of depression.
- a depressed person with dementia.
- a woman who desires to be thin and has missed 3 or more consecutive menstrual cycles, but is not menopausal.
- a person with a history of extreme physical abuse, sexual abuse, and/or post-traumatic stress disorder.

❏ *SUGGESTIONS FOR COLLECTING INFORMATION*

- review records to establish the month and year food refusals began. Note health conditions and medications taken before onset of refusing meals. Check for nausea or vomiting associated with refusing meals.
- check for patterns in the type of food or drink refused, common features of preferred foods, times of day meals are refused, and signs of rebound hunger. Review past successful and unsuccessful methods to get the person to eat and drink.
- assess for obsessive-compulsive features as compulsions can be affecting food choices and quantity, and obsessive thoughts can focus on dieting, thinness, exercise, etc. Collect information using the *Compulsive Behavior Checklist* and, if the person is verbal, the *Obsessive Speech Checklist*.
- assess for depression using instruments or criteria appropriate for this population (e.g., Cooper & Collacott, 1994; Sovner, 1986). Use the *Checklist of Observable Signs of Depression.*
- for those able to read and label emotional states, the "Children's Depression Inventory" (Kovacs, 1985) has been used to screen depression in developmentally disabled people (Benavidez & Matson, 1993; Meins, 1993).
- check for past choking incidents and identify changes in the eating pattern after a serious choking incident.
- rule out pain as a contributing factor; use the *Discomfort Scale* (Hurley et al., 1992) before and after meals to assess for pain in noncommunicative people.
- check for signs of dysphagia, especially in a depressed person with dementia; see ED. 13.

❏ *MEDICAL TESTING / SCREENING ED.10*

- review health status and medication history before and since the onset (or worsening) of meal refusals.
- review medications for ones that have appetite-suppressing effects (e.g., fluoxetine) or that risk causing nausea and vomiting. Frequent nausea can diminish the desire for a wide range of foods except perhaps milk and soft foods.
- review medications for ones that risk worsening obsessive-compulsive symptoms or depression (e.g., benzodiazepines).
- rule out possible pain as a factor in the person's refusing of food and drink; see ED.11.

❏ *POSSIBLE BIOCHEMICAL / ANATOMICAL INVOLVEMENT*

- obsessive-compulsive or depressed patients are often low in central serotonin, a neurotransmitter that helps regulate appetite (Blundell & Hill, 1987; Chafetz, 1990; Wurtman, 1987).
- the hormone cholecystokinin signals satiety and is higher in anorectics than controls (Pirke & Phillips, 1993).

Presenting Concern: **EATING DISTURBANCES**
Dx Category ED.11: *LONG-STANDING REFUSALS TO EAT OR DRINK*

❑ *COMMON FORMS*
- the person has a long-standing pattern of refusing to eat and/or drink.
- the total amount of food consumed is inadequate or the variety of foods eaten is nutritionally limited.
- the person holds food in the mouth for long periods of time (Babbitt et al., 1994).
- a person who is fed by others frequently expels nonpreferred food (Babbitt et al., 1994).
- closing one's mouth, putting a hand over one's mouth, and turning one's head away when caregivers present food or drink (Riordan et al., 1984).
- the person may accept liquids and semi-solid foods, but often rejects solid food.
- at times when the person *has* eaten, he or she tends to be restless and irritable after intake of food.
- a person who frequently refuses food may eat very quickly if "resigned" to having no choice but to eat.
- throwing food, a serving dish, spoon, or tipping the table as part of refusing to eat (Riordan et al., 1980).

❑ *VARIATIONS*
- the person frequently eats small portions or only certain foods.
- the person is more likely to eat breakfast (when the stomach is empty) but does not want snacks or lunch as the food has "stacked up" in the esophagus.
- sometimes in the 3-4 hours after eating, the person shows increased signs of distress such as screaming, loud moaning, self-hitting, or restless pacing.
- severe self-hitting starts when caregivers try to make the person eat.
- the person sobs or screams for 5 seconds or longer between spoonsful (Riordan et al., 1984).
- the person often indicates stomach upset (nausea), and has been vomiting a few times a month for years.
- refusing fluids in a person in the profound range can result in dehydration requiring medical attention.
- the person leaves the table during meals.

❑ *DISTINGUISHING FEATURES FOR ED.11*
- food refusals can be due to (1) organic impairment (e.g., anatomical defects, neurological dysfunction, metabolic imbalances), (2) pain or discomfort, (3) adverse effects of medication, or (4) a combination of these plus "environmental factors" that maintain or exacerbate feeding problems (Riordan et al., 1980).
- if food refusals are due to obsessive-compulsive disorder or depression, see ED.10.
- the person may be experiencing pain from a gastrointestinal problem, e.g., scoliosis (in a nonambulatory person), unrecognized hiatus hernia, sliding hiatus hernia, esophageal narrowing, diverticulosis of the esophagus, stomach covered with infected polyps, stricture in the large colon, undetected parasites, motility problems, or other bowel problems.
- the person may have undiagnosed food allergies not found on skin testing but detected by immunoglobulin testing (ELISA, enzyme-linked immunoabsorbent assay) for food antibodies (see Braly, 1992).
- the person may have health concerns resulting from long-standing food refusals such as malnutrition, growth retardation, lethargy, and weight loss.
- if the nausea and vomiting were adverse effects of one or more medications, they stop after those medications are reduced or stopped. Medications that can cause nausea and vomiting include anti-inflammatories, carbamazepine/Tegretol, buspirone/Buspar, and oral contraceptives.

❑ *FACTORS THAT MAY WORSEN THE CONDITION*
- misinterpreting screaming and refusing food as uncooperative behavior and failing to investigate for possible gastrointestinal dysfunction causing pain.
- in a person with reflux esophagitis: wearing tight clothing; eating before going to bed; sleeping on a level bed (instead of one with the head raised six inches); eating large meals; consuming citrus juices, tomatoes, hot spicy foods, caffeine, or alcohol.
- medication that can reduce appetite, e.g., fluoxetine/Prozac, fluvoxamine/Luvox, sertraline/Zoloft, paroxetine/Paxil.

- withdrawal from a neuroleptic, phenytoin/Dilantin, or phenobarb can cause a temporary loss of appetite, sometimes lasting for weeks.

❏ *PERSONS WHO MAY BE AT RISK*

- a person who often shows signs of physical pain and distress associated with consuming food and drink.
- a nonverbal person who has recurrent diarrhea, abnormal formation of stools, excessive stomach gas, and signs of physical pain associated with eating or digestion.
- a person taking a phenothiazine neuroleptic (e.g., chlorpromazine/Largactil, methotrimeprazine/Nozinan, thioridazine/Mellaril) as this can suppress bowel functioning (De Silva et al., 1992).
- a nonverbal person with a known gastrointestinal problem who is fed by people not trained to know the implications of certain gastrointestinal problems or the signs that indicate a condition is worsening.
- a person in the severe or profound range who eats feces as this increases the risk of having intestinal parasites (Huminer et al., 1992). Some intestinal parasites cause abdominal pain, diarrhea, and anorexia.
- a person in frequent contact with cats who shows lethargy, fatigue, anorexia, and fever of unknown origin, i.e., symptoms of cat scratch fever (Flexman et al., 1995; Margileth, 1992).
- a person who has had dietary restrictions starting in childhood, e.g., childhood diabetes mellitus or a PKU (phenylketonuria) diet (Clarke & Yapa, 1991).

❏ *SUGGESTIONS FOR COLLECTING INFORMATION*

- review records to establish the month and year food refusals began. Note health conditions and medications before and after onset of refusing meals. Check for nausea/vomiting associated with refusing meals.
- check for patterns in the type of food or drink refused, common features of preferred foods, times of day meals are refused, and signs of rebound hunger. Review past successful and unsuccessful methods to get the person to eat and drink.
- check for past choking incidents, and identify changes in eating patterns after a serious choking incident.
- use the *Discomfort Scale* (Hurley et al.,1992) before and after meals to assess pain in nonverbal people.
- if there is a history of unexplained persistent gastrointestinal problems, collect information using the *Risk Factors for Casein-Gluten Peptiduria*.
- check for signs of dysphagia, especially with a person in the late stages of a dementia (see ED.13).

❏ *MEDICAL TESTING / SCREENING ED.11*

- rule out possible gastrointestinal problems (e.g., ulcers, gastroenteritis, parasites) underlying the long-standing refusing of meals. Check for a susceptibility to aspirate food and fluids.
- if there is a history of *unexplained* persistent gastrointestinal problems, test for intestinal parasites, yeast overgrowth, and antibodies to common foods especially casein-gluten antibodies in serum or casein-gluten peptides in urine. Test for celiac disease in Down syndrome (George et al., 1996).
- retest stools in persons with a history of parasites as some types of parasites are difficult to eradicate.
- do immunoglobulin (ELISA, enzyme-linked immunoabsorbent assay) testing for allergies to multiple foods (e.g., Baker, 1997; Braly, 1992) and test for toxins associated with food (Baker, 1997).
- rule out swallowing and positioning difficulties with a dysphagia assessment, especially in aged persons and those taking two or more anticonvulsants for seizures.
- review health status and medication history before and after the meal refusals began.
- review medications for appetite-suppressing effects (e.g., fluoxetine) and for causing nausea or vomiting (which diminish the desire for a wide range of foods except perhaps milk and soft foods).
- rule out cat scratch fever if the person has anorexia, lethargy, fatigue, fever of unknown origin, and contact with a cat.

❏ *POSSIBLE BIOCHEMICAL / ANATOMICAL INVOLVEMENT*

- there may be mild paralysis of facial muscles on one or both sides making tongue movement and/or swallowing difficult causing minor aspirations of fluid over the years, leading to an aversion to drinking.
- pain may occur with food intake and digestion in a person with an undiagnosed gastrointestinal problem.

Presenting Concern: **EATING DISTURBANCES**
Dx Category ED.12: ***RECENT ONSET OF REFUSING TO EAT***

❑ *COMMON FORMS*
- the refusing to eat and drink is a recent behavior, perhaps less than a week.
- persons who recently started refusing food put their fingers in their mouth which initiates the gag reflex and results in vomiting. The vomiting occurs after eating, not before meals.
- the person starts to make retching sounds when the food is being prepared or is approaching.

❑ *VARIATIONS*
- vomiting can occur after even small amounts of food are swallowed.
- the person shows signs of physical pain or discomfort and seeks to lie down in the daytime.
- the person is not showing his or her usual level of physical activity.
- a person with very slow gastrointestinal motility may still feel full by the time of the next meal.
- the refusing to eat had a distinct beginning, e.g., after a serious choking incident.
- the person who started refusing food and fluids can no longer open his or her mouth fully (Dallal et al., 1996).
- a person with a history of eating sharp or durable inedibles suddenly stops eating and drinking.

❑ *DISTINGUISHING FEATURES FOR ED.12*
- the refusing to eat is uncharacteristic of the person, not long-standing.
- the person may be showing signs of pain, discomfort, gagging, or irritability that is unusual for him/her.
- if ulcers are present, there may be excessive salivation or gastrointestinal bleeding.
- if bowel impaction is present, no stool or oozing stool is being passed.
- if there is a narrowing or blockage of the esophagus, food is expelled, vomited out, or vehemently refused.
- if the recent refusing to eat or drink is due to an acute medical condition, the person's eating normalizes after the underlying condition is diagnosed and successfully treated.
- a phobic reaction to eating can occur after a life-threatening choking incident, especially if the person is in the severe, moderate, or mild range of intelligence.

❑ *FACTORS THAT MAY WORSEN THE CONDITION*
- caregivers misinterpreting the refusing of food as uncooperative behavior, and failing to investigate for medical causes.
- caregivers viewing refusals to drink as a person's "right to make a choice" in someone with a mental age below 2-3 years--and severe dehydration develops.

❑ *PERSONS WHO MAY BE AT RISK*
- a person who used to be happy and friendly has become moody, moans often, and cries when touched.
- a person who cannot communicate that he or she is feeling full and is unable to accept more food for several hours. These people may be putting their fingers in their mouths.
- a person who has watery stool that could be bypassing a hard fecal mass (encopresis) or has other fecal retention problems.

- a person with a history of swallowing durable objects as these can get lodged in the pharynx or cause an abscess in the esophagus (Dallal et al., 1996).
- a person who recently had a life-threatening choking episode, and thereafter has difficulty swallowing pills and/or solid food.
- a person with dementia who has lost weight, is eating less, and possibly has an increased interest in sweet foods, especially with Alzheimer-type dementia (Morris et al., 1989).
- adults with Down syndrome are at risk for narrowing of the esophagus.
- adults who have untreated phenylketonuria (PKU) or casein/gluten intolerance, and who are on regular diet, may be at risk for gastrointestinal pain, stomach or intestinal ulcers.
- a person who was recently withdrawn from a neuroleptic and is showing neuroleptic withdrawal signs.
- a person who started taking anticholinergic medication such as benztropine/Cogentin to counter neuroleptic side effects.

❏ *SUGGESTIONS FOR COLLECTING INFORMATION*

- use the *Discomfort Scale* (Hurley et al., 1992) before and after meals to assess a nonverbal person for pain. Chart the timing of signs of pain or screaming (if present) in relation to food intake, insufficient bowel evacuation, attempts to defecate, and so on.
- check bowel charts for the timing and characteristics of recent stool. Check if the person takes medication that can suppress bowel function such as phenothiazine-type neuroleptics (e.g., thioridazine/ Mellaril, chlorpromazine/Largactil).
- record a description of vomited material, e.g., completely undigested, partially digested, blood present, and check for excessive salivation, bloody stools, etc. Provide details to the physician.
- check if the person had a choking incident prior to the onset of food refusals (as this may have resulted in a more sensitive swallowing reflex or a phobic reaction to food chunks in the mouth).
- assess for signs of dysphagia in persons in the late stages of a dementia; see ED.13.
- provide the person's temperature, pulse, and respirations per minute to the nurse and/or physician.

❏ *MEDICAL TESTING / SCREENING ED.12*

- check for gastrointestinal problems, e.g., esophageal blockage or narrowing (stenosis), stomach or intestinal ulcers, severe constipation, bowel impaction or ingestion of a foreign body, if refusing food is acute and vomiting occurs.
- if a nonverbal person with sudden refusing to eat has a history of non-food pica (small toys, twigs, stones, rubber gloves, etc.) consider an X-ray, barium swallow, or endoscopic procedure (see Dallal et al., 1996) to check for foreign objects in the gastrointestinal tract or check for an esophageal abscess related to pica.
- rule out dental or mouth pain.
- rule out dysphagia; see considerations in ED.13.
- for persons taking neuroleptics, check for signs of neuroleptic malignant syndrome (NMS) as food refusals, anorexia, malnutrition, and dysphagia can occur with NMS (Tsutsumi et al., 1994); check for signs of neuroleptic-induced catatonia or neuroleptic malignant syndrome such as muscle rigidity, elevated pulse/ blood pressure/ temperature/ creatinine phosphate kinase level, marked confusional state, and cognitive deterioration (Boyd, 1993; Buckley & Hutchinson, 1995; Tsutsumi et al., 1994; Woodbury & Woodbury, 1992). Neuroleptic malignant syndrome can occur without fever (Hynes & Vikar, 1996) and can be due to carbamazepine/Tegretol (O'Griofa & Voris, 1991; van Amelsvoort, 1994).

❏ *POSSIBLE BIOCHEMICAL / ANATOMICAL INVOLVEMENT*

- the person may have pain associated with food intake/digestion, an inability to ingest more food (the esophagus may be very slow to empty), gingivitis, dental caries, or other dental pathology.
- there may be a serious gastrointestinal tract problem, e.g., esophageal stenosis, stomach ulcers, infected polyps in stomach, looping of bowel, colon stricture, megacolon, or impaction due to a foreign object.

Presenting Concern: **EATING DISTURBANCES**
Dx Category ED. 13: *DYSPHAGIA OR SWALLOWING DIFFICULTIES*

Dysphagia is a swallowing disorder in which there are difficulties controlling food and/or fluid in the mouth, chewing, swallowing, and passing food down the esophagus.

❑ *COMMON FORMS*
- the person coughs or chokes after eating foods, liquids, or medications.
- the person eats very slowly or frequently refuses to eat or drink.
- the person refuses to drink liquids, especially thin liquids, but accepts solid food.
- making rattling sounds, having a change in breathing sounds, or having increased chest congestion.
- frequently showing a negative reaction to a spoon or cup near the person's mouth.
- impaired swallowing--that results in aspirating food or fluid into the lungs--risks aspiration pneumonia.
- showing signs of esophageal reflux such as chronic sore throat, oral thrust, crying/agitation 45-60 minutes after a meal, spitting up, burping after a meal, food in nasal secretions, arching the back during or after eating, preferring only one or two dietary textures, and consistently refusing meals.

❑ *VARIATIONS*
- needing to swallow 3-4 times each mouthful and taking a longer time for meals (Sheppard, 1991).
- showing excessive mouth movement during chewing and swallowing.
- the tongue protrudes from the mouth when eating and/or there is a sucking motion during eating.
- having food lodged in one or both cheeks, as this suggests poor tongue-cheek coordination.
- food or fluids fall out of the person's mouth when being fed, a sign of poor lip closure.
- having excessive drooling during and after meals, increased mucous production, or sputum.
- spitting up undigested food.
- the person with swallowing difficulties may have a spiking temperature of unknown cause.
- showing unexplained weight loss.

❑ *DISTINGUISHING FEATURES FOR ED.13*
- there is impaired swallowing, impaired lip closure, difficulty chewing, poor sucking, abnormal or minimal tongue movement, and/or abnormal swallowing reflex activity (O'Sullivan et al., 1990).
- there may be fluid coming from the nose or mouth while eating or drinking.
- there may be coughing or choking after eating or drinking.
- there are gurgling sounds (or the voice has gurgling quality) after eating or drinking.
- dysphagia that appears suddenly in a person with pica may be caused by foreign objects lodged in the pharynx preventing normal swallowing (Dallal et al., 1996). This resolves when the objects are removed.

❑ *FACTORS THAT MAY WORSEN THE CONDITION*
- having fear or anxiety, especially if it is associated with eating and drinking.
- dehydration that leads to an increased concentration of drug levels in the blood.
- hyperextending the person's neck or poor positioning while feeding the person.
- failing to provide regular in-service education on dysphagia to staff who feed people with dysphagia.
- dental practices such as flushing the mouth with water after scaling or chemical irrigation techniques.
- postictal drowsiness or reduced consciousness that affects chewing and swallowing ability.
- deterioration in skeletal and neurological status due to aging or illness (Sheppard, 1991).
- medication that can cause dry mouth (e.g., tricyclic antidepressants, anticholinergics), vomiting (e.g., oral contraceptives), or reduce the level of consciousness (e.g., clobazam/Frisium).
- medication that risks hyponatremia such as carbamazepine/Tegretol (Bezchlibnyk-Butler et al., 1994).
- medication that impairs tongue and swallowing movements.

❑ *PERSONS WHO MAY BE AT RISK*
- a person who is dependent on others to be fed most or all meals.
- a person with slurred or labored speech due to weak muscles, as these muscles are used for swallowing.

- a person who has hemiplegia, a weakened side, or facial paralysis. "Children with cerebral palsy commonly aspirate during feeding" (Jones, 1993, p. 404).
- a person unable to eat in an upright position, e.g., lies on one's back most of the time due to fused hips.
- persons with Williams syndrome are at risk for frequent tongue thrusting and dental abnormalities (Hertzberg et al., 1994).
- someone who frequently coughs, chokes, gags, and/or does throat-clearing after swallowing.
- someone with signs of reflux such as chronic sore throat, oral thrush, crying/agitation 45-60 minutes after a meal, spitting up, burping after meal, arching the back during or after eating, preferring only one or two dietary textures, and consistently refusing meals.
- someone on long-term use of nutritional supplements.
- a person who often ruminates, regurgitates, or vomits.
- a person with a history of dehydration.
- a person with a history of recurrent clinical pneumonia.
- a person with documented aspiration pneumonia and/or frequent upper respiratory infection.
- a person who regularly takes 45 minutes or more at mealtime, or who takes in less than 50% of the meal.
- a person with significant weight loss or who is chronically under an optimal weight.
- a person in the later stages of a dementia.
- a person who has had a stroke or a non-specific decline in health.
- a nonverbal person about whom staff make comments like, "He likes to eat but doesn't like to drink."
- a person taking medication that can reduce level of consciousness, e.g., clobazam.
- a person with neuroleptic malignant syndrome who is showing loss of the gag reflex (Shamash et al., 1994).

❑ *SUGGESTIONS FOR COLLECTING INFORMATION*
- record the daily/weekly frequency of any features that are listed in *COMMON FORMS*, *VARIATIONS*, and *DISTINGUISHING FEATURES*. Report to the physicians, nurses, dentist, and dysphagia specialists any *FACTORS THAT MAY WORSEN THE CONDITION* that apply to this individual.
- monitor weight closely.
- use the *Discomfort Scale* (Hurley et al., 1992) before and after meals to assess pain in nonverbal people.
- provide the person's temperature, pulse, and respirations per minute to the nurse and/or physician.

❑ *MEDICAL TESTING / SCREENING ED.13*
- check for a tendency to aspirate food or fluids and signs of aspiration pneumonia. "Diagnostic tests, including fiberoptic endoscopy, video fluroscopic swallowing study and upper gastrointestinal series, and tests of esophageal pH, are difficult to perform on this population but may be essential to determine the course of treatment to maintain health." (Sheppard, 1991, p. 84).
- request a dysphagia assessment by an occupational therapist, speech/language pathologist, or dietitian who has training in dysphagia. "Mealtime respiratory distress and chronic lung disease (chronic infiltrates on chest radiographs, recurrent pneumonias, pulmonary fibrosis, chronic obstructive pulmonary disease, bronchiectasis, asthma) should prompt consideration of dysphagia." (Tyler & Bourquet, 1997, p. 491).
- check for foreign objects blocking swallowing movements in nonverbal persons with a history of pica as this can cause the sudden onset of dysphagia (Dallal et al., 1996).
- review medications for ones that can cause vomiting, impair oral motor movements, or reduce level of consciousness (e.g., valproate can impair swallowing in persons with Down syndrome in the late stage of dementia, clobazam has reduced consciousness to the point of coma in some nonambulatory people with mental retardation.)
- rule out decreased salivation from anticholinergic effects of certain medications, as a contributing factor.

❑ *POSSIBLE BIOCHEMICAL / ANATOMICAL INVOLVEMENT*
- dysphagia reflects impaired motor control of the muscles involved in swallowing, chewing, sucking, closing the lips, and/or abnormal reflex activity in the oral area.

Chapter VI

DEMENTIA

Presenting Concern: **DEMENTIA**

Dx Category DM.1: *HYPOTHYROIDISM PRESENTING AS DEMENTIA*

❑ *COMMON FORMS*

Hypothyroidism can cause deterioration in cognitive functioning.

- the person showed a gradual decline in memory and comprehension, not an abrupt decline (Friedman et al., 1989; Thase, 1982).
- the person started occasionally to forget familiar routines, misplace valued objects, and have lapses in comprehension and usual awareness of time.
- the person is more forgetful when tired.
- the person who shows cognitive deterioration may also show signs of hypothyroidism such as weight gain or weight fluctuations, extra sensitivity to the cold, dry skin and hair, excessive sleepiness, extreme muscular sluggishness, marked lethargy, and depression.
- if the cognitive deterioration is due to hypothyroidism, the deterioration might progress to meet the criteria for early or middle stages of dementia, but it does not progress to fit the criteria for late stage dementia or extended care status.

Note: *COMMON FORMS* for dementia in one Diagnostic Category may be similar to *COMMON FORMS* for dementia in other Diagnostic Categories.

❑ *VARIATIONS*

- the person shows increased tiredness and/or an increasing need for sleep about the same time as the onset of memory lapses.
- the person who is declining cognitively has become increasingly reluctant to do activities that require physical exertion, even favorite activities.
- the person may show features of depression in addition to hypothyroidism (Denicoff et al., 1990; Friedman et al., 1989).

❑ *DISTINGUISHING FEATURES FOR DM.1*

- blood test results confirm hypothyroidism or insufficient dosing of supplemental thyroxin.
- in persons with Down syndrome who have hypothyroidism, there may be no overt signs of the condition such as weight gain, tiredness, lethargy, or sensitivity to cold temperatures (Korsager et al., 1978, Mani 1988).
- recovery of previous cognitive and social functioning is evident several weeks after starting thyroxin supplement (McCreary et al., 1993; Thase, 1982).

❑ *FACTORS THAT MAY WORSEN THE CONDITION*

- failing to check blood level of thyroxin at regular intervals (1-2 times a year) in a person taking thyroxin because that person is very resistant to giving a blood sample (i.e., fearful of needles).
- the "bioavailability" of thyroxin medication is reduced when taken with food in the stomach.
- neuroleptics can lower serum thyroxin levels.
- taking anticonvulsive medication (Corbett et al., 1985; Devinsky, 1995; Gupta et al., 1992).
- taking lithium alone or taking it with a medication that potentiates lithium, e.g., carbamazepine/Tegretol as this can interfere with thyroid function.

❏ *PERSONS WHO MAY BE AT RISK*
- persons over age 60-65.
- a person who also showed onset of signs of depression (e.g., lethargy, social withdrawal, loss of daily living skills, change in appetite, increasing need for sleep) about the same time as the decline in memory and comprehension.
- a person with a family history of thyroid dysfunction.
- adults with Down syndrome are at increased risk for hypothyroidism (Dinani & Carpenter, 1990; Friedman et al., 1989) and the risk is even higher if they have Alzheimer disease (Lai & Williams, 1989).
- someone for whom testing thyroid function is not easy because the person is very resistant to giving a blood sample (i.e., fearful of needles).
- someone who has become extra sensitive to cold temperatures and may be gaining weight easily.
- someone whose skin became scaly and whose hair was dry and easily falling out.

❏ *SUGGESTIONS FOR COLLECTING INFORMATION*
- check family history for thyroid disorders and dementia.
- review the history to determine if the onset of cognitive decline occurred in the same overall period as changes in sleep, appetite, weight, mood, or medication.
- rule out depression using instruments or criteria appropriate for this population (e.g., Cooper & Collacott, 1994; Sovner, 1986). Use the *Checklist of Observable Signs of Depression.**
- assess for dementia using instruments appropriate for developmentally disabled people. An instrument called the "Dementia Scale For Down Syndrome" (Gedye, 1995) was designed for tracking recovery--or progressive decline--in persons with mental retardation who show signs of cognitive deterioration. With persons in the mild or moderate range of intelligence, also use tests of cognitive functioning that require direct performance (see Alyward et al., 1997; Devenny et al., 1996).

 * *A chart or checklist listed in italics in this section can be found in the Appendix.*

❏ *MEDICAL TESTING / SCREENING DM.1*
- do thyroid function tests and repeat as necessary if borderline results are obtained. Consider the possible effects of anticonvulsants on thyroid function (Gupta et al., 1992; Isojarvi et al., 1992; Tanaka et al., 1987).
- test the TSH (thyroid stimulating hormone) level in persons with Down syndrome because they can have hypothyroidism yet show a normal T_4 level (Dinani & Carpenter, 1990).
- retest the blood level of thyroxin in a person on thyroxin supplementation to ensure adequate dosing.
- test serum iron, ferritin, and hemoglobin levels. Elevated cholesterol level is a supplementary blood test for investigating thyroid function.
- rule out an underlying medical condition such as a systemic bacterial, fungal or viral infection, or other causes of delirium.
- review the type and timing of medication that might produce cognitive impairment, drowsiness, and/or sedation.
- hypothyroidism can mimic dementia or co-exist with Alzheimer-type dementia in adults with mental retardation (McCreary et al., 1993).

❏ *POSSIBLE BIOCHEMICAL / ANATOMICAL INVOLVEMENT*
- the blood levels of thyroxin might be too low because of autoimmune thyroiditis or other thyroid disorder (e.g., Percy et al., 1990).
- the dose of thyroxin supplement might be too low in persons already receiving treatment for hypo-thyroidism.
- lithium decreases iodine uptake by the thyroid and thereby can affect thyroid functioning.

❑ *COMMON FORMS*

- the onset of lapses in memory and comprehension was accompanied by several of the following: loss of self-help skills, urinary incontinence, apathy, loss of interest in favorite activities, uncooperativeness, irritability, and anger (Burt et al., 1992; Lowry, 1995).
- the person started occasionally to forget familiar routines, have lapses in comprehension, have decreased alertness and awareness, and/or speak less around the same time as becoming more irritable and more reluctant to engage in familiar social or work activities.
- if verbal, the person talks often about funerals, death, others dying, or things associated with death.
- social and functional skills may be lost early in the decline (Adlin, 1993).

❑ *VARIATIONS*

- the lapses in memory and comprehension are observed in one setting but absent in another setting (e.g., evident at the workplace but not at home; evident at the group home but not weekend visits with family).
- a "vacation cure" is observed, i.e., the person showing lapses in memory and comprehension is "back to his usual self" in terms of memory, language, and comprehension when on vacation for a week in an unfamiliar place. By contrast, a person with a progressive dementia would be likely to worsen cognitively, not improve, with the increased demand on new learning in a completely new setting.

❑ *DISTINGUISHING FEATURES FOR DM.2*

- the person shows several of the following signs of depression: sadness; spontaneous crying; reduced interest in activities; social withdrawal; reduced speech or slow speech; decreased energy; loss of self-care skills; impaired concentration; psychomotor retardation; weight loss or appetite change; increased anger or aggression (Burt et al., 1992; Cooper & Collacott, 1994; Lowry 1995; Pary et al., 1996; Prasher & Hall, 1996; Warren et al., 1989). Suicidal thought or action is rare.
- a depressed person may have difficulty with "learning processes and short-term memory (i.e., arousal and attentional processes), whereas long-term memory and retentional processes seem to be intact." (Niederehe, 1986, p. 227).
- other causes of cognitive decline have been be ruled out, e.g., hypothyroidism, folate deficiency, vascular accidents, infection, medication-induced cognitive decline, and so on.
- the time when depressive features started may be closely linked to a distressing life event (Adlin, 1993).
- if the cognitive decline is due to depression, recovery of lost cognitive skills follows spontaneous recovery from the depression or effective treatment for the depression (e.g., grief work, antidepressant medication, deteriorating vision is diagnosed and corrected, a protracted medical condition is corrected).
- if the cognitive decline is due to depression, full recovery to the previous level of cognitive functioning follows successful treatment for depression or a spontaneous recovery from depression.
- if the cognitive decline is due an underlying progressive dementia in a person who is also depressed, then treating the depression may result in modest improvement but not a full recovery of cognitive losses.

❑ *FACTORS THAT MAY WORSEN THE CONDITION*

- failing to meet the person's emotional and/or bereavement needs by not providing grief counseling or not adapting the counseling to the person's mental level (e.g., photos, mementos, visits to the cemetery, counseling picture books (Hollins, 1995), and art therapy techniques can be tried with nonverbal people).
- caregivers misinterpreting frequent crying as attention-seeking and "ignoring it" as a behavioral strategy.
- insomnia caused by sleep apnea, medication, a noisy sleep environment, or poor sleep hygiene practices.
- having undetected hypothyroidism around the same time as a reactive depression.
- acute medical illness can cause delirium (Raskind & Risse, 1986).

- misdiagnosing a depressed person as having manic-depression (bipolar disorder) and using lithium (that can worsen depression, Estroff & Gold, 1986), carbamazepine/Tegretol, or valproic acid/Depakene instead of an antidepressant.
- using medication that may cause depression such as benzodiazepines, beta blockers (especially propanolol/Inderal), cimetidine/Tagamet, ranitidine/Zantac, or oral contraceptives (Lowenthal & Nadeau, 1991; Wise & Taylor, 1990). "The use of a benzodiazepine in a depressed patient or in a patient with a mild or subclinical dementia may cause a worsening of the depression or dementia and occasionally a florid delirium." (Thompson et al., 1983, p. 136). Benzodiazepines in elderly depressed patients can worsen the depression (Thompson et al., 1983).

❑ *PERSONS WHO MAY BE AT RISK*
- adults with Down syndrome have an greater risk for depression than other adults with mental retardation (Collacott et al., 1992). A person with Down syndrome who has a progressive Alzheimer-type dementia may also show depression (McCreary et al., 1993).
- someone who had a personal loss (e.g., a close caregiver, a close relative, a familiar home, or a major decline in vision, hearing or health) because these losses can cause a depressive reaction.
- persons who have recently moved and have lost caregivers as this can also mean loss of familiar programming and lack of consistency in behavioral programming at both residential and work settings. Such changes may be more stressful to people less able to understand the changes, i.e., those in the severe and profound range of intelligence.
- a person with prior depressive episodes or a family history of depression or manic-depressive episodes.
- a person under stress for a protracted period or who shows signs of post-traumatic stress disorder.
- a person who has repeated contact (even if infrequent) with people or places associated with past trauma.

❑ *SUGGESTIONS FOR COLLECTING INFORMATION*
- assess for depression using instruments or criteria appropriate for this population (Cooper & Collacott, 1994; Prasher & Hall, 1996; Sovner, 1986). Use the *Checklist of Observable Signs of Depression.*
- identify major life stressors, e.g., personal loss, relocation, decline in health, inordinate stress.
- for those able to read and label different emotional states, the "Children's Depression Inventory"(Kovacs, 1985) has been used to screen depression in developmentally disabled people (Benavidez & Matson, 1993; Meins, 1993).
- check family history for depression and dementia.
- monitor weight, appetite increases or decreases, and changes in eating patterns (e.g., pica).
- assess for dementia using instruments appropriate for developmentally disabled people. An instrument called the "Dementia Scale For Down Syndrome" (Gedye, 1995) was designed for tracking recovery, progression, and absence of dementia in persons with mental retardation suspected of cognitive decline.

❑ *MEDICAL TESTING / SCREENING DM.2*
- rule out medical conditions associated with depression, e.g., hypothyroidism, abnormally low serum iron/hemoglobin, vitamin B_{12} and folate deficiency (Levitt & Joffe, 1993; Mischoulon, 1996), anemia, congestive heart failure, electrolyte abnormalities, hepatitis, diabetes mellitus (Wise & Taylor, 1990).
- review each medication for ones listing depression as a possible adverse effect; e.g., anticonvulsants, barbiturates, oral contraceptives, propranolol, cimetidine, ranitidine (Wise & Taylor, 1990).
- screen for deterioration in vision or hearing as this is a major loss that can cause a secondary depression.

❑ *POSSIBLE BIOCHEMICAL / ANATOMICAL INVOLVEMENT*
- low central serotonin and/or low noradrenalin in depressed patients can adversely affect short term memory, attention, and concentration. Plasma tryptophan (a serotonin precursor) can be significantly lower in depressed people compared to controls (Lucca et al.,1992).
- free thyroxin can be low in persons with depression (Dorn et al., 1996).
- hippocampal atrophy has been found in adults with recurrent major depression (Sheline et al., 1991).

Presenting Concern: **DEMENTIA**
Dx Category   DM.3:   *FOLATE OR VITAMIN B$_{12}$ DEFICIENCY*

___

❑ *COMMON FORMS*
- symptoms of folate (folic acid) deficiency include poor growth, graying hair, tongue inflammation, gastrointestinal disturbances, irritability, forgetfulness, and mental slowness. It can also cause red blood cell anemia and lesions at the corners of the mouth called cheiloses (Dunne, 1990, p. 39)
- "Symptoms of vitamin B$_{12}$ deficiency may take 5 or 6 years to appear" (Dunne, 1990, p. 32). Initial changes include "soreness and weakness in the legs and arms, diminished reflex response and sensory perception, difficulty walking and speaking (stammering), and jerking of the limbs." (Dunne, 1990, p.32). Further signs include sore mouth, numbness or stiffness, a feeling of deadness, shooting pains, pins-and-needles, hot-and-cold sensations, memory defect, mental slowness, nervousness, neuritis, unpleasant body odor, menstrual disturbances, and difficulty walking (Dunne, 1990).

___

❑ *VARIATIONS*
- the person may fit the criteria for dementia if folate deficiency is present (Boetz et al., 1982).
- with vitamin B$_{12}$ deficiency, the decline in memory may have started around the time other symptoms began, i.e., depression, fear, anxiety, psychosis, paranoia, or delirium (Hector & Burton, 1988).
- the person may start to have memory lapses but might not fit the full criteria for dementia if the decline is due to vitamin B$_{12}$ deficiency (Hector & Burton, 1988).

___

❑ *DISTINGUISHING FEATURES FOR DM.3*
- the person has borderline or abnormally low blood levels of folate or vitamin B$_{12}$.
- the person shows a marked recovery in cognitive and adaptive functioning after folate supplementation and/or vitamin B$_{12}$ supplementation (Gross et al., 1986; Hector & Burton, 1988).
- a person with dementia due to another cause, such as Alzheimer dementia, will not show recovery of memory and cognitive functioning with vitamin B$_{12}$ therapy (Hector & Burton, 1988).
- the person shows a marked recovery in cognitive functioning in the months after anticonvulsive medication is discontinued and no longer interferes with the absorption of folate.
- if the vitamin B$_{12}$ deficiency is caused by excessive bacteria in the stomach or intestines (Dunne, 1990), identifying and treating the condition causing the excessive bacteria and treating the vitamin B$_{12}$ deficiency should result in improvement.

___

❑ *FACTORS THAT MAY WORSEN THE CONDITION*
- having a severe sleep disturbance that causes daytime drowsiness.
- overcooking food as folic acid is easily destroyed by cooking.
- alcohol and anticonvulsants are antagonists for folate (Dunne, 1990).
- oral contraceptives are antagonists for folate and vitamin B$_{12}$ (Dunne, 1990).
- phenytoin/Dilantin is an antagonist for vitamin B$_{12}$ (Dunne, 1990).
- adding another sedating medication.

❑ *PERSONS WHO MAY BE AT RISK*
- a person with frequent vomiting over a long period.
- a person with mental retardation who has chewing and swallowing difficulties may be at risk for folate deficiency (Cole et al., 1985).
- a person with an endogenous depression or schizophrenia may be at risk for folate deficiency (Carney, 1990).
- someone taking medication known to reduce folate concentration such as anticonvulsants (Deb et al., 1987; Goggin et al., 1987), especially phenytoin/Dilantin or phenobarbital (Boetz & Young, 1991; Trimble, 1988).
- a woman taking oral contraceptives may be at risk for folate deficiency (Lambie & Johnson, 1985).
- a person with excessive bacteria in the stomach and intestines is at risk for vitamin B_{12} deficiency (Dunne, 1990).
- a person taking a phenothiazine neuroleptic (e.g., thioridazine/Mellaril), benzodiazepine, tricyclic antidepressant, monoamine oxidase inhibitor, or barbiturate as these medications have been linked to low vitamin B_{12} (Carney, 1990).
- a person with a history of anemia may have vitamin B_{12} deficiency.

❑ *SUGGESTIONS FOR COLLECTING INFORMATION*
- assess for dementia using instruments appropriate for developmentally disabled people. An instrument called the "Dementia Scale For Down Syndrome" (Gedye, 1995) was designed for tracking recovery--or progressive decline--in persons with mental retardation who show signs of cognitive deterioration.
- record the month and year when features that are listed in *COMMON FORMS, VARIATIONS,* and *DISTINGUISHING FEATURES* were first noticed. Report these to the physician involved and any *FACTORS THAT MAY WORSEN THE CONDITION* that apply to this individual.
- rule out depression as a contributing factor using instruments or criteria appropriate for this population (e.g., Cooper & Collacott, 1994; Sovner, 1986). Use the *Checklist of Observable Signs of Depression.*

❑ *MEDICAL TESTING / SCREENING DM.3*
- test red blood cell folate, serum folate, vitamin B_{12} (cobalamin) level, and thyroid hormones (Levitt & Joffe, 1993; Mischoulon, 1996). "Some patients with neuropsychiatric abnormalities develop cobalamin tissue deficiency that can be detected by elevated serum homocysteine and methylmalonic acid levels despite normal serum vitamin B_{12} level without macrocytic anemia. Serum cobalamin testing is neither sensitive nor specific in the low normal range for cobalamin deficiency." (Delva, 1997, p. 917). Therefore testing serum homocysteine and methylmalonic acid levels is recommended for detecting vitamin B_{12} deficiency (also see Carmel et al., 1995).
- screen for vitamin B_{12} deficiency with or without pernicious anemia (Burns & Jacoby, 1988; Gross et al., 1986). Test for pernicious anemia, megaloblastic anemia, Shilling test, and macrocytosis.
- consider testing for vitamin B_6 deficiency as B_6 is a co-factor in maintaining noradrenaline and serotonin levels.
- if the person has unexplained persistent gastrointestinal symptoms, check for intestinal parasites and other causes of "excessive bacteria in the stomach and intestines" which can cause malabsorption of vitamins.

❑ *POSSIBLE BIOCHEMICAL / ANATOMICAL INVOLVEMENT*
- Folate is important in the synthesis of norepinephrine, dopamine, and serotonin (Boetz et al., 1982). These neurotransmitters are important modulators of attention and memory functions (Sommer & Wolkowitz, 1988). Folate affects the turnover of serotonin and dopamine (Godfrey et al., 1990) and folate deficiency can cause low brain serotonin (Young, 1991).
- low vitamin B_{12} is related to high activity of platelet MAO (monoamine oxidase) in patients with dementia (Regland et al., 1988). "...vitamin B_{12} may be involved in modulating mood in depression" (Levitt & Joffe, 1991).

❏ *COMMON FORMS*

- the person showed a gradual cognitive decline, not an abrupt decline.
- the person began to show on occasion many of the following: misplacing valued objects, getting lost in familiar settings, speaking slower or slurring words, reduced alertness/awareness, crying easily, loss of balance at times, droopy eyelids, and being unwilling to do familiar social/work activities.

❏ *VARIATIONS*

- the onset of lapses in memory or comprehension was accompanied by the onset of physical symptoms such as a skin rash, dizziness, unsteadiness, nausea, or reduced appetite.
- the person may still remember how to do their familiar daily routines but have memory lapses for entire moments of 1-5 minutes. For example, the person might forget having a brief conversation, forget having taken pills ten minutes earlier, or forget that a phone call occurred an hour earlier.

❏ *DISTINGUISHING FEATURES FOR DM.4*

- the person is taking one or more anticonvulsive medications.
- in a person whose blood test confirms a toxic level of anticonvulsant(s), the toxicity was probably present for several months, or much longer in some cases if the drug level has not been tested in years. In prolonged cases of toxicity, (1) the person's physical symptoms (rash, dizziness, etc.) overlapped in time with the start of cognitive decline, (2) the drug blood level was unknown during the initial months of the cognitive decline (i.e., had not been tested for many months or even years), and (c) improvement in both physical and cognitive symptoms occurred when the toxicity was corrected.
- in a person with frequent "absence status epilepticus," the criteria for dementia might not be met but the memory and comprehension continue to decline until good control is attained over the seizures.
- the person shows a marked recovery in cognitive functioning in the weeks or months following a reduction in anticonvulsive medication or withdrawal of anticonvulsant medication.
- the person shows partial recovery in cognitive functioning in the weeks following withdrawal of one anticonvulsant, but the gains are lost soon after another anticonvulsant is added or increased.
- other causes of cognitive deterioration have been ruled out, e.g., folate deficiency, hypothyroidism, depression, infections, head injury, vascular accidents, a severe sleep disorder, and so on.

❏ *FACTORS THAT MAY WORSEN THE CONDITION*

- a systemic infection.
- untreated hypothyroidism.
- slower clearance of medication by the liver due to old age (Aman, 1990; Schmucker, 1985; Thomson et al., 1983) or by the kidneys in older people (Adlin, 1993; Anderson & Polister, 1993).
- medication that lowers the seizure threshold (e.g., neuroleptics), leading to higher anticonvulsant doses.
- medication that can in some patients *cause the onset* of absence seizures, myoclonus, or other types of nonconvulsive seizures, e.g., carbamazepine (Aguglia et al., 1987; Dhuna et al., 1991; Horn et al., 1986; Johnsen et al., 1984; Kurlan et al., 1989; Shields et al., 1983; Snead & Hosey, 1985).
- medication that can in some patients worsen the frequency and duration of pre-existing seizures, e.g., carbamazepine (Horn et al., 1986; Pellock, 1987; Sachdeo & Chokroverty, 1985; Snead & Hosey, 1985).
- increasing the dose of anticonvulsants (e.g., phenobarbital, phenytoin/Dilantin, valproic acid/Depakene) or other medication that sedates or impairs cognitive functioning.

❏ *PERSONS WHO MAY BE AT RISK*

- a person who has seizures that have been difficult to control with medication in recent years.
- a person who has absence seizures, 2 or more other types of seizures, and takes multiple anticonvulsants.
- a person who has had no seizures in 3-5 years and no reduction in anticonvulsants in several years.

- a person who has had 6 or more changes in dose and type of anticonvulsant medication in the past year.
- a person taking phenobarbital and another anticonvulsant (Corbett et al., 1985; Meador et al., 1995).
- someone showing confusion, agitation, depression, hyperactivity, and/or psychosis while taking vigabatrin/Sabril (Sander et al., 1991).
- being over age 40 and taking anticonvulsants for many years, perhaps decades.
- a person with a history of toxic levels of anticonvulsants in recent years.
- a person who has generalized seizures that sometimes develop into status epilepticus and require hospitalization (and possibly the use of a general anaesthetic) in order to restore consciousness.
- a person declining cognitively who has not had anticonvulsant blood levels tested in 1-2 years or longer.

❑ SUGGESTIONS FOR COLLECTING INFORMATION
- assess for dementia using instruments appropriate for developmentally disabled people. An instrument called the "Dementia Scale For Down Syndrome" (Gedye, 1995) was designed for tracking recovery--or progressive decline--in persons with mental retardation who show signs of cognitive deterioration. With persons in the mild or moderate range of intelligence, also use more selective tests of cognitive functioning that require direct performance (see Aylward et al., 1997; Devenny et al., 1996).
- review the history to determine if the cognitive decline started around the same time as physical symptoms started (e.g., skin rash, dizziness, unsteadiness, nausea, reduced appetite, slurred speech) which could be adverse effects of anticonvulsant medication.
- monitor cognitive improvement or worsening relative to each medication change.
- monitor for partial cognitive recovery such as improvement in word-finding, comprehension, and/or clarity of speech if the anticonvulsant valproic acid is discontinued in a person with Down syndrome.
- assess for depression using instruments or criteria appropriate for this population (e.g., Cooper & Collacott, 1994; Sovner, 1986). Use the *Checklist of Observable Signs of Depression*.

❑ MEDICAL TESTING / SCREENING DM.4
- check the blood level of each medication and rule out drug toxicity.
- test folate level and thyroid function as anticonvulsants can adversely affect these (Gupta et al., 1992; Tanaka et al., 1987).
- test serum sodium for possible hyponatremia (which can resemble dementia) in those on carbamazepine.
- review each medication for ones that list possible skin rash, dizziness, unsteadiness, nausea, or other physical symptoms that accompanied the person's cognitive decline.
- review medications and doses for possible increased drowsiness without greater seizure control.
- review the person's other medications for risk of additional cognitive impairment such as anti-cholinergics, antihypertensives, lithium, neuroleptics, sedative hypnotics agents (Jain, 1996, p. 83).
- rule out other causes of gradual cognitive decline (severe sleep disorder, systemic infection, head injury).
- consider requesting a neurological investigation to evaluate factors that may be worsening the epilepsy, or a neurological review if the person has had no generalized seizures in 3-5 years or longer.

❑ POSSIBLE BIOCHEMICAL / ANATOMICAL INVOLVEMENT
- anticonvulsants can, in varying degrees, "impair attention, concentration, memory, mental speed or processing, or motor speed. Possible mechanisms of impaired mental function include neuronal damage, or disturbance of folic acid, monoamine or hormonal metabolism." (Reynolds & Trimble, 1985, p. 570).
- with valproic acid, dementia could result from a direct toxic effect on the CNS or an indirect effect mediated by valproic acid-induced hyperammonemia (Jain, 1996, p. 84; Zaret & Cohen, 1986).
- the cognitive deterioration could be due to the toxic level of one or more anticonvulsants.
- brief absence seizures can interfere mid-sentence and impair comprehension. But if they are recognized, caregivers can repeat what they said once the person returns to full consciousness. Unrecognized absence status epilepticus, especially in an adult with a mental age under 4-5 years, can look like the person is "ignoring" caregivers, being uncooperative, and unmotivated.
- long-term use of three or more anticonvulsants, with numerous dosage and medication changes per year, could mean that the cognitive-impairing effects combined with multiple withdrawals, and /or dosage changes contributed to the cognitive deterioration.

Presenting Concern: **DEMENTIA**
Dx Category DM.5: *NEUROLEPTIC-INDUCED COGNITIVE DECLINE*

❑ *COMMON FORMS*

- a person on neuroleptic medication showed a gradual and steady decline in his or her usual cognitive functioning within a 3-6 month period.
- a person on neuroleptic medication started to show most or all of the following within 6 months or less: forgetting familiar routines, misplacing valued objects, having lapses in comprehension, being less alert and aware, being less willing to do familiar social/work activities, being unusually irritable, becoming slow and awkward in moving, and being occasionally incontinent of urine and/or feces.

❑ *VARIATIONS*

- a person on neuroleptic medication, who formerly was independent in self-care skills, has been losing language skills, becoming almost mute, or showing increased muscle rigidity and possibly catatonic episodes.
- urinary incontinence and/or fecal incontinence might have started in this person a few months *before* the cognitive decline was noticed, instead of cognitive decline preceding onset of incontinence.

❑ *DISTINGUISHING FEATURES FOR DM.5*

- the person has been taking neuroleptic medication (antipsychotics) for one month or longer, e.g., chlorpromazine/Largactil/Thorazine, haloperidol/Haldol, trifluoperazine/Stelazine, thioridazine/Mellaril.
- signs of cognitive recovery are evident in the first weeks following the taper and withdrawal of neuroleptic medication.
- the person shows full recovery of cognitive losses in the months following taper and withdrawal of neuroleptic medication (Gedye, 1998; Larson et al., 1987; Learoyd, 1972).
- other causes of cognitive deterioration have been ruled out, e.g., hypothyroidism, depression, infections, head injury, vascular accidents, severe sleep disorder, and so on.

❑ *FACTORS THAT MAY WORSEN THE CONDITION*

- slower clearance of medication by the liver due to old age (Aman, 1990; Schmucker, 1985; Thomson et al., 1983) or by the kidneys in older people (Adlin, 1993; Anderson & Polister, 1993).
- increasing the neuroleptic dose.
- adding another sedating medication.
- adding a short-acting benzodiazepine such as triazolam/Halcion.
- concurrent use of a benzodiazepine, either daily use or frequent use "as needed" (p.r.n.).
- adding a medication with anticholinergic properties (e.g., chlomipramine/Anafranil, amitriptyline/ Elavil).
- tapering neuroleptic medication then increasing it, or withdrawing a neuroleptic then reintroducing it.

❏ *PERSONS WHO MAY BE AT RISK*

- a person who had been on a neuroleptic for many years and the dose was changed in the 6 months prior to starting to deteriorate cognitively (Gedye, 1998).
- a person whose neuroleptic medication was being tapered then the dose was increased, or whose neuroleptic had been tapered and discontinued for a few months, then reintroduced.
- someone over age 50 who has been taking neuroleptics for many years (Learoyd, 1972).
- someone with a previous episode of neuroleptic-induced catatonia or neuroleptic malignant syndrome (Welch, 1993), that is, a previous severe adverse reaction to neuroleptic medication.

❏ *SUGGESTIONS FOR COLLECTING INFORMATION*

- assess for dementia using instruments appropriate for developmentally disabled people. An instrument called the "Dementia Scale For Down Syndrome" (Gedye, 1995) was designed for tracking recovery--or progressive decline--in persons with mental retardation who show signs of cognitive deterioration. With persons in the mild or moderate range of intelligence, also use more selective tests of cognitive functioning that require direct performance (see Aylward et al., 1997; Devenny et al., 1996).
- review the history to determine if the onset of cognitive decline occurred in the same overall period as changes such as incontinence, loss of self-care skills, or social withdrawal (possible signs of neuroleptic-induced catatonia).
- identify the approximate month when each sign of decline began, and list the date for each change in medication dose.
- assess for depression using instruments or criteria appropriate for this population (e.g., Cooper & Collacott, 1994; Sovner, 1986). Use the *Checklist of Observable Signs of Depression*.

❏ *MEDICAL TESTING / SCREENING DM.5*

- review the onset of cognitive and adaptive decline relative to the introduction of a neuroleptic, dose changes in a neuroleptic, or its re-introduction after a withdrawal.
- review the person's other medication(s) to see if cognitive impairment or CNS (central nervous system) depression is listed as a possible adverse effect.
- checking haloperidol serum levels may be useful, but serum levels for other neuroleptics are either unreliable *or* the presence of numerous metabolic breakdown products (e.g., some with neuroleptic effects) makes interpretation of the results difficult (McCreary, 1996).
- check for signs suggesting the spectrum of neuroleptic-induced catatonia and neuroleptic malignant syndrome (NMS) such as muscle rigidity, elevated temperature, elevated pulse, elevated blood pressure, elevated creatinine phosphate kinase level, marked confusional state, and cognitive deterioration (Boyd, 1993; Buckley & Hutchinson, 1995; Tsutsumi et al., 1994; Woodbury & Woodbury, 1992). NMS can occur without fever (Bambrick & Wilson, 1992; Hynes & Vickar, 1996) and can sometimes be caused by carbamazepine/Tegretol (O'Griofa & Voris, 1991; van Amelsvoort, 1994).

❏ *POSSIBLE BIOCHEMICAL / ANATOMICAL INVOLVEMENT*

- neuroleptics adversely affect cholinergic neurotransmission (Jain, 1996, p. 82) which is involved in the ability to concentrate, attend, and remember.

Presenting Concern: **DEMENTIA**
Dx Category DM.6: *OTHER MEDICATION-INDUCED DEMENTIA*

❑ *COMMON FORMS*

- a person on medication showed a gradual decline in memory and comprehension, not an abrupt decline.
- a person taking benzodiazepines daily steadily deteriorated cognitively.

❑ *VARIATIONS*

- the person showed a gradual decline in cognitive functioning that worsened after a third or fourth medication was added.

❑ *DISTINGUISHING FEATURES FOR DM.6*

- the person has been taking two or more medications that can impair cognitive functioning.
- the person shows marked recovery in cognitive functioning in the weeks and months following the reduction and withdrawal of one or more medications (Larson et al., 1987; Learoyd, 1972; Varney et al., 1984).
- other causes of cognitive deterioration have been ruled out, e.g., folate deficiency, vitamin B_{12} deficiency, hypothyroidism, depression, infections, head injury, vascular accidents, a severe sleep disorder, and so on.

❑ *FACTORS THAT MAY WORSEN THE CONDITION*

- slower clearance of medication by the liver due to old age (Aman, 1990; Schmucker, 1985; Thomson et al., 1983) or by the kidneys in older people (Adlin, 1993; Anderson & Polister, 1993).
- increasing the dose of the offending medication(s).
- adding another sedating medication such as the benzodiazepine lorazepam/Ativan (Preston et al., 1989). "All benzodiazepines, given in repeated doses, will accumulate to some degree and may produce excessive sedation." (Thompson et al., 1983, p. 136).
- "...the addition of any medication to an already complicated medication regimen, especially that of an elderly patient, carries with it the potential risk of adversely affecting cognition in the patient. This is particularly worrisome when antidepressant or antipsychotic medications with established anticholin-ergic effects are prescribed." (Tune et al., 1992, p. 1394).

❑ *PERSONS WHO MAY BE AT RISK*

- a person taking two or more medications that have the potential to impair cognitive functioning.
- a person over age 60 who takes three or more medications.
- a person over age 60 who takes antihistamine medication (Thompson et al., 1983).
- a person showing behavioral and/or cognitive deterioration after starting to take corticosteroids (Varney et al., 1984).

❑ SUGGESTIONS FOR COLLECTING INFORMATION

- review the history to determine if the onset of cognitive decline was accompanied by the development of physical symptoms or poor health.
- review the person's medication history for recent changes, especially ones preceding cognitive decline.
- assess for dementia using instruments appropriate for developmentally disabled people. An instrument called the "Dementia Scale For Down Syndrome" (Gedye, 1995) was designed for tracking recovery--or progressive decline--in persons with mental retardation who show signs of cognitive deterioration. With persons in the mild or moderate range of intelligence, also use more selective tests of cognitive functioning that require direct performance (see Aylward et al., 1997; Devenny et al., 1996).
- screen for depression using criteria appropriate for developmentally disabled people (Cooper & Collacott, 1994; Sovner, 1986). Use the *Checklist of Observable Signs of Depression*.

❑ MEDICAL TESTING / SCREENING DM.6

- check the blood level of each medication to rule out drug toxicity (Lowenthal & Nadeau, 1991).
- carefully examine the person at regular intervals for signs of anticholinergic toxicity (Tune et al., 1992).
- "...appropriate laboratory testing should be carried out before treatment to provide a baseline for any changes which occur subsequent to pharmacotherapy." (Aman, 1990, p. 8).
- rule out folate deficiency, thyroid dysfunction, and other causes of gradual cognitive decline such as a severe sleep disorder or a systemic infection.
- review each medication for possible adverse effects that could account for physical symptoms that accompanied the person's cognitive decline. Consider possible drug combinations and drug interactions.
- review each medication for atropine effects and anticholinergic effects which might be additive.
- "The extent and severity of drug side effects can be minimized by proper attention to a drug's half life, dosage, and frequency of administration." (Thompson et al., 1983, p. 136).

❑ POSSIBLE BIOCHEMICAL / ANATOMICAL INVOLVEMENT

- medication-induced cognitive decline could be due to a toxic level of one or more medications.
- medication-induced cognitive decline could be due to adverse interactions between medications (Thompson et al., 1983).
- anticholinergic toxicity "could result from complicated medication regimens in which several medications, some or all of which have modest anticholinergic effects, are prescribed." (Tune et al., 1992, p. 1393).
- "It is possible that the net risk of anticholinergic toxicity from complicated drug-drug interactions is high, even though the patient receives no readily identifiable anticholinergic compound." (Tune et al., 1992, p. 1393). Ten medications commonly prescribed for the elderly produce anticholinergic levels that have been shown to cause significant impairment in recent memory and attention in normal elderly people are: ranitidine, codeine, dipyridamole, warfarin, isosorbide, theophylline, nifedipine, digoxin, Lanoxin, and prednisolone. Most of these drugs have not typically been identified as anticholinergic." (Tune et al., 1992).
- "Antihypertensive drugs adversely affect cognitive function through the central noradrenergic system." (Jain, 1996, p. 82).
- medication-induced cognitive decline could be due to "impairment of calcium and intracellular messenger system. Neurotransmitter release is calcium-dependent. Calcium channel blockers can have an inhibitory influence on neurotransmission. Protein kinase C (PKC) is a calcium dependent enzyme which is inhibited by lithium." (Jain, 1996, p. 82).
- "Benzodiazepine-induced cognitive impairment may be by this mechanism." i.e., the drug is "binding to high affinity sites of $GABA_A$ receptors." (Jain, 1996, p. 82).

Presenting Concern: **DEMENTIA**
Dx Category DM.7: *DELIRIUM*

❏ *COMMON FORMS*

- the person, within a short period of time (usually hours or days), shows signs of delirium, i.e., a reduced level of awareness, reduced ability to focus, disorientation, poor recent memory, language or perceptual disturbance, agitation, and restlessness.
- persons who have recently become disoriented push or strike a caregiver who enters their personal space.
- the person, unlike his or her usual self, is physically resistive during routine care and hits or pushes others.
- the person grabs the arm of a caregiver or supervisor while giving the appearance of needing something.

❏ *VARIATIONS*

- a person started having occasional loss of balance about the same time the cognitive decline started.
- the person's level of altertness fluctuates and the person is sleepy or drowsy at times (Adlin, 1993).
- the person shows confusion, suspicion, agitation, anxiety, speech abnormalities, and a worsening of symptoms at night (Abrams et al., 1995, p. 101).
- the person wakes at night, is disoriented to time and place, does not recognize caregivers, and may hit out at others.
- a person showing signs of delirium might misperceive others as threatening and attack them.

❏ *DISTINGUISHING FEATURES FOR DM.7*

- what began as an acute confusional state (delirium) continued for weeks until the cause of the delirium was identified and treated.
- if the delirium is due to an infection, laboratory tests confirm infection is present (e.g., elevated white blood cell count).
- the delirium clears after the acute or chronic medical illness causing it is successfully treated (Raskind & Risse, 1986).
- if the delirium is drug-induced, the cognitive decline reverses after the toxic state is eliminated (e.g., the offending medication is discontinued).
- other causes of cognitive deterioration have been ruled out, e.g., hypothyroidism, head injury, vascular accidents, a severe sleep disorder, and so on.

❏ *FACTORS THAT MAY WORSEN THE CONDITION*

- "delirious patients often worsen during the night" (Hales & Hershey, 1984, p. 822).
- lack of normal sleep and abnormal REM (rapid eye movement) periods may exacerbate symptoms of delirium (Hales & Hershey, 1984).
- an unstructured, unpredictable environment, especially for persons with dementia (Raskind & Risse, 1986).
- inadequate intake of vitamins and minerals to ensure stable electrolyte balance (Hales & Hershey, 1984).
- inadequate caloric and fluid intake (Hales & Hershey, 1984).
- slower clearance of medication by the liver due to old age (Aman, 1990; Schmucker, 1985; Thomson et al., 1983) or by the kidneys in older people (Adlin, 1993; Anderson & Polister, 1993).
- taking medication that elevates the cortisol level or depresses CNS (central nervous system) function.
- cognitively-impairing drugs (e.g., neuroleptics) can worsen a delirium (Raskind & Risse, 1986).
- benzodiazepine medications can worsen a delirium.
- "withdrawal from an anti-anxiety agent or hypnotic agent can precipitate or exacerbate delirium in the elderly patient" (Raskind & Risse, 1986, p. 21).

❏ *PERSONS WHO MAY BE AT RISK*
- a person over 60-65 years (Evenhuis, 1997).
- a person with reduced immune responsiveness and/or a history of frequent infections.
- older persons with Down syndrome with impaired white blood cell function have a higher risk for infection (Lang, 1992).
- a person who has had frequent courses of antibiotics and responds poorly to the less powerful antibiotics.
- someone taking tricyclic medication as it increases the risk for delirium (Lowenthal & Nadeau, 1991).
- someone taking phenytoin/Dilantin and showing inappropriate affect, confusion, and hallucinations (Hales & Hershey, 1984).
- someone taking the stomach medication cimetidine/Tagamet as it can cause in some people "acute mental confusion, agitation, auditory and visual hallucinations, bizarre speech, fluctuating levels of consciousness, and extreme paranoia" (Estroff & Gold, 1986, p. 175).
- someone taking cimetidine and a benzodiazepine (Hales & Hershey, 1984).
- a person taking cimetidine who is seriously ill or has impaired liver metabolism (Hales & Hershey,1984).

❏ *SUGGESTIONS FOR COLLECTING INFORMATION*
- check for reduced ability to maintain attention or shift attention, impaired memory compared to previous functioning, and disorientation to time, place, or person, i.e., look for signs of delirium.
- assess for dementia using instruments appropriate for developmentally disabled people. An instrument called the "Dementia Scale For Down Syndrome" (Gedye, 1995) was designed for tracking recovery, progression, and absence of dementia in persons with mental retardation suspected of cognitive decline.
- check if physical illness or a medication change preceded or accompanied the cognitive decline.
- provide the person's temperature, pulse, and respirations per minute to the nurse and/or physician.
- rule out sudden-onset bereavement or depression by considering the timing of major life events. Collect information using the *Checklist of Observable Signs of Depression*.

❏ *MEDICAL TESTING / SCREENING DM.7*
- check for a medical condition causing delirium such as dehydration, heart failure, systemic bacterial, fungal or viral infections, especially bladder, chest, vaginal or ear infections (a complete blood count).
- check for metabolic disturbances such as high or low blood sugar, diabetes, uremia, abnormal blood sodium, hyperthyroidism (Adlin, 1993), and hypothyroidism.
- rule out other causes of physical ill-health.
- screen for inadequate vitamin/mineral intake which can increase the risk of infection in elderly people (Chandra, 1992).
- review each medication for possible depression of CNS (central nervous system) functioning.
- review medications for drug-induced delirium. Drugs with established and frequent associations with delirium are benzodiazepines, non-steroidal anti-inflammatory drugs, opioid analgesics, and sedative withdrawal. Other medications associated with delirium are anticholinergics, anticonvulsants, antidepressants, antipsychotics, lithium, beta blockers, and histamine type 2 receptor blockers (Jain, 1996; Medical Letter, 1993). "A toxic delirium associated with confusion, inattention, and visual hallucinations may be seen with higher doses of both neuroleptics and tricyclic agents, particularly when anticholinergic drugs have also been used to treat extrapyramidal side effects. This delirium may produce a paradoxical worsening of psychoses." (Lowenthal & Nadeau, 1991, p.1S-29).

❏ *POSSIBLE BIOCHEMICAL / ANATOMICAL INVOLVEMENT*
- delirium has been associated with high fever, infection, and medication toxicity.
- there may be interference in central cholinergic functioning in patients with delirium (Lowenthal & Nadeau, 1991; Raskind & Risse, 1986).
- "The combination of antipsychotics with other drugs possessing anticholinergic properties can be synergistic, causing anticholinergic delirium that may be misinterpreted as the worsening of the psychosis." (Estroff & Gold, 1986, p.169). "Anticonvulsants can also cause acute delirium."(Ibid, p.172).

Presenting Concern: **DEMENTIA**

Dx Category DM.8: *FREQUENT DISSOCIATION MIMICKING DEMENTIA*

❏ *COMMON FORMS*

"Dissociation can be defined as a state of mind characterized by a break in the continuity of the conscious experience. There are two essential processes in the dissociative experience: splitting or detachment, and loss of control ... in terms of the ability to monitor behavior. Splitting or detachment ... refers to constriction in one's experience of the world and oneself, through detachment, distancing, numbing," (Orbach, 1994, p. 69).

- the person's eyes might look downward or look at the ceiling when they glaze over--lasting a few seconds or much longer--while the person sits or stands motionless.
- the person has moments of motionless staring or a vacant look while being unresponsive to verbal questioning, and these "spells" become frequent, daily.
- the person shows onset of most or all of the following: forgetting partway through familiar tasks, getting lost, lapses in comprehension, word-finding difficulties, reduced speech, speech less clear, reduced alertness. This person also is more fearful, not wanting to be left alone, not initiating ways to occupy self as often, and has moments of motionless staring.
- the onset or worsening of the above features followed contact with people or places associated with past traumatic events. These features may have abruptly become much worse.

❏ *VARIATIONS*

- in addition to many of the features mentioned above, the person might also start to have occasional urinary and/or fecal incontinence in the same period of time.
- the person, who is known to dissociate, may be undergoing acute interpersonal stress or emotional flooding of traumatic memories (e.g., frequently talks about these memories and about death.)

❏ *DISTINGUISHING FEATURES FOR DM.8*

- the person may have had moments of motionless staring before, but these have become very frequent.
- the frequent dissociations disrupt retention and comprehension of conversation and directions.
- the person frequently dissociates and/or fits the criteria for post-traumatic stress disorder.
- intense emotional fear can interfere with the ability to reason and process information.
- improvement in comprehension and ability to attend occurs slowly with efforts to increase the person's feeling of safety and control in his or her life, or with comprehensive treatment for post-traumatic stress disorder adapted for developmentally disabled people (Ryan, 1996a).
- other causes of cognitive deterioration have been ruled out, e.g., hypothyroidism, depression, infections, head injury, vascular accidents, a severe sleep disorder, medication-induced dementia, and so on.
- these dissociative phenomena are not absence seizures (formerly known as "petit mal" seizures).

❏ *FACTORS THAT MAY WORSEN THE CONDITION*

- exposure to people or places or sounds that remind the person of past traumas, e.g., a visit to one's former hometown, distinct smells or sounds associated past traumas.
- special holidays that remind the person of past traumas.
- caregivers engaging in power struggles with a person who has been traumatized.
- psychotherapy that inadvertently causes "emotional flooding" of traumatic memories leading to increased dissociation and/or decompensation (McCann & Pearlman, 1990).
- being questioned about painful past events by other people, especially by a clinician unfamiliar to the person.
- cognitively-impairing medication.
- long-term use of antipsychotic/neuroleptic medication (Ryan, 1996a) in cases where post-traumatic stress disorder has been misdiagnosed as schizophrenia.

❑ *PERSONS WHO MAY BE AT RISK*

- a person who shows dissociative phenomena and/or signs of re-experiencing past traumas (flashbacks).
- a person with a history of sexual abuse, physical trauma, and/or ritualistic abuse.
- a person with a history of witnessing traumatic events or natural disasters.
- a person who has symbols cut into the skin or disfiguring marks on the body.
- a person with unusual scarring on areas out-of-reach for that person, e.g., on the back or buttocks.
- a person with a history of being cruel to animals or insects.
- a person who assumes a defensive or cowering posture when startled, frightened, or threatened.
- someone who shows numbness, a frozen mask-like face, and no eye contact when examined by a physician.
- a person, able to dress properly, sometimes wears trousers backwards with the zipper at the back, wears extra underpants, or does similar things with clothing that suggest extra protection of the genital area.
- someone who is hypervigilant, feels very unsafe at night, and fears the dark.
- a person whose mental retardation was caused by head injury at a young age, possibly by physical abuse.
- someone whose history contains insufficient information about past events, but there are reasonable grounds to suspect previous trauma.

❑ *SUGGESTIONS FOR COLLECTING INFORMATION*

- assess for signs of dissociative states, numbing, and flashbacks.
- check for nightmares, anxious fearful states at bedtime, sleeping in day because of fearing the dark, or other unusual features not typically associated with dementia.
- assess for post-traumatic stress disorder using diagnostic criteria (e.g., DSM-IV, 1994; Ryan, 1994).
- try to identify distinct sounds that trigger fearful or protective responses. Then have staff minimize the occurrence of these triggering cues. Also plan ways to desensitize the person to these triggers.
- review records to determine if the onset of cognitive decline occurred after exposure to persons or places that are associated with traumatizing events.
- assess for dementia using instruments appropriate for developmentally disabled people. An instrument called the "Dementia Scale For Down Syndrome" (Gedye, 1995) was designed for tracking recovery, progression, and absence of dementia in persons with mental retardation suspected of cognitive decline.
- assess for depression using instruments or criteria appropriate for this population (e.g., Cooper & Collacott, 1994; Sovner, 1986). Use the *Checklist of Observable Signs of Depression*.

❑ *MEDICAL TESTING / SCREENING DM.8*

- review medications for ones that list CNS (central nervous system) depressing effects or possible cognitive impairment.
- list scarred areas and indicate which are anatomically incompatible with self-inflicted wounds.
- list areas of past fractures, especially if multiple. There may be no written record to confirm suspected abuse.
- rule out absence seizures if uncertain whether the motionless staring spells are dissociative states or not. Request an EEG and neurological investigation for possible absence seizures.

❑ *POSSIBLE BIOCHEMICAL / ANATOMICAL INVOLVEMENT*

- functional deficits in verbal memory and short-term memory in persons with post-traumatic stress disorder (Bremner et al., 1993) may be due to the significantly smaller volume of the right hippocampus in these patients (Bremner et al., 1995).
- "Dissociation can be defined as a state of mind characterized by a break in the continuity of the conscious experience. There are two essential processes in the dissociative experience: ...detachment [numbing] and loss of ability to monitor behavior [and thoughts]" (Orbach, 1994, p. 69).

Presenting Concern: **DEMENTIA**
Dx Category DM.9: *DETERIORATING HEARING OR VISION MIMICKING DEMENTIA*

❑ *COMMON FORMS*

- the person appeared to be deteriorating cognitively by starting to have difficulty comprehending simple conversation, answering simple questions, following familiar oral instructions, and understanding simple television shows that formerly he/she could. This person also started to show signs of deteriorating hearing such as not understanding directions unless others spoke loudly and clearly, speaking less often, turning up the volume for music, radio, television, and not coming to meals when called.
- the person appeared to be deteriorating cognitively by starting to get lost in familiar places, not recognize familiar people, have difficulty doing ordinary tasks, not comprehend familiar visual cues, and not comprehend simple television shows that formerly he/she could. This person also started to show signs of deteriorating vision such as stumbling or tripping, walking into things, moving slower, and looking up closer at things.

❑ *VARIATIONS*

- the difficulties associated with declining hearing are worse when a second conversation is occurring or there are other noises in the immediate area.
- the person's hearing aide is malfunctioning or turned off.
- the difficulties associated with declining vision are worse at dusk and in dimly lit rooms.
- the person has become fearful of stepping from carpet to tile, from one colored surface to another, or stepping off curbs.
- the person has become fearful of getting into the bathtub, getting in and out of vehicles, or other signs suggesting deterioration in depth perception.

❑ *DISTINGUISHING FEATURES FOR DM.9*

- the person shows a cluster of observable behaviors that could be due to deteriorating hearing or vision.
- deteriorating hearing and/or vision are confirmed by appropriate testing (audiologic, otologic, optometric, or opthalamic consultation).
- the person might have deterioration in both vision and hearing.
- other causes of cognitive deterioration have been ruled out, e.g., hypothyroidism, depression, infections, head injury, vascular accidents, a severe sleep disorder, medication-induced dementia, and so on.

❑ *FACTORS THAT MAY WORSEN THE CONDITION*

- hearing: considerable background noise that is difficult to filter out, e.g., a television on in one room, radio or stereo in another, household appliances in use, kitchen sounds, noisy vehicles, noisy peers.
- hearing: others talking too quickly, talking when not facing the person, or not speaking into the person's "good ear" (Adlin, 1993).
- hearing: lack of regular removal of ear wax build-up, especially in persons with Down syndrome.
- hearing: an ear infection.
- vision: being in rooms dimly lit or darkened with drapes, being outdoors at dusk.
- vision: an eye infection or frequent rubbing of the eyes.

❏ *PERSONS WHO MAY BE AT RISK*
- persons with developmental disabilities over age 70 as the risk of hearing and vision impairment increases markedly after age 70 (van Schrojenstein et al., 1997).
- persons with Down syndrome are at risk for hearing loss, cataracts, and vision loss (Dalton et al., 1993; Evenhuis et al., 1992; France, 1992; Pueshel, 1992; Roeden & Zitman, 1995).
- a person with a previously mild hearing loss that could be worsening.

❏ *SUGGESTIONS FOR COLLECTING INFORMATION*
- identify changes in observable behavior that suggest deterioration in *hearing* such as onset of: not responding to others unless they speak loudly; having to be called several times to come to meals even though the person likes eating; having difficulty comprehending what someone says when another conversation is occurring nearby; asking or motioning for others to repeat what they said; turning music or television up louder than before; trying to be cooperative but following directions only partly as if not hearing them fully; and so on.
- identify changes in observable behavior that suggest deterioration in *vision* such as onset of: looking up close at objects; sitting closer to the television than before; loss of interest in favorite handicrafts, books, or work that requires close-up vision; more cautious on stairs than before; not responding to familiar people until they speak or are up close; unusual tripping or walking into things; and similar signs.
- assess for a depressive reaction secondary to loss of vision or hearing using instruments or criteria appropriate for this population (e.g., Cooper & Collacott, 1994; Meins, 1996; Sovner, 1986). Use the *Checklist of Observable Signs of Depression*.
- check family history for types of hearing and vision losses, and the age at onset for these conditions.
- assess for dementia using instruments appropriate for developmentally disabled people. An instrument called the "Dementia Scale For Down Syndrome" (Gedye, 1995) was designed for tracking recovery, progression, and absence of dementia in persons with mental retardation suspected of cognitive decline.

❏ *MEDICAL TESTING / SCREENING DM.9*
- check for ear wax accumulation, infection, or disease in the ears.
- review results of previous ear exams, otologic/audiologic consultation, and refer to appropriate specialist for reassessment as needed.
- if the person wears a hearing aide(s), ensure the equipment is checked at regular intervals.
- check for infection or disease conditions of the eyes.
- review results of previous eye exams and vision testing, and refer to appropriate specialist for reassessment as needed.

❏ *POSSIBLE BIOCHEMICAL / ANATOMICAL INVOLVEMENT*
- an inability to hear conversation can mimic lapses in comprehending what is being said.
- an inability to see one's way around the house can mimic lapses in spatial recall such as forgetting familiar locations.

Presenting Concern: **DEMENTIA**
Dx Category DM.10: *SEVERE SLEEP APNEA MIMICKING DEMENTIA*

❑ *COMMON FORMS*
- the onset of lapses in memory and comprehension was gradual, not abrupt, in a person who has been getting inadequate sleep.
- the person has periods of reduced alertness and awareness; these wax and wane but worsen when the person is tired.

❑ *VARIATIONS*
- the person shows lapses in memory and comprehension often, but does not show these in the hours after restorative sleep.
- speech becomes less clear when the person is tired and less alert, compared to when he or she is rested.

❑ *DISTINGUISHING FEATURES FOR DM.10*
- the cognitive deterioration might worsen over time but it does not progress to the late stages of a dementia.
- the person shows many of the following observable *daytime* features: sleepy in the daytime, able to fall asleep in a chair easily, slow to awaken in the morning, appears to have morning headaches or reports them, breathes through the mouth often in the day, and has a nasal voice sometimes.
- the person shows many of the following observable *nighttime* features: snoring when asleep, noisy breathing when asleep, coughing frequently during the night in the absence of "cold symptoms,"stops breathing followed by a deep breath or gasping, periods of restlessness during the night, frequent wakenings through the night.
- with obstructive sleep apnea, there is noisy breathing, *snoring in all sleep positions*, and/or exaggerated respiratory muscular effort.
- cognitive recovery does not occur if you restrict daytime napping (to encourage sleeping at night) or use sleeping medication, as these do not correct sleep apnea.
- improvement in memory and comprehension may be uneven, but improvement follows efforts to treat confirmed sleep apnea, e.g., as the person learns to accept wearing a positive pressure mask at night.
- other causes of cognitive deterioration have been ruled out, e.g., hypothyroidism, depression, infections, head injury, vascular accidents, medication-induced dementia, and so on.

❑ *FACTORS THAT MAY WORSEN THE CONDITION*
- high daily intake of caffeine-containing foods, drugs, or beverages.
- marked obesity, as it means added weight on the chest when the person is sleeping on his or her back.
- a nasal obstruction or transient conditions that affect sinus passages, bronchi, or lungs.
- having congested nasal passages or cold symptoms means that a person diagnosed with sleep apnea is temporarily unable to use the CPAP (continuous positive airway pressure) mask during sleep.
- medication that risks inducing or worsening insomnia.
- sedating medication and alcohol can increase the severity of obstructive sleep apnea and worsen cognitive functioning (Hanly & Shapiro, 1995).
- for central sleep apnea, taking medication that can suppress respiratory functioning. Benzodiazepines selectively reduce upper airway muscle tone (Hanly & Shapiro, 1995).

146

❏ *PERSONS WHO MAY BE AT RISK*

- persons with Down syndrome are at risk for both obstructive sleep apnea and central sleep apnea (Silverman, 1988; Strome & Strome, 1992).
- someone with a family member (parent or sibling) who snores/snored may be at risk for obstructive sleep apnea (Strome & Strome, 1992).
- an obese person, especially if male, as obesity increases the risk for obstructive sleep apnea (Hanly & Shapiro, 1995, p. 80).
- a person with Prader-Willi syndrome who is extremely obese (Clarke et al., 1989).
- a person with myotonic dystrophy.
- also read the section on *PERSONS WHO MAY BE AT RISK* in SD.10.

❏ *SUGGESTIONS FOR COLLECTING INFORMATION*

- check for signs suggestive of sleep apnea using the *Checklist of Overt Signs of Sleep Apnea.*
- do overnight charting (e.g., 5 consecutive nights) for signs of sleep apnea using a remote control room monitor or tape recorder. Use the *Overnight Chart for Signs of Sleep Apnea.*
- identify times of day when cognitive lapses occur relative to restorative daytime naps vs. overtired periods.
- identify if there are times of day with no signs of cognitive decline such as after restorative sleep.
- assess for dementia using instruments appropriate for developmentally disabled people. An instrument called the "Dementia Scale For Down Syndrome" (Gedye, 1995) was designed for tracking recovery, progression, and absence of dementia in persons with mental retardation suspected of cognitive decline.
- assess for possible signs of depression using instruments or criteria appropriate for this population (Cooper & Collacott, 1994; Meins, 1996; Sovner, 1986). Use the *Checklist of Observable Signs of Depression.*
- monitor the person's weight regularly if overweight as this can worsen sleep apnea.

❏ *MEDICAL TESTING / SCREENING DM.10*

- check if the person has had a tonsillectomy (e.g., from records or from the family).
- rule out a sinus condition or throat infection (Kryger & Shapiro, 1995).
- refer to an ear/nose/throat (ENT) specialist and to a sleep clinic for overnight polysomnographic recordings. "Central sleep apnea is not a single disease but a final pathway in a large group of heterogeneous disorders." (Hanly & Shapiro, 1995, p. 82).
- review the medications for possible effects on respiratory function and sedation.
- check the heart as obstructive sleep apnea can worsen pre-existing cardiac disease (myocardial ischemia and congestive heart failure) (Fleming, 1996) and, in persons with Down syndrome, worsen pulmonary hypertension.

❏ *POSSIBLE BIOCHEMICAL / ANATOMICAL INVOLVEMENT*

- insufficient sleep for long periods can reduce alertness, impair short term memory, and impair the ability to concentrate.
- frequent hypoxic episodes through the night might adversely affect daytime cognitive functioning.
- with obstructive sleep apnea, the exaggerated respiratory muscular effort may be due to a structural abnormality such as decreased palatal width, micrognathia, and midfacial hypoplasia structurally impinging on the upper airway (Strome & Strome, 1992).
- malformations of the craniofacial bones, skull, cervical spine, and/or rib cage may contribute to obstructive sleep apnea (Fleming, 1996).
- there are lapses in the functioning of respiratory muscles in central sleep apnea, and an "abnormal hypoxic stimulus may serve as a pathway for centrally mediated sleep apnea" (Strome & Strome, 1992, p. 131).

Presenting Concern: **DEMENTIA**
Dx Category DM.11: *COGNITIVE DECLINE AFTER A LENGTHY GENERAL ANAESTHESTIC*

❏ *COMMON FORMS*
- the person did not return to his or her prior level of cognitive functioning after having a general anaesthetic that lasted more than an hour.
- after returning from the hospital for surgery, the person started occasionally to forget familiar routines, forget names, misplace valued objects, have lapses in comprehension and awareness of time, move slower and more awkwardly, and become uncharacteristically irritable. These losses continued 3 to 4 months after the surgery.

❏ *VARIATIONS*
- cognitive deterioration started after the person had two surgeries within a few months time.
- cognitive deterioration started after the person required a lengthy general anaesthetic to terminate severe status epilepticus and restore consciousness.

❏ *DISTINGUISHING FEATURES FOR DM.11*
- prior to the cognitive decline, the person had a lengthy general anaesthetic or had more than one surgery requiring anesthesia less than 6 months apart.
- the onset of the cognitive decline was abrupt, not gradual, and was evident starting the day after surgery.
- other causes of cognitive deterioration have been ruled out, e.g., hypothyroidism, depression, infections, head injury, vascular accidents, a severe sleep disorder, adverse effects of other medication, and so on.

❏ *FACTORS THAT MAY WORSEN THE CONDITION*
- a systemic infection that is not responding well to antibiotic treatment.
- insomnia caused by sleep apnea, medication, a noisy sleep environment, or poor sleep hygiene practices.
- slower clearance of medication by the liver due to old age (Aman, 1990; Schmucker, 1985; Thomson et al., 1983) or by the kidneys in older people (Adlin, 1993; Anderson & Polister, 1993).
- medication that lists central nervous system (CNS) depression as a possible adverse effect (e.g., benzodiazepines).

❏ *PERSONS WHO MAY BE AT RISK*
- a person who has had general anesthesia in recent months (Smith et al., 1986).
- someone over age 60-65 who has had general anaesthesia in recent months (Garfield et al., 1989; Smith et al., 1986).
- someone already showing dementia that such as an Alzheimer-type or vascular dementia.
- a person with a chronic infection who has had surgery recently.
- people who have sleep apnea need an anesthesiologic consultation before having a general anesthetic because anesthesia poses additional risks in people with sleep apnea.

❏ *SUGGESTIONS FOR COLLECTING INFORMATION*
- review the history to determine if the decline in cognitive functioning began only in the days after a general or spinal anesthetic was given.
- monitor for signs of recovery in alertness and cognitive functioning for at least 6-12 months post-surgery.
- assess for dementia using instruments appropriate for developmentally disabled people. An instrument called the "Dementia Scale For Down Syndrome" (Gedye, 1995) was designed for tracking recovery--or progressive decline--in persons with mental retardation who show signs of cognitive deterioration. With persons in the mild or moderate range of intelligence, also use more selective tests of cognitive functioning that require direct performance (see Aylward et al., 1997; Devenny et al., 1996).

❏ *MEDICAL TESTING / SCREENING DM.11*
- review medications for possible additional depression of CNS (central nervous system) functioning.
- rule out possible head injury, tumors, vascular accidents, and other causes of abrupt loss of skills if recovery from general anaesthetic does not occur within a reasonable span of time.
- a small percentage of older adults undergoing lengthy surgery with anesthesia show long-term clinically significant cognitive deterioration (Williams-Russo et al., 1995).
- the lifetime cumulative exposure to general and spinal anesthesia is not a risk factor for developing Alzheimer-type dementia (Bohen et al., 1994a), but it may hasten the age of onset of dementia in a person who does develop Alzheimer-type dementia (Bohen et al., 1994b).

❏ *POSSIBLE BIOCHEMICAL / ANATOMICAL INVOLVEMENT*
- there is "a close relationship between cognitive impairment and cholinergic systems in normal aging, which may mean that those patients who are already showing signs of cognitive deterioration are markedly affected by anticholinergic agents such as atropine [a general anaesthetic]" (Smith et al., 1986, p. 258).
- general anesthetics can adversely affect hippocampal function which is involved in memory functions.

❏ *COMMON FORMS*
- there was an abrupt decline in cognitive functioning after a known or suspected head injury.
- the person had an abrupt decline in cognitive functioning after an accident, after being found dazed, or after a serious fall. The decline in functioning presented as occasionally forgetting familiar routines, forgetting names, misplacing valued objects, having lapses in comprehension and awareness of time, moving slower and more awkwardly, and becoming uncharacteristically irritable.

❏ *VARIATIONS*
- the person had an abrupt deterioration in motor functioning that was accompanied by decline in communication, self-care functioning, body control, movement, and mobility (Klonoff et al., 1986).
- the person had a head injury affecting the left hemisphere and showed depression in addition to cognitive decline (Robinson & Szetela, 1981).

❏ *DISTINGUISHING FEATURES FOR DM.12*
- prior to the cognitive decline, the person had a head injury (possibly unwitnessed) based on the evidence from an X-ray, computed tomography (CT) or other brain scan, pattern of bruising, or the injury was witnessed.
- other causes of abrupt cognitive decline have been ruled out such as cerebral vascular accidents and infection-related delirium.
- causes of a gradual cognitive decline have been ruled out as a contributing factor, e.g., hypothyroidism, a severe sleep disorder, medication-induced dementia, and so on.

❏ *FACTORS THAT MAY WORSEN THE CONDITION*
- a systemic infection.
- insomnia caused by sleep apnea, medication, a noisy sleep environment, or poor sleep hygiene practices.
- slower clearance of medication by the liver due to old age (Aman, 1990; Schmucker, 1985; Thomson et al., 1983) or by the kidneys in older people (Adlin, 1993; Anderson & Polister, 1993).
- medication that lists CNS (central nervous system) depression as a possible adverse effect (e.g., benzodiazepines).

❏ *PERSONS WHO MAY BE AT RISK*
- someone over age 60-65.
- a person who is unsteady walking.
- someone with a history of falling and/or has seizures with loss of consciousness.
- a person in failing health who lives in a house with slippery floors, scatter rugs, and/or stairs.

❏ *SUGGESTIONS FOR COLLECTING INFORMATION*
- review the history to determine if the cognitive decline only started on the day of a suspected head injury.
- determine what was the last day before the cognitive deterioration began abruptly. Then review events for a possible unwitnessed fall, unwitnessed convulsive seizure, injury caused by a vehicle or an aggressive individual.
- identify if there are likely scenarios of this person falling from tripping or being pushed.
- record the location of cuts, bruising, discoloration, or swelling if the fall (or suspected fall) was recent.
- monitor for signs of recovery in motor and cognitive functioning for at least 6-12 months after the head-injury.
- assess for dementia using instruments appropriate for developmentally disabled people. An instrument called the "Dementia Scale For Down Syndrome" (Gedye, 1995) was designed for tracking recovery--or progressive decline--in persons with mental retardation who show signs of cognitive deterioration. With persons in the mild or moderate range of intelligence, also use more selective tests of cognitive functioning that require direct performance (see Aylward et al., 1997; Devenny et al., 1996).

❏ *MEDICAL TESTING / SCREENING DM.12*
- check for possible head injury, subdural hematoma, cranial fractures, etc. Request X-rays or CT scan as warranted.
- rule out tumors, vascular causes of dementia, and other causes of an abrupt loss of cognitive skills.
- rule out causes of gradual cognitive decline that might be a contributing factor, e.g., hypothyroidism, a severe sleep disorder, depression, and so on.
- review medications for cumulative sedating effects or excessive CNS depression.

❏ *POSSIBLE BIOCHEMICAL / ANATOMICAL INVOLVEMENT*
- the sequelae of head injury can result in temporary or irreversible cognitive deterioration.

❑ *COMMON FORMS*

- the person showed an abrupt loss of skills from one day to the next, not a gradual decline.
- the person showed an abrupt impairment of motor function on one side of the body, such as listing to one side when standing or walking, limping, leaning to one side when sitting, or reduced motor control in one hand.
- the person showed abrupt onset of slurred speech, reduced clarity of speech, and slower movements, in addition to other signs of cognitive decline.
- if able to report symptoms, the person reports dizziness, vision problems, sudden weakness, numbness or tingling in the face, arms or legs, in addition to difficulty speaking or slurred speech.

❑ *VARIATIONS*

- there is an abrupt worsening of memory, comprehension, and motor skills in a person who was already in the early or middle stages of a dementia.
- the person showed a sudden loss of consciousness, labored breathing, clammy sweat on the skin, uneven pupils, eyes turned to one side, and paralysis in the face, arm, and leg (usually on one side).
- the person had a stroke affecting the left hemisphere and showed depression in addition to cognitive decline (Robinson & Szetala, 1981).
- the person may show recovery in the skills that were lost--especially motor skills--in the days, weeks or months after an abrupt loss of function.

❑ *DISTINGUISHING FEATURES FOR DM.13*

- there was an abrupt onset of cognitive decline, a stepwise deterioration, a history or presence of hypertension (high blood pressure), somatic complaints, focal neurological signs and symptoms (Rosen et al., 1980).
- a cerebral vascular accident (e.g., stroke, hemorrhage, multi-infarcts) is diagnosed.
- other causes of abrupt cognitive decline have been ruled out, e.g., post head injury cognitive decline, brain tumor, infection-related delirium, and so on.
- causes of a gradual cognitive decline have been ruled out as a contributing factor, e.g., hypothyroidism, depression, a severe sleep disorder, medication-induced dementia, and so on. Depressed mood or major depression was found in about a third of patients with multi-infarct dementia (Reichman & Coyne,1995).

❑ *FACTORS THAT MAY WORSEN THE CONDITION*

- sedating medication.
- stimulants (Thomas, 1993, p. 1890) such as methylphenidate/Ritalin..
- using neuroleptic medication in cases of multi-infarct dementia (van Sweden, 1984).

❑ *PERSONS WHO MAY BE AT RISK*
- a person over age 60-65 (van Schrojenstein et al., 1997).
- a person who has previously had a stroke.
- a person with a family history of stroke.
- an older person with hypertension or a history of hypertension (high blood pressure).

❑ *SUGGESTIONS FOR COLLECTING INFORMATION*
- assess for dementia using instruments appropriate for developmentally disabled people. An instrument called the "Dementia Scale For Down Syndrome" (Gedye, 1995) was designed for tracking recovery--or progressive decline--in persons with mental retardation who show signs of cognitive deterioration. With persons in the mild or moderate range of intelligence, also use more selective tests of cognitive functioning that require direct performance (see Aylward et al., 1997; Devenny et al., 1996).
- review records to determine the exact day (or hour) the deterioration started; record cognitive and motor impairments in the first 24 hours, then days afterward.
- monitor the person closely for recovery of lost motor functions including improved clarity of speech.
- provide the person's temperature, pulse, and respirations per minute to the nurse and/or physician.
- check family history for dementia, stroke, and other cerebral vascular problems.
- assess for depression as a complicating factor using instruments or criteria appropriate for this population (Cooper & Collacott, 1994; Meins, 1996; Sovner, 1986). Use the *Checklist of Observable Signs of Depression*.

❑ *MEDICAL TESTING / SCREENING DM.13*
- check for possible stroke, multi-infarcts, or other cerebral vascular accidents, e.g., using the Hachinski Ischemic Scale (Hachinski, 1974), CT scan, or other brain scans.
- rule out infection-related delirium, possible head injury, brain tumor, and other causes of abrupt loss of cognitive and motor functions.
- rule out causes of gradual cognitive decline that might be a contributing factor, e.g., hypothyroidism, a severe sleep disorder, depression, and so on.

❑ *POSSIBLE BIOCHEMICAL / ANATOMICAL INVOLVEMENT*
- stroke can be caused by different mechanisms including hemorrhage into the brain, formation of an embolus or thrombus (blood clot) that occludes an artery, or rupture of an extracerebral artery causing subarachnoid hemorrhage (Thomas, 1993, p. 1890).

❏ *COMMON FORMS*

- the person gradually started to show several of the following: memory lapses, impaired judgment, difficulty with new learning, loss of vocational skills, loss of self-help skills, disorientation, inability to find one's way, impaired visual recall, urinary incontinence (Burt et al., 1992; Gedye, 1995; Pary, 1992).
- the person showing gradual cognitive decline also started showing features such as loss of interest in familiar activities and/or objects, apathy, withdrawn, and reduced verbal output or nonverbal communication.

❏ *VARIATIONS*

- the person may also show many signs suggesting depression, not as the sole explanation for the cognitive and behavioral decline, but as a co-occurring condition.
- before the onset of a gradual cognitive and functional decline, the person started having seizures with loss of consciousness late in life or had a recurrence of convulsive seizures after many years or decades without any.
- a person who has obsessive-compulsive features may show an increase in the frequency or severity of obsessions and compulsions around the time when the cognitive decline began.

❏ *DISTINGUISHING FEATURES FOR DM.14*

- other causes of dementia have been ruled out such as hypothyroidism, infection, sleep apnea, depression (Holland et al., 1993), and medication-induced dementia (Gedye, 1998). An abrupt onset of dementia is *not* characteristic of Alzheimer-type disease.
- the person meets the criteria for dementia on assessment instruments designed for developmentally disabled adults such as the "Dementia Questionnaire for Mentally Retarded Persons" (Evenhuis, 1990) and the "Dementia Scale For Down Syndrome" (Gedye, 1995).

❏ *FACTORS THAT MAY WORSEN THE CONDITION*

- untreated hypothyroidism.
- a systemic infection.
- a serious sleep disturbance.
- untreated depression in a person with Alzheimer-type dementia (Reifler et al., 1986).
- vitamin B_{12} deficiency (Hector & Burton, 1988). Note that some Alzheimer patients with pathologically low levels of vitamin B_{12} in cerebrospinal fluid show normal serum B_{12} levels (Cole & Prachal, 1984).
- high lifetime cumulative exposure to general or spinal anesthesia may hasten the onset of dementia in a person who develops Alzheimer-type dementia (Bohen et al., 1994b).
- having an operation in which general anaesthesia was used for approximately one hour or longer.
- a head injury with loss of consciousness followed by dizziness, confusion, behavior change in the subsequent days, or loss of consciousness for more than an hour (Gedye et al., 1989; Schofield et al., 1997).
- medication that adversely affects cholinergic neurotransmission, e.g., neuroleptics (Bennett et al., 1992; Brown et al., 1993; Raskind & Risse, 1986; Risse & Barnes, 1986).
- medication that interferes with serotonergic neurotransmission, e.g., benzodiazepines reduce the synthesis and release of serotonin (Saner & Pletscher, 1979; Pei et al., 1989), affect its turnover (breakdown) (Essman & Essman, 1986), and can cause selective or global cognitive impairments (Larson et al., 1987; Preston et al., 1989; Waugaman, 1988).
- "Lithium can cause acute confusional states, even at what are regarded as therapeutic serum levels." (Risse & Barnes, 1986, p. 371).
- valproic acid/Depakene appears to reduce alertness and can worsen dysphagia (and other motor functioning) in persons with Down syndrome in the late stages of a progressive Alzheimer-type dementia.

❑ *PERSONS WHO MAY BE AT RISK*

- adults with Down syndrome are at elevated risk to develop Alzheimer-type dementia (Ball et al., 1980; Dalton et al., 1993; Newroth & Newroth, 1980), and the risk increases in their fifties and sixties (Evenhuis, 1990; Lai & Williams, 1989; Wisniewski et al., 1985; Zigman et al., 1995).
- someone over age 65.
- someone who has two or more first-degree relatives with Alzheimer-type dementia.
- an older person with cognitive decline who shows a noticeable change in eating habits such as eating more, eating less, a change in food choice, or late onset pica as these have been reported in Alzheimer-type dementia (Morris et al., 1989).

❑ *SUGGESTIONS FOR COLLECTING INFORMATION*

- assess for dementia using instruments appropriate for developmentally disabled people such as the "Dementia Questionaire for Mentally Retarded Persons" (Evenhuis, 1990) and the "Dementia Scale For Down Syndrome" (Gedye, 1995). The "Dementia Scale For Down Syndrome" is an instrument designed for tracking recovery, progression, and absence of dementia in persons with mental retardation suspected of cognitive decline. With persons in the mild or moderate range of intelligence, also use more selective tests of cognitive functioning that require direct performance (see Alyward et al., 1997; Devenny et al., 1996).
- assess for depression as a contributing factor (or differential diagnosis) using instruments or criteria appropriate for this population (e.g., Cooper & Collacott, 1994; Meins, 1996; Sovner, 1986). Collect information using the *Checklist of Observable Signs of Depression*.
- rule out cognitive deterioration due to sleep apnea. Collect information using the *Checklist of Overt Signs of Sleep Apnea*.
- check family history for Alzheimer disease, other types of dementia, and depression.

❑ *MEDICAL TESTING / SCREENING DM.14*

- rule out other causes of dementia such as hypothyroidism, vitamin B_{12} and folate deficiency, multi-infarct dementia, head injury, etc. and conditions that can mimic dementia such as delirium, systemic infection, severe sleep apnea, and so on. In future, there may be diagnostic blood tests for certain types of Alzheimer disease.
- check for depression and deteriorating hearing or vision as complicating factors.
- review medications for possible neuroleptic-induced dementia, anticonvulsant-induced dementia, or other medication-related cognitive deterioration.

❑ *POSSIBLE BIOCHEMICAL / ANATOMICAL INVOLVEMENT*

- Alzheimer patients have low central serotonin and low cholinergic functioning (Bowen et al., 1983; Middlemiss et al., 1986; Palmer et al., 1988), and these neurotransmitters are involved in memory and attention functions.
- there are numerous signs of neuropathology in the brains of people with Alzheimer disease, e.g., neuritic plaques, neurofibrillary tangles (e.g., Ball et al., 1980; Wisniewski et al., 1985; Wurtman et al., 1996).

Chapter VII

UNWITNESSED OR UNUSUAL FALLS

❏ *COMMON FORMS*
- the person, who was found on the floor, can no longer get up or walk unassisted.
- after being found on the floor, the person started screaming, showed signs of pain, or reported pain.
- if the fall was witnessed, caregivers have more information such as knowing if the person's body hit an object during the fall, if the person tried to get up but was unsuccessful, if there was loss of consciousness, and so on.
- the person no longer stands up straight but leans forward, almost in a crouched position. The person "guards" the abdominal area after a pelvic, hip or sacral fracture, or if there is inflamed cartilage in the pubic area.
- the person shows an abnormal body alignment, e.g., a dropped shoulder with a collar bone fracture, limping and dragging a leg or a discrepancy in leg length with a hip or leg fracture.
- the person who was found on the floor may thereafter resist or groan if caregivers reposition him/her or try to give routine care (wash the face or body, dress the person).

❏ *VARIATIONS*
- the person, who was found on the floor, thereafter resists or screams when anyone touches a certain part of the body.
- caregivers place the person in bed and notice that an arm or leg does not rotate or move in the usual way.
- the person was found in bed or on a sofa, and is no longer able to get up or walk.
- there may be no signs of pain immediately after the fall, but about a day later the person appears to be in pain. Delayed pain can occur from bleeding into a muscle, then the blood hardens and later causes pain.
- the person walks slowly on level surfaces but can no longer dangle a leg or lift a foot up for a stair step; this can occur with a hip or pelvic fracture.
- the person no longer sleeps on one side (e.g., the left side with a left hip fracture).
- if recently knocked down by a slow-moving vehicle, afterwards the person may still walk but no longer sits normally in a chair. This can occur with a hip or pelvic fracture.
- a hard surface (e.g., porcelain sink or toilet) is close to where the person was found, and it is possible that the person contacted it during a fall.
- if the fracture occurred during a seizure, it may involve a facial bone, vertebra, rib, collarbone, or scapula (Kirby & Sadler, 1995).

❏ *DISTINGUISHING FEATURES FOR FL.1*
- a bone fracture or dislocated joint is confirmed by X-rays.
- often the person loses the ability to do ordinary activities such as walking, rising, sitting, or reaching.

❏ *FACTORS THAT MAY WORSEN THE CONDITION*
- misinterpreting the resistance to walk after a fall as "uncooperative behavior" or misinterpreting the screaming that began after a fall as "attention-seeking".
- a lack of moderate regular exercise to maintain mobility and bone density in older adults with developmental disabilities (Adlin, 1993). Being nonambulatory can lead to lower bone density.
- foot problems such as bunions can cause difficulty with walking and balance due to pain (Adlin, 1993).
- hazards such as slippery footwear, slippery floors, scatter rugs, uneven surfaces, raised thresholds, lack of handrails, stairs, and inadequate lighting.
- medication that can lower blood pressure and increase the risk of falls due to fainting.

❏ *PERSONS WHO MAY BE AT RISK*
- someone who is unsteady walking or has a history of tripping and falling.
- an elderly person or someone in the later stages of a dementia.
- an older person with osteoporosis (Adlin, 1993; van Schrojenstein et al., 1997).

- a person who urinates often at night as frequent nocturia has been associated with falls in elderly people (Abrams et al., 1995, p. 67).
- a person with cerebral palsy has an increased risk for osteoporosis due to lifetime immobility, inadequate calcium intake, and low levels of vitamin D from decreased sunlight (Adlin, 1993).
- a person with a history of cardiac arrhythmias.
- persons with Shy-Drager syndrome (chronic orthostatic hypotension due to autonomic nervous system dysfunction).
- someone with poor vision who walks at night in poorly lit areas.
- a person with a history of convulsive seizures (Kirby & Sadler, 1995).
- elderly people or those with decreased mobility who live in a house with many stairs, a split level, or other inappropriate housing.
- a person with lifetime use of anticonvulsants is at increased risk for osteoporosis (Adlin, 1993).
- elderly people taking histamine type 1 blockers (non-sedating antihistamines) as they have been associated with falls in the elderly population (Cookson, 1993).
- a person taking high doses of two neuroleptics or multiple sedating medications.
- a person with unrecognized lithium neurotoxicity whose motor coordination is deteriorating markedly.
- a person with pre-existing hypotension taking medication that can lower blood pressure, e.g., thioridazine/Mellaril, chlorpromazine/Largactil, risperidone/Risperdal.
- a person with ataxia (poor motor coordination) as a side effect of a medication e.g., phenytoin/Dilantin.
- a person taking antihypertensive medication as this may increase the risk of falls due to fainting.

❑ *SUGGESTIONS FOR COLLECTING INFORMATION*
- record unusual refusals to rise, walk, use the arms, or do ordinary movements following a fall.
- record the location of cuts, bruises, discoloration, swelling, and indicate which are new and not new.
- record any verbal and nonverbal indications of pain subsequent to the fall; use the *Discomfort Scale** (Hurley et al., 1992) to assess noncommunicative people for pain.
- identify if there are likely scenarios that this person was pushed, or tripped and fell independently.
- record unusual features in the minutes, hours and days after the fall such as slowness in comprehending or responding, difficulty speaking, or motor difficulties.
- provide the person's temperature, pulse, and respirations per minute to the nurse and/or physician.

* *A chart or checklist listed in italics in this section can be found in the Appendix.*

❑ *MEDICAL TESTING / SCREENING FL.1*
- examine for possible fractures, dislocations, new paralysis, spinal injury (fractures or subluxation), head injury, X-rays and CT scan as needed. X-ray joints above and below where the injury is suspected.
- rule out stroke-related fall, seizure-related fall, and various causes of fainting.
- take blood pressure supine and sitting or sitting and standing to check for postural hypotension.
- review medications for cumulative sedating effects or possible excessive dosing. Medications associated with falls in elderly people are long-acting benzodiazepines, phenothiazines, tricyclic antidepressants, diuretics, narcotics, and some antihypertensives (Abrams et al., 1995, p. 68.). Excessive medication, especially in persons over 65, can cause disorientation, ataxia, falls, fractures, syncope (Learoyd, 1972).

❑ *POSSIBLE BIOCHEMICAL / ANATOMICAL INVOLVEMENT*
- fractures can result from a fall due to convulsive seizures, fainting, tripping and falling, being pushed, vascular accidents, spontaneous leg fractures, and so on.
- spontaneous fractures associated with degenerative bone conditions can occur without a fall, leaving the person unable to walk, stand, or get up.
- antihypertensives, neuroleptics, or drug toxicity can impair balance and gait, especially in the frail elderly, causing falls and fractures (Larson et al., 1987; Learoyd, 1972; Raskind & Risse, 1986).

Presenting Concern: **UNWITNESSED OR UNUSUAL FALLS**
Dx Category   FL.2: *FAINTING FROM LOW BLOOD PRESSURE*

❏ *COMMON FORMS*

- the person, who was found unconscious on the floor, looked very pale.
- the person stood up from a seated position, took 1-2 steps, then collapsed, knees buckled, and dropped down limply with or without loss of consciousness.
- the person continued to be limp even as caregivers tried to get the person up.
- the person might have put a hand out to break the fall.
- before falling, the person showed warning signs such as dizziness, staggering upon standing, being uncoordinated and losing one's balance, and/or having difficulty focusing visually upon standing.

❏ *VARIATIONS*

- the person occasionally has the need to sit with head down or reports feeling dizzy.
- sometimes the person lowers self to the floor from a standing position, looking very pale.
- dropping to the floor or putting one's head between the knees when getting out of bed or rising quickly from a horizontal position.
- dropping to a horizontal position.
- upon rising, the person gives the appearance of sudden loss of sight, e.g., putting hands out as though not knowing where objects are and appearing confused.
- sometimes the person is walking as usual, then stops, wobbles or looks where to put each foot, holds onto a wall, when normally the person does not do this.
- the person got up to use the toilet and fell while urinating (micturition syncope).

❏ *DISTINGUISHING FEATURES FOR FL.2*

- syncope is a "transient loss of consciousness due to inadequate blood flow to the brain" (Thomas, 1993, p. 1930). Syncope can be associated with nausea and sweating before the fainting, and maintaining one's orientation after the event (which distinguishes it from a seizure). "Occasionally syncope may be accompanied by myoclonic jerks and urinary incontinence which may give the impression of the patient having a seizure." (Jain, 1996, p. 50).
- the person has had spells of turning very pale and lowering self to the floor while remaining conscious prior to fainting with a loss of consciousness.
- the person has a history of low blood pressure or is taking medication that can lower blood pressure.
- the person has episodes of losing facial color very quickly while remaining conscious.
- the person stabilizes momentarily if kept in a head-down position or the head is 12 inches below feet level to promote venous blood return (Guyton, 1986, p. 334).

❏ *FACTORS THAT MAY WORSEN THE CONDITION*

- dehydration from an illness or from long-standing refusing to drink fluids.
- allowing a person with low blood pressure to rise quickly from lying down. (Instead, encourage the person to sit on the edge of the bed before standing.)
- hazards such as slippery footwear, slippery floors, scatter rugs, uneven surfaces, raised thresholds, stairs, lack of handrails, and inadequate lighting.
- medication that can lower blood pressure, e.g., antihypertensives, propranolol/Inderal, thioridazine/ Mellaril (Barnes et al., 1982; Helms, 1985), tricyclic antidepressants except nortriptyline/Aventyl (Lowenthal & Nadeau, 1991).
- medication that can cause a low blood level of sodium (hyponatremia) such as carbamazepine/Tegretol, or medication that can cause a low blood level of potassium (hypokalemia), e.g., diuretics.

❑ *PERSONS WHO MAY BE AT RISK*
- a person with abnormally low blood pressure and low intake of salt.
- a person with a family history of low blood pressure (hypotension).
- a person who is being rapidly withdrawn from thioridazine or other phenothiazine-type neuroleptics as these medications affect blood pressure.
- someone taking medication that can cause hypotension, e.g., antidepressants, antipsychotics, anticholinergics, nitrate vasodilators (Jain, 1996).
- an elderly person taking medication that can cause hypotension, e.g., diuretics, calcium channel blockers, beta blockers, and ACE (angiotension converting enzyme) inhibitors (Jain, 1996, p. 50).
- a person who urinates often at night as frequent nocturia has been associated with falls in elderly people (Abrams et al., 1995, p. 67).

❑ *SUGGESTIONS FOR COLLECTING INFORMATION*
- record all observable features when the person was first found, e.g., unusual body position, skin paleness, slower or weaker movements, level of alertness, or other unusual features.
- identify if the person has a history of the following: voluntarily lowering self to floor from a standing position; staggering upon standing; having difficulty focusing visually upon standing; instances of sudden loss of facial color or dizziness. If present, alert caregivers to watch for these and have the person sit or lie down to prevent falls due to fainting.
- check family history for low blood pressure.
- rule out physical pain as a contributing factor; use the *Discomfort Scale* (Hurley et al., 1992) to assess a noncommunicative person for pain.
- provide the person's temperature, pulse, and respirations per minute to the nurse and/or physician.

❑ *MEDICAL TESTING / SCREENING FL.2*
- review blood pressure history; screen for conditions that could cause fainting due to low blood pressure.
- do baseline and follow-up measurements of blood pressure in both supine and standing positions.
- test blood level of sodium and other electrolytes.
- review medications for possible adverse effects on blood pressure, heart rate, orthostatic tension. Medications associated with falls in elderly people are long-acting benzodiazepines, phenothiazines, tricyclic antidepressants, diuretics, narcotics, and some antihypertensives (Abrams et al., 1995, p. 68.). Medications associated with syncope are antiarrhythmic drugs, beta blockers, calcium channel blockers, diuretics, digitalis, insulin and oral hypoglycemics, vasodilators, anticonvulsants, anticholinergics, antidepressants, antipsychotics, barbiturates, benzodiazepines (Jain, 1996, p. 50). "Most patients stopped falling when the offending drug was stopped" (Larson et al., 1987, p. 173).
- if Subclavian Steel syndrome is present or suspected, take blood pressure readings for both arms. This syndrome occurs when the subclavian artery is occluded thereby affecting blood flow; usually the blood pressure in one arm is significantly lower than in the other arm (Thomas, 1993, p. 1896).

❑ *POSSIBLE BIOCHEMICAL / ANATOMICAL INVOLVEMENT*
- syncope is a "sudden transient loss of consciousness with loss of postural tone usually lasting no more than 15 seconds. Presyncope, which can be characterized as near fainting, light-headedness, or extreme dizziness, may be part of a continuum that leads to syncope or may occur as an isolated event." (Jain, 1996, p. 49).
- syncope can be caused by vasovagal dysfunction, orthostatic hypotension, organic cardiac disease, cardiac arrhythmias, anxiety/panic disorders, cerebrovascular ischemia, transient ischemic attacks, carotid sinus syncope, or drug-induced syncope (Kapoor, 1992).
- antihypertensives or neuroleptics that lower blood pressure can impair balance and gait, especially in the frail elderly, causing falls (Larson et al., 1987).
- excessive medication in persons over age 65 can cause syncope, falls, and fractures (Learoyd, 1972; Raskind & Risse, 1986).

Presenting Concern: **UNWITNESSED OR UNUSUAL FALLS**
Dx Category   FL.3: *BRIEF LOSS OF CONSCIOUSNESS DUE TO A FALL*

❏ *COMMON FORMS*
- the person, who was found on the floor, did not respond cognitively or physically in their usual manner in the moments afterward.
- if the fall was witnessed, caregivers have more information such as knowing if the person's head hit an object, how long the person was motionless on the ground, duration of loss of consciousness, how soon the level of awareness returned to normal, and so on.

❏ *VARIATIONS*
- the person, who was found on the floor, reported pain or showed signs suggesting pain (e.g., holding hand to head, groaning, painful facial expressions, recoiling).
- after the fall, the person may resist or groan if caregivers touch areas of the head when combing hair, washing face or hair, giving mouth care, and so on.
- there are cuts, bruises, or swelling on the head of the person who fell.

❏ *DISTINGUISHING FEATURES FOR FL.3*
- a brief loss of consciousness after a fall may occur from a head injury or concussion. There may be signs of head pain, bruises on the head, blood from the nose or ears, or clear fluid (cerebrospinal fluid) from the ears.
- the fall might have been due to fainting or syncope which is a "sudden transient loss of consciousness with loss of postural tone usually lasting no more than 15 seconds." (Jain, 1996, p. 49).

❏ *FACTORS THAT MAY WORSEN THE CONDITION*
- hazards such as slippery footwear, slippery floors, scatter rugs, uneven surfaces, raised thresholds, lack of handrails, stairs, and inadequate lighting.
- using two or more medications that depress central nervous system (CNS) functioning (e.g., benzodiazepines).

❏ *PERSONS WHO MAY BE AT RISK*

- someone who is unsteady walking or has a history of tripping and falling.
- a person living or working in areas with various hazards such as slippery floors, scatter rugs, uneven surfaces, raised thresholds, lack of handrails, stairs, and inadequate lighting.
- a person in the later stages of a dementia.
- an elderly person.
- a person, especially an elderly person, taking multiple medications that increase the risk of drug-induced fainting (Jain, 1996).
- someone with poor vision who walks at night in poorly lit areas.
- a person with a history of convulsive seizures.
- elderly people taking histamine type 1 blockers as they have been associated with falls in the elderly population (Cookson, 1993).
- a person taking high doses of two neuroleptics or multiple sedating medications.
- a person with unrecognized lithium neurotoxicity whose motor coordination is deteriorating markedly.
- a person with no previous seizures who has severe polydipsia (excessive water drinking) is at risk for a convulsive seizure due to water intoxication (Singh et al., 1985).
- a person who urinates often at night as frequent nocturia has been associated with falls in elderly people (Abrams et al., 1995, p. 67).

❏ *SUGGESTIONS FOR COLLECTING INFORMATION*

- record unusual confusion, difficulty speaking, motor difficulties, abnormal pupil size in the minutes, hours or days following the fall. Check for abnormal reaction of the pupils to light.
- examine the person and record location of cuts, bruising, discoloration, or swelling--especially on the head--with a description of which ones are new or not new.
- identify if there are likely scenarios of this person being pushed, or tripped and fell independently.
- record if there was sweating or possible nausea prior to the fall/fainting; jerking or urinary incontinence during the fall/fainting; and any history of dizziness, near-fainting, or sudden need to sit down or drop to the floor.
- provide the person's temperature, pulse, and respirations per minute to the nurse and/or physician.

❏ *MEDICAL TESTING / SCREENING FL.3*

- rule out stroke-related falls, seizure-related falls, cardiac-related falls, and other physical causes of fainting.
- review medications for cumulative sedating effects or possible excessive dosing.
- review medications for ones that can impair balance and gait, especially in the frail elderly, causing falls, e.g., antihypertensives or neuroleptics (Larson et al., 1987; Learoyd, 1972).
- review medications for ones associated with syncope, e.g., beta blockers, calcium channel blockers, diuretics, antiarrhythmic drugs, digitalis, insulin and oral hypoglycemics, vasodilators, anticonvulsants, anticholinergics, antidepressants, antipsychotics, barbiturates, benzodiazepines (Jain, 1996, p. 50).
- test drug levels because drug toxicity that is sufficient to cause cognitive impairment can also cause the falling (Larson et al., 1987).

❏ *POSSIBLE BIOCHEMICAL / ANATOMICAL INVOLVEMENT*

- loss of consciousness from a head injury or concussion can result from a fall.

Presenting Concern: **UNWITNESSED OR UNUSUAL FALLS**

Dx Category   FL.4: *A SEIZURE WITH LOSS OF CONSCIOUSNESS IN PERSONS NOT KNOWN TO HAVE SEIZURES*

❑ *COMMON FORMS*

- the person, who was found unconscious, is slumped over in a chair or has collapsed onto the floor.
- after being found unconscious, the person is slow in resuming the usual cognitive and/or motor activities.
- the person who is found unconscious may have excessive saliva around the mouth or a small amount of blood from tongue biting.
- the person may have been incontinent of urine during the fall.
- if the fall was witnessed, caregivers have more information about possible limb stiffness or limb jerking, vocalizations at the outset, loss of postural tone or slumping to the ground, and duration of loss of consciousness.
- persons who fall due to a seizure may have soft tissue injuries (cuts, bruises) localized to the head and face (Kirby & Sadler, 1995).

❑ *VARIATIONS*

- the person wants to sleep afterward regardless of the time of day or activities offered.
- the face appears pale, greyish, or bluish (cyanotic) when the person is first found on the ground.
- the person still has stiffness in the limbs in the moments afterward.

❑ *DISTINGUISHING FEATURES FOR FL.4*

- other causes are ruled out and the episode is confirmed as a seizure either due to an epileptic seizure or a non-epileptic seizure (e.g., related to medication withdrawal) (Kirby & Sadler, 1995).
- the person may be undergoing a rapid withdrawal of benzodiazepines or anticonvulsants. (Some people who do not have epilepsy are given anticonvulsants such as carbamazepine/Tegretol or valproic acid/ Depakene for behavioral control, not epilepsy.)

❑ *FACTORS THAT MAY WORSEN THE CONDITION*

- increasing medication that lowers the seizure threshold (e.g., neuroleptics) or using tricyclic antidepressants in a person who is a slow metabolizer of drugs (Dailey & Naritoku, 1996).
- if the seizure is related to use of a selective serotonin reuptake inhibitor (SSRI) (e.g., fluoxetine/Prozac, fluvoxamine/Luvox) (Deahl & Trimble, 1992; Hargrave & Martinez, 1992; Ware & Stewart, 1989; Weber, 1989), increasing the dose may increase the frequency of seizures.

❏ *PERSONS WHO MAY BE AT RISK*

- a person who had convulsive seizures as a child, but has had none for over a decade and does not take anti-seizure medication.
- persons with Down syndrome over age 40 have an increased risk to develop seizures with loss of consciousness. The late onset of convulsive seizures can be an early sign of Alzheimer-type dementia in older adults with Down syndrome.
- a person who is in the middle or late stages of a progressive dementia.
- a person with no history of seizures but who has a family history of seizures.
- a person with no history of convulsive seizures who takes a tricyclic antidepressant (e.g., clomipramine/ Anafranil) or an SSRI antidepressant (e.g., fluoxetine or fluvoxamine).
- a person undergoing a rapid withdrawal from benzodiazepines (e.g., diazepam/Valium, lorazepam/ Ativan, alprazolam/Xanax), anticonvulsants, or alcohol.

❏ *SUGGESTIONS FOR COLLECTING INFORMATION*

- record the presenting features when the person was first found, i.e., unusual body position, limb stiffness or abnormal movements, muscle weakness, speech difficulties, abnormalities in rising or walking, facial color, level of alertness, excess saliva, or other unusual features.
- record features in the first 15 minutes, hours, and days after the fall, e.g., level of alertness, hours of sleeping, comprehension difficulties, speech difficulties, limb stiffness or weakness, any abnormal movements, or unusual activities.
- provide the person's temperature, pulse, and respirations per minute to the nurse and/or physician.
- check family history for epilepsy and ages at onset.

❏ *MEDICAL TESTING / SCREENING FL.4*

- rule out stroke-related falls, seizure-related falls, and various causes of fainting.
- review medications for possible cumulative sedating effects or excessive dosing.
- review medications for risk of a medication-related seizure or withdrawal-related seizure especially in persons without epilepsy or who have had no convulsive seizures for many years.
- in a person with known or suspected polydipsia (excessive water drinking), rule out water intoxication underlying the convulsive seizure (Singh et al., 1985). (See the Diagnostic Categories on polydipsia.)
- if the reason for the seizure remains unknown (i.e., it is not related to a medication, a rapid drug withdrawal, water intoxication, or other known cause), refer the person for an EEG and neurological investigation for possible epileptic activity.

❏ *POSSIBLE BIOCHEMICAL / ANATOMICAL INVOLVEMENT*

- seizures can result from cerebral pathology associated with a progressing dementia.
- GABA is an endogenous anticonvulsant. Selective serotonergic reuptake inhibitors (e.g., fluoxetine, fluvoxamine) have antagonist effects on GABA that may cause seizures in some people (Deahl & Trimble, 1992; Hargrave & Martinez, 1992; Ware & Stewart, 1989; Weber, 1989).
- a rapid withdrawal of anticonvulsants increases the risk of inducing seizures.
- a rapid withdrawal of benzodiazepines increases the risk of withdrawal seizures with loss of consciousness.

❏ *COMMON FORMS*
- the person, who was found unconscious, had collapsed onto the floor.
- the person has recently shown reduced strength and tires easily when using his or her muscles.
- if the fall was witnessed, caregivers have more information about spontaneous slumping or dropping to the ground, marked weakness in efforts to rise or stand, duration of unconsciousness, how long the person was motionlessness, and so on.

❏ *VARIATIONS*
- the person was somewhat limp after the collapse.
- the person has been ill, and may have had frequent vomiting and/or diarrhea in the days preceding the fall.

❏ *DISTINGUISHING FEATURES FOR FL.5*
- laboratory tests (e.g., blood and urine tests) confirm dehydration.
- the mouth is dry, and the saliva is "gummy"or there is less saliva than usual.
- the skin looks dry and lacks elasticity.
- the urine is amber or dark colored in the diaper or toilet.
- the body temperature tends to drop if exposed to even the slightest cold (Guyton, 1986, p. 333).

❏ *FACTORS THAT MAY WORSEN THE CONDITION*
- episodes of vomiting and/or diarrhea.
- water or fluid restriction.
- hot temperatures and excessive sweating.
- medication that can affect sodium or potassium levels, e.g., carbamzaepine/Tegretol can cause a low blood level of sodium (hyponatremia).
- using two or more medications that list sweating as an adverse effect (e.g., using buspirone/Buspar with carbamazepine).
- using diuretic agents.

❏ *PERSONS WHO MAY BE AT RISK*
- a person with recent or long-standing refusals to drink fluids or eat food.
- someone with a marked decrease in urine output.
- someone who has had frequent vomiting and/or diarrhea.
- a person in the profound range of intelligence who has multiple physical abnormalities and requires special techniques/positioning and patience to feed. This person relocates or has several new caregivers who are unfamiliar with the person's typical quantity and speed of intake, urine output, and special handling techniques during feeding.
- someone with dysphagia who acquires a new set of caregivers who are unfamiliar with feeding the person.
- an elderly person in the later stages of dementia who resists drinking fluids and may have dysphagia.

❏ *SUGGESTIONS FOR COLLECTING INFORMATION*
- record the timing of the collapse(s) and review the intake or food/fluids in the previous 5-7 days (e.g., less than 6-8 glasses per 24 hours). Check for a recent decrease in frequency of urination and check the color of the urine as it may be darker and more concentrated.
- record all fluid/food intake in the week(s) after the collapse. Record frequency of urination and, if feasible, amount.
- record any unusual slowness in comprehending or responding, difficulty speaking, or motor difficulties in the minutes, hours, or days following the incident.
- record the location of cuts, bruising, discoloration, swelling (if present), and indicate which ones are new or not new.
- identify if there are likely scenarios of this person falling from tripping or being pushed.
- provide the person's temperature, pulse, and respirations per minute to the nurse and/or physician.

❏ *MEDICAL TESTING / SCREENING FL.5*
- check the electrolyte balance, hemoglobin, blood count, and urine concentration.
- rule out stroke-related falls, seizure-related falls, and various causes of fainting.
- review medications for effect on sodium and potassium, cumulative sedating effects, and possible effects on seizure threshold.
- take blood pressure supine and sitting or sitting and standing to check for postural hypotension.

❏ *POSSIBLE BIOCHEMICAL / ANATOMICAL INVOLVEMENT*
- "...the loss of fluid from all fluid compartments is called dehydration, this can reduce the blood volume and cause hypovolemic shock very similar to that resulting from hemorrhage." (Guyton, 1986, p. 332).
- a marked loss of fluid can lead to an increased concentration of circulating medication which, if sedating, can contribute to reduced consciousness.

❑ *COMMON FORMS*

- the person, who was found on the floor, was weak, probably had bruising or cuts on the face, and may have had a reduced level of awareness when helped up. This person takes medication daily.
- the person was walking unsteadily and suddenly fell forward without attempting to break the fall. This person takes medication daily.
- if the fall was witnessed, caregivers have more information about a sudden forward fall, no attempt to break the fall, or observing the person trip easily.

❑ *VARIATIONS*

- the person who takes medication daily falls straight forward landing on his or her face, possibly fracturing the nose and/or needing stitches (sutures) to close wounds on the face.
- the person who takes medication daily has been falling face-forward directly onto hard surfaces (concrete surfaces, wrought-iron railings).

❑ *DISTINGUISHING FEATURES FOR FL.6*

- the person is shaky and unsteady when walking, but does not have cerebral palsy or a syndrome known to present with ataxia (poor coordination).
- the person is taking two neuroleptics, one or both is at a high dose for the person's body size and/or age.
- the person is taking multiple medications, and most or all of them have sedating properties.
- the person shows psychomotor retardation and decreased reaction time.

❑ *FACTORS THAT MAY WORSEN THE CONDITION*

- dehydration, excessive sweating, or inadequate fluid intake in hot weather that results in concentrating the blood level of medications.
- hazards such as slippery footwear, slippery floors, scatter rugs, uneven surfaces, raised thresholds, lack of handrails, stairs, and inadequate lighting.
- increasing the dose of any current medication.
- adding medication for behavior control which lowers blood pressure (e.g., clonidine/Catapres, propranolol/Inderal).

❑ *PERSONS WHO MAY BE AT RISK*
- a person with little body fat, especially if small-framed, who is on two neuroleptics or multiple sedating medications.
- a person taking two or more benzodiazepines or high doses of one benzodiazepine.
- a person who has recently started taking clobazam/Frisium as this can result in "rag doll" limpness.
- a person on medication who is unable to speak or indicate feeling "light-headed" or "heavily sedated."
- a person whose medications have not been decreased in many years, only increased or more medication has been added.

❑ *SUGGESTIONS FOR COLLECTING INFORMATION*
- examine the person carefully and record the location of cuts, bruising, discoloration, swelling, etc. with a description of which ones are new or not new.
- identify if the unsteadiness in walking worsens in relation to the timing of medications.
- review the history for a period when unsteady walking and tripping were not present. Check if the onset of falling is related to medication increases and/or body weight decreases.
- check for weakness or motor impairment on only one side of the body to help rule out possible stroke as the explanation.
- record any unusual confusion, difficulty speaking, or motor difficulties in the minutes, hours, or days following a severe fall.
- provide the person's temperature, pulse, and respirations per minute to the nurse and/or physician.

❑ *MEDICAL TESTING / SCREENING FL.6*
- review the number and doses of sedating medications in light of the person's body size, fat stores, age if elderly, reduced liver function, and the frequency and severity of injuries incurred in these falls.
- medications associated with falls in elderly people are long-acting benzodiazepines, phenothiazines, tricyclic antidepressants, diuretics, narcotics, and some antihypertensives (Abrams et al., 1995, p. 68.).
- review medications for possible adverse effects on blood pressure, orthostatic tension, and heart rate. "Most patients stopped falling when the offending drug was stopped" (Larson et al., 1987, p. 173).
- review blood pressure history; screen for conditions that could cause fainting due to low blood pressure.
- do baseline and follow-up measurements of blood pressure in both supine and standing positions.
- rule out electrolyte imbalances, dehydration, fractures, seizure-related falls, and cardiovascular causes of fainting/syncope.
- rule out inner ear problems that could be affecting balance.

❑ *POSSIBLE BIOCHEMICAL / ANATOMICAL INVOLVEMENT*
- medication side effects that are associated with falls include decreased alertness, impaired judgment, and dizziness (Abrams et al., 1995, p. 69).
- excessive suppression of central nervous system (CNS) functioning due to medication can result in sudden falls forward, with or without the added complication that some medications also lower blood pressure.

❑ *COMMON FORMS*
- the person, who was found on the floor, was weak, showed facial color change, and may have still been unconscious when found.
- if the fall was witnessed, caregivers have more information about a possible sudden collapse, duration of loss of consciousness, changes in facial color, and possible clutching at the chest.
- common symptoms of mitral valve prolapse are chest pain, fatigue, dizziness, faintness upon standing, fainting, heart palpitations, anxiety, and air hunger resulting in labored or difficult breathing (Galland et al., 1986).

❑ *VARIATIONS*
- the observed loss of consciousness lasted for seconds, then the person was quiet but may report chest pain or make motions suggestive of chest pain.
- the faint may last only a few seconds.

❑ *DISTINGUISHING FEATURES FOR FL.7*
- mitral valve disorders, aortic insufficiency, or other heart abnormalities are present.
- an ischemic attack or other vascular attack is suspected.

❑ *FACTORS THAT MAY WORSEN THE CONDITION*
- engaging in competitive sports by a person with Down syndrome who has mitral valve prolapse or any of the following: arrhythmias, syncope (fainting), mitral insufficiency, chest pain, specific electrocardiographic abnormalities (Pueschel & Werner, 1994, p. 96)
- tricyclic antidepressants, especially in high doses, can have adverse effects on the heart.

❏ *PERSONS WHO MAY BE AT RISK*

- persons with Down syndrome are at increased risk for congenital heart disease (Kidd, 1992; Pueschel & Werner, 1994). Having Down syndrome increases the risk of having mitral valve prolapse (30-50% of adults) and aortic regurgitation (10-15%) (Adlin, 1993).
- persons with past episodes of acute chest pain (Pueschel & Werner, 1994).
- a person with a family history of sudden death (Pueschel & Werner, 1994) and/or heart disease.
- persons with panic disorder are at increased risk for mitral valve prolapse (see Galland et al., 1986).
- persons with hyperthyroidism are at risk for mitral valve prolapse (see Galland et al., 1986).
- persons with a chronic Candida albicans yeast infection may be at risk for mitral valve prolapse due to magnesium-deficiency (Galland et al., 1986).

❏ *SUGGESTIONS FOR COLLECTING INFORMATION*

- observe if the person shows weakness or motor impairment on only one side of the body.
- record any unusual confusion, difficulty speaking, or motor difficulties in the minutes, hours, or days following such an incident.
- check for symptoms of mitral valve prolapse such as chest pain, fatigue, dizziness, faintness upon standing, fainting, heart palpitations, anxiety, and air hunger resulting in labored or difficult breathing.
- review records for mention of past heart defects, heart problems, chronic yeast infection, panic disorder, or hyperthyroidism. Provide any past documentation of these conditions to the physician.
- check family history for sudden deaths and/or heart problems.
- record the location of cuts, bruising, discoloration, swelling, etc. with a description of which ones are new or not new.
- use the *Discomfort Scale* (Hurley et al., 1992) to assess a noncommunicative person for pain.
- provide the person's temperature, pulse, and respirations per minute to the nurse and/or physician.

❏ *MEDICAL TESTING / SCREENING FL.7*

- request an electrocardiogram for abnormalities of electrical activity of the heart (e.g., arrhythmias, myocardial infarction).
- request an echocardiogram (cardiac ultrasound) for heart valve disorders, aortic regurgitation, or other anatomical heart abnormalities. Mitral valve prolapse and aortic regurgitation "are often asymptomatic and an echocardiogram should be obtained if a murmur is noted" (Adlin, 1993, p. 58). Monitor persons with mitral valve prolapse yearly.
- check for other cardiovascular causes of syncope (fainting due to inadequate blood to the brain).
- if mitral valve prolapse is present, check the erythrocyte (red blood cell) magnesium level as the majority of mitral valve patients have low erythrocyte magnesium but normal serum magnesium and calcium (Galland et al., 1986). Treatment of 300 mg/day magnesium lactate for 4 months resulted in improvement in palpitations, chest pain, fatigue, tremor, muscle cramps, and dizziness in mitral valve patients (see Galland et al., 1986).
- rule out medication-related low blood pressure, electrolyte imbalances, dehydration, tripping, fractures, and seizure-related falls.

❏ *POSSIBLE BIOCHEMICAL / ANATOMICAL INVOLVEMENT*

- if the heart fails to pump sufficient blood to the brain, this can cause a transient loss of consciousness. "This low cardiac output is sufficient to sustain life, but is likely to be associated with fainting." (Guyton, 1986, p. 305).
- "Most features of the MVP [mitral valve prolapse] syndrome can be attributed to direct physiological effects of Mg-D [magnesium deficiency] or to secondary effects produced by blockade of EFA [essential fatty acid] desaturation. ...Hypomagnesium LT [latent tetany] is the commonest metabolic disturbance in patients with MVP." (Galland et al., 1986, p. 170).

REFERENCES

Abelson JL, Cameron OG. (1994) Adrenergic dysfunction in anxiety disorders. In: OG Cameron (ed), *Adrenergic Dysfunction and Psychobiology*. pp. 403-446. Washington, DC: American Psychiatric Press.

Abrams WB, Beers MH, Berkow R, Fletcher AJ. (1995) *The Merck Manual of Geriatrics - Second Edition*. Whitehouse Station, New Jersey: Merck Research Laboratories.

Adlin M. (1993) Health care issues. In: E Sutton, AR Factor, BA Hawkins, T Heller, GB Seltzer (eds), *Older Adults with Developmental Disabilities*. pp. 49-60. Baltimore: Brookes Publishing.

Aldenkamp AP, Vermeulen J, Mulder OG, Overweg J, Van Parys AP, Beun AM, Van 't Slot B. (1994) Gamma-vinyl GABA (Vigabatrin) and mood disturbances. *Epilepsia*, 35, 999-1004.

Alemayehu S, Bergey GK, Barry E, Krumholz A, Wolf A, Fleming CP, Frear EJ. (1995) Panic attacks as ictal manifestations of parietal lobe seizures. *Epilepsia*, 36, 824-830.

Aman MG. (1990) Considerations in the use of psychotropic drugs in elderly mentally retarded persons. *Journal of Mental Deficiency Research*, 34, 1-10.

American Psychiatric Association. (1994) *Diagnostic and Statistical Manual of Mental Disorders - Fourth Edition*. Washington, DC: American Psychiatric Association.

Ames D, Cummings JL, Wirshing WC, Quinn B, Nahler M. (1994) Repetitive and compulsive behavior in frontal lobe degenerations. *Journal of Neuropsychiatry*, 6, 100-113.

Anderson DJ, Polister B. (1993) Psychotropic medication use among older adults with mental retardation. In: E Sutton, AR Factor, BA Hawkins, T Heller, GB Seltzer (eds), *Older Adults with Developmental Disabilities*. pp. 49-60. Baltimore: Brookes Publishing.

Anderson LT, Ernst M. (1994) Self-injury in Lesch-Nyhan disease. *Journal of Autism and Developmental Disorders*, 24, 67-81.

Asberg M, Nordstrom L, Traskman-Bendz L. (1986) Cerebrospinal fluid studies in suicide, an overview. *Annals of the American Academy New York*, 487, 243-255.

Ashkenazi I, Shaher E, Brand N, Bartov E, Blumenthal M. (1992) Self-inflicted ocular mutilation in the pediatric age group. *Acta Paediatrica*, 81, 649-651.

Avery D, Wildschiodtz G, Rafaelson O. (1982) REM latency and temperature in affective disorder before and after treatment. *Biological Psychiatry*, 17, 463-470.

Aylward EH, Burt DB, Thorpe LU, Lai F, Dalton A. (1997) Diagnosis of dementia in individuals with intellectual disability. *Journal of Intellectual Disability Research*, 41, 152-164.

Babbitt RL, Hoch TA, Coe DA, Cataldo MF, Kelly KJ, Stackhouse C, Perman JA. (1994) Behavioral assessment and treatment of pediatric feeding disorders. *Journal of Developmental and Behavioral Pediatrics*, 15, 278-291.

Backstrom G, Rubin BR. (1992) *When Muscle Pain Won't Go Away*. Dallas, Texas: Taylor Publishing.

Baker RW, Chengappa R, Baird JW, Steingard S, Christ MAG, Schooler NR. (1992) Emergence of obsessive compulsive symptoms during treatment with clozapine. *Journal of Clinical Psychiatry*, 53, 439-442.

Baker SM. (1997) *Detoxification and Healing: The Key to Optimal Health*. New Canaan, Connecticut: Keats.

Baker SM, Pangborn J. (1997) *Biomedical Assessment Options for Children with Autism and Related Problems* (the Defeat Autism Now/DAN protocol). San Diego, CA: Autism Research Institute.

Baldwin D, Fineberg N, Bullock T, Montgomery S. (1992) Serotonin 1A receptors and obsessive-compulsive disorder. In: SM Stahl, M Gastpar, JM Keppel Hessling, J Traber (eds), *Serotonin 1A Receptors*. pp. 193-200. New York: Raven Press.

Ball MJ, Nutall K. (1980) Neurofibrillary tangles, granulovascular degeneration, and neuron loss in Down syndrome: quantitative comparison with Alzheimer dementia. *Annals of Neurology*, 7, 462-465.

Bambrick M, Wilson D. (1992) Recurrent neuroleptic malignant syndrome in a man with mild mental handicap. *Journal of Intellectual Disability Research*, 36, 377-381.

Bandura A. (1973) *Aggression, A Social Learning Analysis*. Englewood Cliffs, New Jersey: Prentice-Hall.

Barabas G. (1988) Tourette's syndrome: an overview. *Pediatric Annals*, 17, 391-393.

Barak Y, Ring A, Levy D, Granek I, Szor H, Elizur A. (1995) Disabling compulsions in 11 mentally retarded adults: an open trial of clomipramine SR. *Journal of Clinical Psychiatry*, 56, 459-461.

Barnes R, Veith R, Okimoto J, Raskind M, Gumbrecht G. (1982) Efficacy of antipsychotic medications in behaviorally disturbed dementia patients. *American Journal of Psychiatry*, 139, 1170-1174.

Barrett RP, Walters AS. (1992) Comment on treating suicidal behavior in the mentally retarded: the case of Kim. *Suicide and Life-Threatening Behavior*, 22, 506-510.

Bartolucci G, Younger J. (1994) Tentative classification of neuropsychiatric disturbances in Prader-Willi syndrome. *Journal of Intellectual Disability Research*, 38, 621-629.

Baskin DG, Marks JL, Schwartz MW, Figlewicz DP, Woods SC, Porte D. (1993) Insulin and insulin receptors in the brain in relation to food intake and body weight. In: H Lehnert, R Murison, H Weiner, D Hellhammer, J Beyer (eds), *Endocrine and Nutritional Control of Basic Biological Functions.* pp. 209-222. Toronto: Hogrefe & Huber.

Baxter LR. (1992) Neuroimaging studies of obsessive compulsive disorder. *Psychiatric Clinics of North America*, 15, 871-884.

Baxter LR. (1994) Positron emission tomography studies of cerebral glucose metabolism in obsessive compulsive disorder. *Journal of Clinical Psychiatry*, 55, Suppl 54-59.

Beange H, McElduff A, Baker W. (1995) Medical disorders of adults with mental retardation: a population study. *American Journal on Mental Retardation*, 99, 595-604.

Beck AT, Beck R, Kovacs M. (1975) Classification of suicidal behaviors: I. Quantifying intent and medical lethality. *American Journal of Psychiatry*, 132, 285-287.

Beck RW, Morris JB, Beck AT. (1974) Cross-validation of the Suicidal Intent Scale. *Psychological Reports*, 34, 445-446.

Benavidez DA, Matson JL. (1993) Assessment of depression in mentally retarded adolescents. *Research in Developmental Disabilities*, 14, 179-188.

Benjamin E, Buot-Smith T. (1993) Naltrexone and fluoxetine in Prader-Willi syndrome. *Journal of American Academy of Child and Adolescent Psychiatry*, 32, 870-873.

Benjamin S, Seek A, Tresise, Price E, Gagnon M. (1995) Case study: paradoxical response to naltrexone treatment of self-injurious behavior. *Journal of American Academy of Child and Adolescent Psychiatry*, 34, 238-242.

Bennett DA, Gilley DW, Wilson RS. (1992) Rate of cognitive decline and neuroleptic use in Alzheimer's disease. *Neurology*, 42, Suppl 3, 276.

Berg JM, Karlinsky H, Holland AJ. (1993) *Alzheimer Disease, Down Syndrome, and their Relationship.* New York: Oxford University Press.

Berman AL. (1992) Treating suicidal behavior in the mentally retarded: the case of Kim. *Suicide and Life-Threatening Behavior*, 22, 504-506.

Bezchlibnyk-Butler KZ, Jeffrie JJ, Martin BA. (1994) *Clinical Handbook of Psychotropic Drugs - Fourth Edition.* Toronto: Hogrefe & Huber.

Bhatara VS, Carrera J. (1994) Medications for aggressiveness. *Journal of American Academy of Child and Adolescent Psychiatry*, 33, 282.

Blundell JE, Hill AJ. (1987) Serotonergic modulation of the pattern of eating and the profile of hunger-satiety in humans. *International Journal of Obesity*, 11, Suppl 3, 141-155.

Bodfish JW, Crawford TW, Powell SB, Parker DE, Golden RN, Lewis MH. (1995) Compulsions in adults with mental retardation: prevalence, phenomenology, comorbidity with stereotypy and self-injury. *American Journal of Mental Retardation*, 100, 183-192.

Boetz MI, Young SN. (1991) Effects of anticonvulsant treatment and low levels of folate and thiamine on amine metabolites in cerebrospinal fluid. *Brain*, 114, 333-348.

Boetz MI, Young SN, Bachevalier J, Gauthier S. (1982) Effect of folic acid and vitamin B_{12} deficiencies on 5-hydroxyindolacetic acid in human cerebrospinal fluid. *Annals of Neurology*, 12, 479-484.

Bohen NI, Warner MA, Kokmen E, Beard CM, Kurland LT. (1994a) Alzheimer's disease and cumulative exposure to anesthesia: a case-control study. *Journal of the American Geriatrics Society*, 42, 198-201.

Bohen N, Warner MA, Kokmen E, Kurland LT. (1994b) Early and midlife exposure to anesthesia and age of onset of Alzheimer's disease. *International Journal of Neuroscience*, 77, 181-185.

Bonnetblanc JM, Dutheil MJ, Bernard P. (1986) Prurit et porphyrie cutanee tardive. *Annales Dermatologie Venereologie*, 113, 133-136.

Bosch J, Van Dyke DC, Smith SM, Poulton S. (1997) Role of medical conditions in the exacerbation of self-injurious behavior: an exploratory study. *Mental Retardation*, 35, 124-130.

Bowen DM, Allen SJ, Benton JS, Goodhardt MJ, Haan EA, Palmer AN, Sims NR, Smith CCT, Spilane JA, Esiri MM, Neary D, Snowden JS, Wilcock GK, Davidson AN. (1983) Biochemical assessment of serotonergic and cholinergic dysfunction and cerebral atrophy in Alzheimer's disease. *Journal of Neurochemistry*, 41, 266-272.

Boyd RD. (1993) Neuroleptic malignant syndrome and mental retardation: review and analysis of 29 cases. *American Journal on Mental Retardation*, 98, 143-155.

Bradley EA, Udwin O. (1989) Williams syndrome in adulthood: a case study focusing on psychological and psychiatric aspects. *Journal of Mental Deficiency Research*, 33, 175-184.

Braly J. (1992) *Dr. Braly's Food Allergy and Nutrition Revolution.* New Canaan, Connecticut: Keats Publishing.

Bremner AJ, Regan A. (1991) Polydipsia and water intoxication in a mental handicap hospital. *British Journal of Psychiatry*, 158, 244-250.

Bremner JD, Randall P, Scott TM, Bronen RA, Seibyl JP, Southwick SM, Delaney RC, McCarthy G, Charney DS, Innis RB. (1995) MRI-based measurement of hippocampal volume in patients with combat-related posttraumatic stress disorder. *American Journal of Psychiatry*, 152, 973-981.

Bremner JD, Scott TM, Delaney RC, Southwick SM, Mason JW, Johnson DR, Innis RB, McCarthy G, Charney DS. (1993) Deficits in short-term memory in posttraumatic stress disorder. *American Journal of Psychiatry*, 150,

1015-1019.

Brewerton TD. (1989) Seasonal variation of serotonin function in humans, research and clinical implications. *Annals of Clinical Psychiatry*, 1, 153-164.

Brown JW, Chobor A, Zinn F. (1993) Dementia testing in the elderly. *Journal of Nervous and Mental Disease*, 181, 695-698.

Bryson Y, Sakati N, Nyhan WL, Fish CH. (1971) Self-mutilative behavior in the Cornelia de Lange syndrome. *American Journal of Mental Deficiency*, 76, 319-324.

Buchanan N. (1992) The occurrence, management and outcome of antiepileptic drug side effects in 767 patients. *Seizure*, 1, 89-98.

Buckley PF, Hutchinson M. (1995) Neuroleptic malignant syndrome. *Journal of Neurology, Neurosurgery, and Psychiatry*, 58, 271-273.

Bugle C, Rubin HB. (1993) Effects of a nutritional supplement on coprophagia: a study of three cases. *Research in Developmental Disabilities*, 14, 445-456.

Burns A, Jacoby R. (1988) Vitamin B_{12} deficiency in demented patients. *Journal of the American Geriatrics Society*, 36, 85-86.

Burt DB, Loveland KA, Lewis KR. (1992) Depression and the onset of dementia in adults with mental retardation. *American Journal on Mental Retardation*, 96, 502-511.

Cade R, Wagemaker H, Privette RM, Fregly MJ, Rogers J, Orlando J. (1990) The effect of dialysis and diet on schizophrenia. In: CN Stefanis et al (eds), *Psychiatry: A World Perspective - Volume 3.* pp. 494-500. New York: Elsevier.

Carmel R, Gott, PS, Waters CH, Cairo K, Green R, Bondareff W, DeGiorgio CM, Cummings JL, Jacobsen DW, Buckwalter G, et al.(1995) The frequently low cobalamin levels in dementia usually signify treatable metabolic, neurologic and electrophysiologic abnormalities. *European Journal of Haematology* 54, 245-253.

Carney MWP. (1990) Vitamin deficiency and mental symptoms. *British Journal of Psychiatry*, 156, 878-882.

Cascino GD, Sutula TP. (1989) Thirst and compulsive water drinking in medial basal limbic epilepsy: an electro-clinical and neuropathological correlation. *Journal of Neurology, Neurosurgery, and Psychiatry*, 52, 680-681.

Cassone VM, Chesworth MJ, Armstrong SM. (1986) Entrainment of rat circadian rhythms by daily injections of melatonin depends upon the hypothalamic suprachiasmatic nuclei. *Physiology of Behavior*, 36, 1111-1121.

Cavallo A, Holt KG, Hejazi MS, Richards GE, Meter WJ. (1987) Melatonin circadian rhythm in childhood depression. *Journal of American Academy of Child and Adolescent Psychiatry*, 26, 395-399.

Chafetz MD. (1990) *Nutrition and Neurotransmitters, The Nutrient Bases of Behavior.* Englewood Cliffs, New Jersey: Prentice Hall.

Chandra RK. (1992) Effect of vitamin and trace-element supplementation on immune responses and infection in elderly subjects. *Lancet*, 340, 1124-7.

Childs PA, Rodin I, Martin NJ, Allen NHP, Plaskett L, Smythe PJ, Thompson C. (1995) Effect of fluoxetine on melatonin in patients with seasonal affective disorder and matched controls. *British Journal of Psychiatry*, 166, 196-198.

Chinn TA. (1974) Single case study, compulsive water drinking. *Journal of Nervous and Mental Disease*, 158, 78-80.

Clarke DJ. (1993) Prader-Willi syndrome and psychoses. *British Journal of Psychiatry*, 163, 680-684.

Clarke DJ, Waters J, Corbett JA. (1989) Adults with Prader-Willi syndrome: abnormalities of sleep and behavior. *Journal of the Royal Society of Medicine*, 82, 21-24.

Clarke DJ, Yapa P. (1991) Phenylketonuria and anorexia nervosa. *Journal of Mental Deficiency Research*, 35, 165-170.

Claustrat B, Brun J, David M, Sassolas G, Chazot G. (1992) Melatonin and jet lag: confirmatory result using a simplified protocol. *Biological Psychiatry*, 32, 705-711.

Coccaro EF. (1989) Central serotonin and impulsive aggression. *British Journal of Psychiatry*, 155, Suppl 8, 52-62.

Cohen IL. (1995) Behavioral profiles of autistic and nonautistic Fragile X males. *Developmental Brain Dysfunction*, 8: 252-269.

Cole HS, Lopez R, Epel R, Singh BK, Cooperman JM. (1985) Nutritional deficiencies in institutionalized mentally retarded and physically disabled individuals. *American Journal of Mental Deficiency*, 89, 552-555.

Cole MG, Prachal JF. (1984) Low serum vitamin B_{12} in Alzheimer-type dementia. *Age and Ageing*, 13, 101-105.

Coleman M. (1973) *Serotonin in Down's Syndrome.* New York: American Elsevier.

Coleman M. (1994) Clinical presentations of patients with autism and hypocalcinuria. *Developmental Brain Dysfunction*, 7, 63-70.

Collacott RA, Cooper SA, McGrother C. (1992) Differential rates of psychiatric disorders in adults with Down's syndrome compared with other mentally handicapped adults. *British Journal of Psychiatry*, 161, 671-674.

Coltman CA. (1969) Pagophagia and iron lack. *Journal of the American Medical Association*, 207, 513-516.

Commander M, Green SH, Prendergast M. (1991) Behavioural disturbances in children treated with clonazepam.

Developmental Medicine and Child Neurology, 33, 362-364.

Cookson J. (1993) Side-effects of antidepressants. *British Journal of Psychiatry,* Suppl 20, 20-24.

Cooper SA, Collacott RA. (1994) Clinical features and diagnostic criteria of depression in Down's syndrome. *British Journal of Psychiatry,* 165, 399-403.

Corbett JA, Trimble MR, Nichol TC. (1985) Behavioral and cognitive impairments in children with epilepsy: the long-term effects of anticonvulsant therapy. *Journal of American Academy of Child and Adolescent Psychiatry,* 24, 17-23.

Cox IM, Campbell MJ, Dowson D. (1991) Red blood cell magnesium and chronic fatigue syndrome. *Lancet,* 337, 757-760.

Creaby M, Warner M, Jamil N, Jawad S. (1993) Ictal aggression in severely mentally handicapped people. *Irish Journal of Psychological Medicine,* 10, 12-15.

Crook WG. (1996) *The Yeast Connection Handbook.* Jackson, Tennessee: Professional Books.

Czeisler CA, Shapiro CM. (1995) Circadian rhythm disorders. In: CM Shapiro (ed), *Sleep Solutions Manual.* pp. 190-207. Pointe Claire, Quebec: Kommunicom Publications.

Dailey JW, Naritoku DK. (1996) Antidepressants and seizures: clinical anecdotes overshadow neuroscience. *Biochemical Pharmacology,* 52, 1323-1329.

Dallal HJ, Odum J, Ahluwalia NK. (1996) Covert dysphagia in the mentally handicapped: two case reports and a review of published literature. *Dysphagia,* 11, 194-197.

Dalton AJ, Seltzer GB, Adlin MS, Wisniewski HM. (1993) Associations between Alzheimer disease and Down syndrome: clinical observations. In: JM Berg, H Karlinsky, AJ Holland (eds), *Alzheimer Disease, Down Syndrome, and their Relationship.* pp. 53-69. New York: Oxford University Press.

Daniel A, Shekim WO, Koresko RL, Dekirmenjian H. (1980) Congenital sensory neuropathy with anhydrosis--a case report and investigation of autonomic nervous system abnormalities. *Developmental and Behavioral Pediatrics,* 1, 49-53.

Danford DE, Huber AM. (1982) Pica among mentally retarded adults. *American Journal of Mental Deficiency,* 87, 141-146.

Danna PL, Urban C, Bellin E, Rahal JJ. (1991) Role of candida in pathogenesis of antibiotic-associated diarrhoea in elderly patients. *Lancet,* 337, 511-514.

Davidson PW, Cain NN, Sloane-Reeves JE, Speybroech AV, Segel J, Gutkin J, Quijano LE, Kramer BM, Porter B, Shoham I, Goldstein E. (1994) Characteristics of community-based individuals with mental retardation and aggressive behavioral disorders. *American Journal on Mental Retardation,* 98, 704-716.

Deahl M, Trimble M. (1992) Serotonin reuptake inhibitors, epilepsy and myoclonus. *British Journal of Psychiatry,* 159, 433-435.

Deas-Nesmith D, Brewerton TD. (1992) A case of fluoxetine-responsive psychogenic polydipsia: a variant of obsessive-compulsive disorder? *Journal of Nervous and Mental Disease,* 180, 338-339.

Deb S. (1994) Effects of folate metabolism on the psychopathology of adults with mental retardation and epilepsy. *American Journal on Mental Retardation,* 98, 717-723.

Deb S, Bramble D, Drybala G, Boyle A, Bruce J. (1994) Polydipsia amongst adults with a learning disability in an institution. *Journal of Intellectual Disability Research,* 38, 359-367.

Deb S, Cowie VA, Richens A. (1987) Folate metabolism and problem behaviour in mentally handicapped epileptics. *Journal of Mental Deficiency Research,* 31, 163-168.

Decker CJ. (1993) Pica in the mentally handicapped: a 15-year surgical perspective. *Canadian Journal of Surgery,* 36, 551-554.

De Groot CM, Bornstein RA, Baker GB. (1995) Obsessive-compulsive symptom clusters and urinary amine correlates in Tourette syndrome. *Journal of Nervous and Mental Disease,* 183, 224-230.

Delgado-Escueta AV, Swartz BE, Walsh GO, Chauvel P, Bancaud J, Broglin D. (1991) Frontal lobe seizures and epilepsies in neurobehavioral disorders. *Advances in Neurology,* 55, 317-340.

Delva MD. (1997) Vitamin B_{12} replacement, To B_{12} or not to B_{12}? *Canadian Family Physician,* 43, 917-922.

Demisch K, Demisch L, Bochnik HJ, Nickelsen T, Althoff PH, Schoffling K, Rieth R. (1986) Melatonin and cortisol increase after fluvoxamine. *British Journal of Clinical Pharmacology,* 22, 620-622.

Denicoff K, Joffe RT, Rubinow DR, Robbins J. (1990) Neuropsychiatric manifestations of altered thyroid state. *American Journal of Psychiatry,* 147, 94-99.

De Silva P, Deb S, Drummond RD, Rankin R. (1992) A fatal case of ischaemic colitis following long-term use of neuroleptic medication. *Journal of Intellectual Disability Research,* 36, 371-375.

DesNoyers Hurley A. (1996) The misdiagnosis of hallucinations and delusions in persons with mental retardation: a neurodevelopmental perspective. *Seminars in Clinical Neuropsychiatry,* 1, 122-133.

Devenny DA, Silverman WP, Hill AL, Jenkins E, Sersen EA, Wisniewski KE. (1996) Normal ageing in adults with Down's syndrome: a longitudinal study. *Journal of Intellectual Disability Research,* 40, 208-221.

Devinsky O. (1995) Cognitive and behavioral effects of antiepileptic drugs. *Epilepsia,* 36, Suppl 2, S46-S65.

Devinsky O, Bear D. (1984) Varieties of aggressive behavior in temporal lobe epilepsy. *American Journal of Psychiatry*, 141, 651-656.

Dinani S, Carpenter S. (1990) Down's syndrome and thyroid disease. *Journal of Mental Deficiency Research*, 34, 187-193.

Domingues JC, Moreno A, Mariano A, Tellechea O, Correia C, Goncalves O, Poiares Baptista A. (1994) Congenital sensory neuropathy with anhidrosis. *Pediatric Dermatology*, 11, 231-236.

Donnellan AM, Mirenda PL, Mesaros RA, Fassbender LL. (1984) Analyzing the communicative functions of aberrant behavior. *Journal of the Association for Persons with Severe Handicaps*, 9, 201-212.

Donovan NJ, Barry JJ. (1994) Compulsive symptoms associated with frontal lobe injury. *American Journal of Psychiatry*, 151, 618.

Dorn LD, Burgess ES, Dichek HL, Putnam FW, Chrousos GP, Gold PW. (1996) Thyroid hormone concentrations in depressed and nondepressed adolescents: group differences and behavioral relations. *Journal of American Academy of Child and Adolescent Psychiatry*, 35, 299-336.

Dorn MB, Mazzacco MM, Hagerman RJ. (1994) Behavioral and psychiatric disorders in adult male carriers of Fragile X. *Journal of American Academy of Child and Adolescent Psychiatry*, 33, 256-264.

Dossetor DR, Couryer S, Nicol AR. (1991) Massage for very severe self-injurious behaviour in a girl with Cornelia de Lange syndrome. *Developmental Medicine and Child Neurology*, 33, 636-644.

Dunne LJ. (1990) *Nutrition Almanac - Third Edition*. New York: McGraw-Hill.

Dykens EM, Finucane BM, Gayley C. (1997) Brief report: cognitive and behavioral profiles in persons with Smith-Magenis syndrome. *Journal of Autism and Developmental Disorders*, 27, 203-211.

Dykens EM, Hodapp RM, Walsh K, Nash LJ. (1992) Adaptive and maladaptive behavior in Prader-Willi syndrome. *Journal of American Academy of Child and Adolescent Psychiatry*, 31, 1131-1136.

Essman WB, Essman EJ. (1986) Drug effects and receptor changes in aggressive behavior. In: C Shagass, RC Josiassen, WH Bridger, KJ Weiss, D Stoff, GM Simpson (eds), *Biological Psychiatry 1985*. pp. 662-665. New York: Elsevier.

Estroff TW, Gold MS. (1986) Medication-induced and toxin-induced psychiatric disorders. In: I Extein, MS Gold (eds), *Medical Mimics of Psychiatric Disorders*. pp. 163-198. Washington, D.C.: American Psychiatric Press.

Evenhuis HM. (1990) Evaluation of a screening instrument for dementia in ageing mentally retarded persons. *Journal of Intellectual Deficiency Research*, 36, 337-347.

Evenhuis HM. (1997) The natural history of dementia in ageing people with intellectual disability. *Journal of Intellectual Disability Research*, 41, 92-96.

Evenhuis HM, van Zanten GA, Brocaar MP, Roerdinkholder WHM. (1992) Hearing loss in middle-age persons with Down syndrome. *American Journal on Mental Retardation*, 97, 47-56.

Farber LG, Schmaltz LW, Volle FO, Hecht P. (1986) Temporal lobe epilepsy: diagnostic accuracy. *International Journal of Clinical Neuropsychology*, 8, 76-79.

Flanigan MJ, Shapiro CM. (1995) Dangers of sleep. In: CM Shapiro (ed), *Sleep Solutions Manual*. pp. 60-76. Pointe Claire, Quebec: Kommunicom Publications.

Fleming JAE, Shapiro CM. (1995a) Sleep function and insomnia assessment. In: CM Shapiro (ed), *Sleep Solutions Manual*. pp. 2-32. Pointe Claire, Quebec: Kommunicom Publications.

Fleming JAE, Shapiro CM. (1995b) Insomnia management. In: CM Shapiro (ed), *Sleep Solutions Manual*. pp. 34-58. Pointe Claire, Quebec: Kommunicom Publications.

Fleming J. (1996) Sleep disorders and the handicapped. National Association for the Dually Diagnosed Conference Proceedings, November 1996. pp. 75-87. Kingston, New York: NADD.

Flexman JP, Lavis NJ, Kay ID, Watson M, Metcalf C, Pearman JW. (1995) Bartonella henselae is a causative agent of cat scratch disease in Australia. *Journal of Infection*, 31, 241-245.

France TD. (1992) Ocular disorders in Down syndrome. In: IT Lott, EE McCoy (eds), *Down Syndrome, Advances in Medical Care*. pp. 147-154. New York: John Wiley & Sons.

Franks RD, Richter AJ. (1979) Schizophrenia-like psychosis associated with anticonvulsant toxicity. *American Journal of Psychiatry*, 136, 973-974.

Friedman DL, Kastner T, Plummer AT, Ruiz MQ, Henning D. (1992) Adverse behavioral effects in individuals with mental retardation and mood disorders treated with carbamazepine. *American Journal on Mental Retardation*, 96, 541-546.

Friedman DL, Kastener T, Pond WS, O'Brien DR. (1989) Thyroid dysfunction in individuals with Down syndrome. *Archives of Internal Medicine*, 149, 1990-1993.

Fukuda K, Etoh T, Okuma T. (1986) Affective disorders in mentally retarded adolescents--report of two cases with lithium treatment. *Japanese Journal of Psychiatry and Neurology*, 40, 551-557.

Fusco L, Iani C, Faedda T, Manfredi M, Vigevano F, Ambroetto G, Ciarmatori C, Tassinari CA. (1990) Mesial frontal lobe epilepsy: a clinical entity not sufficiently described. *Journal of Epilepsy*, 3, 123-135.

Gabler-Halle D, Halle JW, Chung B. (1993) The effects of aerobic exercise on psychological and behavioral variables of individuals with developmental disabilities: a critical review. *Research in Developmental Disabilities*, 14, 359-386.

Galderisi S, Mucci A, Catapano F, Colucci D'Amato A, Maj M. (1995) Neuropsychological slowness in obsessive-compulsive patients, Is it confined to tests involving the fronto-subcortical systems? *British Journal of Psychiatry*, 167, 394-398.

Galland L. (1992) Magnesium, stress and neuropsychiatric disorders. *Magnesium Trace Elements*, 10, 287-301.

Galland LD, Baker SM, McLellan RK. (1986) Magnesium deficiency in the pathogenesis of mitral valve prolapse. *Magnesium*, 5, 165-174.

Gardener AR, Gardener AJ. (1975) Self-mutilation, obsessionality and narcissism. *British Journal of Psychiatry*, 127, 127-132.

Gardos G. (1980) Disinhibition of behavior by antianxiety drugs. *Psychosomatics*, 21, 1025-1026.

Garfield JM, Cassens G, Gugino L, Bizzarri-Schmid M, Williams E. (1989) Preliminary studies of postoperative cognitive deficits following general anesthesia in elderly patients. Paper presented to the International Neurological Society, Vancouver, Canada.

Garioch JJ, Lewis HM, Sargent SA, Leonard JN, Fry L. (1994) 25 years' experience of a gluten-free diet in the treatment of dematitis herpetiformis. *British Journal of Dermatology*, 131, 541-545.

Gedye A. (1989a) Episodic rage and aggression attributed to frontal lobe seizures. *Journal of Mental Deficiency Research*, 33, 369-379.

Gedye A. (1989b) Extreme self-injury attributed to frontal lobe seizures. *American Journal on Mental Retardation*, 94, 20-26.

Gedye A. (1990) Dietary increase in serotonin reduces self-injurious behaviour in a Down's syndrome adult. *Journal of Mental Deficiency Research*, 34, 195-203.

Gedye A. (1991a) Frontal lobe seizures in autism. *Medical Hypotheses*, 34, 174-182.

Gedye A. (1991b) The self-injury hypothesis: addressing a neurologist's concerns. *American Journal on Mental Retardation*, 96, 85-94.

Gedye A. (1991c) Tourette syndrome attributed to frontal lobe dysfunction: numerous etiologies involved. *Journal of Clinical Psychology*, 47, 233-252.

Gedye A. (1991d) Serotonergic treatment for aggression in a Down's syndrome adult showing signs of Alzheimer's disease. *Journal of Mental Deficiency Research*, 35, 247-258.

Gedye A. (1991e) Buspirone alone or with serotonergic diet reduced aggression in a developmentally disabled adult. *Biological Psychiatry*, 30, 88-91.

Gedye A. (1992a) Recognizing obsessive-compulsive disorder in clients with developmental disabilities. *Habilitative Mental Healthcare Newsletter*, 11, 73-77.

Gedye A. (1992b) Anatomy of self-injurious, stereotypic, and aggressive movements: evidence for involuntary explanation. *Journal of Clinical Psychology*, 48, 766-778.

Gedye A. (1992c) Serotonin-GABA treatment is hypothesized for self-injury in Lesch-Nyhan syndrome. *Medical Hypotheses*, 38, 325-328.

Gedye A. (1995) *Dementia Scale For Down Syndrome*, Instruction Manual and Test Booklet. Vancouver, Canada: Author.

Gedye A. (1996a) Issues involved in recognizing obsessive-compulsive disorder in developmentally disabled clients. *Seminars in Clinical Neuropsychiatry*, 1, 142-147.

Gedye A. (1996b) Recognizing involuntary movements with vocalizations and autonomic changes: a Nonconvulsive Ictal Signs Checklist. *Habilitative Mental Healthcare Newsletter*, 15, 71-80.

Gedye A. (1998) Neuroleptic-induced dementia documented in four adults with mental retardation. *Mental Retardation*, 36, 182-186.

Gedye A, Beattie BL, Tuokko H, Horton A, Kosarek E.(1989) Severe head injury hastens age of onset of Alzheimer's disease. *Journal of the American Geriatrics Society*, 37, 970-973.

Gedye A, Russell J. (1995) Common concerns in Down syndrome: initial signs and steps to take. *Habilitative Mental Healthcare Newsletter*, 14, 31-33.

George EK, Mearin ML, Bouquet J, von Blomberg BME, Stapel SO, van Elburg RM, de Graaf EAB. (1996) High frequency of celiac disease in Down syndrome. *Journal of Pediatrics*, 128, 555-557.

Gershon ES, Goldstein RE, Moss AJ, van Kammen DP. (1979) Psychosis with ordinary doses of propranolol. *Annals of Internal Medicine*, 90, 938- 939.

Gillberg C, Coleman M. (1992) *The Biology of the Autistic Syndromes - 2nd Edition*. New York: Cambridge University Press.

Gillberg C, Uvebrant P, Carlsson G, Hedstrom A, Silfvenius H. (1996) Autism and epilepsy (and tuberous sclerosis?) in two pre-adolescent boys: neuropsychiatric aspects before and after epilepsy surgery. *Journal of Intellectual Disability Research*, 40, 75-81.

Glover D, Maltzman I, Williams C. (1996) Food preferences among individuals with and without Prader-Willi syndrome. *American Journal on Mental Retardation*, 101, 195-205.

Gobbi G, Bouquet F, Greco L, Lambertini A, Tassinari CA, Ventura A, Zaniboni MG. (1992) Coeliac disease, epilepsy, and cerebral calcifications. *Lancet*, 340, 439-443.

Godfrey PSA, Toone BK, Carney MWP, Flynn TG, Bottiglieri T, Laundy M, Chanarin I, Reynolds EH. (1990) Enhancement of recovery from psychiatric illness by methylfolate. *Lancet*, 336, 392-395.

Goggans FC, Allen RM, Gold MS. (1986) Primary hypothyroidism and its relationship to affective disorders. In: I Extein, MS Gold (eds), *Medical Mimics of Psychiatric Disorders*. pp. 93-109. Washington, D.C.: American Psychiatric Press.

Goggin T, Gough H, Bissessar A, Crowley M, Baker M, Callahan N. (1987) A comparative study of the relative effects of anticonvulsant drugs and dietary folate on the red cell folate status of patients with epilepsy. *Quarterly Journal of Medicine*, Series 65, 911-919.

Goodhart SP, Savitsky N. (1933) Self-mutilation in chronic encephalitis. Avulsion of both eyeballs and extraction of teeth. *American Journal of Medical Sciences*, 185, 674-684.

Goodman WK, McDougle CJ, Price LH, Riddle MA, Pauls DL, Leckman JF. (1990) Beyond the serotonin hypothesis: a role for dopamine in some forms of obsessive compulsive disorder? *Journal of Clinical Psychiatry*, 51, 8 Suppl, 36-43.

Goodwin FK, Wirz-Justice A, Wehr TA. (1982) Evidence that the pathophysiology of depression and the mechanism of action of antidepressant drugs both involve alterations in circadian rhythms. In: E Costa, G Racagni (eds), *Typical and Atypical Antidepressants: Clinical Practice*. pp. 1-11. New York: Raven Press.

Green AR. (1986) Changes in gamma-aminobutyric acid biochemistry and seizure threshold. *Annals of New York Academy of Sciences*, 462, 105-119.

Greenberg A, Coleman M. (1973) Depressed whole blood serotonin levels associated with behavioral abnormalities in the de Lange syndrome. *Pediatrics*, 52, 720-724.

Greenwald BS, Marin DB, Silverman SM. (1986) Serotoninergic treatment of screaming and banging in dementia. *Lancet*, i, 464-65.

Gross JS, Weintraub NT, Neufeld RR, Libow LS. (1986) Pernicious anemia in the demented patient without anemia or macrocytosis. *Journal of the American Geriatrics Society*, 34, 612-614.

Gualtieri CT. (1989) The differential diagnosis of self-injurious behavior in mentally retarded people. *Psychopharmacology Bulletin*, 25, 358-363.

Gualtieri CT. (1991) *Neuropsychiatry and Behavioral Pharmacology*. New York: Springer-Verlag.

Gualtieri CT, Schroeder SR, Hicks RE, Quade D. (1986) Tardive dyskinesia in young mentally retarded individuals. *Archives of General Psychiatry*, 43, 335-340.

Guberman A, Cantu-Reyna G, Stuss D, Broughton R. (1986) Nonconvulsive generalized status epilepticus: clinical features, neuropsychological testing, and long-term follow-up. *Neurology*, 36, 1284-1291.

Gupta A, Eggo MC, Uetrecht JP, Cribb AE, Daneman D, Reider MJ, Shear NH, Cannon M, Spielberg SP. (1992) Drug-induced hypothyroidism: the thyroid as a target organ in hypersensitivity reactions to anticonvulsants and sulfonamides. *Clinical Psychopharmacology Therapy*, 51, 56-67.

Guyton AC. (1986) *Textbook of Medical Physiology, 7th Edition*. Philadelphia: WB Saunders.

Hachinski VC, Iliff KLD, Zilhka E, Du Boulay GH, McAllister VL, Marshall J, Russell RWR, Symon L. (1975) Cerebral blood flow in dementia. *Archives of Neurology*, 32, 632-637.

Hageman G, Hilhorst BGJ, Rozeboom AR. (1992) Is there involvement of the central nervous system in hereditary sensory radicular neuropathy? *Clinical Neurology and Neurosurgery*, 94, 49-54.

Hales RE, Hershey SC. (1984) Psychopharmacologic issues in the diagnosis and treatment of organic mental disorders. *Psychiatric Clinics of North America*, 7, 817-829.

Hanifin JM. (1991) Atopic dermatitis: new therapeutic considerations. *Journal of American Academy of Dermatology*, 24, 1097-1101.

Hanly PJ, Shapiro CM. (1995) Excessive daytime sleepiness. In: CM Shapiro (ed), *Sleep Solutions Manual*. pp. 78-103. Pointe Claire, Quebec: Kommunicom Publications.

Hare RD. (1993a) *Without Conscience. The Disturbing World of Psychopaths Among Us*. New York: Simon & Schuster.

Hare RD. (1993b) *Hare Psychopathy Checklist-Revised*. Toronto: Multi-Health Systems.

Hargrave R, Martinez AJ. (1992) Fluoxetine-induced seizures. *Psychosomatics*, 33, 236-237.

Harper M, Reid AH. (1987) Use of a restricted protein diet in the treatment of behaviour disorder in a severely mentally retarded adult female phenylketonuric patient. *Journal of Mental Deficiency Research*, 31, 209-212.

Hector M, Burton JR. (1988) What are the psychiatric manifestations of vitamin B_{12} deficiency? *Journal of the American Geriatrics Society*, 36, 1105-1112.

Helms P. (1985) Efficacy of antipsychotics in the treatment of the behavioral complications of dementia: a review of the literature. *Journal of the American Geriatrics Society*, 33, 206-209.

Hennig J, Daume E, Netter P. (1993) Patterns of periodicity in eating behavior during the menstrual cycle in healthy women and their relations to hormones and behavior. In: H Lehnert, R Murison, H Weiner, D Hellhammer, J Beyer (eds), *Endocrine and Nutritional Control of Basic Biological Functions*. pp. 151-159. Toronto: Hogrefe & Huber.

Hertzberg J, Nakisbendi L, Needleman HL, Pober B. (1994) Williams syndrome--oral presentation of 45 cases. *Pediatric Dentistry*, 16, 262-267.

Hillbrand M. (1992) Self-directed and other-directed aggressive behavior in a forensic sample. *Suicide and Life-Threatening Behavior*, 22, 333-341.

Hiyoshi T, Masakazu S, Mihara T, Matsuda K, Tottori T, Yagi K, Wada JA. (1989) Emotional facial expressions at the onset of temporal lobe seizures: observations on scalp and intracranial EEG recordings. *Japanese Journal of Psychiatry and Neurology*, 43, 421-426.

Holland AJ, Karlinsky H, Berg JM. (1993) Alzheimer disease in persons with Down syndrome: diagnostic and management considerations. In: JM Berg, H Karlinsky, AJ Holland (eds), *Alzheimer Disease, Down Syndrome, and their Relationship*. pp. 95-114. New York: Oxford University Press.

Holland AJ, Treasure J, Coskeran P, Dallow J. (1995) Characteristics of the eating disorder in Prader-Willi syndrome: implications for treatment. *Journal of Intellectual Disability Research*, 39, 373-381.

Hollins S. (1995) Managing grief better: people with developmental disabilities. *Habilitative Mental Healthcare Newsletter*, 14, 50-52.

Horn CS, Ater SB, Hurst DL. (1986) Carbamazepine-exacerbated epilepsy in children and adolescents. *Pediatric Neurology*, 2, 340-345.

Huminer D, Symon K, Groskopf I, Pietrushka D, Kremer I, Schantz PM, Pitlik SD. (1992) Seroepidemiologic study of toxocariasis and strongyloidiasis in institutionalized mentally retarded adults. *American Journal of Tropical Medicine and Hygiene*, 46, 278-91.

Hunt A. (1993) Development, behaviour and seizures in 300 cases of tuberous sclerosis. *Journal of Intellectual Disability Research*, 37, 41-51.

Hurley AC, Volicer BJ, Hanrahan PA, Houde S, Volicer L. (1992) Assessment of discomfort in advanced Alzheimer patients. *Research in Nursing and Health*, 15, 369-377.

Hyman SL, Fisher W, Mercugliano M, Cataldo MF. (1990) Children with self-injurious behavior. *Pediatrics*, 85, Suppl, 437-441.

Hynes AFM, Vickar EL. (1996) Case study: neuroleptic malignant syndrome without pyrexia. *Journal of American Academy of Child and Adolescent Psychiatry*, 35, 959-962.

Intrator J, Hare R, Stritzke P, Brichtswein K, Dorfman D, Harpur T, Bernstein D, Handelsman L, Schaefer C, Keilp J, Rosen J, Machac J. (1997) A brain imaging (single photon emission computerized tomography) study of semantic and affective processing in psychopaths. *Biological Psychiatry*, 42, 96-103.

Ishii N, Kawaguchi H, Miyakawa K, Nakajima H. (1988) Congenital sensory neuropathy with anhidrosis. *Archives of Dermatology*, 124, 564-566.

Isojarvi JI, Pakarinen AJ, Myllyla VV. (1992) Thyroid function and antiepileptic drugs. *Epilepsia*, 33, 142-148.

Jain KK. (1996) *Drug-Induced Neurological Disorders*. Toronto: Hogrefe & Huber.

Jan JE, Espezel H, Appleton RE. (1994a) The treatment of sleep disorders with melatonin. *Developmental Medicine and Child Neurology*, 36, 97-107.

Jan JE, Good WV, Freeman RD, Esperzel H. (1994b) Eye-poking. *Developmental Medicine and Child Neurology*, 36, 321-325.

Jawed SH, Krishnan VHR, Prasher VP, Corbett JA. (1993) Worsening of pica as a symptom of depressive illness in a person with severe mental handicap. *British Journal of Psychiatry*, 162, 835-837.

Jenike MA. (1992) Pharmacologic treatment of obsessive compulsive disorders. *Psychiatric Clinics of North America*, 15, 895-919.

Jenike MA, Hyman S, Baer L, Holland A, Minichiello WE, Buttolph L, Summergrad P, Seymour R, Riccardi J. (1990) A controlled trial of fluvoxamine in obsessive compulsive disorder: implications for a serotonergic theory. *American Journal of Psychiatry*, 147, 1209-1215.

Jones NP. (1990) Self-enucleation and psychosis. *British Journal of Ophthalmology*, 74, 571-573.

Jones PM. (1989) Feeding disorders in children with multiple handicaps. *Developmental Medicine and Child Neurology*, 31, 404-406.

Kalachnik JE, Hanzel TE, Harder SR, Bauernfeind JD, Engstrom EA. (1995) Antiepileptic drug behavioral side effects in individuals with mental retardation and the use of behavioral measurement techniques. *Mental Retardation*, 33, 374-382.

Kales A, Soldatos CR, Bixler EO, Kales JD. (1983) Rebound insomnia and rebound anxiety: a review. *Pharmacology*, 26, 121-137

Kanemoto K, Kawasaki J, Kawai I. (1996) Postictal psychosis: a comparison with acute interictal and chronic psychoses. *Epilepsia*, 37, 551-556.

Kaplan PW. (1996) Nonconvulsive status epilepticus in the emergency room. *Epilepsia*, 37, 643-650.

Kapoor WN. (1992) Evaluation and management of the patient with syncope. *Journal of the American Medical Association*, 268, 2553-2560.

Kastener T, Friedman DL, Pond WI. (1992) Carbamazepine-induced hyponatremia in patients with mental retardation. *American Journal on Mental Retardation*, 96, 536-546.

Keeling PJ, Ramsay J, Shand WS. (1987) Pica, paper, and pseudoporphyria. *Lancet*, ii, 1095.

Kellner CH, Best CL, Roberts JM, Bajorksten O. (1985) Self-destructive behavior in hospitalized medical and surgical patients. *Psychiatric Clinics of North America*, 8, 279-89.

Kidd L. (1992) Cardiorespiratory problems in children with Down syndrome. In: IT Lott, EE McCoy (eds), *Down Syndrome, Advances in Medical Care*. pp. 61-69. New York: John Wiley & Sons.

Kinnell HG. (1985) Pica as a feature of autism. *British Journal of Psychiatry*, 147, 80-82.

Kirby S, Sadler RM. (1995) Injury and death as a result of seizures. *Epilepsia*, 36, 25-28.

Klonoff EA, Moore DJ. (1984) Compulsive polydipsia presenting as diabetes insipidus: a behavioral approach. *Journal of Behavior Therapy and Experimental Psychiatry*, 15, 353-358.

Klonoff PS, Costa L, Snow WG. (1986) Predictors and indicators of quality of life in patients with closed-head injury. *Journal of Clinical and Experimental Neuropsychology*, 8, 469-485.

Knivsberg AM, Wiig, Lind G, Nodlund M, Reichelt KL. (1990) Dietary intervention in autistic syndromes. *Brain Dysfunction*, 3, 315-327.

Knivsberg AM, Reichelt KL, Nodlund M, Hoien T. (1995) Autistic syndromes and diet: a follow-up study. *Scandinavian Journal of Educational Research*, 39, 223-236.

Koopman C, Classen C, Spiegel D. (1994) Predictors of posttraumatic stress symptoms among survivors of the Oakland/Berkeley, Calif., firestorm. *American Journal of Psychiatry*, 151, 888-894.

Korsager S, Chatham EM, Kristensen HPQ. (1978) Thyroid tests in adults with Down's syndrome. *Acta Endocrinologica*, 88, 48-54.

Kotagal P, Luders H, Morris HH, Dinner DS, Wylie E, Godoy J, Rothner AD. (1989) Dystonic posturing in complex partial seizures of temporal lobe onset: a new lateralizing sign. *Neurology*, 39, 196-201.

Kovacs M. (1985) The Children's Depression Inventory (CDI). *Psychopharmacology Bulletin*, 21, 995-998.

Kramer DS, Drake ME. (1983) Acute psychosis, polydipsia, and inappropriate secretion of antidiuretic hormone. *American Journal of Medicine*, 75, 712-714.

Kroll L, Drummond LM. (1993) Temporal lobe epilepsy and obsessive-compulsive symptoms. *Journal of Nervous and Mental Disease*, 181, 457-458.

Kryger M, Shapiro CM. (1995) Pain and distress at night. In: CM Shapiro (ed), *Sleep Solutions Manual*. pp. 106-146. Pointe Claire, Quebec: Kommunicom Publications.

Lacey EP. (1990) Broadening the perspective of pica: literature review. *Public Health Reports*, 105, 29-35.

Lai F, Williams RS. (1989) A prospective study on Alzheimer disease in Down syndrome. *Archives of Neurology*, 46, 849-853.

Lambie DG, Johnson RH. (1985) Drugs and folate metabolism. *Drugs*, 30, 145-155.

Lang DJ. (1992) Susceptibility to infectious disease in Down syndrome. In: IT Lott, EE McCoy (eds), *Down Syndrome, Advances in Medical Care*. pp. 83-92. New York: John Wiley & Sons.

Lapierre O, Dumont M.(1995) Melatonin treatment of a non-24-hour sleep-wake cycle in a blind retarded child. *Biological Psychiatry*, 38, 119-122.

Larson EB, Kukull WA, Buchner D, Reifler BV. (1987) Adverse drug reactions associated with global cognitive impairment in elderly persons. *Annals of Internal Medicine*, 107, 102-104.

Lauerma H. (1994) Ear stuffing and psychoses. *Journal of Nervous and Mental Disease*, 182, 412-413.

Learoyd BM. (1972) Psychotropic drugs and the elderly patient. *Medical Journal of Australia*, 1, 1131-1133.

Leonard TA, Watson RR, Mohs ME. (1987) The effects of caffeine on various body systems: a review. *Journal of the American Dietetic Association*, 87, 1048-1053.

Levitas A. (1996) Neuropsychiatric aspects of Fragile X. *Seminars in Clinical Neuropsychiatry*, 1, 154-167.

Levitt AJ, Joffe RT. (1993) Folate, B_{12} and thyroid function. *Biological Psychiatry*, 33, 52-53.

Ley R. (1988a) Panic attacks during sleep: a hyperventilation-probability model. *Journal of Behavior Therapy and Experimental Psychiatry*, 19, 181-192.

Ley R. (1988b) Panic attacks during relaxation and relaxation-induced anxiety: a hyperventilation interpretation. *Journal of Behavior Therapy and Experimental Psychiatry*, 19, 253-259.

Lichtigfield FJ, Gillman MA. (1996) Role of dopamine mesolimbic system in opioid action of psychotropic analgesic nitrous oxide in alcohol and drug withdrawal. *Clinical Neuropharmacology*, 19, 246-51.

Lieb JP, Dashieff RM, Engel J Jr. (1991) Role of the frontal lobes in the propagation of mesial temporal lobe seizures. *Epilepsia*, 32, 822-837.

Linaker OM. (1994) Assaultiveness among institutionalised adults with mental retardation. *British Journal of Psychiatry*, 164, 62-68.

Linnoila M, Virkkunen M, Scheinin M, Nuutila A, Rimon R, Goodwin FK. (1983) Low cerebrospinal fluid

5-hydroxyindoleacetic acid concentration differentiates impulsive from nonimpulsive violent behavior. *Life Sciences*, 33, 2609-214.

Lipinski JF, Jr. (1991) Clomipramine treatment of self-mutilating behaviors. *New England Journal of Medicine*, 324, 1441.

Lofts RH, Schroeder SR, Maier RH. (1990) Effects of serum zinc supplementation on pica behavior of persons with mental retardation. *American Journal on Mental Retardation*, 95, 103-109.

Lou HC, Guttler F, Lykkelund C, Bruhn P, Niederweiser A. (1985) Decreased vigilance and neurotransmitter synthesis after discontinuation of dietary treatment for phenylketonuria in adolescents. *European Journal of Pediatrics*, 144, 17-20.

Lowenthal DT, Nadeau SE. (1991) Drug-induced dementia. *Southern Medical Journal*, 84, 1S, 4-43.

Lowry MA. (1995) Anger: a root of problem behaviors in the depressed. *Habilitative Mental Healthcare Newsletter*, 14, 101-106.

Lucca A, Lucini V, Piatti E, Ronchi P, Smeraldi E. (1992) Plasma tryptophan levels and plasma tryptophan/neutral amino acids ratio in patients with mood disorder, patients with obsessive-compulsive disorder, and normal subjects. *Psychiatry Research*, 44, 85-91.

Luciano D. (1993) Partial seizures of frontal and temporal origin. *Neurologic Clinics*, 11, 805-822.

Lum LC. (1976) The syndrome of habitual chronic hyperventilation. In: OW Hill (ed), *Modern Trends in Psychosomatic Medicine - Third Edition*. pp. 196-229. London: Butterworth.

Lum LC. (1981) Hyperventilation and anxiety state. *Journal of the Royal Society of Medicine*, 74, 1-4.

Maclean G, Robertson BM. (1976) Self-enucleation and psychosis. Report of two cases and discussion. *Archives of General Psychiatry*, 33, 242-249.

Mader TH, Stulting RD. (1992) Corneal transplantation in a patient with congenital sensory neuropathy. *Cornea*, 11, 270-271.

Maeda N, Watanabe K, Negoro T, Aso K, Haga Y, Kito M, Shylaja N, Ohki T, Sakuma S, Ito K, Tadokoro M, Kato T. (1992) Usefulness of PET scan in a child with mesial frontal lobe epilepsy. *Brain Development*, 14, 161-164.

Maj J, Palider W, Rawlow A. (1979) Trazodone, a central serotonin antagonist and agonist. *Journal of Neural Transmission*, 44, 237-248.

Mani C. (1988) Hypothyroidism in Down's syndrome. *British Journal of Psychiatry*, 153, 102-104.

Mann JJ, McBride A, Brown RP, Linnoila M, Leon AC, Demeo M, Mieczkowski T, Myers JE, Stanley M. (1992) Relationship between central and peripheral serotonin indexes in depressed and suicidal psychiatric inpatients. *Archives of General Psychiatry*, 49, 442-446.

Margileth AM. (1992) Antibiotic therapy for cat-scratch disease: clinical study of therapeutic outcome in 268 patients and a review of the literature. *Pediatric Infectious Diseases Journal*, 11, 474-478.

Marks DA, Kim J, Spencer DD, Spencer SS. (1995) Seizure localization and pathology following head injury in patients with uncontrolled epilepsy. *Neurology*, 45, 2051-2057.

Martin WJ. (1995) Stealth virus isolated from an autistic child. *Journal of Autism and Developmental Disorders*, 25, 223-224.

Martin WJ. (1996) Severe stealth virus encephalopathy following chronic fatigue syndrome-like illness: clinical and histopathological features. *Pathobiology*, 64, 59-63.

Martin WJ, Anderson D. (1997) Stealth virus epidemic in the Mohave Valley. *Pathobiology*, 65, 51-56.

Mass E, Gadoth N. (1994) Oro-dental self-mutilation in familial dysautonomia. *Journal of Oral Pathological Medicine*, 23, 273-276.

Mass E, Sarnat H, Ram D, Gadoth N. (1992) Dental and oral findings in patients with familial dysautonomia. *Oral Surgery Oral Medicine Oral Pathology*, 74, 305-311.

Mathew G. (1988) Psychiatric symptoms associated with carbamazepine. *British Medical Journal*, 296, 1071.

Matilainen R, Pitkanen A, Ruutianinen T, Mervaala E, Piekkeinen AP. (1989) Vigabatrin in epilepsy in mentally retarded patients. *British Journal of Clinical Pharmacology*, 27, 1135-1185.

Mayhew LA, Hanzel TE, Ferron FR, Kalachnik JE, Harder SR. (1992) Phenobarbital exacerbation of self-injurious behavior. *Journal of Nervous and Mental Disease*, 180, 732-733.

McAlpine C, Singh NN. (1986) Pica in institutionalized mentally retarded persons. *Journal of Mental Deficiency Research*, 30, 171-178.

McCann IL, Pearlman LA. (1990) *Psychological Trauma and the Adult Survivor, Theory, Therapy, and Transformation*. New York: Bruner/Mazel.

McCartney JR, Palmateer LM. (1985) Assessment of cognitive deficit in geriatric patients, a study of physician behavior. *Journal of the American Geriatrics Society*, 33, 467-471.

McCoy EE. (1992) Endocrine function in Down syndrome. In: IT Lott, EE McCoy (eds), *Down Syndrome, Advances in Medical Care*. pp. 71-82. New York: John Wiley & Sons.

McCreary BD. Personal communication. November 6, 1996.

McCreary BD. Personal communication. July 28, 1997.

McCreary BD, Thompson J. Personal communication. February 24, 1997.

McCreary BD, Fotheringham JB, Holden JA, Oulette-Kuntz H, Robertson DM. (1993) Experiences in an Alzheimer clinic for persons with Down syndrome. In: JM Berg, H Karlinsky, AJ Holland (eds), *Alzheimer Disease, Down Syndrome, and their Relationship*. pp. 115-131. New York: Oxford University Press.

McDougle CJ, Krech LE, Goodman WK, Naylor ST, Volkmar FR, Cohen DJ, Price LH. (1995) A case-controlled study of repetitive thoughts and behavior in adults with autistic disorder and obsessive-compulsive disorder. *American Journal of Psychiatry*, 152, 772-777.

McLoughlin IJ. (1988) Pica as a cause of death in three mentally handicapped men. *British Journal of Psychiatry*, 152, 842-845.

McNally RJ, Calamari JE, Hansen PM, Kaliher C. (1988) Behavioral treatment of psychogenic polydipsia. *Journal of Behavioral Therapy and Experimental Psychiatry*, 19, 57-61.

McNamara ME, Fogel BS. (1990) Anticonvulsant-responsive panic attacks with temporal lobe EEG abnormalities. *Journal of Neuropsychiatry*, 2, 193-196.

McNeil JK, LeBlanc EM, Joyner M. (1991) The effect of exercise on depressive symptoms in the moderately depressed elderly. *Psychology and Aging*, 6, 487-488.

Meador KJ, Loring DW, Moore EE, Thompson WO, Nichols ME, Oberzan RE, Durkin MW, Gallagher BB, King DW. (1995) Comparative cognitive effects of phenobarbital, phenytoin, and valproate in healthy adults. *Neurology*, 45, 1494-1499.

Medical Letter (1993) Drugs that cause psychiatric symptoms. *Medical Letter*, 35, 55-70.

Mega MS, Cummings JL. (1994) Frontal-subcortical and neuropsychiatric disorders. *Journal of Neuropsychiatry*, 6, 358-370.

Meins W. (1993) Assessment of depression in mentally retarded adults: reliability and validity of the Children's Depression Inventory (CDI). *Research in Developmental Disabilities*, 14, 299-312.

Meins W. (1996) A new depression scale designed for use with adults with mental retardation. *Journal of Intellectual Disability Research*, 40, 222-226.

Middlemiss DN, Palmer AM, Edel N, Bowen DM. (1986) Binding of the novel serotonin agonist 8-hydroxy-2-(di-n-propylamino) tetralin in normal and Alzheimer brain. *Journal of Neurochemistry*, 46, 993-996.

Mischoulon D. (1996) The role of folate in major depression: mechanisms and clinical implications. *American Society of Clinical Psychopharmacology Progress Notes*, 7, 4-5.

Mixter RC, David DJ, Perloff WH, Green CG, Pauli RM, Popic PM. (1990) Obstructive sleep apnoea in Apert's and Pfeiffer's syndromes: more than a craniofacial abnormality. *Plastic and Reconstructive Surgery*, 86, 457-463.

Mizuno T, Ohta R, Kodama K, Kitazumi E, Minejima N, Takeishi M, Segawa M. (1979) Self-mutilation and sleep stage in the Lesch-Nyhan syndrome. *Brain Development*, 2, 121-125.

Moos RH. (1968) The development of a Menstrual Distress Questionnaire. *Psychosomatic Medicine*, 6, 853-866.

Morris CH, Hope RA, Fairburn CG. (1989) Eating habits in dementia, a descriptive study. *British Journal of Psychiatry*, 154, 801-806.

Munari C, Stoffels C, Bossi L, Bonis A, Talairach J, Bancaud J. (1981) Automatic activities during frontal and temporal lobe seizures: are they the same? In: M Dam, L Gram JK, Penry (eds), *Advances in Epileptology: 12th Epilepsy International Symposium*. pp. 287-291. New York: Raven Press.

Nagy LM, Morgan CA, Southwick SM, Charney DS. (1993) Open prospective trial of fluoxetine for posttraumatic stress disorder. *Journal of Clinical Psychopharmacology*, 13, 107-113.

Naumann M, Supprian T, Kornhuber J, Lange KW, Reiners K. (1994) Bipolar affective psychosis after vigabatrin. *Lancet*, 343, 606-607.

Nathan C. (1993) Serotonergic control on food intake in man. In: H Lehnert, R Murison, H Weiner, D Hellhammer, J Beyer (eds), *Endocrine and Nutritional Control of Basic Biological Functions*. pp. 107-117. Toronto: Hogrefe & Huber.

Neill JC, Cooper SJ. (1989) Selective reduction by serotonergic agents of hypertonic saline consumption in rats: evidence for possible 5-HT1C receptor mediation. *Psychopharmacology*, 99, 196-201.

Neilsen J, Lou HC, Guttler F. (1988) Effects of diet discontinuation and dietary tryptophan supplementation on neurotransmitter metabolism in phenylketonuria. *Brain Dysfunction*, 1, 51-56.

Neville J. (1959) Paranoid schizophrenia in a mongoloid defective: some theoretical considerations derived from an unusual case. *Journal of Mental Science*, 105, 444-448.

Newroth A, Newroth S. (1980) Coping with Alzheimer's disease: a growing concern. Mental Retardation Health Care Services. pp. 3-26. Downsview, Ontario: National Institute of Mental Retardation.

Niederehe G. (1986) Depression and memory impairment in the aged. In: LW Poon (ed) *Clinical Memory Assessment of Older Adults*, pp. 226-237. Washington, D.C.: American Psychological Association.

Nixon PGF. (1994) Effort syndrome: hyperventilation and reduction of anaerobic threshold. *Biofeedback and Self-Regulation*, 19, 155-169.

O'Brien G, Whitehouse AM. (1990) A psychiatric study of deviant eating behaviour among mentally handicapped adults. *British Journal of Psychiatry*, 157, 281-284.

O'Connor DW, Pollitt PA, Hyde JB, Brook CPB, Roth M. (1988) Do general practitioners miss dementia in elderly patients? *British Medical Journal*, 297, 1107-1110.

O'Gorman MA, Orenstein SR, Proujansky R, Wadowsky RM, Putnam PE, Kocoshis SA. (1993) Prevalence and characteristics of Blastocystis hominis infection in children. *Clinical Pediatrics*, 32, 91-96.

O'Griofa FM, Voris JC. (1991) Neuroleptic malignant syndrome associated with carbamazepine. *Southern Medical Journal*, 84, 1378-1380.

Okawa M, Mishima K, Hishikawa Y. (1991) Vitamin B_{12} treatment for sleep-wake rhythm disorders. *Japanese Journal of Psychiatry and Neurology*, 45, 165-166.

Okawa M, Takahashi K, Sasaki H. (1986) Disturbance of circadian rhythms in severely brain-damaged patients correlated with CT findings. *Journal of Neurology*, 233, 274-282.

O'Loughlin V, Dickie AC, Ebmeier KP. (1991) Serum iron and transferrin in acute neuroleptic-induced akathisia. *Journal of Neurology, Neurosurgery, and Psychiatry*, 54, 363-364.

Orbach I. (1994) Dissociation, physical pain, and suicide: a hypothesis. *Suicide and Life-Threatening Behavior*, 24, 68-79.

Orlikov A, Rykov I. (1991) Caffeine-induced anxiety and increase in kynurenine concentration in plasma of healthy subjects: a pilot study. *Biological Psychiatry*, 29, 391-396.

O'Sullivan N, Godfrey M, van Boldrik A, Puntil J. (1990) *Dysphagia Care, Team Approach with Acute and Long Term Patients*. Los Angeles, California: Cottage Square.

Page TJ, Finney JW, Parrish JM, Iwata BA. (1983) Assessment and reduction of food stealing in Prader-Willi children. *Applied Research in Mental Retardation*, 4, 219-228.

Palm L, Blennow G, Wetterberg L. (1991) Correction of non-24-hour sleep-wake cycle by melatonin in a blind retarded boy. *Annals of Neurology*, 29 336-339.

Palmer AM, Stratmann GC, Procter AW, Bowen D. (1988) Possible neurotransmitter basis of behavioral changes in Alzheimer's disease. *Annals of Neurology*, 23, 616-620.

Pandey GN, Pandey SC, Dwivedi Y, Sharma RP, Janicak PG, Davis JM. (1995) Platelet serotonin 2A receptors: a potential biological marker for suicidal behavior. *American Journal of Psychiatry*, 152, 850-855.

Pary RJ. (1992) Differential diagnosis of functional decline in Down's syndrome. *Habilitative Mental Healthcare Newsletter*, 11, 37-41.

Pary RJ, Loschen EL, Tomkowiak SB. (1996) Mood disorders and Down syndrome. *Seminars in Clinical Neuropsychiatry*, 1, 148-153.

Pasion RC, Kirby SG. (1993) Trazodone for screaming. *Lancet*, 341, 970.

Patel B, Tandon R. (1993) Development of obsessive-compulsive symptoms during clozapine treatment. *American Journal of Psychiatry*, 150, 836.

Paterson AJ, Tulloch EN, Hughes AM. (1992) Self-inflicted mutilation of the dentition in a schizophrenic patient. *British Dental Journal*, 173, 314-316.

Patil VJ. (1992) Development of transient obsessive-compulsive symptoms during treatment with clozapine. *American Journal of Psychiatry*, 149, 272.

Paykel ES. (1977) Depression and appetite. *Journal of Psychosomatic Research*, 21, 401-407.

Pei Q, Zetterstrom T, Fillenz M. (1989) Both systemic and local administration of benzodiazepine agonists inhibit the in vivo release of 5-HT from ventral hippocampus. *Neuropharmacology*, 28, 1061-1066.

Percy ME, Dalton AJ, Markovic VD, Crapper McLachlan DR, Gera E, Hummel JT, Rusk ACM, Somerville MJ, Andrews DF, Walfish PG. (1990) Autoimmune thyroiditis associated with mild "subclinical" hypothyroidism in adults with Down syndrome: a comparison of patients with and without manifestations of Alzheimer disease. *American Journal of Medical Genetics*, 36, 148-154.

Pies R. (1992) Proposed model for self-injurious behavior. *American Journal of Psychiatry*, 149, 420.

Pirke KM, Phillips E. (1993) Gastrointestinal peptides and amino acids in anorexia and bulimia nervosa. In: H Lehnert, R Murison, H Weiner, D Hellhammer, J Beyer (eds), *Endocrine and Nutritional Control of Basic Biological Functions*. pp. 119-124. Toronto: Hogrefe & Huber.

Pleak R, Birmaher B, Gavrilescu A, Abichandani C, Williams DT. (1988) Mania and neuropsychiatric evaluation following carbamazepine. *Journal of American Academy of Child and Adolescent Psychiatry*, 27, 500-503.

Podboy JW, Mallory WA. (1977) Caffeine reduction and behavior change in the severely retarded. *Mental Retardation*, 15, 40.

Poindexter AR. (1996) *Assessment and Treatment of Anxiety Disorders in Persons with Mental Retardation*. Kingston, New York: National Association for the Dually Diagnosed.

Ponce de Leon P, Svetaz MJ, Zdero M. (1991) [Importance of the diagnosis of Blastocystis hominis in the parasitological examination of feces]. *Revista Latinoamericana de Microbiologia*, 33, 159-164.

Pontieri FE, Tanda G, Orzi F, Chiara G. (1996) Effects of nicotine on the nucleus accumbens and similarity to those of addictive drugs. *Nature*, 382, 6588, 255-257.

Pope HG, McElroy SL, Satlin A, Hudson JI, Keck PE, Kalish R. (1988) Head injury, bipolar disorder, and response to valproate. *Comprehensive Psychiatry*, 29, 34-38.

Post RM, Uhde TW, Joffe RT, Bierer L. (1986) Psychiatric manifestations and implications of seizure disorders. In: I Extein, MS Gold (eds), *Medical Mimics of Psychiatric Disorders*. pp. 33-91. Washington, D.C.: American Psychiatric Press.

Prasher VP. (1995) Overweight and obesity amongst Down's syndrome adults. *Journal of Intellectual Disability Research*, 39, 437-441.

Prasher VP, Day S. (1995) Brief report: obsessive-compulsive disorder in adults with Down's syndrome. *Journal of Autism and Developmental Disorders*, 25, 453-458.

Prasher VP, Hall W. (1996) Short-term prognosis of depression in adults with Down's syndrome: association with thyroid status and effects on adaptive behaviour. *Journal of Intellectual Disability Research*, 40, 32-38.

Preston GC, Ward CE, Broks P, Traub M, Stahl SM. (1989) Effects of lorazepam on memory, attention, and sedation in man: antagonism by Ro 15-1788. *Psychopharmacology*, 97, 222-227.

Primeau F, Fontaine R. (1987) Obsessive disorder with self-mutilation: a subgroup responsive to pharmacotherapy. *Canadian Journal of Psychiatry*, 32, 699-701.

Pueshel SM, Werner JC. (1994) Mitral valve prolapse in persons with Down syndrome. *Research in Developmental Disabilities*, 15, 91-97.

Puri BK, El-Dosiky A, Barrett JS. (1994) Self-inflicted intracranial injury. *British Journal of Psychiatry*, 164, 841-2.

Quesney LF, Cendes F, Olivier A, Dubeau F, Andermann F. (1995) Intracranial electroencephalographic investigation in frontal lobe epilepsy. *Advances in Neurology*, 66, 243-258.

Quesney L, Kreiger C, Leitner C, Gloor P, Olivier A. (1984) Frontal lobe epilepsy: clinical and electrographical presentation. In: *Advances in Epileptology: XVth Symposium*. pp. 503-508. New York: Raven Press.

Quine L. (1991) Sleep problems in children with mental handicaps. *Journal of Mental Deficiency Research*, 35, 269-90.

Rao ML, Braunig P, Papassotiropoulos A. (1994) Autoaggressive behavior is closely related to serotonin availability in schizoaffective disorder. *Pharmacopsychiatry*, 27, 202-206.

Rapoport JL. (1989a) The biology of obsessions and compulsions. *Scientific American*, 260, 83-89.

Rapoport JL. (1989b) *The Boy Who Couldn't Stop Washing, The Experience and Treatment of Obsessive-Compulsive Disorder*. New York: Dutton.

Raskind MA, Risse SC. (1986) Antipsychotic drugs and the elderly. *Journal of Clinical Psychiatry*, 47, Suppl 5, 17-22.

Rasmussen SA, Eisen JL. (1990) Epidemiology of obsessive compulsive disorder. *Journal of Clinical Psychiatry*, 51, 2S10-13.

Reeves AG, Plum F. (1969) Hyperphagia, rage, and dementia accompanied by ventromedial hypothalamic neoplasm. *Archives of Neurology*, 20, 616-624.

Regland B, Gottfries CG, Oreland L, Svenerholm L. (1988) Low B_{12} levels related to high activity of platelet MAO in patients with dementia disorders. *Acta Psychiatrica Scandinavica*, 78, 451-457.

Reichelt KL, Knivsberg AM, Nodlund M, Lind G. (1994) Nature and consequences of hyperpeptiduria and bovine casomorphins found in autistic syndromes. *Developmental Brain Dysfunction*, 7, 71-85.

Reichelt KL, Seim AR, Reichelt WH. (1996) Could schizophrenia be reasonably explained by Dohan's hypothesis on genetic interaction with a dietary peptide overload? *Progress in Neuro-Psychopharmacology and Biological Psychiatry*, 20, 1083-1114.

Reichelt WH, Knivsberg AM, Nodland M, Stensrud S, Reichelt KL. (1997) Urinary peptide levels and patterns in autistic children from seven countries, and the effect of dietary intervention after 4 years. *Developmental Brain Dysfunction*, 10, 44-55.

Reichman WE, Coyne AC. (1995) Depressive symptoms in Alzheimer's disease and multi-infarct dementia. *Journal of Geriatric Psychiatry and Neurology*, 8, 96-99.

Reid AD, Naylor GJ, Kay DS. (1981) A double-blind placebo controlled crossover trial of carbamazepine in over-active severely mentally handicapped patients. *Psychological Medicine*, 11, 109-113.

Reifler BV, Larson E, Teri L, Poulsen M. (1986) Dementia of the Alzheimer's type and depression. *Journal of the American Geriatrics Society*, 34, 855-859.

Reiss, S. (1994) *Handbook of Challenging Behavior: Mental Health Aspects of Mental Retardation*. Worthington, Ohio: IDS Publishing.

Reiss S, Rojahn J. (1993) Joint occurrence of depression and aggression in children and adults with mental retardation. *Journal of Intellectual Disability Research*, 37, 287-294.

Reppert SM, Weaver DR, Rivkees SA, Stopa EG. (1988) Putative melatonin receptors in a human biological clock. *Science*, 242, 78-81.

Resnick HS, Yehuda R, Pitman RK, Foy DW. (1995) Effect of previous trauma on acute plasma cortisol level following rape. *American Journal of Psychiatry*, 152, 1675-1677.

Reynolds EH, Trimble MR. (1985) Adverse neuropsychiatric effects of anticonvulsant drugs. *Drugs*, 29, 570-581.

Riordan MM, Iwata BA, Finney JW, Wohl MK, Stanley AS. (1984) Behavioral assessment and treatment of chronic food refusal in handicapped children. *Journal of Applied Behavioral Analysis*, 17, 327-341.

Rimland B, Baker SM. (1996) Brief report: alternative approaches to the development of effective treatments for autism. *Journal of Autism and Developmental Disorders*, 26, 237-41.

Riordan MM, Iwata BA, Wohl MK, Finney JW. (1980) Behavioral treatment of food refusal and selectivity in developmentally disabled children. *Applied Research in Mental Retardation*, 1, 95-112.

Risse SC, Barnes R. (1986) Pharmacologic treatment of agitation associated with dementia. *Journal of the American Geriatrics Society*, 34, 368-376.

Rivinus TM. (1982) Psychiatric effects of the anticonvulsant regimens. *Journal of Clinical Psychopharmacology*, 2, 165-192.

Roberts RJ, Gorman LL, Lee GP, Hines ME, Richardson ED, Riggle TA, Varney NR. (1992) The phenomenology of multiple partial seizure-like symptoms without stereotyped spells: an epilepsy spectrum disorder? *Epilepsy Research*, 13, 167-177.

Robinson RG, Szetela B. (1981) Mood change following left hemisphere brain injury. *Annals of Neurology*, 9, 447-453.

Roeden JM, Zitman FG. (1995) Ageing in adults with Down's syndrome in institutionally based and community-based residences. *Journal of Intellectual Disability Research*, 39, 399-407.

Romans SE, Martin JL, Anderson JC, Herbison GP, Mullen PE. (1995) Sexual abuse in childhood and deliberate self-harm. *American Journal of Psychiatry*, 152, 1336-1342.

Rosemberg S, Nagahashi Marie SK, Kliemann S. (1994) Congenital insensitivity to pain with anhidrosis (hereditary sensory and autonomic neuropathy type IV). *Pediatric Neurology*, 11, 50-56.

Rosen SD, King JC, Wilkinson JB, Nixon PFG. (1990) Is chronic fatigue syndrome synonymous with effort syndrome? *Journal of the Royal Society of Medicine*, 83, 761-765.

Rosen WG, Terry RD, Fuld PA, Katzman R, Peck A. (1980) Pathological verification of ischemic score in differentiation of dementias. *Annals of Neurology*, 7, 486-488.

Roy A. (1994) Recent biologic studies on suicide. *Suicide and Life-Treatening Behavior*, 24, 10-14.

Russ MJ, Shearin EN, Clarkin JF, Harrison K, Hull JW. (1993) Subtypes of self-injurious patients with borderline personality disorder. *American Journal of Psychiatry*, 150, 1869-1871.

Ryan R. (1994) Posttraumatic stress disorder in persons with developmental disabilities. *Community Mental Health Journal*, 30, 45-54.

Ryan R. (1996a) Post-traumatic stress disorder in persons with developmental disabilities. In: AR Poindexter (ed), *Assessment and Treatment of Anxiety Disorders in Persons with Mental Retardation*. pp. 41-52. Kingston, New York: National Association for the Dually Diagnosed.

Ryan R. (1996b) *Handbook of Mental Health Care for Persons with Developmental Disabilities*. Evergreen, Colorado: S&B Publishing.

Ryan R, Sunada K. (1997) Medical evaluation of persons with mental retardation referred for psychiatric assessment. *General Hospital Psychiatry*, 19, 274-280.

Sachdev A, McNuff C. (1989) Pica. In IL Rubin, AC Crocker (eds), *Developmental Disabilities: Delivery of Medical Care for Children and Adults*. pp.361-365. Philadelphia: Lea & Febiger.

Sachdev P, Smith JS, Matheson J, Last P, Blumbergs P. (1992) Amygdalo-hippocampectomy for pathological aggression. *Australian and New Zealand Journal of Psychiatry*, 26, 671-676.

Saint-Hillaire JM, Gilbert M, Bouvier G, Barbeau A. (1980) Epilepsy and aggression: two cases with depth electrode studies. In: P Robb (ed), *Epilepsy Updated: Causes and Treatment*. pp. 145-176. Miami: Symposium Specialist Medical Books.

Saliga CA, Kirchener L, Loschen EL. (1996) Nonpharmacologic treatment of anxiety disorders: one woman's story. In: AR Poindexter (ed), *Assessment and Treatment of Anxiety Disorders in Persons with Mental Retardation*. pp. 53-63. Kingston, New York: National Association for the Dually Diagnosed.

Sander JWAS, Hart YM, Trimble MR, Shorvon SD. (1991) Vigabatrin and psychosis. *Journal of Neurology, Neurosurgery, and Psychiatry*, 54, 435-439.

Sanders VJ, Felisan SL, Waddell AE, Conrad AJ, Schmid P, Swartz BE, Kaufman M, Walsh GO, De Salles AAF, Tourtellotte WW. (1997) Presence of herpes simplex DNA in surgical tissue from human epileptic seizure foci detected by polymerase chain reaction. *Archives of Neurology*, 54, 954-960.

Sandman CA, Barron JL, Colman H. (1990) An oral administered blocker, naltrexone, attenuates self-injurious behavior. *American Journal on Mental Retardation*, 95, 93-102.

Sandyk R, Bamford CR. (1987) Deregulation of hypothalamic dopamine and opioid activity and the patho-physiology of self-mutilatory behavior in Tourette's syndrome. *Journal of Clinical Psychopharmacology*, 7, 367.

Saner A, Pletscher A. (1979) Effect of diazepam on cerebral 5-hydroxytryptamine synthesis. *European Journal of Pharmacology*, 55, 315-318.

Schmucker DL. (1985) Aging and drug disposition: an update. *Pharmacological Reviews*, 37, 133-148.

Shafti M, MacMillan DR, Key MP, Derrick AM, Kaufman N, Nahinsky ID. (1996) Nocturnal serum melatonin profile in major depression in children and adolescents. *Archives of General Psychiatry*, 53, 1009-1013.

Shah AK. (1992) Violence, death and associated factors on a mental handicap ward. *Journal of Intellectual Disability Research*, 36, 229-239.

Shamash J, Miall L, Williams F, Creamer D, Robinson S, Johnston DG. (1994) Dysphagia in the neuroleptic malignant syndrome. *British Journal of Psychiatry*, 164, 849-850.

Shaunesey K, Cohen JL, Plummer B, Berman A. (1993) Suicidality in hospitalized adolescents: relationship to prior abuse. *American Journal of Orthopsychiatry*, 63, 113-119.

Shah PJ, Greenberg WM. (1992) Polydipsia in a state hospital population. *Hospital and Community Psychiatry*, 43, 509-511.

Shaw W, Rimland B, Semon B, Lewis L, Seroussi K, Scott P. (1998) *Biological Treatments for Autism and PDD. What's going on? What can you do about it?* Overland Park, Kansas: The Great Plains Laboratory.

Shear CS, Nyhan WL, Kirman BH, Stern J. (1971) Self-mutilative behavior as a feature of the de Lange syndrome. *Pediatrics*, 78, 506-509.

Sheline YJ, Wang PW, Gado MH, Csernansky JG. (1996) Hippocampal atrophy in recurrent major depression. *Proceedings of the National Academy of Science*, 93, 3908-3913.

Sheppard JJ. (1991) Managing dysphagia in mentally retarded adults. *Dysphagia*, 6, 83-87.

Shukla S, Cook BL, Mukherjee S, Godwin C, Miller MG. (1987) Mania following head trauma. *American Journal of Psychiatry*, 144, 93-96.

Silverman M. (1988) Airway obstruction and sleep disruption in Down's syndrome. *British Medical Journal*, 296, 1618-1619.

Silverstein FS, Parrish MA, Johnston MJ. (1982) Adverse behavioral reactions in children treated with carbamazepine (Tegretol). *Journal of Pediatrics*, 101, 785-787.

Simeon D, Stanley B, Frances A, Mann JJ, Winchel R, Stanley M. (1992) Self-mutilation in personality disorders: psychological and biological correlates. *American Journal of Psychiatry*, 149, 221-226.

Simila S, Kokkonen J. (1990) Coexistence of celiac disease and Down syndrome. *American Journal on Mental Retardation*, 95, 120-122.

Singh NN, Pulman RM. (1979) Self-injury in the de Lange syndrome. *Journal of Mental Deficiency*, 23, 79-84.

Singh S, Padi MH, Bullard H, Freeman H. (1985) Water intoxication in psychiatric patients. *British Journal of Psychiatry*, 146, 127-131.

Smith RJ, Roberts NM, Rodgers RJ, Bennett S. (1986) Adverse cognitive effects of general anesthesia in young and elderly patients. *International Clinical Psychopharmacology*, 1, 253-259.

Smith WO, Clark ML. (1980) Self-induced water intoxication in schizophrenic patients. *American Journal of Psychiatry*, 137, 1055-1060.

Snead C, Hosey LC. (1985) Exacerbation of seizures in children by carbamazepine. *New England Journal of Medicine*, 313, 916-921.

Sommer BR, Wolkowitz OM. (1988) RBC folic acid levels and cognitive performance in elderly patients: a preliminary report. *Biological Psychiatry*, 24, 352-354.

Sovner R. (1986) Limiting factors in the use of DSM-III criteria with mentally ill/mentally retarded persons. *Psychopharmacology Bulletin*, 22, 1055-1059.

Sovner R. (1995) Thioridazine withdrawal-induced behavioral deterioration treated with clonidine: two case reports. *Mental Retardation*, 33, 221-225.

Sovner R, DesNoyers Hurley A. (1990) Assessment tools which facilitate psychiatric evaluations and treatment. *Habilitative Mental Healthcare Newsletter*, 9, 91-99.

Spencer SS, Spencer DD, Williamson PD, Mattson RH. (1983) Sexual automatisms in complex partial seizures. *Neurology*, 33, 527-533.

Sperling MR, O'Connor MJ, Saykin AJ, Plummer C. (1996) Temporal lobectomy for refractory epilepsy. *Journal of the American Medical Association*, 276, 470- 475.

Sprague RL, Kalachnik JE. (1991) Reliability, validity, and total score cut-off for the Dyskinesia Identification System (DISCUS) with mentally ill and mentally retarded populations. *Psychopharmacology Bulletin*, 27, 51-58.

Starkstein SE, Pearlson GD, Boston J, Robinson RG. (1987) Mania after brain injury, a controlled study of causative factors. *Archives of Neurology*, 44, 1069-1073.

Stebbens VA, Dennis J, Samuels MP, Croft CB, Southall DP. (1991) Sleep related upper airway obstruction in a cohort with Down's syndrome. *Archives of Disease in Children*, 66, 1333-1338.

Steinhausen HC, Willms J, Spohr HL. (1994) Correlates of psychopathology and intelligence in children with fetal alcohol syndrome. *Journal of Child Psychology and Psychiatry*, 35, 323-331.

Stenzel DJ, Boreham PFL. (1996) Blastocystis hominis revisited. *Clinical Microbiology Reviews*, 9, 563-584.

Sternlicht M, Pustel G, Deutsch MR. (1969) Suicidal tendencies among institutionalized retardates. *Journal of*

Mental Subnormality, 15, 93-102.

Stone TW. (1989) *Quinolinic Acid and the Kynurenines*. Boca Raton, Florida: CRC Press.

Stores G. (1992) Annotation: sleep studies in children with a mental handicap. *Journal of Child Psychology and Psychiatry*, 33, 1303-1317.

Stores G, Zaiwalla Z, Bergel N. (1991) Frontal lobe complex partial seizures in children: a form of epilepsy at particular risk of misdiagnosis. *Developmental Medicine and Child Neurology*, 33, 998-1009.

Strome M, Strome S. (1992) Recurrent otitis and sleep obstruction in Down syndrome. In: IT Lott, EE McCoy (eds), *Down Syndrome: Advances in Medical Care*. pp. 127-133. New York: Wiley-Liss.

Stuss DT, Benson DF. (1986) *The Frontal Lobes*. New York: Raven Press.

Sugita K, Izumi T, Yamaguchi K, Fukuyama Y, Sato A, Kajita A. (1986) Cornelia de Lange syndrome associated with a suprasellar germinoma. *Brain Development*, 8, 541-546.

Summers JA, Allison CB, Lunch PS, Sandler L. (1995) Behaviour problems in Angelman syndrome. *Journal of Intellectual Disability Research*, 39, 97-106.

Tanaka K, Kodama S, Yokoyama S, Komatsu M, Konishi H, Momota K, Matsuo T. (1987) Thyroid function in children with long-term anticonvulsant treatment. *Pediatric Neuroscience*, 13, 90-94.

Takeda A. (1988) Complex partial status epilepticus of frontal lobe origin. *Japan Journal of Psychiatry and Neurology*, 42, 525-530.

Thase ME. (1982) Reversible dementia in Down's syndrome. *Journal of Mental Deficiency Research*, 26, 111-113.

Thomas CL. (1993) *Taber's Cyclopedic Medical Dictionary 17th Edition*. Philadelphia: FA Davis Co.

Thompson TL, Moran MG, Nies AS. (1983) Psychotropic drug use in the elderly. *New England Journal of Medicine*, 308, 134-138.

Toren P, Samuel E, Weizman R, Golomb A, Eldar S, Laor N. (1995) Case study: emergence of transient compulsive symptoms during treatment with clothiapine. *Journal of American Academy of Child and Adolescent Psychiatry*, 34, 1469-1472.

Trimble MR. (1988) Cognitive hazards of seizure disorders. *Epilepsia*, 29, Suppl 1, S19-S24.

Tsutsumi Y, Yamamoto K, Hata S, Sakai M, Shirakura K. (1994) Incidence of "typical cases" and "incomplete cases" of neuroleptic malignant syndrome and their epidemiological study. *Japanese Journal of Psychiatry and Neurology*, 48, 789-799.

Tu JB, Shafey H, Van Dewetering C. (1994) Iron deficiency in two adolescents with conduct, dysthymic and movement disorders. *Canadian Journal of Psychiatry*, 39, 371-375.

Tu J, Partington MW. (1972) 5-Hydroxyindole levels in the blood and CSF in Down's syndrome, phenylketonuria and severe mental retardation. *Developmental Medicine and Child Neurology*, 14, 457-46.

Tucker GJ, Price TR, Johnson VB, McAllister T. (1986) Phenomenology of temporal lobe dysfunction: a link to atypical psychosis--a series of cases. *Journal of Nervous and Mental Disease*, 174, 348-356.

Tune L, Carr S, Hoag E, Cooper T. (1992) Anticholinergic effects of drugs commonly prescribed for the elderly: potential means for assessing risk of delirium. *American Journal of Psychiatry*, 149, 1393-1394.

Tyler CV, Bourquet C. (1997) Primary care of adults with mental retardation. *Journal of Family Practice*, 44, 487-94.

van Amelsvoort T. (1994) Neuroleptic malignant syndrome and carbamazepine? *British Journal of Psychiatry*, 164, 269-270.

van der Kolk BA. (1988) The trauma spectrum: the interaction of biological and social events in the genesis of the trauma response. *Journal of Traumatic Stress*, 1, 273-290.

van Schrojenstein Lantman-de Valk HMJ, van den Akker M, Maaskant MA, Haverman MJ, Urlings HFJ, Kessels AGH, Crebolder HFJM. (1997) Prevalence and incidence of health problems in people with intellectual disability. *Journal of Intellectual Disability Research*, 41, 42-51.

van Sweden B. (1984) Drug-induced repetitive sharp-wave EEG discharges in multi-infarct dementia. *Gerontology*, 30, 397-402.

Varney NR, Alexander B, MacIndoe JH. (1984) Reversible steroid dementia in patients without steroid psychosis. *American Journal of Psychiatry*, 141, 369-372.

Varney NR, Hines ME, Bailey C, Roberts RJ. (1992) Neuropsychiatric correlates of theta bursts in patients with closed head injury. *Brain Injury*, 6, 499-508.

Veilleux F, Saint Hilaire JM, Giard N, Turmel A, Bernier GP, Rouleau I, Mercier M, Bouvier G. (1992) Seizures of the human medial frontal lobe. *Advances in Neurology*, 57, 245-255.

Vieweg WVR, Godleski LS. (1989) Polydipsia, hyponatremia, and psychosis. *American Journal of Psychiatry*, 146, 124.

Vieweg WVR, Karp BI. (1994) Severe hyponatremia in the polydipsia-hyponatremia syndrome. *Journal of Clinical Psychiatry*, 55, 355-361.

Virkkunen M. (1976) Self-mutilation and anti-social personality disorder. *Acta Psychiatrica Scandinavica*, 54, 347-352.

Vitiello B, Behar D, Hunt J, Stoff D, Ricciuti A. (1990) Subtyping aggression in children and adolescents. *Journal of*

Neuropsychiatry, 2, 189-192.

Vitiello B, Spreat S, Behar D. (1989) Obsessive-compulsive disorder in mentally retarded patients. *Journal of Nervous and Mental Disease*, 177, 232-236.

Vitiello B, Stoff DM. (1997) Subtypes of aggression and their relevance to child psychiatry. *Journal of American Academy of Child and Adolescent Psychiatry*, 36, 307-315.

Voitk AJ. (1987) Acute abdomen in severely mentally retarded patients. *Canadian Journal of Surgery*, 30, 195-196.

Wakham MD, Burtner AP, McNeal DR, Garvey TP, Bedinger S. (1992) Pica: a peculiar behavior with oral involvement. *Special Care in Dentistry*, 12, 207-210.

Ware MR, Stewart RB. (1989) Seizures associated with fluoxetine therapy. *DICP Annals of Pharmacotherapy*, 23, 428.

Warren AC, Holroyd S, Folstein MF. (1989) Major depression in Down's syndrome. *British Journal of Psychiatry*, 155, 202-205.

Waterman K, Purves SJ, Kosaka B, Strauss E, Wada JA. (1987) An epileptic syndrome caused by mesial frontal lobe seizure foci. *Neurology*, 37, 577-582.

Waugaman WR. (1988) Surgery and the patient with Alzheimer disease. *Geriatric Nursing*, 9, 227-229.

Waxman SG, Geschwind N. (1975) The interictal behavior syndrome of temporal lobe epilepsy. *Archives of General Psychiatry*, 32, 1580-1586.

Weber JJ. (1989) Seizure activity associated with fluoxetine therapy. *Clinical Pharmacy*, 8, 296-298.

Wehr TA. (1991) Sleep loss as a possible mediator of diverse causes of mania. *British Journal of Psychiatry*, 159, 576-578.

Welch JB. (1993) Dementia as a consequence of neuroleptic syndrome. *American Journal of Psychiatry*, 150, 1561-1562.

Wiggs L, Stores G. (1996) Severe sleep disturbance and daytime challenging behaviour in children with severe learning disabilities. *Journal of Intellectual Disability Research*, 40, 518-528.

Williamson PD. (1995) Frontal lobe epilepsy, some clinical characteristics. *Advances in Neurology*, 66, 127-152.

Williams-Russo P, Sharrock NE, Mattis S, Szatrowski TP, Charlson ME. (1995) Cognitive effects after epidural vs general anesthesia in older adults. *Journal of the American Medical Association*, 274, 44-50.

Winchel RM, Stanley M. (1991) Self-injurious behavior: a review of the behavior and biology of self-mutilation. *American Journal of Psychiatry*, 148, 306-317.

Wise CD, Berger BD, Stein L. (1972) Benzodiazepines: anxiety-reducing activity by reduction of serotonin turnover in the brain. *Science*, 177, 180-83.

Wise MG, Taylor SE. (1990) Anxiety disorders in medically ill patients. *Journal of Clinical Psychiatry*, 51, 1S, 27-32.

Wisniewski KE, Dalton AJ, Crapper McLachlan DR, Wen GY, Wisniewski HM. (1985) Alzheimer's disease in Down's syndrome: clinicopathologic studies. *Neurology*, 35, 957-961.

Wolfe F, Ross K, Anderson J, Russell IJ. (1995) Aspects of fibromyalgia in the general population: sex, pain, threshold, and fibromyalgia symptoms. *Journal of Rheumatology*, 22, 151-156.

Woodbury MW, Woodbury MA. (1992) Neuroleptic-induced catatonia as a stage in the progression toward neuroleptic malignant syndrome. *Journal of American Academy of Child and Adolescent Psychiatry*, 31, 1161-1164.

Woods NF, Most A, Longenecker GD. (1985) Major life events, daily stressors, and perimenstrual symptoms. *Nursing Research*, 34, 263-267.

Wright JBD. (1993) Mania following sleep deprivation. *British Journal of Psychiatry*, 163, 679-680.

Wurtman J. (1987) Recent evidence from human studies linking central serotoninergic function with carbohydrate intake. *Appetite*, 8, 211-213.

Wurtman R. (1982) Nutrients that modify brain function. *Scientific American*, 246, 50-59.

Wurtman RJ. (1993) Effects of dietary carbohydrates and proteins on the brain: impact for selective control of macronutrient intake. In: H Lehnert, R Murison, H Weiner, D Hellhammer, J Beyer (eds), *Endocrine and Nutritional Control of Basic Biological Functions*. pp. 97-106. Toronto: Hogrefe & Huber.

Wurtman RJ, Corkin S, Growdon JH, Nitsch RM.(eds) (1996) The neurobiology of Alzheimer's disease. *Annals of the New York Academy of Sciences*, 777, 1-430.

Yehuda R, Boisoneau D, Mason JW, Giller EL. (1993b) Glucocorticoid receptor number and cortisol excretion in mood, anxiety, and psychotic disorders. *Biological Psychiatry*, 34, 18-25.

Yehuda R, Kahana B, Binder-Byrnes K, Southwick SM, Mason JW, Giller EL. (1995) Low urinary cortisol excretion in holocaust survivors with posttraumatic stress disorder. *American Journal of Psychiatry*, 152, 982-986.

Yehuda R, Resnick HS, Kahana B, Giller EL. (1993a) Long-lasting hormonal alterations to extreme stress in humans: normative or maladaptive? *Psychosomatic Medicine*, 55, 287-297.

Young SN. (1991) Some effects of dietary components (amino acids, carbohydrate, folic acid) on brain serotonin synthesis, mood, and behavior. *Canadian Journal of Physiology and Pharmacology*, 69, 893-903.

Zaret BS, Cohen RA. (1986) Reversible valproic acid-induced dementia: a case report. *Epilepsia*, 27, 234-240.

Zigman WB, Schupf N, Sersen E, Silverman W. (1995) Prevalence of dementia in adults with and without Down syndrome. *American Journal on Mental Retardation*, 100, 403-412.

Ziring PR. (1987) A program that works. *Mental Retardation*, 25, 207-210.

Zohar J, Mueller EA, Insel TR, Zohar-Kadouch RC, Murphy DL. (1987) Serotonergic responsivity in obsessive-compulsive disorder. *Archives of General Psychiatry*, 44, 946-951.

Zwil AS, McAllister TW, Cohens I, Halpern LR. (1993) Ultra-rapid cycling bipolar affective disorder following closed-head injury. *Brain Injury*, 7, 147-152.

Zucker DK, Livingston RL, Nakra R, Clayton PJ. (1981) B_{12} deficiency and psychiatric disorders: a case report and literature review. *Biological Psychiatry*, 16, 197-205.

ABOUT THE AUTHOR

The author is a psychologist and researcher who began consulting for people with developmental disabilities in 1981. Since 1987, Dr. Gedye has been doing research on serotonergic treatments, self-injurious movements, frontal lobe seizures, obsessive-compulsive disorder, and dementia assessment in adults with developmental disabilities. She earned her Ph.D. at the University of California, Berkeley, California, USA and was a research assistant for five years at the Institute for Human Development, University of California, Berkeley. Dr. Gedye is a member of the College of Psychologists of British Columbia, Canadian Psychological Association, Canadian Register of Health Service Providers in Psychology, American Psychological Association, and American Association for the Advancement of Science. The idea for this book came from a desire to help individuals with difficult behaviors who were being misdiagnosed, wrongly treated for conditions they did not have, and who continued to suffer from unrecognized conditions.

APPENDIX

LIST OF ITEMS IN THE APPENDIX

* Reprinted with written permission from the publishers.

CHECKLIST FOR DESCRIBING PHYSICAL AGGRESSION

For use with the *Behavioral Diagnostic Guide* © A. Gedye, 1998

NAME:_____ SEX: M F BIRTHDATE:_____/____/_____

OBSERVER:_____ Years Known: ____ REPORT DATE:_____/____/_____

Estimate the number times you have observed this person being aggressive: 2-5, 6-10, 11-20, 21-50, >50.

This checklist is for collecting details about movements, targets, speech, vocalizations, etc. that occur when a developmentally disabled person is "aggressive." Have this form completed by at least two people who have seen the person's aggressive episodes. This information is intended for use with Chapter 1 of the *Behavioral Diagnostic Guide*.

HOW FREQUENT DURING EPISODES			AGGRESSIVE MOVEMENTS INVOLVING OTHERS	AGGRESSIVE MOVEMENTS INVOLVING OBJECTS
F	Oc	R	___ one hand hits another 1-2 times	___ hits objects:_____
F	Oc	R	___ both hands hit out repeatedly	___ hits objects repeatedly:_____
F	Oc	R	___ grabs another	___ grabs objects:_____
F	Oc	R	___ chokes another	
F	Oc	R	___ scratches another	___ scratches objects:_____
F	Oc	R	___ pinches another	
F	Oc	R	___ rips/tears others' clothing	___ rips/tears apart:_____
F	Oc	R	___ throws another	___ throws object:_____
F	Oc	R	___ stabs another	___ using a:_____
F	Oc	R	___ bites another	___ bites objects:_____
F	Oc	R	___ spits on another	___ spits on objects:_____
F	Oc	R	___ head-butts another	___ head thrusting on:_____
F	Oc	R	___ kicks another	___ kicks objects:_____
F	Oc	R	___ charges another	___ runs into:_____
F	Oc	R	___ jumps on another	___ jumps on objects:_____
F	Oc	R	___ shows inordinate strength	
F	Oc	R	___ other:_____	

F = Frequent during an aggressive episode   **Oc** = Occasional   **R** = Rare

TARGETS:

___ anyone within close reach   ___ weak, vulnerable peers   ___ staff smaller than the person
___ mostly/only females   ___ mostly/only males   ___ people unfamiliar to person
___ people disliked by the person   ___ people liked by the person
___ other, give examples:_____

PROVOKED VS. UNPROVOKED:

How often do these episodes occur without provocation, "out of the blue?

   Circle: 75 %   50 %   25 %   Rare   Other:_____

What seems to occur just before the most intense episodes?_____

_____

_____

_____

CHECKLIST FOR DESCRIBING PHYSICAL AGGRESSION

For use with the *Behavioral Diagnostic Guide* © A. Gedye, 1998

FACIAL EXPRESSIONS	AT THE START OF MOST EPISODES	DURING SOME OR MOST AGGRESSIVE EPISODES
mild anger	_____	_____
intense anger	_____	_____
fixed staring	_____	_____
blank/vacant look	_____	_____
wild look	_____	_____
fear	_____	_____
disgust	_____	_____
surprise	_____	_____
other:_____	_____	_____

SPEECH DURING AGGRESSIVE EPISODES:

___ a single word, e.g.,_____ a single word repeated, e.g.,_____

___ a short phrase repeated, e.g.,_____

___ sentences relevant to the situation, e.g., _____

___ sentences unrelated to the situation, e.g.,_____

___ other examples:_____

___ no words during the aggressive episode

VOCALIZATIONS DURING AGGRESSIVE EPISODES:

___ screaming sounds   ___ laughing   ___ humming

___ moaning and/or groaning   ___ grunting   ___ hooting

___ ah-ah-ah   ___ one syllable repeated   ___ squealing

___ garbled words (dysphasia)   ___ other:_____

MOVEMENTS THAT ARE COUNTERPRODUCTIVE (if one is trying to be aggressive):

_____

DURATION OF EPISODES:

Examples: 2-5 seconds,   10-30 seconds,   30-60 seconds,   1-2 minutes,   2-5 minutes,
      5-10 minutes,   10-20 minutes,   20-30 minutes,   1 hour,   2 hours.

Short Episodes:_____   Long Episodes:_____   Average Length:_____

STATE AFTER AGGRESSIVE EPISODES:

___ winds down gradually   ___ continues complaining about the topic

___ suddenly back to usual self   ___ seems unaware of what happened during some episodes

___ is apologetic if objects/people were hurt   ___ no remorse shown if objects/people were hurt

___ is very tired afterward   ___ holds a grudge

___ other:_____   ___ other:_____

OTHER DETAILS ABOUT THESE EPISODES YOU CONSIDER IMPORTANT:

_____

_____

_____

COMPULSIVE BEHAVIOR CHECKLIST
For Clients with Mental Retardation

NAME:_____ ETIOLOGY:_____

BIRTHDATE:_____/___/____ REPORT DATE:_____/___/_____

RECORDER:_____ INFORMANTS:_____

This is a guide for collecting information to aid in determining if OCD criteria have been met.
Instructions: Checkmark behaviors present and underline words that apply.
Mark "N" if the behavior has not been observed.
Sum the *types* of compulsions present (of the 25 listed).

---

1. ORDERING COMPULSIONS

___ Arranges objects (cutlery, dresser items, toys) in a certain pattern.
___ Arranges certain items (pencils, toys, specific clothes) in one spot.
___ Wants chairs in fixed arrangement (at table, in living room).
___ Wants/arranges peers to sit in certain chairs.
___ Insists on using the same chair or location when in a particular room.
___ Insists on doing a certain activity/ chore at same time each day.
    Other compulsions (e.g., "evening up" actions), describe: _____

_____

2. COMPLETENESS/ INCOMPLETENESS COMPULSIONS

___ Insists on closing open doors, open cupboards; turns lights off (or on) repeatedly.
___ Takes all items out of clothes closet, linen closet, cupboard, drawer, purse, spice rack, etc.
___ Removes many items, then puts each back one by one, repeats process.
___ Tries to empty all toiletry bottles in bathroom; wants serving jug or dish to be empty at end of meals;
    or similar activity.
___ Puts garment on then off, or hangs it up then puts it on, over and over; insists on wearing same
    garment(s) for many days, weeks, or months.
___ Insists on doing a certain chore, resists letting anyone else do it.
    Other related compulsion, describe: _____

_____

3. CLEANING/ TIDINESS COMPULSIONS

___ Insists on doing hygiene steps (dressing/toileting/grooming) in a fixed sequence, may start at
    beginning of sequence if interrupted.
___ Cleans body part excessively, e.g., hands, part of face, teeth.
___ Insists on picking up stray bits off the ground; does the motion of picking lint off clothes even when
    there is no lint.
___ Picks at loose threads, seams of clothing, edges of upholstery; picks at or rips tags or garments/
    linens/ grass/ shrubs often if not prevented.
___ Insists that a certain activity be done: taking out garbage when full; having dishwasher started once
    full; clearing dishes off table right after the meal; or similar insistence.
___ Hides particular objects away or collects/ hoards objects.
    Other related compulsion, describe: _____

_____

COMPULSIVE BEHAVIOR CHECKLIST
For Clients with Mental Retardation

4. CHECKING/ TOUCHING COMPULSIONS

___ Opens cupboard door, may look in, closes door, repeats with other cupboard doors; opens and closes drawer repeatedly.

___ Touches or taps item repeatedly (doors, walls, window panes, floor).

___ Touching or stepping pattern predictably touches item B after touching item A so many times; takes 2-3 steps forward then steps backward before going forward.

___ Does unusual sniffing; sniffs one item many times, sniffs hair often, sniffs items that have no smell.

Other related compulsion, describe: _____

_____

5. DEVIANT GROOMING COMPULSIONS

___ Picks at face/ hands/ legs to point of gouging skin.

___ Checks teeth, hair, face, etc.; checks self in mirror excessively.

___ Inappropriately cuts hair, eyebrows or pubic hair; pulls at hair as if "to make it longer"; pulls out hair when sitting calmly. (Do not could hair-pulling during a screaming outburst).

Other related compulsion, describe: _____

_____

☐	**NUMBER OF TYPES OF COMPULSIONS (OF THE 25 LISTED).**
☐	**NUMBER OF CATEGORIES REPRESENTED (OF THE 5 LISTED).**

EXTENT OF INTERFERENCE WITH DAILY LIVING   (Checkmark items that apply)

Compulsions take more than an hour a day (if not prevented) . . . . ☐

Compulsions significantly interfere with the person's normal routine. . . . . ☐

Compulsions significantly interfere with usual social activities. . . . . ☐

Compulsions significantly interfere with relationships with others. . . . . ☐

RESPONSE TO STAFF INTERRUPTION OF COMPULSIONS

(Circle: 0 = Never, 1 = Rare, 2 = Occasional, 3 = Often)

	0	1	2	3
Halts momentarily, then resumes compulsive activity.	0	1	2	3
Waits until caregiver is not in immediate area then resumes.	0	1	2	3
Becomes angry, may hit or kick staff who intervene.	0	1	2	3
Becomes upset, may bite self, hit self, or headbang.	0	1	2	3
Other response:_____	0	1	2	3

COMMENTS:_____

_____

_____

OBSESSIVE SPEECH CHECKLIST
For Clients with Mental Retardation
For use with the *Behavioral Diagnostic Guide* © A. Gedye, 1998

NAME:_____ ETIOLOGY:_____

BIRTHDATE:_____/___/___ REPORT DATE:_____/__/_____

RECORDER:_____ INFORMANTS:_____

This is a guide for collecting information on obsessive speech patterns that can occur in obsessive-compulsive disorder. This is to be used in conjunction with the **Compulsive Behavior Checklist** (Gedye, 1992a; 1996a).

Instructions: Use only with people who can speak in complete sentences or use hand signs fluently.
Do not use this checklist with people who are in the profound range of intelligence, who have only echolalic speech, or who speak only single words and short phrases.
Write **"YES"** if the speech pattern occurs and record examples.
Write **"NO"** if the speech pattern has not been observed.

1. REPEATING A SENTENCE VERBATIM

___ Asks the same question with the same inflection repeatedly, like a "broken record." The question is asked as if in conversation. The person asks the same question to anyone including strangers, e.g., "Are you married?" or "Me go to dance tonight?" anytime of day, regardless of the circumstances. Record examples here:_____
(Do not count if the person immediately *repeats word for word what another just said,* i.e. echolalia.
Do not count *excessive need for reassurance about self-worth* as with Generalized Anxiety Disorder, e.g.,
Do you like me? You like me, don't you? Am I pretty? Do I look nice? Help me? You help me?
The wording and inflection of such questions tends to vary slightly and not be exactly the same each time.)

___ Says the same sentence with the same inflection, for weeks or months. The content may resemble a piece of conversation or may describe an image not seen by others (an intrusive image).
Example:_____

2. REPEATING A SENTENCE TO EVOKE A FIXED REPLY

___ Repeats a question relentlessly until a *particular reply* is given that "completes the fixed dialogue." No other answers or explanations halt this questioning. Later, the person initiates the exchange again. e.g., "All clean now?" & "You're all clean now" is the only reply that ends the persistent questioning.
Example:_____

___ Asks a question over and over, even if the key reply is given: the person wants to repeat this "fixed dialogue" several times in a row (5-6 times, not just 1-2) or with more than one listener.
Example:_____
Makes other statement(s) to evoke a fixed exchange of comments between self and others.
Example:_____

3. EXCESSIVE TALKING ABOUT CERTAIN PEOPLE, OBJECTS, OR EVENTS

___ Repetitive comments and questions about someone in the person's past or current life, e.g., girl or boy friend, caregiver of the opposite sex, neighbor, doctor. He/she may insist on seeing or phoning them.
Example:_____
(Try not to count celebrities, but look for individuals in the person's life.)

___ Excessive comments about certain topics, e.g., money (not wanting to spend it); clothing (new clothes, excessive planning of what to wear); a memorable experience (past vacation); other objects or events.
Example:_____

OBSESSIVE SPEECH CHECKLIST
For Clients with Mental Retardation

4. INORDINATE CONCERN ABOUT ONE'S HEALTH / WEIGHT

___ Comments often about: weight, staying thin, diet, not eating too much, needing to exercise often, etc.
Example:_____
    (Do not count if the person is obese and trying to stay motivated to lose weight.)

___ Comments frequently about a health issue, out of proportion to the issue.
Example:_____
Other excessive concerns about one's body:_____

5. EXCESSIVE COMMENTS ABOUT TIME, CALENDARS, SCHEDULING

___ Refers often to calendars, number of days until a given event, which days staff work or don't work,etc.
Example:_____

___ Speaks frequently about the timing of routine events: dinner must be at 6:00PM, laundry must only be done on Tuesday nights, excessive concern over who has a birthday coming up next, etc.
Example:_____

6. STATEMENTS INDICATING IRRATIONAL FEARS

___ Comments about wanting to avoid certain places: specific buildings, crowded settings, areas with people in lab coats, unfamiliar washrooms, or any unfamiliar place.
Example:_____
    (Do not count fears associated with actual traumas or "common" fears--heights, needles--unless inordinate.)

___ Comments about avoiding certain people or fearing certain activities (social events, new people).
Example:_____
    (Do not count fears associated with actual traumas or "common" fears--heights, needles--unless inordinate.)

___ Excessive or irrational comments about fearing death, harming self, or other abstract irrational fear.
Example:_____
    (Do not count grief reactions, appropriate concern for ailing relatives, or "realistic" concerns.)

[ ]   **OVERALL NUMBER OF EXAMPLES OF OBSESSIVE SPEECH (of the 13 listed)**

[ ]   **NUMBER OF PATTERNS OF OBSESSIVE SPEECH (of the 6 listed)**

EXTENT OF INTERFERENCE WITH DAILY LIVING   (Checkmark items that apply)

Obsessive speech occurs for more than an hour a day . . . . ☐
Obsessive speech significantly interferes with person's normal routine . . . . ☐
Obsessive speech significantly interferes with usual social activities. . . . . ☐
Obsessive speech significantly interferes with relationships with others. . . . . ☐

RESPONSE TO CAREGIVERS INTERRUPTING OBSESSIVE TALKING
(Circle: 0 = Never, 1 = Rare, 2 = Occasional, 3 = Often)

	0	1	2	3
Halts momentarily, then resumes obsessive talking	0	1	2	3
Seeks a different person to resume obsessive talking	0	1	2	3
Other response:_____	0	1	2	3

COMMENTS:_____

AN OBSESSIVE SPEECH CHECKLIST FOR SCREENING OCD IN VERBAL CLIENTS WITH DEVELOPMENTAL DISABILITIES

by A. Gedye (1998)

Obsessive-compulsive disorder (OCD) can present as either obsessions or compulsions, although most cases have both.[9] Obsessions are recurring thoughts, urges or images, phenomena largely inaccessible to clinicians working with nonverbal people. Compulsions are *observable* phenomena, hence are very helpful for diagnosing OCD, especially in people unable to report inner thoughts. The importance of using observable phenomena for detecting OCD in developmentally disabled people lead to the creation of a checklist that focused solely on compulsions: the *Compulsive Behavior Checklist*.[7,8] That instrument has been used in recent studies[5,11,15] for detecting OCD in developmentally disabled people. Certain patterns of repetitive speech reflect obsessions, hence are also observable phenomena. The purpose of this article is to present the companion instrument to the *Compulsive Behavior Checklist*, namely, the *Obsessive Speech Checklist* for use in verbal individuals with developmental disabilities.

Speech Patterns That Reflect Obsessive Thought

Obsessions can be silent unspoken thoughts, or spoken thoughts. When obsessive thoughts are spoken aloud, this provides "observable" evidence of obsessions. There are certain patterns of repetitive speech that reflect obsessive thought. For example, a person with OCD might *repeat a sentence verbatim with the same inflection* each time--regardless of the situation or conversation--as if speaking aloud an intrusive thought. Or they may feel that they have to have the words exactly right.[16] People with OCD might have urges to *repeat a dialogue* the same way it was said previously, and may repeat a question until another person replies with very specific words. Someone with OCD might *repeat questions* to which "he already has heard answers a hundred times before."[16] Having *irrational fears* or avoiding people and places based on irrational fears can also occur in OCD.[10] *Talking excessively* about people, places, health, dying,[17] calendars, or time can reflect obsessive thinking and/or difficulty inhibiting inner thoughts in people with OCD. These patterns of obsessive speech occur in people with developmental disabilities who have OCD and who are verbal.

Some forms of repetitive talk are not obsessive-compulsive disorder. Repetitive speech that reflects intrusive thoughts characteristic of OCD can be quite different from ruminating thoughts during bereavement, reliving traumatic memories, realistic fears, or immediate echolalia. Excessive talking about real-life problems such as an ailing friend or recent death is not considered an obsession. Repeatedly asking others about one's self-worth can indicate a long-standing need for reassurance and self-validation as occurs with Generalized Anxiety Disorder; this kind of questioning by itself, in the absence of compulsions, would not be considered OCD. Although some people with OCD have a tendency to mimic the actions or verbalizations of others,[2,13] echolalic speech is not a criterion for OCD.[1] Nor is repetitive screaming or repetitive humming used for diagnosing OCD.

The content of obsessive speech will vary depending on the person's comprehension level. Obviously, we should not look for obsessions that require abstract thinking in people only capable of concrete reasoning. Obsessions that require concepts like aesthetic comparison (symmetry), spread of disease (contamination), or complicated doctrines (religious obsessions) were more common in OCD cases from the general population than 50 autistic people with OCD (35 had mental retardation).[12] Developmentally disabled people with OCD who talk obsessively about money are more likely to be in the mild or moderate range of intelligence than those in the severe range who cannot make change. People with OCD who talk obsessively about calendars and specific times of day understandably have greater comprehension of time concepts than people with OCD who are unable to tell time.

Obsessive speech can remain as "words without actions" or lead directly to actions. Obsessive thoughts can lead to difficult-to-manage behaviors. A developmentally disabled person who has been talking obsessively about a favorite "someone" for weeks might start insisting strenuously on seeing that someone. This can range from demanding to phone him or her any time of the day, yelling loud and long in public about wanting to see the other, to "running away" to go and see that someone. During intense periods of insisting on seeing, talking to, or being with "that someone," caregiver attempts to reason with the obsessive person can be futile, worsen the yelling and public displays, or result in aggression. Irrational concern about one's weight can lead to strenuous exercise regimes, rigid eating habits, refusing meals, anorexia, or induced vomiting. Irrational fears in people with OCD can lead to avoidance behaviors that severely limit social and recreational life, by not going to certain places or any unfamiliar place. By learning to recognize patterns of repetitive speech that reflect obsessive irrational concerns, we can better understand certain avoidance behaviors, fearful reactions, and unusual preoccupations as part of a disorder, not deliberate misbehavior.

Using the Obsessive Speech Checklist

The *Obsessive Speech Checklist* was designed for use only with developmentally disabled people who talk in sentences and use meaningful speech. This checklist is **not for use with** individuals who are in the profound range of intelligence, who have only echolalic speech, or who speak only single words and short phrases. The checklist was intended to be used by a consultant (e.g., psychologist, behavior therapist, physician) to interview two or more caregivers familiar with the person being assessed. Users are to record examples of the person's speech patterns on the checklist form. It is very important to complete the *Compulsive Behavior Checklist* on the same individual, preferably before doing the *Obsessive Speech Checklist*. The information collected is then discussed with clinicians who evaluate whether the diagnostic criteria for OCD have been met. The *Obsessive Speech Checklist* is a guide for obtaining information to aid the diagnostic process; it is not a standardized test. The "test" is whether the presenting symptoms fit the diagnostic criteria for OCD.

Clinical Criteria for Obsessive-Compulsive Disorder

Clinicians can use the information gathered from the *Compulsive Behavior Checklist* and the *Obsessive Speech Checklist* to determine if the person fits the clinical criteria for OCD, or possibly "subclinical OCD."[6] The portions of the DSM-IV[1] criteria that are relevant to this discussion follow.

"A. Either obsessions or compulsions:
Obsessions as defined as (1), (2), (3), and (4):

(1) recurrent and persistent thoughts, impulses, or images that are experienced, at some time during the disturbance, as intrusive and inappropriate and that cause marked anxiety or distress;
(2) the thoughts, impulses, or images are not simply excessive worries about real-life problems;
(3) the person attempts to ignore or suppress such thoughts, impulses or images, or to neutralize them with some other thought or action;
(4) the person recognizes that the obsessional thoughts, impulses, or images are a product of his or her own mind (not imposed from without as in thought insertion).

C. The obsessions or compulsions ...are time consuming (take more than 1 hour a day), or significantly interfere with the person's normal routine, ...usual social activities or relationships."[1]

An additional requirement (B.) that people recognize the obsessions or compulsions are excessive or unreasonable does not apply to children. By extrapolation, this would not apply to adults with mental ages of children. Moreover, the diagnosis of OCD can be made when insight is lacking by specifying "With Poor Insight."[1]

Comment

Why try to identify obsessive speech patterns? First, it helps clinicians detect OCD in people with few or no compulsions where the diagnosis might be missed. Secondly, it helps us understand that obsessive speech is a difficulty inhibiting certain thoughts and urges, not deliberate misbehavior. Thirdly, it helps caregivers understand the futility of trying to change obsessional behavior by arguing or focusing on how irrational the person's concerns are. Arguing tends to make it worse, in contrast to efforts to desensitize, distract, change the topic or the situation. Identifying the problem is a first step toward better treatment, and certain medications have been reported useful in developmentally disabled adults with OCD.[3,4,11,14]

The purpose of this article is to help professionals recognize obsessive speech patterns--and therefore OCD--in verbal people with developmental disabilities. The *Obsessive Speech Checklist* was designed for identifying obsessive speech patterns in persons in the mild, moderate or severe range of intelligence. It can help to differentiate obsessive speech patterns from other forms of repetitive speech, and is a guide for gathering information to assist clinicians in diagnosing OCD.

References

1. American Psychiatric Association. (1994) *Diagnostic and Statistical Manual - Fourth Edition. Washington*, DC: American Psychiatric Association.

2. Ames D, Cummings JL, Wirshing WC, Quinn B, Mahler M. (1994) Repetitive and compulsive behavior in frontal lobe degenerations. *Journal of Neuropsychiatry and Clinical Neuroscience*, 6, 100-113.

3. Barak Y, Ring A, Levy D, Granek I, Szor H, Elizur A. (1995) Disabling compulsions in 11 mentally retarded adults: an open trial of clomipramine SR. *Journal of Clinical Psychiatry*, 56, 459-461.

4. Bodfish JW, Madison JT. (1993) Diagnosis and fluoxetine treatment of compulsive behavior disorder of adults with mental retardation. *American Journal on Mental Retardation*, 98, 360-367.

5. Bodfish JW, Crawford TW, Powell SB, Parker DE, Golden RN, Lewis MH. (1995) Compulsions in adults with mental retardation: prevalence, phenomenology, and comorbidity with stereotypy and self-injury. *American Journal on Mental Retardation,*100, 183-192.

6. Flament MF, Whitaker A, Rapoport JL, Davies M, Berg CZ, Kalikow K, Sceery W, Shaffer D. (1988) Obsessive compulsive disorder in adolescence: an epidemiological study. *Journal of the American Academy of Child and Adolescent Psychiatry*, 27, 764-771.

7. Gedye A. (1992) Recognizing obsessive-compulsive disorder in clients with developmental disabilities. *Habilitative Mental Healthcare Newsletter*, 11, 73-77.

8. Gedye A. (1996) Issues involved in recognizing obsessive-compulsive disorder in developmentally disabled clients. *Seminars in Clinical Neuropsychiatry*, 1, 142-147.

9. Insel TR. (1985) Obsessive-compulsive disorder. *Psychiatric Clinics of North America*, 8, 105-117.

10. Khanna S, Kaliaperumal VG, Channabasavanna SM. (1990) Clusters of obsessive-compulsive phenomena in obsessive-compulsive disorder. *British Journal of Psychiatry*, 156, 51-54.

11. Lewis MH, Bodfish JW, Powell SB, Golden RN. (1995) Clomipramine treatment for stereotypy and related repetitive movement disorders associated with mental retardation. *American Journal on Mental Retardation,* 100, 299-312.

12. McDougle CJ, Kresch LE, Goodman WK, Naylor ST, Volkmar Fr, Cohen DJ, Price LH. (1995) A case-controlled study of repetitive thoughts and behavior in adults with autistic disorder and obsessive-compulsive disorder. *American Journal of Psychiatry*, 152, 772-777.

13. Mega MS, Cummings JL. (1994) Frontal-subcortical circuits and neuropsychiatric disorders. *Journal of Neuropsychiatry and Clinical Neuroscience*, 6, 358-370.

14. O'Dwyer J, Holmes J, Collacott RA. (1992) Two cases of obsessive-compulsive disorder in individuals with Down's syndrome. *Journal of Nervous and Mental Disease,* 180, 603-604.

15. Prasher VP, Day S. (1995) Brief report: obsessive-compulsive disorder in adults with Down's syndrome. *Journal of Autism and Developmental Disorders*, 25, 453-458.

16. Rapoport JL. (1989) *The Boy Who Couldn't Stop Washing, The Experience and Treatment of Obsessive-Compulsive Disorder.* New York: Dutton.

17. Rapoport JL. (1989) The biology of obsessions and compulsions. *Scientific American*, 260, 83-89.

OCD SEVERITY SCALE - For Persons with Mental Retardation
by Vitiello B, Spreat S, and Behar D (1989)

This page from the *Journal of Nervous and Mental Disease*, 1989, vol. 177, p. 236 has been reprinted with written permission from the publishers. However, the publishers did not give permission for others to photocopy this page. Therefore, users of the *Diagnostic Behavioral Guide* have been provided with a simple recording sheet that they may photocopy for clinical use when using this OCD Severity Scale. See the "Recording Sheet for the OCD Severity Scale" on page 205.

Severity of Symptoms

Rate the following aspects of severity of the repetitive behaviors:

During the last week:

1. Time spent with all symptoms daily
   0 = less than 15 minutes
   1 = 15 to 30 minutes
   2 = 30 minutes to 1 hour
   3 = 1 to 3 hours
   4 = more than 3 hours   0 1 2 3 4

2. Subjective resistance or attempt to stop the symptoms
   0 = not interested in stopping
   1 = would like to stop, but didn't try
   2 = has tried a little
   3 = has tried hard
   4 = has tried very hard   0 1 2 3 4

3. Ability to stop symptoms when desired
   0 = always
   1 = most of the time
   2 = only in front of other people
   3 = very little, even when with other people
   4 = not at all   0 1 2 3 4

4. Interference with work/school
   0 = no work/school missed
   1 = often late arriving at work/school
   2 = often late completing tasks at work/school
   3 = unable to complete tasks at work/school
   4 = completely unable to attend work/school   0 1 2 3 4

5. Interference with self-care
   0 = no interference with daily self-care
   1 = hygiene poor occasionally
   2 = frequent delays in hygiene and/or dressing and/or emptying bladder or bowels
   3 = has to be showered and/or dressed by others and/or constipated often
   4 = completely dependent on other people for survival functions such as feeding   0 1 2 3 4

6. Interference with social contacts and leisure activities
   0 = no interference
   1 = has sometimes given up opportunities to see friends or play sports/hobbies
   2 = has often refused to meet friends or to enjoy sports/hobbies
   3 = needs to be constantly pushed in order to have any social contact
   4 = unable to engage in any social or leisure time activities   0 1 2 3 4

7. Slowness of walking, talking, or moving in general:
   0 = none at all
   1 = sometimes slow in movements
   2 = often slowed
   3 = constantly slowed
   4 = extremely slow, often needs help to move   0 1 2 3 4

8. Interventions by others required:
   0 = no external intervention is required
   1 = verbal intervention from other people is sometimes necessary
   2 = verbal intervention is often necessary
   3 = physical intervention is necessary
   4 = strenuous physical intervention with struggling is necessary   0 1 2 3 4

9. Suffering and distress from symptoms or their consequences:
   0 = none at all
   1 = a little, occasional
   2 = moderately, often
   3 = a lot, every day
   4 = intense, unremitting distress   0 1 2 3 4

Total severity score = _____

Recording Sheet for the OCD SEVERITY SCALE

For use with the *Behavioral Diagnostic Guide* © A. Gedye, 1998

NAME:_____ ETIOLOGY:_____

BIRTHDATE:_____/___/___ REPORT DATE:_____/__/_____

RECORDER:_____ INFORMANTS:_____

This is a recording sheet for use with the "OCD Severity Scale" for persons with mental retardation by Vitiello, Spreat and Behar (1989) in the *Journal of Nervous and Mental Disease*, vol. 177, p. 236. Rate severity before and after any changes in treatment for obsessive-compulsive disorder (OCD). It is advisable to first complete the *Compulsive Behavior Checklist* (Gedye, 1992) and, if applicable, the *Obsessive Speech Checklist* (Gedye, 1997) before rating severity of obsessive-compulsive features.

Record the *level of severity*
for the obsessive-compulsive
behaviors:

COMMENTS IF ANY:

1. **0 1 2 3 4** _____

2. **0 1 2 3 4** _____

3. **0 1 2 3 4** _____

4. **0 1 2 3 4** _____

5. **0 1 2 3 4** _____

6. **0 1 2 3 4** _____

7. **0 1 2 3 4** _____

8. **0 1 2 3 4** _____

9. **0 1 2 3 4** _____

Total Severity Score _____ (maximum 36).

Note: In an unpublished study of 100 developmentally disabled adults screened for (OCD), Gedye found certain score ranges using the "OCD Severity Scale" by Vitiello et al., (1989). The mean severity score for those with OCD was 16.6, the standard deviation (S.D.) was 4.5, and the range was 10 - 28. Gedye found:

OCD Severity Scores 22 + - very difficult-to-manage individuals who had OCD (> 1 S.D. above the mean)

12 - 21 - persons with mental retardation who met the criteria for OCD ($\pm$ 1 S.D.)

8 - 11 - marginal range

1 - 7 - persons with "subclinical OCD" (i.e., they had many obsessive-compulsive features but these were not significantly interfering in their lives) had a mean severity score of 3.9.

CHECKLIST OF INTENTIONAL SELF-RESTRAINT AND INVOLUNTARY SELF-INJURIOUS MOVEMENTS

For use with the *Behavioral Diagnostic Guide* © A. Gedye, 1998

NAME:_____ ETIOLOGY:_____

BIRTHDATE:_____/___/___ REPORT DATE:_____/__/_____

RECORDER:_____ INFORMANTS:_____

> This is a guide for collecting information to aid in evaluating if certain self-injurious movements are involuntary muscle contractions. Some, but not all, persons with involuntary self-injurious movements try to restrain their limbs from doing these involuntary contractions by assuming postures or using clothing/objects that are incompatible with the movements.

TOPOGRAPHY OF MUSCLE CONTRACTIONS THAT CAUSE TISSUE DAMAGE:

__ hand hits head/cheek/ear   (Median Nerve supplies muscles involved)

__ hand hits mouth/jaw, no biting   (Median Nerve)

__ hand/forearm hits mouth, is bitten   (Median N., masseteric reflex)

__ digits 2 & 3 forced onto side of thumb   (Musculocutaneous branch, Median N.)

__ digits 2 & 3 & thumb pinch cheek/neck   (Musculocutaneous branch, Median N.)

__ hand hits table/chair/wall   (Radial Nerve supplies muscles involved)

__ hand hits leg   (Radial Nerve)

__ head thrusting forward   (Accessory branch 11th Cranial Nerve)

__ head thrusting backward   (Accessory branch 11th Cranial Nerve)

__ side of head contacts shoulder

CONSISTENCY OF TOPOGRAPHY AS EVIDENT FROM TISSUE DAMAGE:

Thickened (Cauliflower) Areas: __ R ear, __ L ear, __ forehead, __ jaw, __ cheek, __ outer edge of hand, other:_____

Wounds/Scarred Areas: __ side of thumb (from pressing fingers on it), __ cheek/neck pinch areas, __ forearm area bitten, __ hand area bitten, __ shoulder area from side of head-to-shoulder hitting.

Detached Retina: __ R eye, __ L eye. Other:_____

SEVERITY OF THESE INJURIOUS MOVEMENTS:

Currently: ___ Severe; ___ Moderate; ___ Mild; ___ Rarely occurs.

In past years: ___ Severe; ___ Moderate; ___ Mild; ___ Rarely occurred.

AGE OF ONSET (Self-Hitting, Self-Biting, or Headbanging):

__ before 3 years, __ 3-4 years, __ between 4-10 years, __ in childhood, as adult at age:_____

CHECKLIST OF INTENTIONAL SELF-RESTRAINT AND INVOLUNTARY SELF-INJURIOUS MOVEMENTS

For use with the *Behavioral Diagnostic Guide* © A. Gedye, 1998

USE OF CLOTHING (that is incompatible with self-injurious muscle contractions):

___ tucking one or both arms under a shirt or sweatshirt.
___ wrapping a shirt around hands/arms.
___ pulling a shirt sleeve over one or both hands.
___ pulling a shirt over one's head.   *Circle* HB *if the person does headbanging:*   HB
___ putting a shoe or cushioned object in a position to receive   HB
the impact of the head during forward thrusting.

_____

USE OF LINENS, FURNITURE, ETC. (incompatible with self-injurious muscle contractions):

___ rigidly holding an object with both hands, elbows close to body.
___ entangling one's hands/arms in another person's hands or arms.
___ entangling one's hands/arms in the rungs of a chair or other parts of furniture.
___ lying in a confining space, e.g., under a bench with a blanket.
___ wanting bedsheets pulled tightly.
___ covering the head or whole self with a blanket or sheet in daytime.   HB

_____

POSITIONS THAT ARE INCOMPATIBLE WITH INJURIOUS MUSCLE CONTRACTIONS:

___ sitting on one's hands (in a chair, on a bed, on the floor).
___ lying facedown on one's hands/arms.
___ crossing one's arms and tucking the hands under the armpits.
___ leaning forward on crossed arms while sitting.
___ holding one's hands at the back of the head or neck.
___ stiffening one's arms while walking or while leaning against an object or person.
___ bending forward, head resting on one's hands that are cupped in front.   HB
___ lying on bed/sofa in day (the head hits a soft surface during thrusting).   HB

_____

OTHER:

___ putting on a protective device or motioning for a caregiver to put it on the person (e.g., mitts, head cover, helmet, elbow tubes, neck cushion).
___ the person sometimes wakes from sleep with head-thrusting or hand-hitting-head.

_____

TIME SPENT IN POSITIONS OR USING OBJECTS IN CERTAIN WAYS (that are incompatible with self-jurious muscle contractions):

___ more that 90% of the day;   ___ about 75% of the day;   ___ about 50% of day

___ about 25% or less of day;   ___ not daily but occurs weekly.

Other:_____

Comments (past head injury, current medication, treatments): _____

_____

The Habilitative Mental Healthcare Newsletter

Co-Editors
Robert Sovner, M.D.
Anne DesNoyers Hurley, Ph.D.
Managing Editor
Maggie Zwilling
Contributing Editors
Joan Beasley, M.Ed. Mental Healthcare Policy
Betsey A. Benson, Ph.D. Psychosocial Interventions
William H. Benefield, Jr., Pharm.D., FASCP Drug Information
David Hingsburger, M.Ed. Sexuality
Andrew Levitas, M.D. Fragile-X Syndrome
Michael A. Lowry, Ph.D. Behavioral Psychology
James Luiselli, Ed.D. Clinical Behavior Therapy
Robert Pary, M.D. Down Syndrome/Aging
Al Pfadt, Ph.D. Community-Based Support Services
Stephen Ruedrich, M.D. Psychopathology
Judith J. Saklad, Pharm.D., FASCP Drug Information
Daniel J. Tomasulo, Ph.D., C.P. Psychotherapy

RECOGNIZING INVOLUNTARY MOVEMENTS WITH VOCALIZATIONS AND AUTONOMIC CHANGES:

A NONCONVULSIVE ICTAL SIGNS CHECKLIST

A. GEDYE, PH.D.

There may be features evident during outbursts that shed light on the voluntary or involuntary nature of certain "behaviors."

Episodes of uncontrollable aggressive and/or self-injurious movements occur in some people with developmental disabilities. A phenomenon that is much discussed in neurology journals and rarely mentioned in mental retardation journals is: frontal lobe seizures. Myriad involuntary movements can occur during this type of seizure that typically involves some loss of contact but not complete loss of consciousness.[2,10,45] It is typically followed by rapid recovery and rarely do convulsive seizures follow.[2,33] Amnesia for episodes may or may not occur.[10] Frontal lobe seizures can present with movements as diverse as running, flailing arms, turning head to one side, shifting one's weight from side to side, throwing oneself to the ground, and rocking.[16,24,36,45] Many movements can occur in quick succession along with intense vocalizations such as screaming, swearing, mumbling, groaning, growling, or laughing.[2,24,45,47] Autonomic features such as facial flushing, facial pallor, noisy breathing, pupil dilation and/or sweating can accompany the episodes.[2,25,45]

Some movements during nonconvulsive seizures appear aggressive: repetitive arm movements that forcefully contact nearby objects[10,31,34,35,38] or nearby people,[36,38,42] or repetitive leg movements such as kicking and stamping.[35,38,43] Repetitive head-thrusting,[36,45] hitting the hands to the ears,[26] slapping one's chest,[35] or scratching oneself[10,34,35,40] are ictal movements that have been reported. ("Ictal" pertains to an epileptic seizure.) Ictal aggression has been documented in epileptics with normal intelligence, but it is considered rare.[41] Ictal aggression in developmentally disabled people[4,17,32] and ictal headbanging in this population[29] are not new. However, no guide for listing observable ictal signs in developmentally disabled people has been available.

What might a person of normal intelligence do if he or she started to have nonconvulsive seizures? That person could report the involuntary phenomena to medical specialists. Family and friends could attest to the person's lack of control during episodes. What might happen if the person who has such

*Reprinted from volume 15(4):71-80, July/August 1996

Subscription rates: Personal $49.00 per year in the **US** ($58.00 in **Canada/Mexico** and $66.00 in **all other countries**); Institutional $63.00 per year in the US ($74.00 in **Canada/Mexico** and $85.00 in **all other countries**). Subscriptions must be prepaid in **US currency** (make checks payable to Psych-Media). Issues are published bimonthly, January/February, March/April, May/June, July/August, September/October, November/December. **Subscriptions run from January through December of the current year.** Back issues are available; please call for index and prices.

Address all editorial and circulation correspondence to: The Editors, PO Box 57, Bear Creek, NC 27207-0057; **Phone No.** 910-581-3700 **Fax No.** 910-581-3766 or **E-Mail** to magz@aol.com. **The Habilitative Mental Healthcare Newsletter** (ISSN: 1057-3291) is published bimonthly by Psych-Media, Inc. Copyright © 1996 by Psych-Media, Inc. **The Habilitative Mental Healthcare Newsletter** is indexed in the National Rehabilitation Information Center bibliographic database.

Information to authors: We invite readers to submit manuscripts for consideration as newsletter review articles and case reports. Manuscripts should be between eight and fourteen pages in length and follow the newsletter format.

episodes had little or no ability to speak? What if family and caregivers had no idea what involuntary episodes look like? Caregivers might misinterpret the movements and sounds as deliberate, and search for reasons behind such "behavior" (communication? attention?).

The purpose of this article is to alert clinicians to the possibility that certain aggressive and self-injurious movements may be involuntary movements (often accompanied by vocalizations and autonomic changes), *not intentional behavior*. To assist clinicians, a Checklist is provided of observable ictal features from over 60 neurologic articles on frontal lobe seizures. (A complete reference list is available from the author.) Classic signs of temporal lobe epilepsy such as chewing, lipsmacking, licking, and swallowing are not listed in order to focus on frontal lobe ictal signs which neurologists report are more difficult to recognize and confirm than temporal lobe seizures.[37]

ICTAL AGGRESSION VS. RESISTANCE DURING POST-ICTAL PERIOD

This article addresses involuntary movements that appear aggressive, self-injurious, or otherwise uncontrollable. An epileptic may show physical resistance during moments following a seizure, i.e., the post-ictal period. Treiman[41] differentiated "ictal aggression" and "violent automatisms lacking aggressive intent" from aggression during a post-ictal confused state and from post-ictal psychosis. The present article addresses movements that occur **during the ictus** (the attack), namely ictal aggression, ictal destruction of objects, or ictal self-injury. A case of **ictal aggression** in a developmentally disabled woman age 20 — confirmed by implanted depth electrodes — follows.

The aggressive outbursts happen suddenly, without warning. She quickly moves toward a target and physically assaults it...When the targets are objects, she breaks them and/or throws them. When she directs these behaviors toward humans, she will often grab the eyeglasses and break them; if a person does not wear glasses, she will direct her attack toward the face while grabbing and/or hitting. The outbursts suddenly abate...[32]

REPORTS OF DIFFICULTY IN DETERMINING ORIGIN OF INVOLUNTARY MOVEMENTS, VOCALIZATIONS AND AUTONOMIC SIGNS

Each feature on the Checklist has been reported during EEG-confirmed frontal lobe seizures; each was selected as a frontal lobe ictal sign. However, neurologists and neurosurgeons often report how difficult it can be to identify a cerebral focus in frontal lobe seizures.[10,37,46,47] "Normal ictal recordings are frequent"[25] and many patients had normal ictal EEGs before EEG confirmation was finally made.[22,29,36,45] Some continued to have normal EEGs, but showed frontal abnormalities on MRI, SPECT or PET scans.[18,26,36] For others with normal ictal and interictal EEGs (during seizures and between seizures), the observable pattern of features was the basis for the diagnosis.[10,39,47] This type of seizure can originate in the temporal lobe and spread to the frontal lobe, or vice versa.[23,25,30,42,47]

In short, identifying the site of origin can reportedly be very difficult with some patients. The important point is that this is a list of movements, vocalizations and autonomic changes that can occur as *involuntary phenomena*, even if localization or cause can be difficult to determine.

WAYS THAT THESE ICTAL EVENTS DIFFER FROM INTENTIONAL BEHAVIOR

Researchers report that EEG-confirmed frontal lobe seizures have been misdiagnosed as: acute mania,[20] behavior problems,[36] hysteria,[36,39,45] hysterical with potential for violence,[6] pseudoseizures,[1,3,36] psychogenic attacks,[25,31,47] psychological disorder,[36] psychiatric problem,[34,35,45] or temper tantrums.[27] Close scrutiny of episodes, however, can reveal observable ways that ictal events differ from intentional behavior.

1. **Nonconvulsive ictal events that appear aggressive differ from intentional aggression because they include movements that are counterproductive or irrelevant to intentional aggression.**

    There may be hitting or kicking during an ictal event, but there may also be running in circles,[47] bicycling movements,[25,44,45] head and eyes turning to one side,[22,37] rocking,[25,47] bending at the waist while flapping one's arms up and down,[21] holding one's arms in an elevated position,[6,18,22] rubbing one's head[10,40] or legs,[6,38] arching one's back,[10,22,36,38] losing postural tone,[22,36,38] or throwing oneself to the floor.[5,16,36]

2. **Certain ictal signs tend to appear at the beginning of most or all of a person's episodes.[2,3,32]**

    Initial ictal signs for one person may differ from initial features for another person. In deliberate expressions of anger, people often comment on the immediate situation; angry comments may vary from one circumstance to another. Facial expressions might gradually shift from disapproval to frustration to anger. It is unlikely that people expressing intentional anger would almost always start immediately with the same facial expression, same physical movements, same autonomic changes whenever they got angry. The tendency for ictal events to have similar initial features (specific to the individual) contrasts with the ordinary variation in facial changes, verbal comments, and physical actions that occurs with intentional aggression.

3. **Nonconvulsive status epilepticus is reported as fairly common with frontal lobe seizures.[39,40,48]**

    Indeed, some frontal lobe seizures **can last many hours or even days.**[47] With prolonged voluntary movements, fatigue eventually occurs, whereas involuntary movements continue as long as nonconvulsive ictal events persist. It is rather unlikely that "attention-seeking displays" or intentional aggression would continue for several hours nonstop, the way some nonconvulsive seizures can.

4. **Certain autonomic features are beyond conscious control and could not be voluntarily produced by the average person.**

People cannot willfully dilate their pupils or produce—within seconds—enough saliva for drooling. Nor can people voluntarily sweat on short notice; this can be done after vigorous activity but not instantly at will. People can intentionally breathe faster or noisily, but this requires continual mental attention. Intense physical activity for several minutes can speed up breathing, but with ictal episodes the change in breathing rate can occur right at the outset, before an oxygen debt could develop. People's faces can become flushed when angered[8,9] or pale when frightened. However, some ictal episodes erupt suddenly with no provocation, no angering or frightening stimulus. In short, autonomic changes are too sudden or too prolonged to be produced voluntarily, or are simply beyond conscious control.

5. **Another aspect that underscores the involuntary nature of these episodes is the extreme difficulty in mimicking such a memory-motor feat.**

Twenty developmentally disabled adults who exhibited these ictal signs[12] had an average of 27 (range 18-43) involuntary movements/vocalizations/autonomic features during their episodes. Preliminary work by J.W. Bodfish (personal communication, 1996) indicates similar high numbers of features from this list during outbursts in certain severely and profoundly disabled adults.

One would have to (I) remember 10-20 different eye/face/bodily movements, (ii) intentionally execute 15 or more different movements and vocalizations in a few minutes or less, (iii) deliberately alter one's breathing rate, produce facial flushing and autonomic changes beyond conscious control, and (iv) sometimes continue this memory-motor feat for over 30 minutes. To *remember and execute* so many eye, face, arm, and leg movements plus vocalizations would be very difficult for adults of above-average intelligence. It is highly improbable that people with young mental ages or IQS below 35 have learned (or taught themselves) to do 10-20 different movements in rapid succession, often at high speed. People functioning in the severe or profound range of intelligence have difficulty learning sequences of two-, three- and four-steps. They could neither remember over 15 movements and vocalizations, nor voluntarily perform them in rapid succession.

NONCONVULSIVE ICTAL SIGNS CHECKLIST (NISC)

The **Nonconvulsive Ictal Signs Checklist** is a guide to aid clinicians in distinguishing **involuntary** episodes with numerous ictal signs from **voluntary** behavior. It provides a framework for observing and collecting empirical data on particular clients. It helps identify phenomena that might otherwise have been missed, hence not considered in analyzing "behavior." It helps identify antecedent conditions and possible stressors for uncontrollable outbursts. Interviewing informants who have witnessed the person during many outbursts is crucial. Videotaping several episodes might yield further information. Reviewing clinical records might reveal clues as to age of onset, unusual strength or duration, antecedent stressors, or other patterns.

Candidates for screening include those with "uncontrollable" episodes, sudden-onset aggression, relentless self-injurious movements, relentless screaming, or clusters of unusual movements. The Checklist can be used with clients who have minimal or no speech. There are extra questions specifically for clients who can converse and relate experiences.

Comments on interpreting the findings are given on the first page of the Checklist. Even people with EEG-confirmed nonconvulsive seizures might at times be intentionally aggressive. However, voluntary verbal/physical aggression should have a discernibly different profile than episodes with high scores on this Checklist. If clinicians suspect nonconvulsive seizures after using this Checklist, such cases could be referred to a neurologist. As many neurologists have reported, normal EEG results are common and misdiagnosis as psychiatric disorders or pseudoseizures is also common with frontal lobe seizures.

DISCUSSION

Great variation can occur in ictal presentations *between* affected individuals and *within* affected individuals. A large number of ictal signs can occur during intense outbursts or only 2-3 ictal signs occur during brief versions. Examples are: eyes deviating to the side, a grimace and hand moving to the mouth lasting 1-2 seconds; or a brief involuntary vocalization with an involuntary hand/arm movement. The individual differences in length/brevity of outbursts, combined with frequently normal EEG results, further complicate diagnosis.

If the people affected show EEG changes in the frontal/mesiobasal area during long or short outbursts, they are likely to be diagnosed with frontal lobe seizures. If the people affected tend to have mostly short versions and show normal EEGs during these, they are likely to receive the descriptive label of "Tourette syndrome." Extensive overlap between frontal lobe ictal features and a cluster of symptoms labeled "Tourette syndrome" is discussed in detail elsewhere.[13] If the people affected have mostly long versions and show normal EEGs during such outbursts, they are likely regarded as intentionally misbehaving or psychiatrically disturbed. If the people affected have no ability to report subjective experiences—as with many developmentally disabled people—they are likely seen as intentionally "aggressive" or "self-injurious." Such diagnostic imprecision may continue until more sensitive techniques for scanning deep cortical areas are available.

It is illogical to argue that a type of nonconvulsive seizure, which occurs in people of normal intelligence (minimal brain dysfunction), does not occur among a group of people with extensive brain dysfunction. One obvious difference between these groups is the ability or inability to report symptoms and relate experiences. Identifying observable ictal signs during outbursts can be especially important in people with little or no speech. People in the severe and profound range of intelligence—who display ictal phenomena—might know that they need help, but cannot articulate what happens to them in order to inform medical specialists.

Using a checklist of ictal signs helps alert observers to look for certain eye movements, certain mouth movements, autonomic signs and so on, that might otherwise be missed. It is crucial that clinicians interview caregivers/family who have witnessed dozens of the client's outbursts. If a client does not show a large number of features on this Checklist, *that finding* should be a verifiable fact, not the result of ill-informed sources who have witnessed few of the episodes.

If outbursts are involuntary, this has implications for treatment. First, using negative consequences is unlikely to reduce the frequency of involuntary phenomena. This may explain how some cases of severe aggression or self-injurious movements have persisted for years, despite numerous behavioral approaches. Second, analysis of behavior might shift away from consequences toward what occurs *before* these episodes and toward possible somatic factors. Identifying antecedent stressors[14] and then reducing them may be beneficial. Educating caregivers not to add further stress or pressure *during* involuntary episodes, may avoid prolonging episodes inadvertently. Third, allowing clients to restrain their arms/hand (using clothing, objects, or limb-restricting postures) is advisable and humane if involuntary contractions of arm adductors[15] result in hands repeatedly impacting the head or chest. Fourth, it becomes obvious that involuntary episodes are not a form of communication, self-stimulation, or "self-induced endorphin high."

Discussion of pharmacologic approaches to nonconvulsive seizures is beyond the scope of this article. However, it is worth mentioning there are several reports of anticonvulsants being ineffective or exacerbating frontal lobe seizures.[7,10,19,36]

CONCLUSION

There may be features evident during outbursts that shed light on the voluntary or involuntary nature of certain "behaviors." The **Nonconvulsive Ictal Signs Checklist** is a guide for collecting data on phenomena evident during "uncontrollable" episodes (possibly aggressive or self-injurious) in persons known to have brain dysfunction. The use of this Checklist is not a substitute for thorough neurological investigation for nonconvulsive seizures. However, information collected with this Checklist can assist professionals in making clinical judgments about the **voluntary-involuntariness** of particular episodes. These judgments alone may lead to improved understanding and more effective approaches to previously enigmatic episodes.

1. Boone KB, Miller BL, Rosenberg L, Durazo A, McIntyre H, Weil M. Neuropsychological and behavioral abnormalities in an adolescent with frontal lobe seizures. **Neurology** 1988;38:583-586.

2. Chauvel P, Kliemann F, Vignal JP, Chodkiewicz JP, Talairach J, Bancaud J. The clinical signs and symptoms of frontal lobe seizures, phenomenology and classification. **Adv Neurol** 1995;66:115-126.

3. Connolly MB, Langill L, Wong KH, Farrell K. Seizures involving the supplementary sensorimotor area in children: A video-EEG analysis. **Epilepsia** 1995;36:1025-1032.

4. Creaby M, Warner M, Jamil N, Jawad S. Ictal aggression in severely mentally handicapped people. **Irish J Psychol Med** 1993;10:12-15.

5. Delgado-Escueta AV, Bacsal FE, Treiman DM. Complex partial seizures on closed-circuit television and EEG: A study of 691 attacks in 79 patients. **Ann Neurol** 1982;11:292-300.

6. Delgado-Escueta AV, Swartz BE, Maldonado HM, Walsh GO, Rand RW. Complex partial seizures of frontal lobe origin. In Weiser HG & Elger CE (eds), **Presurgical Evaluation of Epilepsies.** Berlin: Springer-Verlag, 1987.

7. Delgado-Escueta AV, Swartz BE, Walsh GO, Chauvel P, Bancaud J, Broglin D. Frontal lobe seizures and epilepsies in neurobehavioral disorders. **Adv Neurol** 1991;55:317-340.

8. Fava M, Rosenbaum F, McCarthy MK, Pava J, Steingard R, Bless E. Anger attacks in depressed outpatients and their response to fluoxetine. **Psychopharmacol Bull** 1991;27:275-279.

9. Fava M. Rosenbaum JF, Pava J, McCarthy MK, Steingard R, Boufides E. Anger attacks in unipolar depression, Part 1: Clinical correlates and response to fluoxetine treatment. **Am J Psychiatry** 1993;150:1158-1163.

10. Fusco L, Iani C, Faedda T, Manfredi M, Vigevano F, Ambroetto G, Ciarmatori C, Tassinari CA. Mesial frontal lobe epilepsy: A clinical entity not sufficiently described. **J Epilepsy** 1990;3:123-135.

11. Gedye A. Extreme self-injury attributed to frontal lobe seizures. **Am J Ment Retard** 1989;94:20-26.

12. Gedye A. Episodic rage and aggression attributed to frontal lobe seizures. **J Ment Defic Res** 1989;33:369-379.

13. Gedye A. Tourette syndrome attributed to frontal lobe dysfunction: Numerous etiologies involved. **J Clin Psychol** 1991;47:233-252.

14. Gedye A. The self-injury hypothesis: Addressing a neurologist's concerns. **Am J Ment Retard** 1991;96:85-94.

15. Gedye A. Anatomy of self-injurious, stereotypic, and aggressive movements: Evidence for involuntary explanation. **J Clin Psychol** 1992;48:766-778.

16. Geier S, Bancaud J, Talairach J, Bonis A, Enjelvin M, Hossard-Bouchaud H. Automatisms during frontal lobe epileptic seizures. **Brain** 1976;99:447-458.

17. Gillberg C, Uvebrant P, Carlsson G, Hedstrom A, Silfvenius H. Autism and epilepsy (and tuberous sclerosis?) in two pre-adolescent boys: Neuropsychiatric aspects before and after epilepsy surgery. **J Intellect Disabil Res** 1996;40:75-81.

18. Harvey AS, Hopkins IJ, Bowe M, Cook DJ, Shield K, Berkovic SF. Frontal lobe epilepsy: Clinical seizure characteristics and localization with ictal 99mTcHMPAO SPECT. **Neurology** 1993;43:1966-1980.

19. Horn CS, Ater SB, Hurst DL. Carbamazepine-exacerbated epilepsy in children and adolescents. **Ped Neurol** 1986;2:340-345.

20. Jambaque I, Dulac O. Syndrome frontal reversible et epilesie chez un enfant de 8 ans. **Arch Fr Pediatr** 1989;46:525-529.

21. Kanner AM, Morris HH, Luder H, Dinner DS, Wyllie E, Medendorp SV, Rowan AJ. Supplementary motor seizures mimicking pseudoseizures: Some clinical differences. **Neurology** 1990;40:1404-1407.

22. Laskowitz DT, Sperling MR, French JA, O'Connor MJ. The syndrome of frontal lobe epilepsy: Characteristics and surgical management. **Neurology** 1995;45:780-787.

23. Lieb JP, Dashieff RM, Engel J.Jr. Role of the frontal lobes in the propagation of mesial temporal lobe seizures. **Epilepsia** 1991;32:822-837.

24. Loiseau P, Cohadon F, Cohadon S. Gelastic epilepsy, a review and report of five cases. **Epilepsia** 1971;12:313-323.

25. Luciano D. Partial seizures of frontal and temporal origin. **Neurol Clinics** 1993;11:805-821.

26. Maeda N, Watanabe K, Negoro T, Aso K, Haga Y, Kito M, Shylaja N, Ohki T, Sakuma S, Ito K, Tadokoro M, Kato T. Usefulness of PET scan in a child with mesial frontal lobe epilepsy. **Brain Dev** 1992;14:161-164.

27. Mazars G. Criteria for identifying cingulate epilepsies. **Epilepsia** 1970;11:41-47.

28. Pincus JH, Tucker GJ. **Behavioral Neurology 2nd Edition**. New York: Oxford University Press, 1978.

29. Quesney LF. Seizures of frontal lobe origin. In Pedley TA & Meldrum BS (eds), **Recent Advances in Epilepsy**. New York: Churchill Livingstone, 1986.

30. Quesney LF, Cendes F, Olivier A, Dubeau F, Andermann F. Intracranial electroencephalographic investigation in frontal lobe epilepsy. **Adv Neurol** 1995;66:243-258.

31. Riggio S, Harner RN. Repetitive motor activity in frontal lobe epilepsy. **Adv Neurol** 1995;66:153-164.

32. Saint-Hilaire JM, Gilbert M, Bouvier G, Barbeau A. Epilepsy and aggression: Two cases with depth electrode studies. In Robb P (ed), **Epilepsy Updated: Causes and Treatment**. Miami: Symposium Specialist,1980.

33. Salanova V, Morris HH, Van Ness P, Kotagal P, Wyllie E, Luders H. Frontal lobe seizures: Electroclinical syndromes. **Epilepsia** 1995;36:16-24.

34. Scheffer IE, Bhatia KP, Lopes-Cendes I, Fish DR, Marsden CD, Andermann F, Andermann E, Desbiens R, Cendes F, Manson JI, Berkovic SF. Autosomal dominant frontal epilepsy misdiagnosed as sleep disorder. **Lancet** 1994;343:515-517.

35. Spencer SS, Spencer DD, Williamson PD, Mattson RH. Sexual automatisms in complex partial seizures. **Neurology** 1983;33:527-533.

36. Stores G, Zaiwalla Z, Bergel N. Frontal lobe complex partial seizures in children: A form of epilepsy at particular risk of misdiagnosis. **Dev Med Child Neurol** 1991;33:998-1009.

37. Sutherling WW, Risinger MW, Crandall PH, Becker DP, Baumgartner C, Cahan LD, Wilson C, Levesque MF. Focal functional anatomy of dorsolateral frontocentral seizures. **Neurology** 1990;40:87-98.

38. Swartz BE, Halgren E, Delgado-Escueta AV, Mandelkern M, Gee M, Quinones N, Blahd WH, Repchan J. Neuroimaging in patients with seizures of probable frontal lobe origin. **Epilepsia** 1989;30:547-558.

39. Takeda A. Complex partial status epilepticus of frontal lobe origin. **Japan J Psychiatry Neurol** 1988;42:525-530.

40. Tomson T, Svanborg E, Wedlund JE. Nonconvulsive status epilepticus: High incidence of complex partial status. **Epilepsia** 1986;27:276-285.

41. Treiman DM. Psychobiology of ictal aggression. **Adv Neurol** 1991;55:341-356.

42. Veilleux F, Saint Hilaire JM, Giard N, Turmel A, Bernier GP, Rouleau I, Mercier M, Bouvier G. Seizures of the human medial frontal lobe. **Adv Neurol** 1992;57:245-255.

43. Vigevano F, Fusco L. Hypnic tonic postural seizures in healthy children provide evidence for a partial epileptic syndrome of frontal lobe origin. **Epilepsia** 1993;39:110-119.

44. Waterman K, Purves SJ, Kosaka B, Strauss E, Wada JA. An epileptic syndrome caused by mesial frontal lobe seizure foci. **Neurology** 1987;37:577-582.

45. Williamson PD. Intensive monitoring of complex partial seizures: Diagnosis and subclassification. **Adv Neurol** 1986;46:69-84.

46. Williamson PD. Frontal lobe seizures, problems of diagnosis and classification. **Adv Neurol** 1992;57:289-309.

47. Williamson PD. Frontal lobe epilepsy, some clinical characteristics. **Adv Neurol** 1995;66:127-152.

48. Yaki K, Oka E. Nonconvulsive status epilepticus. **Japan J Psychiatry Neurol** 1988;42:531-532.

A. Gedye, Ph.D. is an independent researcher and psychologist who provides consultation services to people with mental handicaps. Address correspondence to Dr. Gedye at P.O. Box 39081 Point Grey, Vancouver, BC V6R 4P1, Canada.

NONCONVULSIVE ICTAL SIGNS CHECKLIST

© A. Gedye, 1996

CLIENT: _____ ETIOLOGY: _____

BIRTHDATE: _____/_____/_____ REPORT DATE: _____/_____/_____
            month   day   year   month   day   year

MENTAL LEVEL: _____ RECORDER: _____

INFORMANT: _____ YEARS KNOWN: _____

INFORMANT: _____ YEARS KNOWN: _____

CURRENT MEDICATION: _____

PAST HEAD INJURY? (year, severity, other details): _____
_____

There are involuntary events due to abnormal neural discharges that have been mistaken for volitional behavior, both in persons with mental retardation and those from the general population. Observable features of these involuntary events appear in this Checklist. To understand the purpose and rationale for using this Checklist, clinicians must read the accompanying article.

This Checklist is a guide for collecting information to aid clinicians in distinguishing **involuntary** movements and vocalizations from **voluntary** behavior. Clusters of certain movements, vocalizations and autonomic changes occur during sudden-onset "uncontrollable episodes." The episodes often include movements of the eyes/face, intense vocalizations and arm/trunk/leg movements. Involuntary phenomena can last a second, minutes, half an hour or more. Typically, there is no loss of consciousness but amnesia can occur. Candidates for screening include those with "uncontrollable" episodes, sudden-onset aggression, relentless self-injurious movements, relentless screaming, or clusters of unusual movements.

GENERAL INSTRUCTIONS:

1. Interview informants who have witnessed the client during many outbursts. These often present with features mentioned above, and start with a certain look in the eyes. Explain that these questions pertain to features that occur *during an outburst*. Clinicians questioning informants might say:

   FIRST I WILL ASK QUESTIONS ABOUT THE FACE AND EYES, THEN VOCALIZATIONS, MOVEMENTS, AND OTHER FEATURES THAT OCCUR DURING THIS PERSON'S OUTBURSTS.

2. Check off features that occur during outbursts, indicating if they occur during most/all outbursts or only some. (See columns next page.) If a feature has not been observed, mark the column NOT OBSERVED.

3. After identifying the features for each Domain, ask which ones occur AT THE START of most outbursts and record this.

4. Informants might spontaneously remark that this person displays certain features when relatively calm, i.e., not in an outburst. Such information can be recorded by checking off the circle (**O**) on the left.

5. Ask informants the remaining questions. Then ask the questions specifically for CLIENTS WHO CAN CONVERSE. If clients report additional autonomic changes or speech arrest, add this before tallying.

6. Tally the features that occur *during outbursts* for the four Domains.

COMMENTS ON INTERPRETING THE FINDINGS:

A person with *intentional* outbursts will likely (a) have few entries on this Checklist, (b) show physical actions consistent with aggressive or destructive intent, and (c) show a lack of movements that are counterproductive or irrelevant to intentional aggression. There might also be (d) evidence of prior planning or premeditation.

A person with outbursts of *involuntary* movements/vocalizations/autonomic changes will likely have (a) a large number of features on this Checklist (severe cases tend to have 15 - 35+) and (b) entries in all four Domains. There will likely be other evidence consistent with an *involuntary explanation*, such as:

1. Movements that are *counterproductive or irrelevant* to intentional aggression;
2. A pattern of certain motor, vocal and autonomic features at the *start* of episodes;
3. Past examples of inordinately long episodes of intense movements and sounds, surpassing normal limits of fatigue;
4. The impossibility of a client intentionally altering certain autonomic functions instantly; and
5. The improbability of a person with limited memory capacity (e.g., a young mental age) achieving a memory-motor feat that would be extremely difficult for even highly intelligent adults to imitate.

Use of this Checklist is not a substitute for neurological investigation for frontal lobe seizures.

DOMAIN 1. FACE AND EYES

DURING OUTBURSTS, DOES HE/SHE SHOW:	AT THE START	MOST/ALL OUTBURSTS	SOME OUTBURSTS	NOT OBSERVED
o Staring, glaring or vacant look				
o "Wild look," eyes wide open, eyebrows back				
o Frightened look, look of fear				
o Grimacing				
o Head and eyes turn to right or left side				
o Blinking				
o Eyes moving side to side (darting)				
o Eyes looking to the ceiling (roll upward)				
o Jaw jutting or jerking, teeth grinding				
o Bites down (not chewing motion)				
o Spitting				
Other:				

DOMAIN 1. TALLY: ⇩ ⇩
_____ + _____ = ◯

DOMAIN 2. VOCALIZATIONS

UNDERLINE WORDS THAT APPLY:	AT THE START	MOST/ALL OUTBURSTS	SOME OUTBURSTS	NOT OBSERVED
o Repeating word or phrase over & over (N/A if no speech)				
o Swearing, saying expletives (N/A if no speech)				
o Muttering, garbled words (dysphasic) (N/A if no speech)				
o Speech arrest, momentarily unable to speak (N/A)				
o Repetitive screaming or shrieking				
o Laughing				
o Grunting				
o Moaning or groaning				
o Humming				
o Barking, growling or howling				
o Hissing, quacking, roaring, snorting or squealing				
Other:				

DOMAIN 2. TALLY: ⇩ ⇩
_____ + _____ = ◯

DOMAIN 3. MOTOR ACTIVITY

UNDERLINE WORDS THAT APPLY:	AT THE START	MOST/ALL OUTBURSTS	SOME OUTBURSTS	NOT OBSERVED
○ Flailing or flapping arms/hands				
○ Slapping/patting own chest with hand				
○ Hand(s) hit ear, arm, leg or: _____				
○ Hands move to mouth (underline if bitten)				
○ Rubbing mouth/head/face/stomach/legs				
○ Pulls own hair with hand(s)				
○ Hand clapping or hand rubbing				
○ Scratching self or other(s)				
○ Tearing at one's clothes, may remove clothing				
○ Arms extend & adduct repeatedly, may hit nearby objects or person				
○ Grabbing/grasping nearby objects or person				
○ Throwing nearby object(s)				
○ Arm(s) held in elevated position, may point				
○ Mimicry, performs the action of words spoken				
○ Running or charging				
○ Running in circles or twirling				
○ Kicking (hard surfaces or nearby person)				
○ Stamping foot or feet				
○ Bicycling movements, alternating leg movements				
○ Jumping				
○ Body rocking, trunk flexion, bending at the waist				
○ Head thrust backward or forward, head nodding				
○ Arching one's back				
○ Throws self on floor or hard surface				
○ Thrashing, rolling side to side				
○ Pelvic thrusting				
○ Loss of postural tone				

DOMAIN 3. TALLY:

⇩ ⇩

_____ + _____ = ◯

DOMAIN 4. AUTONOMIC SIGNS				
UNDERLINE WORDS THAT APPLY:	AT THE START	MOST/ALL OUTBURSTS	SOME OUTBURSTS	NOT OBSERVED
o Face becomes flushed				
o Face becomes pale (or blue/cyanotic)				
o Noisy breathing, blowing air or whistling				
o Gasping, difficulty breathing				
o Dilation of pupils, eyes appear darker				
o Excess saliva or drooling				
o Urinary incontinence (or desire to urinate afterward)				
o Evidence of vomitus or sudden release of bowels				
o Piloerection, hair stands up on skin				
o Sweating				
Other autonomic signs:				
DOMAIN 4. TALLY:	⇩ _____	⇩ + _____	= ◯	
Mark here if sexual automatisms (e.g., masturbation) occur during outbursts, but exclude from final tally.				

TALLY:

Tally for **DOMAIN 1.** _____ during outbursts.   (Showing at least 4 is common.)

Tally for **DOMAIN 2.** _____ during outbursts.   (Showing at least 2 is common.)

Tally for **DOMAIN 3.** _____ during outbursts.   (Showing at least 6 is common.)

Tally for **DOMAIN 4.** _____ during outbursts.   (Showing at least 2 is common.)

TOTAL NUMBER = _____ possible ictal signs observed during outbursts.

DURATION AND FREQUENCY OF OUTBURSTS   *Check off if some episodes last:*

_____ a few seconds or a minute   _____ 2 - 5 minutes   _____ 5 - 30 minutes   _____ more than an hour.
Circle the average length: 2   5   5-10   10   10-15   20   25   30   or _____ minutes.
The average number of outbursts this person has is _____ in a day   (or _____ in a week).
The highest number of outbursts this person had was _____ in a day   (or _____ in a week).
The longest outburst this person has had was approximately _____.

PRE- AND POST-OUTBURST FEATURES   *Does the person indicate the following:*

Report having a strange feeling in the stomach before outbursts?	YES	NO
Point to his/her stomach at the beginning of some outbursts?	YES	NO
Show a pattern of signs *at the start* of most outbursts?	YES	NO
Resume pre-outburst activity as if the outburst did not occur?	YES	NO
Apologize or show regret if activity during outbursts was inappropriate or harmful?	YES	NO
Make comments like "I don't know why I did that." (N/A if no speech)	YES	NO
Make comments showing awareness that such activity was unwanted; e.g., "I'll be good." (N/A if no speech)	YES	NO
Show no awareness when asked about events during outbursts? SOMETIMES	YES	NO

POSSIBLE STRESSORS AND HIGH-RISK TIMES FOR INVOLUNTARY EPISODES

Do these outbursts tend to occur if there is:
- _____ a high noise level
- _____ a startling event
- _____ bright sunlight or flickering light (through trees or fences)
- _____ other environmental stressor: _____

Do these outbursts tend to occur when the person:
- _____ is lacking sleep or is overtired
- _____ is hungry or possibly low in blood sugar (e.g., before breakfast)
- _____ has a fever or is ill
- _____ is experiencing seasonal allergies   N/A
- _____ has recently had insect bites
- _____ has just had caffeine and/or chocolate (_____ only drinks decaf. beverages)
- _____ has consumed alcohol   N/A
- _____ is menstruating or in premenstrual days   N/A
- _____ other related stressor: _____

Are these outbursts likely to occur when the person:
- _____ is overly excited about an upcoming special event
- _____ is stressed, and/or pressured to perform certain activities
- _____ is frustrated or angry
- _____ has a change in plans or routine sequence
- _____ is mentally concentrating on TV, reading, calculating, computer work, etc. N/A
- _____ has a protective device (e.g., helmet) removed   N/A
- _____ other circumstance: _____

How often do these episodes occur without provocation, "out of the blue"?
Circle: 75%   50%   25%   Rare   Other: _____

Are there certain times of the day when the outbursts are more likely, such as:
- _____ in the waking hours of the morning (during shift in consciousness)
- _____ when falling off to sleep (during shift in consciousness)
- _____ late afternoon about 4:00 PM to 6:00 PM
- _____ at mealtime: breakfast lunch supper *(underline words that apply)*
- _____ other risk times: _____

QUESTIONS ONLY FOR CLIENTS WHO CAN CONVERSE

Establish rapport if new to this person. Simplify the wording if necessary. Ask questions in the order shown.

1. I want to talk about your sudden outbursts or spells.   What do you call them? _____
   At the beginning of your _____s, do you sometimes have a strange feeling in your body? YES NO

2. If YES, in what part of your body do you feel this? _____
   Tell me what this feels like. _____

3. During these _____s (outbursts), have you ever felt:
   - a strange feeling in your stomach (like "butterflies")   YES NO
   - a feeling that starts in your stomach then moves up your body YES NO
   - a tingling in your body   YES NO
   - a numbness in your body   YES NO
   - your heart racing (tachycardia)   YES NO
   - your body shivering   YES NO
   - other sensations/feelings in your body: _____

4. During these _____s, are there times when it is hard to breathe? YES NO
   Are there times during these when you cannot speak any words at all? YES NO

5. Is there anything else you want to tell me about these outbursts?
   _____

62 References for the "Nonconvulsive Ictal Signs Checklist" (Gedye, 1996b).

Boone KB, Miller BL, Rosenberg L, Durazo A, McIntyre H, Weil M. (1988) Neuropsychological and behavioral abnormalities in an adolescent with frontal lobe seizures. *Neurology*, 38, 583-586.

Chang CN, Ojemann LM, Ljemann GA, Lettich E. (1991) Seizures of fronto-orbital origin: a proven case. *Epilepsia*, 32, 487-491.

Chauvel P, Kliemann F, Vignal JP, Chodkiewicz JP, Talairach J, Bancaud J. (1995) The clinical signs and symptoms of frontal lobe seizures, phenomenology and classification. *Advances in Neurology*, 66, 115-126.

Connolly MB, Langill L, Wong KH, Farrell K. (1995) Seizures involving the supplementary sensorimotor area in children: a video-EEG analysis. *Epilepsia*, 36, 1025-1032.

Creaby M, Warner M, Jamil N, Jawad S. (1993) Ictal aggression in severely mentally handicapped people. *Irish Journal of Psychological Medicine*, 10, 12-15.

Delgado-Escueta AV, Bacsal FE, Treiman DM. (1982) Complex partial seizures on closed-circuit television and EEG: a study of 691 attacks in 79 patients. *Annals of Neurology*, 11, 292-300.

Delgado-Escueta AV, Swartz BE, Maldonado HM, Walsh GO, Rand RW. (1987) Complex partial seizures of frontal lobe origin. In Weiser HG & Elger CE (eds), *Presurgical Evaluation of Epilepsies*. Berlin: Springer-Verlag.

Delgado-Escueta AV, Swartz BE, Walsh GO, Chauvel P, Bancaud J, Broglin D. (1991) Frontal lobe seizures and epilepsies in neurobehavioral disorders. *Advances in Neurology*, 55, 317-340.

Fava M, Rosenbaum F, McCarthy MK, Pava J, Steingard R, Bless E. (1991) Anger attacks in depressed outpatients and their response to fluoxetine. *Psychopharmacology Bulletin*, 27, 275-279.

Fava M. Rosenbaum JF, Pava J, McCarthy MK, Steingard R, Boufides E. (1993) Anger attacks in unipolar depression, Part 1: Clinical correlates and response to fluoxetine treatment. *American Journal of Psychiatry*, 150, 1158-1163.

Fusco L, Iani C, Faedda T, Manfredi M, Vigevano F, Ambroetto G, Ciarmatori C, Tassinari CA. (1990) Mesial frontal lobe epilepsy: a clinical entity not sufficiently described. *Journal of Epilepsy*, 3, 123-135.

Geier S, Bancaud J, Talairach J, Bonis A, Enjelvin M, Hossard-Bouchaud H. (1976) Automatisms during frontal lobe epileptic seizures. *Brain*, 99, 447-458.

Geier S, Bancaud J, Talairach J, Bonis A, Szikla G, Enjelvin M. (1977) The seizures of frontal lobe epilepsy, study of clinical manifestations. *Neurology*, 27, 951-958.

Harvey AS, Hopkins IJ, Bowe M, Cook DJ, Shield K, Berkovic SF. (1993) Frontal lobe epilepsy: clinical seizure characteristics and localization with ictal 99mTcHMPAO SPECT. *Neurology*, 43, 1966-1980.

Jambaque I, Dulac O. (1989) Syndrome frontal reversible et epilesie chez un enfant de 8 ans. *Archives of French Pediatrics*, 46, 525-529.

Joseph TP, Pratap Chand R. (1993) Rotary seizures of frontal lobe origin. *Clinical Neurology and Neurosurgery*, 95, 237-240.

Kanner AM, Morris HH, Luder H, Dinner DS, Wyllie E, Medendorp SV, Rowan AJ. (1990) Supplementary motor seizures mimicking pseudoseizures: some clinical differences. *Neurology*, 40, 1404-1407.

Laskowitz DT, Sperling MR, French JA, O'Connor MJ. (1995) The syndrome of frontal lobe epilepsy: characteristics and surgical management. *Neurology*, 45, 780-787.

Lieb JP, Dashieff RM, Engel J.Jr. (1991) Role of the frontal lobes in the propagation of mesial temporal lobe seizures. *Epilepsia*, 32, 822-837.

Loiseau P, Cohadon F, Cohadon S. (1971) Gelastic epilepsy, a review and report of five cases. *Epilepsia*, 12, 313-323.

Luciano D. (1993) Partial seizures of frontal and temporal origin. *Neurology Clinics*, 11, 805-821.

Ludwig B, Marsden CA, Van Buren J. (1975) Cerebral seizures of probable orbito-frontal origin. *Epilepsia*, 16, 141-158.

Maeda N, Watanabe K, Negoro T, Aso K, Haga Y, Kito M, Shylaja N, Ohki T, Sakuma S, Ito K, Tadokoro M, Kato T. (1992) Usefulness of PET scan in a child with mesial frontal lobe epilepsy. *Brain Development*, 14, 161-164.

Mazars G. (1970) Criteria for identifying cingulate epilepsies. *Epilepsia*, 11, 41-47.

Munari C, Stoffels C, Bossi L, Bonis A, Talairach J, Bancaud J. (1981) Automatic activities during frontal and temporal lobe seizures: are they the same? In M Dam, L Gram, JK Penry (eds) *Advances in Epileptology: 12th Epilepsy International Symposium*, pp. 287-291, New York: Raven Press.

Penfield W, Jasper H. (1954) *Epilepsy and the Functional Anatomy of the Human Brain*, Boston: Little, Brown.

Pincus JH, Tucker GJ. (1978) *Behavioral Neurology 2nd Edition*. New York: Oxford University Press, p. 17.

Quesney LF, Kreiger C, Leitner C, Gloor P, Olivier A. (1984) Frontal lobe epilepsy: clinical and electrographic presentation. In RJ Porter et al. (eds) *Advances in Epileptology: 15th Epilepsy International Symposium*, pp. 503-508, New York: Raven Press.

Quesney LF. (1986) Seizures of frontal lobe origin. In Pedley TA & Meldrum BS (eds) *Recent Advances in Epilepsy*, pp. 81-110, New York: Churchill Livingstone.

Quesney LF, Constain M, Fish DR, Rasmussen T. (1990) The clinical differentiation of seizures arising in the parasagittal and anterolaterodorsal frontal convexities. *Archives of Neurology*, 47, 677-679.

Quesney LF, Cendes F, Olivier A, Dubeau F, Andermann F. (1995) Intracranial electroencephalographic investigation in frontal lobe epilepsy. *Advances in Neurology*, 66, 243-258.

Rasmussen T. (1975) Surgery of frontal lobe epilepsy. *Advances in Neurology*, 8, 197-205.

Rasmussen T. (1983) Characteristics of a pure culture of frontal lobe epilepsy. *Epilepsia*, 24, 482-493.

Riggio S, Harner RN. (1995) Repetitive motor activity in frontal lobe epilepsy. *Advances in Neurology*, 66, 153-164.

Roger J, Bureau M, Dravet C. (1988) Distinctive characteristics of frontal lobe versus generalized epilepsies. *Epilepsia*, 29, 213.

Rougier A, Loiseau P. (1988) Orbital frontal epilepsy: a case report. *Journal of Neurology, Neurosurgery and Psychiatry*, 51, 146-147.

Saint-Hilaire JM, Gilbert M, Bouvier G, Barbeau A. (1980) Epilepsy and aggression: two cases with depth electrode studies. In Robb P (ed) *Epilepsy Updated: Causes and Treatment*, pp. 145-176, Miami: Symposium Specialist.

Salanova V, Quesney LF, Rasmussen T, Andermann F, Olivier A. (1995) Reevaluation of surgical failures and the role of reoperation in 39 patients with frontal lobe epilepsy. *Epilepsia*, 35, 70-80.

Salanova V, Morris HH, Van Ness P, Kotagal P, Wyllie E, Luders H. (1995) Frontal lobe seizures: electroclinical syndromes. *Epilepsia*, 36, 16-24.

Scheffer IE, Bhatia KP, Lopes-Cendes I, Fish DR, Marsden CD, Andermann F, Andermann E, Desbiens R, Cendes F, Manson JI, Berkovic SF. (1994) Autosomal dominant frontal epilepsy misdiagnosed as sleep disorder. *Lancet*, 343, 515-517.

Spencer SS, Spencer DD, Williamson PD, Mattson RH. (1983) Sexual automatisms in complex partial seizures. *Neurology*, 33, 527-533.

Stores G, Zaiwalla Z, Bergel N. (1991) Frontal lobe complex partial seizures in children: a form of epilepsy at particular risk of misdiagnosis. *Developmental Medicine and Child Neurology*, 33, 998-1009.

Sutherling WW, Risinger MW, Crandall PH, Becker DP, Baumgartner C, Cahan LD, Wilson C, Levesque MF. (1990) Focal functional anatomy of dorsolateral frontocentral seizures. *Neurology*, 40, 87-98.

Swartz BE, Halgren E, Delgado-Escueta AV, Mandelkern M, Gee M, Quinones N, Blahd WH, Repchan J. (1989) Neuroimaging in patients with seizures of probable frontal lobe origin. *Epilepsia*, 30, 547-558.

Swartz BE. (1994) Electrophysiology of bimanual-bipedal automatisms. *Epilepsia*, 35, 264-274.

Takahaski I, Miura K, Nomura K, Furune S, Machara M, Negoro T, Watanabe K. (1988) Frontal lobe epilepsy in childhood. *Japan Journal of Psychiatry and Neurology*, 42, 597-598.

Takeda A. (1988) Complex partial status epilepticus of frontal lobe origin. *Japan Journal of Psychiatry and Neurology*, 42, 525-530.

Tharp BR. (1972) Orbital frontal seizures: an unique electroencephalographic and clinical syndrome. *Epilepsia*, 13, 627-642.

Tomson T, Svanborg E, Wedlund JE. (1989) Nonconvulsive status epilepticus: high incidence of complex partial status. *Epilepsia*, 27, 276-285.

Tottori T, Yagi K, Mihara T, Matsude K, Baba K, Hiyoshi T, Watanabe Y, Inoue Y, Kubota Y, Seino M. (1993) Frontal lobe epilepsy with supplementary motor seizures successfully treated with cortical resection following intracranial EEG/CCTV monitoring and functional mapping. *Japan Journal of Psychiatry and Neurology*, 47, 267-270.

Treiman DM. (1991) Psychobiology of ictal aggression. *Advances in Neurology*, 55, 341-356.

Veilleux F, Saint Hilaire JM, Giard N, Turmel A, Bernier GP, Rouleau I, Mercier M, Bouvier G. (1992) Seizures of the human medial frontal lobe. *Advances in Neurology*, 57, 245-255.

Vigevano F, Fusco L. (1993) Hypnic tonic postural seizures in healthy children provide evidence for a partial epileptic syndrome of frontal lobe origin. *Epilepsia*, 39, 110-119.

Wada JA. (1988) Nocturnal recurrence of brief, intensely affective vocal and facial expression with powerful bimanual, bipedal, axial, and pelvic activity with rapid recovery as manifestations of mesial frontal lobe seizures. *Epilepsia*, 29, 209.

Wada JA, Purves SJ. (1984) Oral and bimanual-bipedal activity as ictal manifestations of frontal lobe epilepsy. *Epilepsia*, 25, 668.

Waterman K, Purves SJ, Kosaka B, Strauss E, Wada JA. (1987) An epileptic syndrome caused by mesial frontal lobe seizure foci. *Neurology*, 37, 577-582.

Weiser HG. (1988) Differentiating frontal from temporal lobe seizures. *Epilepsia*, 29, 208-209.

Williamson PD, Spencer DD, Spencer SS, Novelly RA, Mattson RH. (1985) Complex partial seizures of frontal lobe origin. *Annals of Neurology*, 18, 497-504.

Williamson PD. (1986) Intensive monitoring of complex partial seizures: diagnosis and subclassification. *Advances in Neurology*, 46, 69-84.

Williamson PD. (1992) Frontal lobe seizures, problems of diagnosis and classification. *Advances in Neurology*, 57, 289-309.

Williamson PD. (1995) Frontal lobe epilepsy, some clinical characteristics. *Advances in Neurology*, 66, 127-152.

Yaki K, Oka E. (1988) Nonconvulsive status epilepticus. *Japan Journal of Psychiatry and Neurology*, 42, 531-532.

CHECKLIST OF OBSERVABLE SIGNS OF DEPRESSION

For use with the *Behavioral Diagnostic Guide* © A. Gedye, 1998

NAME:_____ ETIOLOGY:_____

BIRTHDATE:_____/___/___ REPORT DATE:_____/___/_____

RECORDER:_____ INFORMANTS:_____

This is a guide for collecting information to aid in determining if the criteria for depression (e.g., DSM-IV, 1994) been met. It is for use with developmentally disabled people who are unable to report inner feelings.

FEATURES SUGGESTIVE OF DEPRESSION:

(Record the month or season when a feature became evident. Underline words that apply.)

_____ *sadness*, cries easily, unhappy more often, cries at reminders/photos of deceased relatives.

_____ *depressed or irritable mood*, apathetic expression, reduced emotional responsiveness, *or* easily angered, the onset or worsening of angry displays.

_____ *loss of interest in favorite activities*, began refusing to do social or work activities.

_____ *talks much less often*, almost mute now, less interest in others, withdraws socially. [No speech]

_____ *appetite disturbance*, started to eat excessively, began stealing food, the onset or worsening of pica (eating inedibles), started refusing meals, weight loss or weight gain.

_____ *sleep disturbance*, sleeps excessively, onset/worsening of difficulty falling or staying asleep.

_____ *decreased energy*, became lethargic and tired most of the day.

_____ *loss in interest in self-care*, may become incontinent, hygiene worsens, is becoming increasingly dependent on others.

_____ *psychomotor retardation*, slower reaction time, slower to comprehend things and to respond.

_____ *difficulty concentrating* compared to an earlier time, uncharacteristic memory lapses.

_____ *talk of death*, frequent talk about funerals or someone's death, suicidal talk (rare). [No speech]

POSSIBLE PRECIPITATING EVENTS OR STRESSORS: *(Record the date or month.)*

_____ Loss of a close caregiver   _____ Death of a close family member

_____ Marked reduction in family contact _____ Loss of friends or housemates

_____ Moved to a new residence   _____ Poor acceptance of new housemate

_____ Major illness or decline in health _____ Deterioration in vision

_____ Deterioration in hearing that affects daily life _____ Onset of blindness

_____ Visiting people/places associated with trauma   _____ Visit or contact with former abuser

_____ Onset of a major worry/concern (e.g., change in financial status, lost a job, a parent became very ill)

_____ Other major change or event:_____

(See also Burt et al., 1992; Cooper & Collacott, 1994; DesNoyers Hurley, 1996; Prasher & Hall, 1996; Sovner, 1986).

© A. Gedye, 1998 Author grants permission to photocopy this page for clinical use only.

CHECKLIST OF OBSERVABLE SIGNS OF PSYCHOSIS
In Persons with Mental Retardation*
For use with the *Behavioral Diagnostic Guide* © A. Gedye, 1998

NAME:_____ ETIOLOGY:_____

BIRTHDATE:_____/___/___ REPORT DATE:_____/__/_____

RECORDER:_____ INFORMANTS:_____

> This is a guide for collecting information to aid in determining if the criteria for psychosis have been met. This is intended for use with individuals who are unable to report their inner feelings.

FEATURES THAT CAN BE INDICATIVE OF PSYCHOSIS:

____ stares into corners and nods head as if involved in a conversation (unless the person is in full control and engaging in self talk).

____ appears to be shadow-boxing. (Do not count if this occurs during a flashback.)

____ glares angrily at strangers or favorite people. (Do not count if this occurs during a flashback or altered mood state associated with temporal lobe dysfunction/epilepsy.)

____ wears several layers of clothing. (Do not count if person has obsessive-compulsive disorder, hypothyroidism, or has learned this from living on the streets.)

____ brushes non-existent material off the body. (Do not count if the person has numbness or tingling sensations or is having flashback phenomena.)

____ covers ears or eyes. (Do not count if person has pain, infections, migraine, extra sensitive hearing/ vision, or strong preferences.)

____ inspects or refuses food with fearful or intense emotion. (Do not count if the person often vomits, has gastrointestinal problems, allergies, had pills put in food previously, or is having a flashback.)

____ whinces as if smelling/tasting something foul.
(Do not count if the person is having an aura, seizure, migraine, or flashback.)

____ puts wrappings around collar, ears, sleeves, ankles or other "openings."
(Do not count if the person has obsessive-compulsive disorder or is feeling cold.)

____ often wears costumes. (Do not count if this reflects a person's wish, not a belief.)

____ wears a scarf or bandanna around his or her head. (Do not count if done for fashion.)

FEATURES NOT USUALLY CHARACTERISTIC OF PSYCHOSIS:

- having imaginary friends (common in persons with Down syndrome) ❑
- speaking in altered voices (can occur with echolalia or involuntary vocalizations) ❑
- seeing deceased relatives or friends ❑
- phenomena that the person can start and stop at will ❑

---

* Adapted from Ryan, R. (1994) Recognizing psychosis in persons with developmental disabilities who do not use spoken communication. In *Spectrum of Psychosis*, R. Ancill (Ed.), pp. 339-344, John Wiley & Sons Ltd.

RISK FACTORS FOR CASEIN-GLUTEN PEPTIDURIA

For use with the *Behavioral Diagnostic Guide* © A. Gedye, 1998

NAME:_____ ETIOLOGY:_____

BIRTHDATE:_____/___/____ REPORT DATE:_____/___/_____

RECORDER:_____ INFORMANTS:_____

This is a guide for collecting information to assist physicians (or others) in deciding whether or not to screen for casein and gluten abnormalities. See comments at the bottom of the page.

---

1. EARLY DEVELOPMENT   As a child, the person:
- was developing normally until sometime in the first year   YES   NO
- was developing normally until sometime between 1-3 years   YES   NO
- was developing normally until age:_____
- had delayed milestones but started *losing* skills (e.g., language skills) about age _____

2.a) MILK, WHEAT, AND/OR INTESTINAL SYMPTOMS   As a child, did the person have:
- a problem with cow's milk in the first year   YES   NO
- normal development until after breast-feeding stopped at ____ months   YES   NO
- persistent redness or skin rash that waxed and waned   YES   NO
- diarrhea and/or vomiting often in the first or second year   YES   NO
- excessive intestinal gas, often associated with discomfort   YES   NO
- a suspected or confirmed leaky gut (intestinal permeability)   YES   NO

 b) Later in life: excess stomach acid or ulcers in the stomach/intestines   YES   NO
- other stomach-bowel problem, describe:_____   YES   NO

3. FAMILY HISTORY   Does this person have a family relation with:
- milk intolerance or milk allergy   NO   YES, relationship:_____
- wheat intolerance or wheat allergy   NO   YES, relationship:_____
- celiac disease   NO   YES, relationship:_____
- schizophrenia   NO   YES, relationship:_____
- manic-depression (Bipolar Disorder)   NO   YES, relationship:_____
- autism or Asperger syndrome   NO   YES, relationship:_____

OTHER POSSIBLE FEATURES:
- sleeps for brief periods and can stay awake without being tired   YES   NO
- seems to have an unusual pain threshold at times   YES   NO
- has normal facial appearance (e.g., no asymmetries)   YES   NO
- has unusually large pupils at times or unusual pupillary changes   YES   NO
- has seizures   YES   NO
- skin allergy tests were unrevealing   YES   NO
- an intestinal overgrowth of yeast is present   (NOT YET TESTED) YES   NO

Peptiduria is an overload of peptides in the urine and usually entails peptidemia, which is an overload of peptides in the blood; this can be caused by inhibition or an absence of enzymes (peptidases) that metabolize certain peptides.

Screening for casein-gluten abnormalities is recommended if the person (a) has an entry marked for part #1 and at least one entry for part #2 **or** #3, or (b) has a diagnosis of Autism or Asperger syndrome and an entry marked for part #2 **or** #3. Specialized labs test the urine for casein and gluten peptides: Karl Reichelt, MD, PhD, Dept. of Pediatric Research, Rikshospitalet National Hospital, Pilestredet 32, N 0027 Oslo, NORWAY, Phone 47-22-86-9110; and later in 1998 at The Great Plains Laboratory, 9335 West 75 St., Overland Park, Kansas USA 66204 Phone 913-341-8949. Also consider testing the blood for antibodies (IgA and IgG) to casein and gluten.

MENSTRUAL DISTRESS CHART* For use with the *Behavioral Diagnostic Guide* © A. Gedye, 1998

NAME: _____

MONTH/YEAR: _____ / _____

RECORDER: _____

□ = absent, not observed ■ = present, mild-moderate ■ = severe s = suspected

Possible Menstrual Features	1	2	3	4	5	6	7	8	9	10	11	12	13	14	15	16	17	18	19	20	21	22	23	24	25	26	27	28	29	30	31
P cramps in stomach area																															
A general aches/pains																															
I backache																															
N muscle stiffness																															
C insomnia																															
O motor coordination worse																															
N accidents																															
C more difficulty concentrating																															
N more distractible than usual																															
B stays at home, not typical																															
E takes naps, stays in bed																															
H avoids social activities																															
R reduced work performance																															
W weight gain/clothes tighter																															
A swelling																															
T painful breasts																															
R skin disorders onset/worsen																															
N crying																															
E anxiety onset/worsening																															
G more irritable																															
A restlessness																															
T loneliness																															
Menses/bleeding this day																															
Temporary illness/cold, flu, etc.																															

© A. Gedye, 1998 Author grants permission to photocopy this page for clinical use only.   * See original work by Moos (1968).

DISCOMFORT SCALE
by Hurley AC, Volicer BJ, Hanrahan PA, Houde S, and Volicer L (1992)

This page from *Research in Nursing & Health*, 1992, 15, p. 373 has been reprinted with written permission from the publishers. However, the publishers did not give permission for others to photocopy this page. Therefore, users of the *Diagnostic Behavioral Guide* have been provided with a recording sheet that they may photocopy for clinical use when using 7 items from this Scale. See the "Recording Sheet for a Modified Scoring of the DISCOMFORT SCALE."

Behavioral Indicators for Discomfort Scale Items

Noisy breathing: negative sounding noise on inspiration or expiration;
    breathing looks strenuous, labored, or wearing;
    respirations sound loud, harsh, or gasping;
    difficulty breathing or trying hard at attempting to achieve a good gas exchange;
    episodic bursts of rapid breaths or hyperventilation.

Negative vocalization: noise or speech with a negative or disapproving quality;
    hushed low sounds such as constant muttering with a guttural tone;
    monotone, subdued, or varying pitched noise with a definite unpleasant sound;
    faster rate than a conversation or drawn out as in a moan or groan;
    repeating the same words with a mournful tone;
    expressing hurt or pain.

* *Content facial expression:* pleasant calm looking face; tranquil, at ease, or serene;
    relaxed facial expression with a slack unclenched jaw; overall look is one of peace.

Sad facial expression: troubled looking face;
    looking hurt, worried, lost, or lonesome;
    distressed appearance;
    sunken, "hang dog" look with lackluster eyes;
    tears; crying.

Frightened facial expression: scared, concerned looking face;
    looking bothered, fearful, or troubled;
    alarmed appearance with open eyes and pleading face.

Frown: face looks strained;
    stern or scowling looks;
    displeased expression with a wrinkled brow and creases in the forehead;
    corners of mouth turned down.

* *Relaxed body language:* easy openhanded position; look of being in a restful position
    and may be cuddled up or stretched out; muscles look of normal firmness and joints are
    without stress; look of idle, lazy, or "laid back;" appearance of "just killing the day;" casual.

Tense body language: extremities show tension;
    wringing hands, clenched fist, or knees pulled up tightly;
    look of being in a strained and inflexible position.

Fidgeting: restless impatient motion;
    acts squirming or jittery;
    appearance of trying to get away from hurt area;
    forceful touching, tugging, or rubbing of body parts.

---

* These two items reflect the absence of pain or discomfort, and were omitted from the "Modified Scoring"
    on p. 229 by Gedye (1998).

Recording Sheet for a Modified Scoring of the DISCOMFORT SCALE

For use with the *Behavioral Diagnostic Guide* © A. Gedye, 1998

NAME:_____ ETIOLOGY:_____

BIRTHDATE:_____ / ___ / ____ REPORT DATE:_____ / ___ / _____

RECORDER:_____ (one recorder observes at least twice on the same day)

The *Discomfort Scale* is a standardized scale developed by Hurley, Volicer, Hanrahan, Houde, and Volicer (1992) *Research in Nursing & Health*, 15, 369-377. It was developed to assess discomfort in people with advanced dementia of the Alzheimer type. However, it might be useful in screening for pain in other people who are unable to report pain.

This recording sheet lists 7 of the 9 items* on the *Discomfort Scale* and provides a modified scoring method that is recommended for screening purposes only. This modified scoring is not the scoring that Hurley et al. (1992) used to standardize the scale. (Readers are free to use the original scoring in the 1992 publication.)

* The *Discomfort Scale* items are reprinted with permission on page 228 in the *Behavioral Diagnostic Guide*.

Instructions: Learn the 7 items in advance so you can watch the person and not need to read the items while observing. Wait 15 - 30 minutes after any event that is potentially stressful or discomforting before starting. Be unobtrusive and observe the person for a **5 minute** period. Rate severity for the 7 items. Rate the person at least two times on the same day. People with several 2s or 3s may be in pain and may need further investigation for conditions that cause pain.

0 = Not observed in the 5 minute period   **1** = Infrequent, low intensity
2 = Fairly often, or very intense but brief   **3** = Continuous, or very intense and often

START TIME: _____ AM / PM   STOP TIME: _____
LOCATION:_____ POSITION: lying   sitting   standing   pacing
RESTRAINT: (type, body parts)_____

Noisy Breathing	0	1	2	3
Negative Vocalizations	0	1	2	3
Sad Facial Expression	0	1	2	3
Frightened Facial Expression	0	1	2	3
Frown Facial Expression	0	1	2	3
Tense Body Language	0	1	2	3	*Discomfort Score* _____
Fidgeting Body Language	0	1	2	3	(maximum 21)

START TIME: _____ AM / PM   STOP TIME: _____
LOCATION:_____ POSITION: lying   sitting   standing   pacing
RESTRAINT: (type, body parts)_____

Noisy Breathing	0	1	2	3
Negative Vocalizations	0	1	2	3
Sad Facial Expression	0	1	2	3
Frightened Facial Expression	0	1	2	3
Frown Facial Expression	0	1	2	3
Tense Body Language	0	1	2	3	*Discomfort Score* _____
Fidgeting Body Language	0	1	2	3	(maximum 21)

CHECKLIST OF OVERT SIGNS OF SLEEP APNEA
In Persons with Mental Retardation
For use with the *Behavioral Diagnostic Guide* © A. Gedye, 1998

NAME:_____ ETIOLOGY:_____

BIRTHDATE:_____/___/____ REPORT DATE:_____/__/_____

RECORDER:_____ INFORMANTS:_____

This is a guide for collecting preliminary information that may indicate a need to do overnight charting of sleep sounds. The information collected can assist physicians in their decision to refer to an ear-nose-throat (ENT) specialist and to request overnight polysomnographic recording at a sleep clinic.

OBSERVABLE DAYTIME SIGNS

1. Is the person sleepy in the daytime?   YES   NO

2. Is the person easily able to fall asleep in a chair?   YES   NO

3. Does the person snore during daytime naps or brief snoozes?   YES   NO

4. Is the person slow to awaken in the morning?   YES   NO

5. Does the person report or appear to have morning headaches?   YES   NO

6. Does the person often breath through his or her mouth?   YES   NO

FAMILY HISTORY

1. Is there a family member who often snored during sleep?   YES   NO
   Circle: Father   Mother   Brother   Sister   other: _____

TONSILS & ADENOIDS

1. Has this person had his or her tonsils and/or adenoids removed?   YES   NO

NIGHTTIME SIGNS

If necessary, collect this information using the *Overnight Charting for Signs of Sleep Apnea* for 5 nights. Staff find it helpful to use a battery-operated room monitor to record sounds without disturbing the person.

1. Does the person snore or breathe noisily when asleep?   YES   NO

2. During sleep are there moments when breathing stops,   YES   NO
   then the person gasps or takes a deep breath?

3. Does the person cough often during the night?   YES   NO

4. Does the person have periods of restless movements at night?   YES   NO

5. Does the person wake frequently during the night?   YES   NO

6. Does the person snore in all positions?   YES   NO

© A. Gedye, 1998 Author grants permission to photocopy this page for clinical use only.

OVERNIGHT CHARTING FOR SIGNS OF SLEEP APNEA

For use with the *Behavioral Diagnostic Guide* © A. Gedye, 1998

NAME: _____ RECORDER (upper date): _____ RECORDER (lower date): _____

Enter the hour (e.g., "10" for 10:00 PM) that is close to the person's bedtime in the box with the asterisk.* Then that box represents 10:00 - 10:14 PM, the second box represents the time interval 10:15 - 10:29 PM, the third is 10:30 -10:44 PM, and so on. Checkmark each 15-minute-interval-box during which the person snores, gasps, etc. Do not disturb the person; use a room monitor or tape recorder to record sleep sounds. Record for 5 nights. Show data to MD.

DATE:	*	15	30	45	15	30	45	15	30	45	15	30	45	15	30	45	15	30	45	15	30	45
Snoring																						
Noisy breathing																						
Breathing stops, a gasp or deep breath																						
Coughing																						
Awake																						
Other (describe)																						
DATE:																						
Snoring																						
Noisy breathing																						
Breathing stops, a gasp or deep breath																						
Coughing																						
Awake																						
Other (describe)																						

MONTH: _____

CLIENT'S NAME: _____

TABLE 3.   MONTHLY SLEEP CHART*

INSTRUCTIONS: Place an "X" in the appropriate box if the patient is awake for any time during the indicated 30 minute time period. Do not consider whether or not the client gets out of bed. Consider only if his or her eyes are open.

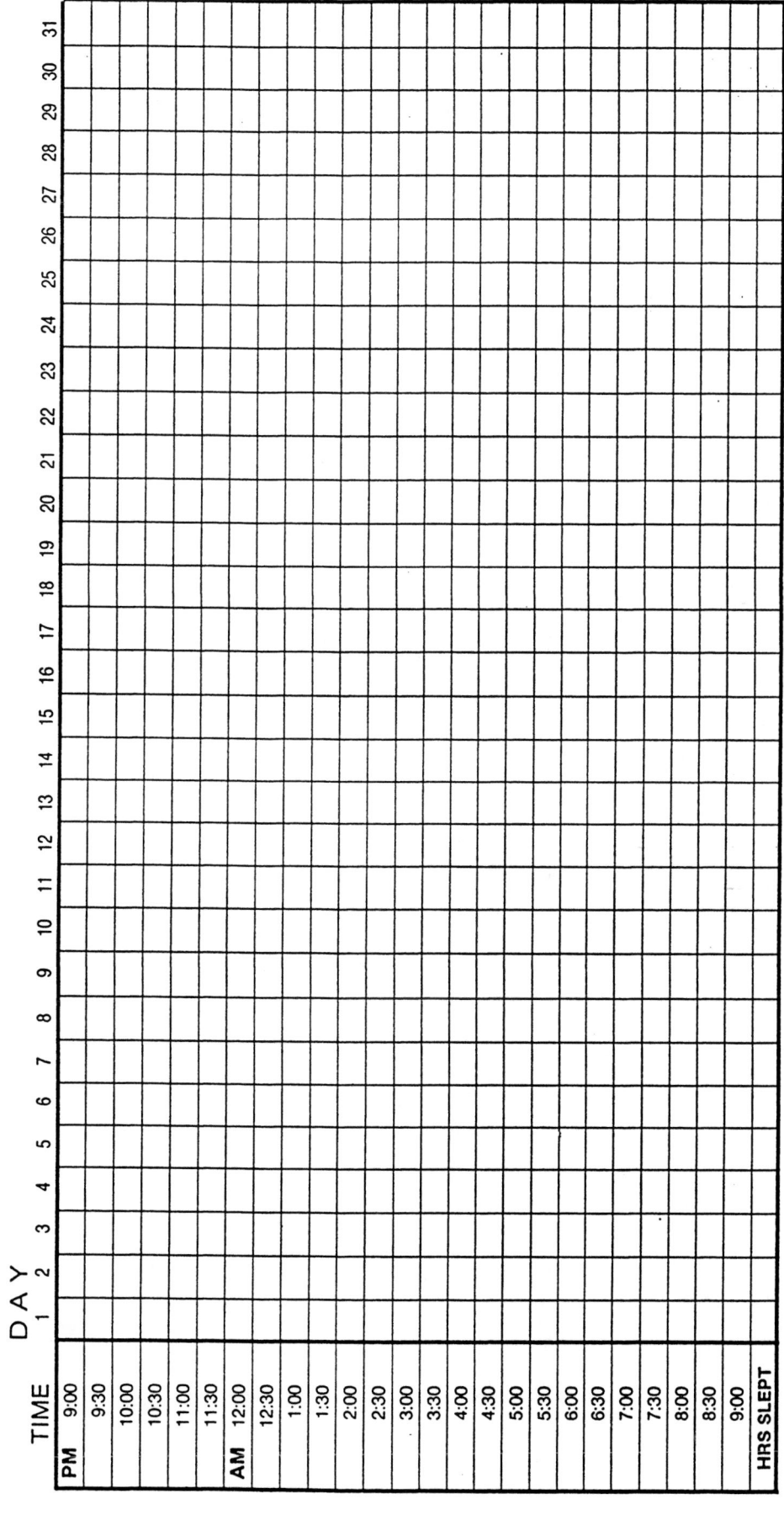

TIME		D A Y 1	2	3	4	5	6	7	8	9	10	11	12	13	14	15	16	17	18	19	20	21	22	23	24	25	26	27	28	29	30	31
PM	9:00																															
	9:30																															
	10:00																															
	10:30																															
	11:00																															
	11:30																															
AM	12:00																															
	12:30																															
	1:00																															
	1:30																															
	2:00																															
	2:30																															
	3:00																															
	3:30																															
	4:00																															
	4:30																															
	5:00																															
	5:30																															
	6:00																															
	6:30																															
	7:00																															
	7:30																															
	8:00																															
	8:30																															
	9:00																															
HRS SLEPT																																

The Habilitative Mental Healthcare Newsletter

The Habilitative Mental Healthcare Newsletter

Co-Editors
Robert Sovner, M.D.
Anne DesNoyers Hurley, Ph.D.
Managing Editor
Maggie Zwilling
Contributing Editors
Betsey A. Benson, Ph.D. Psychosocial
  Interventions
Kathy Bungay, Pharm.D. Drug Information
David Hingsburger, M.Ed. Sexuality
Andrew Levitas, M.D. Fragile-X Syndrome
Michael A. Lowry, Ph.D. Behavioral Psychology
James Luiselli, Ed.D. Clinical Behavior Therapy
Robert Pary, M.D. Down Syndrome/Aging
Al Pfadt, Ph.D. Prader-Willi Syndrome
Stephen Ruedrich, M.D. Psychopathology

COMMON CONCERNS IN DOWN SYNDROME: INITIAL SIGNS AND STEPS TO TAKE

A. GEDYE, PH.D.
J. E. RUSSELL, M.D.

PROBLEMS COMMON IN DS ADULTS	POSSIBLE INDICATIONS	INITIAL STEPS	FOLLOW-UP STEPS
Vision - cataracts, deteriorating vision, changes in depth perception.	- moving around less - reduced interest in TV or handicrafts - fear of walking on uneven ground - increasing falls	- visit G.P. and/or optometrist - referral to eye specialist	- regular check-ups by eye specialist and/or optometrist
Hearing - ear wax build-up, conductive hearing loss, ear infections, etc. - approximately 40% develop sensori-neural hearing loss.	- staff have to repeat instructions or speak louder to be understood - apparent difficulty in comprehending - there may be no sign of hearing loss	- G.P. to remove ear wax build-up, check for infection - referral to audiologist	- ensure ear wax is removed at regular intervals (2-3 times per year) - repeat hearing testing by audiologist every 2-3 years - monitor possible hearing loss
Heart - congenital heart defects in less than 50% DS.	- there may be no signs obvious to nonmedical people - blueness of lips, hands and/or feet - shortness of breath - increased fatigue	- congenital heart problems have usually been identified in childhood - visit G.P. - possible cardiology consultation - baseline echocardiogram	- G.P. is likely already aware and is monitoring this - cardiology follow-up
Bone/Joint Problems - degenerative arthritis, atlantoaxial instability, cervical and lumbar abnormality.	- complains of pain in neck, back, etc. - holds neck in awkward position - arthritic symptoms - limping, loose joints or recurring dislocation or deformity - no overt signs	- have G.P. screen for atlantoaxial (AA) instability, disc changes, etc. - neurological examination - X-ray c. spine in flexion and extension for every person with Down syndrome - this is very important if athletic activities are being considered	- neck brace worn on car rides may be necessary if significant AA instability present - G.P. follow-ups and specialist referral as required

COMMON CONCERNS IN DOWN SYNDROME: INITIAL SIGNS AND STEPS TO TAKE
(Cont.)

PROBLEMS COMMON IN DS ADULTS	POSSIBLE INDICATIONS	INITIAL STEPS	FOLLOW-UP STEPS
Seizures - late onset or recurrence of seizures.	- found on the floor, onset of "falling" - slumps over in chair, obvious loss of consciousness	- record details of all falls, or periods of unresponsiveness - provide detailed accounts to G.P.	- referral for EEG and/or to neurologist - keep seizure records
Respiratory Difficulties - weakened immunological response	- chronic or recurrent cough - noisy, wheezy respirations - recurrent pneumonia and/or other respiratory infections	- appropriate medical investigation and treatment	- appropriate medical follow-up
Sleep Apnea, Obstructive or Central in Origin	- snoring - interrupted breathing when sleeping - difficulty awakening - chronic nocturnal cough - daytime sleepiness - mouth breathing - morning headaches	- visit G.P. - possible referral to ENT specialist - change the sleeping position to side lying - weight reduction program if over weight	- possible T & A - possible uvulopatalo-pharyngoplasty, etc.
Dental Problems	- halitosis, gingivitis - loss of teeth	- scrupulous oral hygiene - dental exam	- continuing oral hygiene - dental exam twice yearly
Hepatitis B and Propensity to Carrier State and/or Chronic Hepatitis	- former resident of institution - sexual activity, being bitten, or accident with blood or other body fluids	- visit G.P. for Hepatitis B screen - Hepatitis B screen for both people involved	- Hepatitis B vaccine if Hepatitis B screen shows no antibodies - Hepatitis B immune globulin and/or vaccine series if determined necessary
Thyroid Dysfunction - hypothyroidism, auto-immune thyroiditis, hyperthyroidism, etc.	- weight gain or weight fluctuations - lethargy, tires easily - onset cognitive decline	- thyroid tests, especially TSH annually	- regular screening - regular blood tests for thyroxin levels if being treated (TSH can be normal in auto-immune thyroiditis)
Depression - more common in DS than non-DS mentally handicapped adults	- reduced interest in activities and others - speaks less than before - disturbed sleeping or eating patterns - may follow a move or major change in life	- record changes in eating, sleeping, activity level, and when they began - discuss with G.P. - referral to mental health team/psychiatrist	- monitor for changes in mood, crying spells, sleep, appetite, and interest level; provide feedback to attending physicians

COMMON CONCERNS IN DOWN SYNDROME: INITIAL SIGNS AND STEPS TO TAKE
(Cont.)

PROBLEMS COMMON IN DS ADULTS	POSSIBLE INDICATIONS	INITIAL STEPS	FOLLOW-UP STEPS
Dementia* - reversible types or progressive Alzheimer-type dementia	- onset of lapses in memory, comprehension, spatial recall - needs more staff help in daily tasks - DS adults under age 40 are more likely to have a reversible type of dementia, not progressive type	- dementia assessment by psychologist or other qualified professional - visit G.P. to screen for physical causes of decline including thyroid testing	- record unusual changes - reassessments by qualified professionals for cognitive changes - thyroid testing
Other Behavioral Disorders	- self-hitting, headbanging - clinical or subclinical obsessive- compulsive disorder - hyperactivity, unusual movements - no proper drug review in years - long term use of neuroleptics - unusual loss of appetite, unusual irritability	- visit G.P. - proper drug review - referral to psychiatric/ psychological services - ulcer screening for G.I. symptoms	- monitor - follow-up drug reviews

*Examples of Reversible Dementias in DS Adults -

Undetected hypothyroidism can occur because the T4 test can be normal in DS adults with hypothyroidism; TSH test must be done. In rare cases of auto-immune thyroiditis, microsomal antibody test is done because TSH can be normal. Reversible dementia may also occur after adjustment to a personal loss or move, or after discontinuing cognitively-impairing medication.

A. Gedye, Ph.D. is an independent researcher and provides psychological services to mentally handicapped people for the Province of British Columbia, Canada. Address correspondence to Dr. Gedye at P.O. Box 39081, Point Grey RPO, Vancouver, BC V6R 4P1, Canada. J.E. Russell, M.D. is a physician at Glendale Hospital, P.O. Box 4250, Stn. A, Victoria, British Columbia, V8X 3X9, Canada with over 20 years experience with the developmentally disabled.

Reprinted from volume 14(2):31-33, March/April 1995

Subscription rates: Personal $49.00 per year in the **US** ($58.00 in **Canada/Mexico** and $66.00 in **all other countries**); Institutional $63.00 in the **US** ($74.00 in **Canada/Mexico** and $85.00 in **all other countries**). Subscriptions must be prepaid in **US currency** (Make checks payable to Psych-Media). Issues are published bimonthly, January/February, March/April, May/June, July/August, September/October, November/December. **Subscriptions run January through December of the current year.** Back issues are available; please call for index and prices.

Address all editorial and circulation correspondence to: The Editors, PO Box 57, Bear Creek, NC 27207-0057; **Phone No.** 910-581-3700 **Fax No.** 910-581-3766. **The Habilitative Mental Healthcare Newsletter** (ISSN: 1057-3291 is published bimonthly by Psych-Media, Inc. Copyright © 1995 by Psych-Media, Inc. **The Habilitative Mental Healthcare Newsletter** is indexed in the National Rehabilitation Information Center bibliographic database.

Information to authors: We invite readers to submit manuscripts for consideration as newsletter review articles. Manuscripts should be between eight and fourteen pages in length and follow the newsletter format.

A description of the:

DEMENTIA SCALE FOR DOWN SYNDROME (*DSDS*) © A. Gedye, 1995

The *DSDS* is an informant-based instrument for use by psychologists and psychometrists in assessing dementia in adults with Down syndrome. It has also been effective in assessing the presence or absence of dementia in developmentally disabled adults without Down syndrome. The *DSDS* was designed so that persons in the severe or profound range of mental retardation can be assessed. The scale was standardized in British Columbia on 70 adults with DS followed longitudinally over 7 years. The original longitudinal study also included 37 adults with other causes of mental retardation. A separate validation and reliability study was done in the province of Ontario in 1993 with follow-ups to double check the accuracy of initial diagnoses. The *DSDS* showed high interrater reliability when given by a psychologist and psychometrist on the same 50 adults with Down syndrome (kappa coefficient = .91). It had good concurrent validity when diagnoses were given independently by a psychiatrist (who specializes in the field of mental retardation and is very experienced in assessing dementia) and a psychologist (A.G.) (kappa coefficient = .81).

As author of this instrument, I designed the *DSDS* to address certain assessment concerns and I regard this instrument as having the following psychometric advantages:

Wide Range of Clients Can Be Assessed:

- Psychologists can assess the full range of mental retardation including people considered "untestable" or who have little or no speech, i.e., those in the profound or low severe range of intelligence.
- One can assess adults who have mental retardaton due to Down syndrome or other causes.

Low Risk of Making False Positive Diagnoses:

- Features that are typical of the person are distinguished from features that represent a cognitive loss. The *DSDS* allows one to distinguish the inability to do everyday tasks due to *lifelong physical or sensory impairment* from the inability to do everyday tasks because of cognitive deterioration.
- This scale takes *premorbid level* of intelligence into account for rating the severity of dementia.

Addresses Differential Diagnosis:

- *Differential diagnosis screening questions* are provided.
- Psychologists can look for patterns in the *DSDS* items that suggest seven other explanations.

Test Construction:

- It provides *objective criteria* for the presence or absence of dementia in adults with mental retardation.
- It provides a *rating of severity*, i.e., early stage, middle stage, late or very late stage.
- It helps identify *when onset* occurred (e.g., the season and year).
- It is designed for *charting progression* of dementia over time.
- It aids in *charting recovery* when there are reversible dementias.
- The test items were analyzed for *discriminative value*, and weak items were discarded.
- The standardized scoring criteria were based on 7-year *longitudinal data*.

Cost-Savings: One Test Booklet can be used **10** times on the same individual.

Safeguards When Using Informant-Based Tests:

- The *DSDS* is available for use only by psychologists and psychometrists.
- The Manual stresses that informants must meet certain criteria, indicates when to reassess in 6 or 12 months, and suggests obtaining a *DSDS* baseline on older adults with mental retardation.

As of 1997, the *DSDS* was being used in 33 American States, most Canadian provinces, Australia, Belgium, England, Germany, Italy, Ireland, Japan, Spain, Sweden, and Wales. So far it has been translated into two foreign languages. Psychologists and psychometrists can obtain a Purchaser Qualification Form and Order Form from: A. Gedye, PhD, PO Box 39081 Point Grey, Vancouver, BC V6R 4P1 Canada Phone: 604-733-1950.

Please **Mail** ☐ or **Fax** ☐ the *Order Form* for the

BEHAVIORAL DIAGNOSTIC GUIDE
for Developmental Disabilities

to:

NAME:_____

ADDRESS:_____

_____

CITY:_____STATE / PROVINCE:_____

COUNTRY:_____ POSTAL CODE:_____

PHONE: (_____) _____ FAX: (_____) _____

Send this Request Form to A. Gedye, PhD, PO Box 39081 Point Grey,
Vancouver, B.C. V6R 4P1 CANADA. Phone or Fax 604-733-1950.

— —

Please **Mail** ☐ or **Fax** ☐ the *Order Form* for the

BEHAVIORAL DIAGNOSTIC GUIDE
for Developmental Disabilities

to:

NAME:_____

ADDRESS:_____

_____

CITY:_____STATE / PROVINCE:_____

COUNTRY:_____ POSTAL CODE:_____

PHONE: (_____) _____ FAX: (_____) _____

Send this Request Form to A. Gedye, PhD, PO Box 39081 Point Grey,
Vancouver, B.C. V6R 4P1 CANADA. Phone or Fax 604-733-1950.